William Shakespeare, Richard Simpson, J. W. M Gibbs

The School of Shakespeare

Vol. II

William Shakespeare, Richard Simpson, J. W. M Gibbs

The School of Shakespeare
Vol. II

ISBN/EAN: 9783744685559

Printed in Europe, USA, Canada, Australia, Japan

Cover: Foto ©Thomas Meinert / pixelio.de

More available books at **www.hansebooks.com**

THE
SCHOOL OF SHAKSPERE

INCLUDING

'THE LIFE AND DEATH OF CAPTAIN THOMAS STUKELEY,'
WITH A NEW LIFE OF STUCLEY, FROM UNPUBLISHED SOURCES;
'NOBODY AND SOMEBODY;' 'HISTRIO-MASTIX;'
'THE PRODIGAL SON;' 'JACK DRUM'S ENTERTAINEMENT;'
'A WARNING FOR FAIR WOMEN,'
WITH REPRINTS OF THE ACCOUNTS OF THE MURDER;
AND 'FAIRE EM.'

EDITED,

With Introductions and Notes,

AND AN ACCOUNT OF ROBERT GREENE, HIS PROSE WORKS, AND HIS QUARRELS WITH SHAKSPERE,

By RICHARD SIMPSON, B.A.

AUTHOR OF
'THE PHILOSOPHY OF SHAKSPERE'S SONNETS,' THE 'LIFE OF CAMPION,' ETC:

IN TWO VOLUMES.—VOL. II.

NEW YORK:
J. W. BOUTON, 706 BROADWAY.
1878.

Bungay, Suffolk:
CLAY AND TAYLOR, PRINTERS.

CONTENTS OF VOL. II.

	PAGE
HISTRIO-MASTIX; OR, THE PLAYER WHIPT	1
THE PRODIGAL SON	90
JACKE DRUMS ENTERTAINEMENT	125
A WARNING FOR FAIRE WOMEN	209
FAIRE EM, THE MILLER'S DAUGHTER OF MANCHESTER	337
AN ACCOUNT OF ROBERT GREENE, HIS LIFE AND WORKS, AND HIS ATTACKS ON SHAKSPERE AND THE PLAYERS	339
INDEX AND GLOSSARY	469

HISTRIO-MASTIX;

OR,

𝔗𝔥𝔢 𝔓𝔩𝔞𝔶𝔢𝔯 𝔚𝔥𝔦𝔭𝔱.

PRINTED FOR TH: THORP. 1610.

[STORY OF THE PLAY.]

[This play has too many characters to have much story. It is rather a review of the vices of the time, and their influence upon the community generally, than a story, or the evolvement of a dramatic plot. It shows four Lords (Mavortius, &c.) and four Citizens (Fourcher, &c.), each group in its several ways of life seduced from the study of the Arts (whose virtues are set forth in the initial scene) by the prevalence of the luxurious ways consequent upon the reign of Plenty, the ill-advised daughter and successor of Peace. The gentlefolk throw over the Arts, and deride the teaching of the Scholar (Chrisoganus—who, however, continues to teach and preach right through the play, and so is a sort of chorus to its action), in order that they may indulge in frivolous amusements, amongst which the newly fashionable patronage of companies of players has a prominent place. Play-acting patronage, in the humbler form of play-going, is also shown as being a principal vice of the citizens. The Players, with Post-haste the poet for their most active member and writer, are depicted as a set of tippling 'mechanicals,' who have abandoned their respective trades for the profit, combined with dissipation, which the formation of their number into a 'company' (known as 'Sir Oliver Owlet's') affords. These players are further shown, by means of a play in part given by them (Act 2), an 'extempore song' given by their poet upon the same occasion, and by incidents in other scenes of the play, as being men of the poorest ability. Indeed the play they give in the Hall of Lord Mavortius (Act 2) is stopped in mid-career for its badness; and it and Post-haste's 'extempore song' are declared by Landulpho, an Italian lord, one of Mavortius's guests, to be 'base trash' by comparison with the drama and poetry of Italy. Indulgence on the part of the two groups of gentlemen and citizens brings upon each the influence of vice upon vice—Pride and Vainglory, for example, leading to Envy, Ambition, &c., which, in turn, bring about War, &c., amongst the gentry, and Riot, &c., amongst the common people. When War comes, the players are pressed, despite their 'privilege,' and their gay stage apparel is taken to clothe soldiers; and when Poverty and Famine come, these 'idle fellows' are arrested for the amounts of their tavern scores, and are shipped off and 'banished out o' the land.' When, through the general Ruin which has ensued, Mavortius and the other gentlemen and their wives are reduced to beggary, and the group of citizens and their wives are almost as badly off, they all repent; and, thereupon, Peace reappears, bringing with her Fame, Fortitude, Religion, &c., and driving out Poverty, &c. At the same time the Arts reappear to end the play as they began it, by supporting 'Peace sitting in Majestie.' The extensive list of 'dramatis personæ,' with their succession, almost tells the story of the play.—G.]

INTRODUCTION.

I HAVE included the play of *Histriomastix* in the 'School of Shakspere' for several reasons :—

First, because of its general importance for the history of the Stage.

Secondly, because of an allusion, which, if it really relate to Shakspere, is of great importance. I refer to the parody of *Troilus and Cressida*, p. 39, l. 273, where one of the lines seems even to name Shakspere—

That when he *shakes* his furious *Speare*.

And thirdly, because it is manifestly one of the parcel works of Marston, who is perhaps of all our dramatists the one who made the most manifest attempt to form his style on that of Shakspere.

The drama as it has come to us is manifestly the work of two hands, and of two times. This is proved both by the confusion of the sub-play in Act II., and by the alternative endings of the play. As originally written, the sub-play was that of the *Prodigal child*; as it stands now, we have both the original sub-play, and another perfectly distinct one on *Troilus and Cressida* foisted in on its shoulders.

Again, there are two incompatible endings to the play. In one, Queen Elizabeth in the person of Astræa 'mounts unto the throne' and receives the homage of Peace. In the other, Plenty, Pride,

Envy, War, and Poverty enter and resign their sceptres to 'Peace sitting in majesty.'

This alternative arrangement seems to show that the play was originally written in the reign of Elizabeth, and was remodelled when it was no longer necessary to flatter her.

The author of the new additions to the play is clearly Marston. His unmistakeable swagger begins to appear in Act II., where he begins to transmute the Academic Philosopher Crysoganus of the old play into the Poet-scholar Crysoganus of the new, and Hariot becomes Jonson or Marston.

> How you translating scholar? you can make
> A stabbing *Satir*, or an *Epigram*,
> And thinke you carry just *Ramnusia's* whippe
> To lash the patient. (p. 30, l. 63, et seq.)

The translating scholar, or the epigrammatist, is more like Jonson; the satirist, armed with Ramnusia's whip, more like Marston himself. Yet Horace (Jonson) in the *Poetaster* is made a satirist, and in the very title of the *Satiromastix* is termed so, while in its scenes he flings about his epigrams. In this same act the sub-play of *Troilus* is also Marston's. In the 3rd Act Marston's work begins with the entrance of Crysoganus, and it continues at least to the beginning of the 6th Act. Perhaps I ought to except the scenes where the players appear. These may belong to the older drama; as they are either in prose or in doggrel, the tests which prove Marston's blank verse fail us.

Marston then being the author of the recension of this play, it remains to inquire the date of his rewriting it. I have said that the alternative endings would suggest that the new additions were made after the death of Elizabeth. But external testimony forces me to conclude that Marston had worked upon the play, even before 1599. In that year Ben Jonson brought out his *Every man out of his humour*. In that play, as Dr Brinsley Nicholson has shown me, Jonson introduces two characters, Clove and Orange, whom he means for Marston and Dekker. In Act III. he puts into Clove's mouth a speech crammed with Marston's fustian words, in which he mentions the *Histriomastix* by name. 'Now sir, whereas the *ingenuity* of the time, and the *soul's synderisis* are but *embrions* in nature, added to the *paunch of Esquiline*, and the intervallum of the zodiac, besides the *ecliptic line being optic* and not mental, but by the contemplative and *theoric* part thereof, doth demonstrate to us the vegitable circumference, and the *ventosity* of the tropics; and whereas our *intellectual*, or *mincing capreal*, (according to the metaphysics) as you may read in Plato's *Histriomastix*,' .... &c. The language shows that Clove is meant for Marston, and the mention by him of the *Histriomastix* leads almost irresistibly to the conclusion that Marston had a finger in that composition before the Christmas of 1599, when Jonson's play appeared.

Jonson's sneer at the play seems also to suggest that it was written in opposition to him. 'He had,' as he told Drummond, 'many quarrels with Marston, beat him, and took his pistol from him, wrote his *Poetaster* on him.' But Marston was modelling himself on Jonson when he wrote the first part of *Antonio and Mellida* in 1598; was quarrelling with him when he satirized him as Torquatus in the *Scourge of Villany*, 1599; was lashed by Jonson in 1599 as Clove; in 1600 in *Cynthia's revels* as Hedon or Anaides; in 1601 in the *Poetaster* as Crispinus. And then Jonson said that for three years Marston and Dekker had been lampooning him. But in 1604 Marston dedicated his *Malcontent* (a work of 1600) to Jonson, 'amico suo candido et cordato,' and in 1605 joined him in writing *Eastward Ho.*

But though Marston wrote *Antonio and Mellida* while a kind of disciple of Jonson, yet Jonson made no scruple of ridiculing it in the *Poetaster.* So it is possible, even though Marston's Crysoganus was intended for Jonson, that Jonson should afterwards reject the compliment, and ridicule the courtier who made it. We must therefore rely only on the internal evidence to determine whether Marston's Crysoganus was intended for Jonson, or for Marston himself.

I have already quoted a passage from Act II., which seems to be more applicable to Jonson than to Marston. Another of the same import occurs in Act III., where the comedians ask him,

'Chrisoganus, faith, what's the lowest price?'

and he answers,

'You know as well as I, ten pound a play.'

(p. 50, ll. 179-80.)

Now if this play was written in 1598 or 1599 it seems preposterous to suppose that Marston, 'the new poet,' as Henslowe calls him Sept. 28, 1599, would be paid even more than the old ones. Here is an entry eighteen days later :—'Received .... for the first part of the *Life of Sir John Oldcastle,* and in earnest of the second part, ten pounds.' The earnest was either 20s. or 40s., so that the payment for the play was £8 or £9. It proved successful, and in November Henslowe bestowed on Munday and the rest of the poets 10s. more 'as a gift.'

A study of Henslowe's diary will show that before 1600 the

highest price ever paid by him was £8 or £9. The usual price varied from £4 to £6. Jonson was the first to charge £10. It was for *Richard Crookback*, about 1600. Greene sold *Orlando Furioso* for 20 nobles, or £7 10s., in 1592. Antonio (Munday) in *The Case is Altered*, says 'an they'll give me £20 a play, I'll not raise my vein,'—an impossible price for an impossibility.

And again, no one can doubt that the position of Crysoganus in Marston's part of the play is altogether similar to that of Asper in *Every man out of his humour*, Crites in *Cynthia's revels*, and Horace in the *Poetaster*. To us, Jonson seems to be the inventor of the method which introduced the author of the play upon the stage, as the great critic of the characters, and the censor of the morals of the age. It is true that in Marston's first play, *Antonio and Mellida*, which was earlier than any of the plays just named, Feliche plays the same part. But I think that any one who reads the play will agree with me, that Feliche does not carry off his character naturally; he does not seem to be an original, but a copy. And Jonson had written many plays now lost, in which I have little doubt that he introduced himself as chorus to criticize his own drama and its persons, as Asper, Crites, and Horace do in his three extant plays. Though Marston in the Induction to the first part of *Antonio and Mellida*, promises a further development of Feliche's character in the second part, he seems to have repented of his purpose, and to have given up his Jonsonese ideal before he wrote again. So that we may probably date his quarrel with Jonson as having occurred between the writings of the two parts of *Antonio and Mellida*.

The part of Crysoganus, as developed by Marston, is precisely similar in principle to that of Feliche and to those of Jonson's

Asper, Crites, and Horace. Hence it is additionally probable that his recension of the *Histriomastix* was made about the time when he wrote the first part, and before he wrote the second part of *Antonio and Mellida*. Hence again it is also easily to be accounted for, if, though he meant Crysoganus for himself, he also completed the sketch with many characteristics taken from Ben Jonson. Jonson was the ideal which he thought he should like to imitate. Consequently in describing himself he, consciously or unconsciously, posed himself in the station and gait of Jonson.

And now I must inquire whether the reference to *Troilus and Cressida* is meant for Shakspere's play. That play was not published till 1609, and then had never been acted in a public theatre. It might however have been exhibited before a private audience, such as would be collected at the revels of one of the Inns of Court. Then comes the question, is Shakspere's *Troilus and Cressida* as early as 1599? Mr Fleay says part of it is, probably, 1597: he recognizes two constituents of the play, one much earlier than the other; the earlier being the Cressida story, the later the Agamemnon story. It is not at all impossible that the short Cressida story may have been first dramatized as a kind of masque for some private revels, and afterwards enlarged into the play as we have it. The date therefore is, I take it, no objection to the supposition that the short play was alluded to in the *Histriomastix*.

And this supposition, founded on the line 'when he *shakes* his furious *Speare*,' seems to gain immense support from the line in the later *Troilus and Cressida*, I. iii. 73, 'When rank Thersites opes his mastic jaws.' Commentators have concluded from this that Thersites was Dekker, and that his *mastic* jaws referred to his *Satiromastix*. But this is unlikely, as that play was written expressly for the company at the Globe in reply to the abuse of them by Jonson in his *Poetaster*. The interpretation of the passage would be much more natural if this mastic Thersites was the author of the *Histriomastix* who had provoked the sarcasm by his attack on the first sketch of the very play where the sarcasm is now found.

After having stated my reasons for believing that Marston is the author of the amended *Histriomastix* of 1599, and that in it he attacks Shakspere, it remains that I should, with all diffidence, propose my hypothesis as to the author and date of the original play. Enough remains of this play, after Marston's additions and alterations are taken out, to show what its main intention was. It was to show the utter unworthiness of actors to any place in the commonwealth, in peace or war, plenty or poverty. With such an object it could hardly have been intended to be acted on any public stage. It was an academical exercise for young men at the universities or for schoolboys to act. In its revised form it is clearly one of the series of plays in which the boy-actors went to buffets with the men-actors of the common stages, and the boys' poets abused the men's poets. There is no indication that in the original play Crysoganus, who in the 3rd Act comes out as Marston-Jonson, was a poet at all; he is a man who professes the seven liberal sciences, and prefers the mathematics to all. In the 1st Act, when the merchants and lawyers propose to go see a play[1] as being all in fashion, one replies, 'See a play! a proper pastime indeed! to hear a deal of prating to so little purpose.' So they all go to Crysoganus' study to hear him read mathematics. And after hearing him they agree to ' design some place for exercise, and

[1] p. 23, l. 170.

every morning have a lecture,' and give Chrisoganus 'competent exhibition'—in other words, to set up an academy, where its members should 'dote in rusty art, plodding upon a book to dull the sense.'[1] The centre of this pedantic institute was quite a different Crysoganus from the one afterwards delineated by Marston.[2]

The earlier Crysoganus seems to one to be of the time when the Earl of Northumberland, Raleigh, and Hariot strove to set up an academy in London. And the spirit of the play, and even its expressions, were quite in unison with Peele's dedication of his *Honour of the Garter* (1593) to the Earl—

> The Muses love, patron, and favourite,
> That *artisans* and scholars dost embrace,
> And clothest *Mathesis* in rich ornaments,
> That admirable mathematic skill
> Familiar with the stars and Zodiac,
> To whom the heaven lies open as her book.

After much more in this style, equally like the matter of the earlier play, Peele begins to speak of

> these unhappy times
> Disfurnished wholly of heroical spirits
> That learning should with glorious hands uphold,

in which only Northumberland has,

> in regard the true philosophy
> That in pure wisdom seats her happiness.

[1] p. 29, l. 20.
[2] How differently Marston treated the Scholastic questions of the first Act of *Histriomastix* may be seen in the character of Lampatho, in Act II. of his *What you will*.

Augustus is dead, and Sidney, and Walsingham—why then do not the poets follow? What has Spenser to do here below, and Harrington, and Daniel, and Campion, and Fraunce? Why do they not go also,

> And leave behind our ordinary grooms
> With trivial humours to pastime the world
> That favours Pan and Phœbus both alike? . . . .
> Why go not all into th' Elysian fields
> And leave this centre barren of repast,
> Unless in hope Augusta will restore
> The wrongs that learning bears of covetousness.

This last line calls to mind the complaints of Nash and Greene in 1589 and 1592 against the covetous players, who would not give proper pay to the scholar poets, because they found that one of their own fellows was *Johannes Factotum* enough to write plays for them. Peele was precisely one of the play-makers whom Greene addressed in his dying protest, and urged to forswear the trade of dramatist. This prologue to his *Honour of the Garter* in 1593 reads like an echo of Greene's words in 1592. And if the original *Histriomastix* was a further contribution by Peele to the same cause, then it follows that the original Post-hast of the play was meant for the Shake-scene of Greene's *Groatsworth of Wit*, the monopolizing factotum Shakspere. In this case Marston, by foisting in the allusion to Troilus, would not have given the old satire any new application, but would simply have amplified it, and brought it down to a later date.

In searching for any external or internal evidence to confirm or contradict this hypothesis, I have tried to find some play of the

Prodigal Child, which in the earlier *Histriomastix* was presented as the masterpiece of the poet Post-hast. I have found none, except that which exists only in the German collection of English tragedies and comedies published in 1620. Of the eight pieces of that collection, one is *Titus Andronicus*, another *Julio and Hypolita*, an alteration of the *Two Gentlemen of Verona;* another Dekker's *Fortunatus*, another *Nobody and Somebody* (referred to by Shakspere in the *Tempest*), another *Sidonea and Theagenea*, another a triumphant comedy of a son of the King of England and a daughter of the King of Scotland. With these secular pieces there are two spiritual plays, the *Prodigal Son*, and the *History of Esther and Haman*, probably the same piece that was played by the Lord Chamberlain's Company at Newington, June 3, and June 10, 1594. It seems to me probable that all these German plays belonged, at the date of their representation in Germany, to a travelling detachment of Shakspere's company. And this hypothesis would lead to the belief that the *Prodigal Son*, as well as *Hester*, was a spiritual play belonging to the Lord Chamberlain's Company in 1593 or 1594. This would bring us a step nearer to the possibility of its being by Shakspere. Another step is, that in the *Groatsworth of Wit* the player who employs Roberto, who is presumably the same player who is afterwards attacked as Shake-scene, is said to be a country author, passing as a moral—'for it was I that penned the moral of *Man's Wit*, the *Dialogue of Dives*, and for seven years space was absolute interpreter of the puppets.' Post-hast the poet is also said in the *Histriomastix* to have began as a ballad-writer, and when his trade as a dramatist fails, he says he will write ballads again. Certainly the tradition is that Shakspere began as a ballad-maker (on Sir Thomas Lucy). And he makes Hamlet say, in a way that may be autobiographic, that he is 'your only jig-maker,' and that he can interpret any action which he sees puppets exhibiting. So that there is some slight evidence both of his jig-making or ballading, of his interpreting to the puppets, and of his writing spiritual plays. Possibly, then, he may have written a *Prodigal Child*, as Post-hast is said to have done.

And when we come to examine the structure of the *Prodigal Son*, we find that it is in great measure borrowed from Greene's autobiographical novel the *Mourning Garment*. And then it becomes one of a series of plays reflecting on Greene, Peele, and Nash, all of which have traditionally been attributed to Shakspere, if we take Posthaste to mean Shakspere. This series of plays includes *Fair Em*, the *London Prodigal*, the *Prodigal Son*, the *Puritan*, and the *Yorkshire Tragedy*. I made some remarks on them in a paper published in the Transactions of the New Shakspere Society, Vol. II. pp. 160, 161, a portion of which I will transcribe. I say, then, that the tradition that *Fair Em* was Shakspere's must be taken in connection with "the curious fact that *Fair Em* is not a solitary phenomenon. There is another play, evidently referring to Greene,[1] and making a mock at his 'Never too late,'—a play of the same date as *Fair Em*, apparently by the same hand, and containing a line identical with one in *Fair Em*—

'Pardon, dear Father, my follies that are past.'

This other play, the *London Prodigal*, was printed in 1605 with Shakspere's name on the title-page. But there is also another play, now only existing in a miserable German translation of the end of

---

[1] Greene is 'Flowerdale' in the play, and it is said of him,
'If e'er his heart doth turn, 'tis ne'er too late.'

the 16th century, which treats the Scriptural story of the Prodigal Son very much as Greene treats it in his more or less autobiographical novel, the *Mourning Garment*. In the old play of *Histriomastix* (which, as we have it, is a hash of two distinct forms of the play, one perhaps as written by Peele about 1590, the other as rewritten by Marston in one of his transient alliances with Ben Jonson about 1600) the *Prodigal Son* is attributed to the poet Posthaste, who, at least in Marston's recension of the play, is pretty clearly identified with Shakspere. Thus we have three plays, the plots of which more or less closely refer to Greene and to his autobiographical novels, all in very early times attributed to Shakspere. Nor does this list exhaust these coincidences. There is another play of which George Peele is the hero, under the synonym of George Pyeboard, and where his tricks and vices are exhibited in the same unsparing fashion as Greene's are in the *London Prodigal*. This play also, *The Puritan, or the Widow of Watling Street*, was printed in Shakspere's life-time with his initials on the title, and reproduced as his in the 4th Folio. Nor does my list end here. For in the *Yorkshire tragedy*, also printed with Shakspere's name on the title during his life, some penitent verses of Thomas Nash, from his *Pierce Penniless*, are put into the mouth of the murderer. Supposing that this was meant to hint at some similarity between Nash and the criminal, we should be obliged to reckon this play as an attack on Nash's memory—he was dead before it was written—and then we have this curious fact, that five plays, exhibiting Greene, or Peele, or Nash in a ludicrous or offensive way, were all traditionally ascribed to Shakspere. Are we to suppose that this tradition of Shakspere's quarrel with these men arose from Greene's letter to his brother playmakers in his *Groatsworth of wit*? Why, then, is none of the various extant attacks on Marlowe's character attributed to Shakspere? But in truth the age was too uncritical to have built so much on the interpretation of an enigmatical letter. The rivalry of the poets was a fact living in the memory of men at the time in question, and it seemed the most natural thing in the world, that whenever any play reflecting on his enemies appeared, it should at once be attributed to Shakspere. And this tradition included plays like *Fair Em* and the *London Prodigal*, which were anterior to Greene's letter. The quarrel therefore did not originate in the latter months of Greene's life, nor was his peevish and splenetic reference to the *Shakescene* a mere sudden and passing expression of wrath."

After these remarks it seems clearly desirable to print a translation of the *Prodigal Son*, in order that readers should be enabled to judge of the hypothesis I put forward. It is only necessary to remark that in all these German translations the original play is strangely metamorphosed and barbarized, all poetry squeezed out, characters and motives ridiculously misrepresented, and nothing but a bare outline of the plot preserved with any approach to truth. The translation will only enable readers to judge of the treatment of the plot, and to trace its resemblance to Greene's treatment of the same matter in his *Mourning Garment*.

HISTRIO-MASTIX.

DRAMATIS PERSONÆ.[1]

PEACE,
GRAMMAR,
LOGIC,
RHETORIC,
ARITHMETIC,
GEOMETRY,
MUSIC,
ASTRONOMY.
MAVORTIUS.
PHILARCHUS.
LARIUS.
HILETUS.
CHRISOGANUS.
INCLE,
BELCH,
GUT, } *players.*
POSTHASTE,
BOUGLE.
FOURCHER.
VOUCHER.
VELURE.
LYONRASH.
Harvest-folks.
PLENTY,
PLUTUS,
CERES,
BACCHUS.
Countrymen.
Clerk of the market.
Merchant's wife.
Prentice.
GULCH, } *players.*
CLOWT,
Ballad-singer.
Vintner.
Usher of the Hall,
Clerk of the kitchen, } to Mavor-
Porter, tius.
Sewer,
Servants,
PROLOGUE,
TROILUS,   VICE,
CRESSIDA,   INIQUITY,
DEVIL,   JUVENTUS.

LANDULPHO, *an Italian Lord.*
Lady.
PRIDE,
VAIN-GLORY,
HYPOCRISY,
CONTEMPT.
Steward.
4 Serving men.
2 Pages.
PERPETUANA.
FILLISELLA.
BELLULA.
Jeweller.
Tyrewoman.
Tailor.
CHAMPERTY.
CALAMANCA.
ENVY.
INGLE.
WAR.
AMBITION.
FURY.
HORROR.
RUIN.
Captain.
Officer.
Russettings and Mechanicals.
Soldiers.
Noblemen.
Peasants.
Citizens.
POVERTY.
FAMINE.
SICKNESS.
BONDAGE.
SLUTTISHNESS.
Hostess.
Constable.
Sailors.
ASTRÆA.
FAME.
FORTITUDE.
RELIGION.
VIRGINITY.
7 Arts.

---

[1] Not in original.

HISTRIO-MASTIX.

ACTUS PRIMI, SCÆNA PRIMA.

Enter PEACE, GRAMMAR, LOGICK, RHETORICK, ARITHMATICK, GEOMETRIE, MUSICK *and* ASTRONOMIE.

Peace. Unmaske thy face thou minister of Time!
Looke forth bright mirror, let thy golded hand
Ride (with distinctlesse motion) on the eyes
Of this fayre *Chorus*, till the Raigne of *Peace*   4
Hath propagated *Plenty*, and increase.
Now sit wee high (tryumphant in our sway)
Encircled with the seaven-fold flower of Art,
[1] To tread on *Barbarisme* with silver feete;   8
These, these are adjuncts fit to waite on *Peace*,
Who beeing courted by most searching spirits,
Have alwayes borne themselves in God-like state
With lofty fore heads, higher then the starres.   12
Draw neere fayre Daughters of eternity,
Your Fostresse *Peace*, is (like the aged Nursse)
Growne proud to see her Children florish thus.
  Gram. We know not how to turne these bounties backe   16
But with continuance of obsequious love.

[1] Suggests the date 1585—95.

Whil'st *Peace* tryumphes, it lyes in *Grammers* might
To make the rudest braine both speake and write.
 Log. Logick shall furnish them with Argument,   20
And make them apt and able to dispute;
The theame shall be of *Peace*, and her sweet name,
And every Sillogism shall prove her fame.
 Rhe. Rhetorick will put her richest habite on,   24
Of gestures, Voice, and exornation.
Her *Tropes* and *Scheames* shall dignifie her sence,
And Honours *Peace*, with clearest eloquence.
 Ar. Her graces in my numbers shall be seene,   28
So full that nothing can be added more,
Nor ought subtracted: true *Arithmetick*
Will multiply and make them infinit.
 Musick. Musick shall feast the bounteous eares of *Peace*,   32
Whil'st she inspires her numme conceipt with life,
Varying each concord, moode and faculty,
In flowing straynes, and rapting *Symphonie*.
 Astr. The motions of the Planets and their Spheares,   36
The starres, their influence, quantities, consents,
All that *Astronomie* can teach or know,
She doth professe from sacred *Peace* to flow.
 Geo. And I will make her powers demonstrative   40
In all my angles, circles, cubes or squares,
The very state of *Peace* shall seeme to shine
In every figure or dimensive lyne.
 Peace. Inough, fayre Virgins, Time shall proove this true;   44
Whil'st you do honor *Peace* shee'le cherish you.

Enter MAVORTIUS, PHILARCHUS, LARIUS, HILETUS, CHRISOGANUS.

Omnes. Honor and safety still attend fayre *Peace.*
Peace. Thankes noble Lords and worthy Gentlemen.
But wherefore looke you so askaunce on these,
As if they were not worthy your salutes?
   Omnes. Because wee know.them not.
   Chri. The more your blame.
   Peace. O pittied state! most weake, where nobles want
The love and knowledge of the liberall Arts;[1]
Are you the men (for birth and place) admir'd?
By whose great motions, lesser wheeles turne round?
And shall your mindes affect so dull a course?
As if your sence where most irrationall?
What is a man superior to a beast
But for his mind? nor that ennobles him,
While hee dejects his reason; making it
The slave unto his brutish appetite.
Make then your mindes illustrious in your deedes,
And each choose (in this troupe) a spowsall mate.
   Mavo. Wee doe obay: And I choose Musick first—
   Phil. I *Geometry.*
   Hile. I *Rhetorick.*
   Lar. And *I Astronomie.*
   Chri. And I to be a servant unto all.
   Peace. But now beware yee injure not the fame

---

[1] This portion of the play seems to belong to the period when there was great talk of setting up academies for the young nobles.

Of these bright Virgins with adulterate love. 70
Meane time their servant (heere) *Chrisoganus*
Shall teach of every Art the misterie. [*Exeunt* PEACE *and Arts.*
  Mavo. But if (by Art) as all our Artists say,
There is no reall truth to be attain'd, 74
Why should wee labour in their loves bestow?
The wisest said : *I know I nothing know.*
  Chri. The wisest was a foole for saying soe :
That Oracle pronounc'd wise *Socrates :* 78
For doe I know I see you, or the light?
Or do you know you heere mee, or I touch you?
  Phil. All this wee needes must know, assuredly.
  Chri. If this bee certaine then which comes from sence? 82
The knowledg proper to the soule is Truer;
For that pure knowledg by the which wee know
A thing to bee, with true cause how it is,
Is more exact then that which knowes it is, 86
And reacheth not to knowledge of the cause.
Besides ; that knowledge (that considers things
Abjunct from sencive matter) is exacter
Then that which joynes it selfe with elements. 90
Arithmetick ever considers numbers
Abstract from sencive matter : *Musick* still
Considers it with sence, as mixt with sound.
Therefore *Arithmeticque* is more exact, 94
And more exact then is *Geometrie :*
Since *unitas* is still *simplicior puncto,*
And number simpler then is magnitude.
For *Unitas* may still be *sine puncto,* 98

But *Punctus* never without Unitie,
Nor, *Magnitudo sine Numero*.
Dum (enim) punctus ponitur, ponitur (ex necessitate) unitas.
    Mavor. But all this prooves not wee may know a truth.   102
    Chri. If wee have this wee call *Scientia*
We must have truth of meere necessity,
For *Acriveia* doth not signifie
Onely a certainty in that wee know,   106
But certainty with all perfection.
    Phil. Although I am not satisfied in this,
It doth me good to heare him thus discourse.
    Mavor. My Lords, let's betake us to our studies.   110
    Phil. In nothing am I better pleas'd, let's goe.   [*Exeunt.*

    Enter INCLE, BELCH, GUTT, POST-HAST.
            The Players Song.

The nut-browne ale, the nut-browne ale
Puts downe all drinke when it is stale.
The toast, the nut-meg, and the ginger   114
Will make a sighing man a singer.
Ale gives a buffet in the head,
    But ginger under-proppes the brayne.
When ale would strike a strong man dead,   118
    Then nut-megge tempers it againe.
The nut-browne ale, the nut-browne ale
Puts downe all drinke when it is stale.
    Inc. This peace breeds such plenty, trades serue no turnes. 122
    Bel. The more fooles wee to follow them.
    Post. Lett's make up a company of Players,

For we can all sing and say,
And so (with practise) soone may learne to play. 126
   Inc. True, could our action answer your extempore.
   Post. Ile teach ye to play true *Politicians*.[1]
   Inc. Why, those are the falsest subtle fellows lives.
   Bel. I pray sir, what titles have trauailing *players?* 130
   Post. Why, *proper-fellowes*, they play Lords and Kings.
   Inc. What parts would best become us (sir) I pray?
   Bel. Faith, to play Roagues, till we be bound for running away.
   Post. Content: Scrivener, ho! 134
You must tye a knott of Knaves togither.

                Enter a SCRIVENER.

   Scri. Your appellations?
   Post. Your names he meanes. The man's learn'd.
   Bel. I, Belch the beard-maker. 138
   Gut. I, Gut the fiddle-string maker.
   Inc. I, Incle the pedlar.
   Post. I, Maister Posthast, the poet.
   Scr. Your nomenclature? 142
   Post. O stately Scrivener! That's: where dwell ye?
   Omnes. Townsmen, townsmen all.
   Scr. The Obligatory's Condition? 145
   Post. Politician players. [*Exit* SCRIVENER
   Bel. But whose men are wee all this while?
   Post. Whose but the merry Knights, Sir Oliver Owlets?
There was never a better man to Players.
   Gut. If our 'parrell be not point-device the fat's i' th' fire. 150

---

[1] Politics the arena of Players. See l. 146.

Post. What a greasy phrase. This playing will furnish ye.
Bel. What ho, Master Bougle, a word.
Post. Here's half a dozen good fellows.
Clout. Soft sir, we are but four or five.   154
Post. The liker to thrive.

Enter BOUGLE.

Bou. What sawcy knaves are these.
Post. A [1] speaks to you *players :* I am the *poet.*
Bel. As concerning the King and the Clowne.   158
Boug. Will you have rich stuff indeed?
Post. Tis not to be dealt on without store of drink.
Boug. Store of money you would say.
Post. Nay, tis well said, for drink must clap up the bargain. 162
Lets away.   [*Exeunt.*

Enter FOURCHER, VOUCHER, VELURE, LYON-RASH, *and* CHRISOGANUS *in his study. These Merchants and Lawyers enter two and two at severall doores.*

Lyon. Maister *Fourcher,* how fares your body sir? come you from your booke?
Four. Troth Master *Lyon-rash,* this *Peace* gives Lawyers leave to play.   166
Velure. Maister *Vourcher?* you are very well incountred sir.
Voucher. Maister Velure, I value your friendship at as high a price as any mans.
Lion. Gentlemen, how shall wee spend this afternoone?   170
Four. Fayth, lets goe see a Play.

[1] *A speaks*—He speaks.

Vel. See a Play, a proper pastime indeed : to heere a deale of prating to so little purpose.

Vour. Why this going to a play is now all in the fashion.   174

Lyon. Why then lets goe where wee may heare sweet musick and delicate songs, for the Harmonie of musick is so Heavenlike that I love it with my life.   177

Four. Nay, faith, this after-noone weele spend in hearinge the Mathematickes read.

Vel. Why then lets to the *Academy*[1] to heare *Crisoganus*.

Omnes. Content.

So all goe to CHRISOGANUS *study, where they find him reading.*

Four. Maister *Chrisoganus :* by your leave, sir.   182

Chri. Gentlemen, you are welcome.

Fur. I pray, sir, what were the best course for a scholler ?

Chri. Why, no man can attaine to any truth,
But he must seeke it *Mathematicé*.   186

Vour. Which are the *Mathematicque* sciences ?

Chri. Arithmetic and Geometry are chiefe.

Vel. What difference is there twixt *philosophy*
And knowledge which is *Mathematicall ?*   190

Chri. This, sir : The natural Philosopher
Considers things as meerely sensible ;
  The *Mathematician ; ut mente abjunctas a materia sensibili.*
But this requireth time to satisfy ;   194
For 'tis an Axiome with all men of Art,
[2] *Mathematicum abstrahentem non comittere mendacium.*

[1] See remarks on the attempt of the Earl of Northumberland, Raleigh, and Hariot to set up an *Academy* in London. Introduction to this play, *ante*, p. 10.

[2] Jonson's *discoveries* are quite contradictory to this notion of Art. He evidently knew little, and cared less, for mathematics and the exact sciences,

And (for the beauty of it,) what can be
Urg'd (more extractive) then the face of heaven? 198
The misteries that Art hath found therein.
It is distinguisht into Regions;
Those Regions fil'd with sundry sorts of starres:
They (likewise) christned with peculiar names. 202
To see a dayly use wrought out of them,
With demonstrations so infallible,
The pleasure cannot bee but ravishing.
    Fur. The very thought thereof enflameth mee. 206
    Chri. Why you shall meet with projects so remov'd
From vulgar apprehension (as for instance)
The Sunne heere riseth in the East with us,
But not of his own proper motion, 210
As beeing turn'd by *primum mobile*
(The heaven above *Cœlum stellarum*)
Whereas his true asscent is in the West.
And so hee consummates his circled course 214
In the Ecliptick line, which partes the Zodiack,
Being borne from Tropick to Tropick. This time
Wee call a yeere; whose *Hierocliphick* was
(Amongst the *Egyptians* figured in a Snake 218
Wreath'd circular, the tayle within his mouth)
As (happily) the Latines (since) did call
A Ring (of the word *Annus*) *Annulus*.
    Vour. I apprehend not in my ablest powers, 222
That once in every foure and twenty houres,

or for the Aristotelian metaphysic. With him, as with the later and altered Chrisoganus, Poetry is the queen of arts.

The sunne should rise and sette; yet be a yeare
In finishing his owne dessigned course.
    Chri. Why, that I will demonstrate to you, thus;   226
Turne a huge wheele: contrary to the sway
Place me a flye uppon't: the flye (before
It can arrive the poynt from whence it went)
Shall sundry times be circumvolv'd about;   230
Even so the Sunne and the affinities:
For if you wonder how at one selfe houre
Two of discordant natures may be borne,
As one a King, another some base Swaine,   234
One valiant, and the other timerous,
Let but two droppes of incke or water fall
Directly on so swift a turning wheele,
And you shall find them both cast farre in sunder.   238
Even so the heavenly *Orbs*, whirling so fast
And so impetuously (project mens fates)
Most full of change and contrariety.
    Four. Good faith these knowledges are very rare,   242
And full of admiration; are they not?
    Chri. The *Mathematicques* are the strength of truth,
A *Magazine* of all perfection.
    Vour. Shall we designe some place for exercise,   246
And every morning have a Lecture read?
    Four. Content, (if soe Chrisoganus stand pleaz'd)
His exhibition shall be competent: wee'le all be Patrons.
    Chri. To make you Artists, answeres my desire,   250
Rather then hope of[1] mercenary hire.   [*Exeunt.*

[1] 'or' in original.

Enter harvest-folkes with a bowle: after them PEACE *leading in* PLENTY: PLUTUS *with ingottes of gold;* CERES *with sheaves:* BACCHUS *with grapes.*

The harvest-folkes Song.

Holyday, O blessed morne!
This day *Plenty* hath beene borne.
Plenty is the child of *Peace;*   254
To her birth the Gods do prease.
Full crown'd Mazors Bacchus brings,
With liquor which from grapes hee wringes.
Holliday, O blessed morne!   258
This day *Plenty* hath bin borne.
Holliday, let's loudly cry,
For joy of her nativity.
Ceres, with a bounteous hand,   262
Doth at *Plenties* elbo stand,
Binding mixed Coronets
Of wheat which on her head she sets.
Holliday, O blessed morne!   266
This day *Plenty* hath bin borne.
Holliday, lets loudly cry
For joy of her nativity.
 Peace. Reach me the bowle with rich *Autumnian* Juice,   270
That I may drinke a health to your new Queene.
Times winged howers (that poynted out my raygne,)
Are fled; I am no more your Soveraigne.
Wound Ayre, with shrill tun'd Canzonets,   274

I robbe my selfe to make my Daughter rich.
Peace doth resigne her pure imperiall Crowne,
(Wrought by the Muses) in whose Circle grow 277
All flowers that are to Phœbus consecrate. [*Exeunt.*
Finis Actus primi.

ACTUS SECUNDI, SCENA: 1.

Enter PLENTY *in Majesty, upon a Throne; heapes of gold;* PLUTUS,
CERES & BACCHUS *doing homage.*

Plen. What heavenly soveraignty supports my state
That *Plenty* raignes (as Princesse) after *Peace?*
Then if this powerfull arme can turne the hower,
It is my will, (and that shall stand for law) 4
That all things on the earth be plentifull.
I crush out bounty from the amber grape,
And fill your barnes with swelling sheaves of Corne.
How can this but engender blessed thought, 8
Especially when Gods our good have sought?
 Ceres. For thee, thy servants captivate the Earth;
Her fruitfulnes fals down at *Plentyes* feete.
 Bach. Bachus will cheere her melancholly sence, 12
With droppes of Nectar from this Crimson Juyce.
 Plut. Her body shall sustaine ten thousand wounds,
And swarthy India be transform'd to Sea,
Disgorging golden choller to the waves 16
Before sweet *Plenty* find the least defect.
 Plen. For this aboundance pour'd at *Plenties* feet
You shall be *Tetrarchs* of this petty world.

Enter MAVORTIUS, PHILARCHUS, CHRISOGANUS.

Mavo. What dullards thus would dote in rusty Arte, 20
Plodding upon a booke to dull the sence,[1]
And see the world become a treasure-house,
Where Angels swarme like Bees in *Plenties* streets,
And every Peasant surfets on their sweetes? 24
   Phil. Give mee a season that will sturre the blood;
I like not Nigardice to hungar-starve.
Tis good when poore men frolicke in the hall,
The whil'st our fathers in the Chambers feast, 28
And none repines at any straunger-guest.
   Chri. Who was the authour of this store, but Peace?
That common-welth is never well at ease
Where Parchment skinnes, whose use should bear records, 32
Must head their brawling Drummes and keepe a coyle,
As if they threatned Plenty with a spoyle.
   Plenty. Your houses must bee open to the poore,
Your dusty Tables fill'd with store of meate. 36
Let goodly yeomen at your elboes stand,
Swords by their sides and trenchers in their hand:
Long-skirted coates, wide-sleeves with cloth 'inough:
Thus Lords, you shall my government enlarge; 40
Reverence your Queene, by practizing her charge.
   Omnes. Ours be the charge, and thine the Empire.
                                  [*Exit* PLENTY
   They bring her to the doore and leave her.
   Mavor. Gallants, let us invent some pleasing sportes,

---

[1] Compare with Biron's speech in *Love's Labour Lost*, IV. iii. 289.

To fit the Plentuous humor of the Time. 44
    Chri. What better recreations can you find
Then sacred knowledge in divinest thinges?
    Phil. Your bookes are Adamants, and you the Iron
That cleaves to them till you confound yourselfe. 48
    Mavor. Poore Scholler spend thy spirits so and dye.
    Phil. Let them doe soe that list; so will not I.
    Mavor. I cannot feed my appetite with Ayre
I must pursue my pleasures royally: 52
That, spung'd in sweat, I may returne from sport,
Mount mee on horseback, keepe the Hounds and Haukes,
And leave this Idle contemplation
To rugged Stoicall Morosophists. 56
    Chri. O, did you but your own true glories know,
Your judgements would not then decline so low!
    Phil. What! Maister *Pedant*, pray forbeare, forbeare.
    Chri. Tis you my Lord that must forbeare to erre. 60
    Phil. Tis still safe erring with the multitude.
    Chri. A wretched morall; more than barbarous rude.
    Mavor. How you translating-scholler? you can make
A stabbing *Satir*,[1] or an *Epigram*, 64
And thinke you carry just *Ramnusia's* whippe,
To lash the patient; goe, get you clothes,
Our free-borne blood such apprehension lothes.
    Chri. Proud Lord, poore Art shall weare a glorious crowne 68
When her despisers die to all renowne. [*Exeunt*

---

[1] Here begins the alteration; from this point Chris. is Ben Jonson. The additions perhaps by Marston. See *ante*, p. 4.

Enter Contrimen, to them, Clarke of the Market: hee wrings a bell, and drawes a curtaine; whereunder is a market set about a Crosse.

Con. Wher's this drunkard Clarke to ring the bell?
Clar. Heigho, bottle Ale has buttond my cappe.
Corne-b. Whats a quarter of Corne?   72
Seller. Two and six-pence.
Corne-b. Ty't up tis mine.

Enter a Marchants wife, with a Prentice, carrying a hand-basket

Wife. Ha' y' any Potatoes?
Seller. Th' aboundance will not quite-cost the bringing.   76
Wife. What's your Cock-sparrowes a dozen?
Sel. A penny, Mistresse.
Wife. Ther's for a dozen; hold.

Enter GULCH, BELCH, CLOWT *and* GUT. *One of them steppes on the Crosse, and cryes, A Play.*

Gulch. All they that can sing and say,   80
Come to the Towne-house and see a play.
At three a clock it shall beginne,
The finest play that ere was seene.
Yet there is one thing more in my minde: 84
Take heed you leave not your purses behinde.

Enter a Ballet-singer and sings a Ballet

Bal. Whats your playes name? Maisters, whose men are ye?
How, the signe of the Owle i' th' Ivybush? Sir Oliver Owlets?

Gul. Tis a sign ye are not blind, Sir. 88
Belch. The best that ever trode on stage!
The Lascivious Knight, and *Lady Nature!*
Post. Have you cryd the play, maisters!
Omnes. I, I, I. No doubt we shall have good dooings, but 92
How proceed you in the new plot of the *Prodigall Childe?*
Post. O sirs, my wit's grown no less plentiful than the time;
Thers two sheets done in folio, will cost two shillings in rime.
Gul. Shall we heere a flurt before the audience come? 96
Post. I, that you shall, I sweare by the Sunne. Sit down sirs.

(*He reades the Prologue—they sit to heare it*)
'When Aucthours quill in quivering hand
　His tyred arm did take,
His wearied Muse bad him devise 100
　Some fine play for to make.'
And now, my Maisters, in this bravadoe,
I can read no more without Canadoe.
Omnes. What ho! some Canadoe quickly! 104

Enter VINTNER *with a quart of Wine.*

Post. Enter the Prodigal Child—fill the pot, I would say.
'Huffa, huffa, who calls for me?
I play the Prodigall child in jollytie.'
Clowt. O detestable good! 108
Post. Enter to him Dame Vertue:
'My sonne, thou art a lost childe'
(This is a passion, note you the passion?)
'And hath many poore men of their goods beguild: 112

O prodigall child, and child prodigall'—
Read the rest sirs, I cannot read for teares.
Fill me the pot I prethe fellow Gulch.
 Gut. Faith, we can read nothing but riddles.   116
 Post. My maisters, what tire wears your lady on her head?
 Bel. Four squirrels tails tied in a true loves knot.
 Post. O amiable [1] good, 'tis excellent!
 Clout. But how shall we do for a Prologue for lords?   120
 Post. Ile do it extempore.
 Bel. O might we hear a spurt if need require?
 Post. Why, *Lords, we are here to shew you what we are:*
Lords, we are here although our clothes be bare.   124
Instead of flowers in season ye shall gather Rime and Reason
I never pleasd myself better, it comes off with such suavity.
 Gul. Well fellows, I never heard happier stuff.
Heres no new luxury or blandishment,   128
But plenty of Old Englands mothers words.
 Clout. [2] Ist not pity this fellow's not employd in matters of State?
But wheres the Epilogue must beg the plaudite?
 Post. Why man, *The glass is run, our play is done:*   132
Hence; Time doth call, we thank you all.
 Gulsh. I, but how if they do not clap their hands?
 Post. No matter so they thump us not.
Come come, we poets have the kindest wretches to our Ingles. 136
 Belch. Why, whats an Ingle, man?
 Post. One whose hands are hard as battle doors with clapping
  at baldness.
 Clowt. Then we shall have rare ingling at the prodigall child. 140

---

[1] admirable (?)   [2] Characteristics of Posthaste. See Note 2, p. 87.

Gul. I, ant be played upon a good night. Lets give it out for Friday.

Post. Content.

Enter Steward.

Stew. My maisters, my Lord Mavortius is disposed to hear what you can do. 144

Belch. What! fellows, shall we refuse the Town play?

Post. Why, his reward is worth the Mayor and all the Town.

Omnes. Weele make him merry i' faith; wele be there. [*Exeunt.*

Enter VELURE *and* LYON-RASH, *with a Water-spaniell and a Duck.*

Vel. Come, sirs, how shall we recreate our selves? 148
This plentious time forbids aboad at home.

Lyon. Let's Duck it with our Dogs to make us sport,
And crosse the water to eate some Creame. What hoe! Sculler.

Vel. You doe forget; *Plenty* affoords us Oares. 152

Enter FURCHER *and* VOURCHIER, *with bowes and arrowes.*

Four. What, shall we shoote for a greene Goose, sir?

Vour. Ther's a wise match.

Fur. Faith, we may take our bowes and shafts and sleepe,
This dreaming long vacation gives us leave. 156

Vel. Gentlemen, well met. What? *Pancrace*[1] Knights?

---

[1] The Pancras knights are no doubt so calld from their gay dress, like 'The Earl of Pancridge' [Pancras], one of the ridiculous personages in the burlesque procession called Arthur's Show. Jonson mentions him....
                        C. Or our Shoreditch duke.
    M. Or *Pancridge earl.*   *P.* Or Bevis, or sir Guy.—*Tale of a Tub,* iii. 3.
Also in some lines against Inigo Jones, he says:
        Content thee to be *Pancridge* earl the while,
        An earl of show, for all thy worth is show.
            To Inigo Marquis Would be.'   Nares.—F. J. F.

Vour. The bounty of the time will have it so.

Four. You are prepared for sport, as well as we.

Vour. One of the goodliest Spaniels I have seene.   160

Lyon. And heere's the very quintessence of Duckes.

Fur. For diving meane yee?

Lyon. I, and thriving too,
For I have wonne three wagers this last weeke;   164
What? will you goe with us and see our sport?

Vour. No faith, sir, Ile go ride and breath my horse.

Vel. Why whether ride you? we will all go with you.

Vour. Lets meet some ten miles hence, to hawke and hunt. 168

Lyon. Content: This plenty yeelds us choise of sports;
Our trades and we are now no fit consorts.   [*Exeunt.*

Enter Usher of the Hall; and Clarck of the Kitchin:

Usher. Maister Clarke of the Kitchin, faith what's your dayly expence.   172

Clar. Two beeves; a score of Muttons;
Hogsheads of Wine and Beere, a doozen a day.

Ush. Never was Age more plentifull.

Clar. Usher, it is my Lords pleasure all comers bee bounteously entertaind.   177

Ush. I, but its my Ladies pleasure?

Clar. What else? She scornes to weare cloth-breeches [1] man.

Enter Porter.

Porter. A Morrice-daunce of neighbours crave admittance. 180

---

[1] Allusion to Greene's pamphlet, 1592. "A Quip for an Upstart Courtier: Or, a quaint dispute between Velvet breeches and Cloth-breeches." (Imitated from the anonymous "Debate Betweene Pride and Lowlines," ab. 1570, *not* by Francis Thynne.)—F. J. F.

Clar. Porter, let them in man.

Enter Morrice-dancers.

Butler, make them drinke their skinnes full.

Omnes mor. dan. God blesse the founder.

Clar. Porter, are these Players come? 184

Port. Halfe an houre a goe sir.

Clar. Bid them come in and sing. The meat's going up. [*Exit.*

Ush. Gentlemen and yeomen, attend upon the Sewer.

Enter Players, with them POST-HAST *the Poet.*[1]

Ush. Sir *Oliver Owlets* men, welcome. By Gods will, 188
It is my Lords pleasure it should be so.

Post. Sir we have carowst like Kings;
For heere is plenty of all things.

Ush. Looke about you Maisters; be uncover'd. 192

Enter Sewer with service, in side livery coates.
The Players Song.

Brave ladds come forth and chant it, and chant it,
   for now 'tis supper time.
See how the dishes flaunt it, and flaunt it,
   with meate to make up rime. 196
Pray for his honor truly, and truly,
   in all hee under takes.
He serv's the poore most duely, and duely,
   as all the country speakes. 200

Post. God blesse my Lord Mavortius and his merry men all:
To make his honour merry we sing in the hall.

---

[1] Post-hast not reckoned a " Player " amongst the rest, but a " poet." See Note 2, p. 87.—G.

Usher. My maisters, for that we are not only (for causes)
Come new to the house; but also (for causes) 204
I marvaile where you will lodge.
  Post. We hope (for causes) in the house, though drink be in our
    heads,
Because to Plenty we carowse for beefe, and beere, and beds.
  Ush. Sed like honest men : what playes have you? 208
  Belch. Heres a Gentleman scholar[1] writes for us.
I pray, maister Post-hast, declare for our credits.
  Post. For mine own part, though this summer season,
I am desperate of a horse. 212
  Ush. Tis well. But what plays have you?
  Post. A gentleman's a gentleman that hath a clean shirt on, with
    some learning   And so have I.
  Ush. One of you answer the names of your playes. 216
  Post. Mother Gurtons neadle (a tragedy)
The Devel and Dives (a comedie)
A russet coat and a knaves cap (an Infernal)
A proud heart and a beggars purse (a pastoral) 220
The widdowes apron stringes (a nocturnall)
  Ush. I promise ye, pritty names.
I pray, what ye want in any thing, to take it out in drink. 223
And so go, make ye ready masters. [*Exeunt Players.*

Enter MAVORTIUS, PHILARCHUS, *with* LANDULPHO (*an Italian
  Lord*) *and other nobles and gentles to see the play.*
  Mavor. My lords, your entertainment is but base
Coarser your cates, but welcome with the best.

---

[1] Gentleman-scholar. See note on characteristics of Post-hast, p. 87.

Fellowes, some cushions; place faire ladies heere.
Signoour Landulpho, pray be merry sir.   228
    Lady. I'st th' Italian guise to be so sad,
When Love and Fancie should be banquetting?
    Land. Madam, your kindnesse hath full power to command.
    Lady. These admirable wits of Italy,   232
That court with lookes, and speake in sillables,
Are curious sepervisours over strangers;
And when we covet so to frame our selves,
(Like over-nice portraying picturers,)   236
We spoyle the counterfeit in colouring.
England is playne, and loves her mothers guyse;
Enricht with cunning, as her parents rise.
    Land. Lady, these eyes did ever hate to scorne, 240
This toung's unur'd to carpe or contrary:
The bozome where this heart hath residence
I wish may seeme the seat of curtesie
    Usher Rowme, my Maisters, take your places.   244
Hold up your torches for dropping there!
    Mavor. Usher, are the Players ready? bid them beginne.

Enter Players and sing.

Some up and some down, there's players in the Town:
You wot well who they bee.   248
The sum doth arise to three companies:
    One, two, three, foure, make we.
Besides we that travel, with pumps full of gravell,[1]

[1] Ben Jonson, *Poetaster*. 'If he pen for thee once thou *shalt not need to travel with thy pumps full of gravel* any more, after a blind jade and a hamper, and stalk upon boards and barrell-heads to an old crackt trumpet.'

Made all of such running leather,   252
That once in a week, new masters we seeke,
And never can hold together.

Enter PROLOGUE.

Phillida was a fair maid—I know one fairer than she.
Troilus was a true lover—I know one truer than he.   256
And Cressida, that dainty dame, whose beauty fair and sweet,
Was clear as is the crystal stream that runs along the street.
How Troyl he, that noble knight, was drunk in love, and bade
    good night.
So bending leg likewise, do you not us despise.   260
    Land. Most ugly [1] lines and base-browne-paper [1]-stuffe
Thus to abuse our heavenly poesie,
That sacred off-spring from the braine of Jove,
Thus to be mangled with prophane absurds,   264
Strangled and chok't with lawlesse bastards words.
    Mavor. I see (my Lord) this home-spun country stuffe
Brings little liking to your curious eare,
Be patient, for perhaps the play will mend.   268

Enter TROYLUS *and* CRESSIDA.

    Tro. Come Cressida, my Cresset light,
Thy face doth shine both day and night
Behold behold thy garter blue . . . .
Thy knight his valiant elbow wears,   272
That when he shakes his furious Speare [2]
The foe in shivering fearful sort

---

[1] Marston-like.   [2] The Shakspere allusion.   See Introduction, p. 3.

May lay him down in death to snort.

Cres. O knight, with valour in thy face,   276
Here take my skreene, wear it for grace,
Within thy helmet put the same,
Therewith to make thine enemies lame.

Land (Lame stuff indeed, the like was never heard.)   280

Enter a roaring DEVIL *with the* VICE *on his back,* INIQUITY *in one hand, and* JUVENTUS *in the other.*

Vice. Passion of me sir, puff, puff, how I sweat, sir;
The dust out of your coat I intend for to beat, sir.

Juven. I am the prodigal child, I, that I am,
Who says I am not, I say he is to blame.   284

Iniq. And I likewise am Iniquity,
Belov'd of many, alas for pity.

Devil. Ho! ho! ho! these babes mine are all;
The Vice, Iniquity, and child Prodigall.   288

Land. Fie! what unworthy foolish foppery
Presents such buzzardly simplicity.

Mavor. No more, no more, unlesse twere better,
And for the rest yee shall be our debter.   292

Post. My Lords, of your accords,
Some better pleasure for to bring,
If you a theame affords,
You shall know it,   296
That I, *Post-haste*, the Poet,
Extempore can sing.

Lan. I pray my Lord let's ha'te; the Play is so good
That this must needs be excellent.   300

Mavo. Content (my Lord) pray give a theame.

Theam.

Land. Your Poetts and your Pottes [1]
Are knit in true-Love knots.

The Song extempore

Give your scholar degrees, and your lawyer his fees,   304
   And some dice for Sir Petronell flash : [2]
Give your Courtier grace, and your Knight a new case,
   And empty their purses of cash.
Give your play-gull a stool, and my lady her fool,   308
   And her Usher potatos and marrow;
But your poet were he dead, set a pot to his head
   And he rises as peart as a sparrow.
O delicate wine, with thy power so divine   312
   Full of ravishing sweet inspiration,
Yet a verse may run clear that is tap'd out of beer,
   Especially in the vacation.
But when the term comes that with trumpets and drums   316
   Our play houses ring in confusion
Then Bacchus me murder—but rime we no further—
   Some sack now, upon the conclusion!

Mavor. Give them forty pence,[3] let them go.   320

[Exeunt players

---

[1] Earle in his *Microcosmography* gives a character of 'A Pot-Poet,' p. 45. Ed. Arber.

[2] In *Eastward Hoe*, Act I., 'Sir Petronel' is called also 'Sir Flash,' Marston, iii. p. 114.

[3] 40 pence, or 3s. 4d., the fee to a company of players for a play. This points to an early date—say 1592. (The fee rises in the next act to £10: See p. 53, l. 266. So much for *Plenty's* reign.—G.)

How likes Landulpho this extempore song?

Land. ¹I blush in your behalfes at this base trash.
In honour of our Italy we sport
As if a synod of the holly Gods, 324
Came to triumph within our Theatres —
(Always commending English courtesy)
Our Amphitheatres and Pyramides
Are setuate like three-headed Dindymus, 328
Where stand the Statues of three striving Queens
That once contended for the goulden ball,
(Alwaies commending English curtesie)
Are not your curious Dames of sharper spirit? 332
I have a mistresse whose intangling wit,
Will turne and winde more cunning arguments
Then could the *Crœtan Labyrinth* ingyre.
(Alwayes commending English courtesie.) 336

 Mavo. Good sir, you give our English Ladyes cause
Respectively to applaud th' Italian guise,
Which proudly hence-forth we will prosecute.

 Land. Command what fashion Italy affoords. 340

 Phil. By'r Lady sir, I like not of this pride.
Give me the ancient hospitallity:
They say, Tis merry in hall, when beards wag all.
The Italian Lord is an Asse: the song is a good song. 344

 ¹ This speech of Landulpho is in the vein of Greene or Peele.

ACTUS TERTIJ, SCÆNA 1.

Enter PRIDE, VAINE-GLORY, HYPOCRISIE, *and* CONTEMPT :
PRIDE *casts a mist, wherein* MAVORTIUS *and his company vanish off the Stage, and* PRIDE *and her attendants remaine.*

Pride. Brave mindes, now beautifie your thoughts with pompe,
Send forth your Shipps unto the furthest Seas,
Fetch me the feathers of th' Arabian Birds,
Bring Mermaides combes, and glasses for my gaze :   4
Let all your sundry imitating shapes
Make this your native soyle the land of Apes.
Then Ladies trick your traines with Turkish pride,
Plate your disheavled haire with ropes of Pearle,   8
Weare sparkling Diamonds like twinkling starres,
And let your spangled crownes shine like the Sunne :
' *If you will sit in throne of state with Pride*
The newest fashion (still) must be your guide.   12
    Vain. Vaine-glory vowes to lackey by thy foote,
Till she hath swolne mens hearts with Arrogance.
    Hyp. In like designes, *twofac'd Hypocrisie*
Is prest to spend her deepest industry.   16
    Cont. And (till her soveraignty decline and bow)
Contempt shall be enthron'd in every browe.
    Pry. Then thus, (as soveraigne Empresse of all sinnes)
Pryde turnes her houre, and heere her Sceane beginnes.   20

Enter FURCHER, *and* VOURCHER;[1] *two Lawyers.*

Vour. How shall we best imploy this idle time?
Four. Lets argue on some case for exercise.
Vour. You see the full-gorg'd world securely sleepes, 24
And sweet contention (Lawyers best content)
Is sent by drowsie *Peace* to banishment.
Pryd. O these be Lawyers! Concords enemies;
Prydes fuell shall their fire of strife increase. [*aside.*]

Enter VELURE *and* LYON-RASH.

Four. Signior *Vourcher*, know you those Cittizens? 28
Vour. They are two wealthy merchants and our friends.
Four. Yt may be they have brought us welcome fees.
Pry. Lawyers and Merchants met! bestir thee *Pride*. [*aside.*]
Vel. In faith no sute sir; quiet, quiet all. 32
Pry. Fortune and health attend you, Gentlemen.
Four. We thank you, Lady; may we crave your name?
Pry. Men call me *Pryde*, and I am *Plenties* heire:
Immortal, though I beare a mortal showe. 36
Are not you Lawyers, from whose reverend lippes
Th' amazed multitude learne Oracles?
Are not you Merchants, that from East to West,
From the Antarcticke to the Arctick Poles, 40

---

[1] These are law terms. Davis, Epigram 24, says that when Gallus talks to him in military slang—

'With words of my profession I reply;
I tell of fourching, vouchers, and counterpleas
Of withernams, essoins, and champarty.'

Bringing all treasure that the earth can yeeld?

Omnes. We are (most worthy Lady)

Pry. Then use your wisedome to enrich your selves:
Make deepe successe high Steward of your store.
Enlarge your mighty spirits: strive to excede
In buildings, ryot, garments, gallantry.
For take this note: *The world the show affects:*
Playne Vertue, (*vilie clade*) *is counted Vice;*
And makes high blood indure base præjudice.

Vour. But wee have Lawes to limitte our attire.[1]

Pry. Broke with the least touch of a golden wyer.

Vel. Yet wisedome still commands to keepe a meane.

Pry. True, had you no meanes to excell the same;
But having power labour to ascend,
The fames of mighty men do never end.

Four. Is not Ambition an aspiring sinne?

Pry. Yes for blind batts and birds of lazy wing.

Lyon. Me seemes tis good to keepe within our bounds.

Pry. Why beasts themselves of bounds are discontent.
Spend me your studies to get offices,
Then stooping suiters and uncovered heads
May groaning come, unbowelling[2] the bagges
Of their rich burthens in your wide-mouth'd deskes.

Lyon. But men will taxe us to want charity.

---

[1] Sir Geo. Bond, L. Mayor in 1587-8, wrote from the city to the P. Council, to say that in order to maintain comely order (which could not be without some further toleration) they had drawn up a book containing a certain order for apparel of citizens and their wives, and desiring that they might not be impeached for wearing it. (Nichols, Prog. of Q. Eliz., ii. p. 543.)

[2] Incomplete note in Mr Simpson's MS.—'if some expression of Sh.'

Pry. True charity beginneth first at home.
Heere in your bosomes dwell your deere-lov'd hearts;
Feed them with joy; first crowne their appetites,
And then cast water on the care-scorcht face. 68
Let your owne longings first be satisfied;
All other pitty is but foolish pryde.

Four. Sweet councell; worthy of most high regard.
All our endeavours shall be to aspire. 72

Vour. Ours to be rich and gallant in attire.

Pry. All to be brave, else all of no respect;
It is the habit doth the mind deject.[1]

Vour. Lets brave it out, since *Pride* hath made us knowe, 76
Nothing is grac'd that wants a glorious showe.

Exeunt : manet PRYDE.

Pry. The puft up spirits of the greater sort
Shall make them scorne the abject and the base;
Th' impatient spirit of the wretched sort 80
Shall think imposed duties their disgrace,
Poore naked neede shall be as full of pryde,
As he that for his wealth is Deifide. [*Exit.*

Enter Steward, with foure Serving-men, with Swords and Bucklers, in their hose and doublets.

1. *ser.* No Steward with discharge shall us disgrace. 84

Stew. Why, all the Lords have now cashierd their traines.

---

[1] *deiect*—perhaps *detect.* (Compare Polonius's advice to Laertes:
  Costly thy habit as thy purse can buy,
  But not expresst in fancy; rich, not gaudy;
  For the apparel oft proclaims the man.
              Hamlet, I. iv. 70-2.—F. J. F.)

2. *ser.* But we have serv'd his father in the field.

3 *ser.* What, think they boyes can serve to beard their foes?

Enter MAVORTIUS *and* PHILARCHUS *with their pages.*

Page. Be patient, fellow, seest thou not my Lord? 88

1. *ser.* What an I see him? puppet, prating ape!

2. *ser.* We are no stocks, but we can feele disgrace.

3 *serv.* Nor tonglesse blocks; but since we feele, weele speak.

Mavo. What a coyle keepes those fellows there? 92

Stew. These impudent, audatious, serving-men,
Scarcely beleeve your honours late discharge. [*Exit*

1. *ser.* Beleeve it? by this sword and buckler, no:
Stript of our liveries, and discharged thus? 96

Mavo. Walke sirs, nay walke; awake yee drowsie drones
That long have suckt the honney from my hives:
Begone yee greedy beefe-eaters; y'are best:
The Callis Cormorants[1] from Dover roade 100
Are not so chargeable as you to feed.

Phil. 'Tis true my Lord, they carelessly devoure.
In faith, good fellowes, get some other trade;
Ye live but idle in the common-wealth. 104

Mavo. Broke we not house up, you would breake our backs.

1. *ser.* We breake your backs? no, 'tis your rich lac'd sutes,
And straight lac'd mutton; those breake all your backs.

Phil. Cease, Ruffians! With your swords and bucklers, hence.

2. *ser.* For service, this is savage recompence. 109

---

[1] Refers most easily to the year when the English in Henry IV.'s pay were discharged. But the returners from the Low Countries must have kept up always a procession on the Dover Road. Calais Cormorants however are men who have served in France.

Your fathers bought lands and maintained men:
You sell your lands, and scarse keepe rascall boyes;
Who ape-like jet, in garded coates, are whipt 112
For mocking men.   Though with a shamlesse face,
Yet gracelesse boyes can never men disgrace.

   3. *Ser.* Desertfull vertue: O impiety! [*Exeunt*

   Mavo. My Lord *Philarchus*, follow all my course, 116
I keepe a Taylor, Coach-man, and a Cooke,
The rest for their boord-wages may goe looke.
A thousand pound a yeare will so be sav'd,
For revelling and banquetting and playes 120

   Phil. Playes, well remembred: we will have a play.
Steward, lets have Sir *Olliver Owlets* men.

   Mavo. *Philarchus*, I mislike your fashion.

   Phil. Faith, Ile fly intoo't with a sweeping wing. 124
Methinkes your honours hose sit very well;
And yet this fashion is growne so stale.

   Mav. Your hat is of a better blocke then mine.

   Phil. Is on a better block, your Lordship meanes. 128

   Mav. Without all question 'tis; he that denies
Either, he hath no judgement or no eyes.

   Phil. Your Lordships doublet-skirt is short and neate.

   Mav. Who sits there, finds the more uneasie seate. 132

Enter a Page

   Pag. My Lords, your Supper staies; tis eight a clock.

   Mav. What, is't so late?   That fashion's not so good. [*Exeunt.*

Enter PERPETUANA, FILLISELLA, BELLULA; *with them a Jewel-*
ler, a Tyre-woman, and a Taylour; with every one their severall
furniture.

Perp. Of our three Jewells (sir) which likes you best?
Jew. An excellent piece. This those excells as farre   136
As glorious *Tytan* staines a silly Starre.
Filli. Tush, be not partiall, but peruse mine well.
See you not proud *Ulisses* carrying spoyles?
Jew. The rest are but (to this) in sooth base foyles,   140
And yet they all are ritch, and wondrous faire.
Bell. But trash: Ile have a Jewell Amatist
Whose beauty shall strike blind the gazers Eye;
Perp. Ile put it downe. One promisd to devise   144
A Globe—like Jewell, cut transparently,
And in the place of fixed starres to set
The richest stones that mightiest summes could get.
Fill. Nay, Ile be matchlesse for a carckanet,   148
Whose Pearles and Diamonds, placed with ruby[1] rocks,
Shall circle this fair necke to set it forth.
Bell. Well Goldsmith, now you may be gone.—[*Exit Jeweller*]
     Taylour,   152
Ile have a purfled Roabe, loose boddied wise,
That shall enjoy my jewells maydenhead.
Tay. The loosest bodies are in fashion most.
Perp. We better know what likes us best, then you.   156
Let me have flaring fashions, tuck't and pinn'd[2],
That powerfull winds may heave it all a huffe.

[1] *orig.* ruly.   [2] *i.e.* winged or flounced.

Bell. True measure of my body shalbe tane:
Plaine dealing is the best when all is done. 160
That fall Pride taught us when we first begun.

Fill. Ile have a rich imbost imbrothery,
On which invaluable pretious Roabe
Ile hang the glorious brightnesse of my Globe. 164
Mistresse Pinckanie, is my new ruffe done?

Pinc. Beleeve me, Madam, tis but new begun.

Bell. Let pinching citty-dames orecloud their Eies,
Our brests lie forth like conduicts of delight, 168
Able to tice the nicest appetite.
Mistresse Pinckanie, shall I have this Fanne?

Pink. Madam, not this weeke, doe what I can.

Fill. Pleasure as bond-slave to our wills is tyed. 172
We Ladies cannot be defam'd with Pride.
Come, lets have a play: let poore slaves prate;
Ranck pride in meanest sort, in us is state.
Remember promise, mistres Pinkanie. 176

Pink. Well Ladies, though with worke I am opprest,
Workewomen alwaies live by doing, best. [*Exeunt*

Enter CHRISOGANUS, POST HAST, GULCH, CLOUT, GUT *and* BELCH.

Bel. Chrisoganus, faith, what's the lowest price?

Chri. You know as well as I; tenne pound a play. 180

Gul. Our Companie's hard of hearing of that side.

Chri. And will not this booke passe? alasse for pride!
I hope to see you starve and storme for books;
And in the dearth of rich invention, 184

When sweet smooth lines are held for pretious,
Then will you fawne and crouch to Poesy.
   Clout. Not while goosequillian Posthast holds his pen.
   Gut. Will not our own stuffe serve the multitude?   188
   Chri. Write on, crie on, yawle to the common sort
Of thick-skin'd auditours such rotten stuffs,
More fit to fill the paunch of Esquiline [1]
Than feed the hearings of judiciall eares.   192
Yee shades, triumphe, while foggy Ignorance
Clouds bright Apollos beauty!   Time will cleere
The misty dulnesse of Spectators Eyes:
Then, woeful hisses to your fopperies!   196
O age, when every Scriveners boy shall dippe
Profaning quills into Thessaliaes spring;
When every artist prentice that hath read
The pleasant pantry of conceipts shall dare   200
To write as confident as Hercules;
When every ballad-monger boldly writes
And windy forth [2] of bottle-ale [3] doth fill
Their purest organ of invention—   204
Yet all applauded and puft up with pride,
Swell in conceit, and load the stage with stuff
Rakt from the rotten imbers of stall jests;
Which basest lines best please the vulgar sense,   208
Make truest rapture lose preheminence!
   Bel. The fellow doth talke like one that can talke.
   Gut. Is this the well-learn'd man Chrisoganus?
He beats the ayre the best that ere I heard.   212

[1] This is Marston's. See p. 5.   [2] froth.   [3] cf. Ben Jonson.

Chri. Ye scrappes of wit, base Ecchoes to our voice,
Take heed ye stumble not with stalking hie,
Though fortune reels with strong prosperity.   [*Exit.*
   Clout. Farwell the Muses, poor Poet adiew!   216
When we have need, 't may be weele send for you.

Enter STEWARD.

   Stew. My Lord hath sent request to see a play.
   Post. Your Lord? What, shall our pains be soundly recompenc'd
With open hand of honours francke reward?   220
   Stew. Ye shall have four faire Angells gentlemen.
   Clout. Faire ladies, meane you? We have four i' th' play.
   Stew. Nay, my good friends, I meane in faire pure gold.
   Gul. Fie, 'tis to much, too long ere it be told.   224
   Stew. Mas, these are single jests indeed;
But I will double it once, ye shall have eight.
   Post. But are you sure that none will want the weight
To wey downe our expense in sumptuous Clothes?   228
   Bel. Well, pleasure's pride shall mount to higher rate;
Tenne pound a play will scarce maintaine our state.
   Stew. Fat *Plenty* brings in *Pride* and *Idleness;*
The world doth turn a maze in giddy round;   232
This time doth rayse what other times confound.
   Post. O sir, your moral lines were better spent
In matters of more worthy consequent.
   Gul. Well, whilest occasion helpes to clime aloft   236
Wee'le mount Promotions highest battlement.
   Stew. And breake your neckes I hope.   Clime not too fast:
A heady course confusion ends at last.

Post. Preach to the poore. Look, Steward, to your compt. 240
Direct your houshold, teach not us to mount.

Stew. Farewell ye proud (I hope they heare me not)
Proud Statute rogues.[1]   [*Exit they follow.*

Enter FOURCHER, VELURE, LYON-RASH, CHAMPERTY *and* CALA-
MANCHA, *their wives.*

Champ. Faith, husband, Ile have one to beare my traine; 244
Another bare before, to usher me.

Cala. Nay, I my selfe will learne the Courtly grace;
Honour shall give my wealth a higher place.
Out on these velvet gards, and black-lac'd sleeves, 248
These simpering fashions simply followed.

Cham. Well, through the streetes in thundring coache Ile ride:
Why serves our wealth, but to maintaine our pride?
Lawe, Armes, and Merchandize, these are three heads, 252
From whence Nobility first tooke his spring.
Then let our haughty mindes our fortune spend;
Pleasure and honour shall our wealth attend.

Calla. Nay I will have it, I, that I will. 256

Four. Containe your speech within your private thoughts,
Wee are encountred with the honour'd traine.

Enter MAVORTIUS, PHILARCHUS, FILLISSELLA, BELLULA, *and
others.*

Mavo. Faire Ladies, could these times affoord you cates,

---

[1] The act of 1597, cap. IV., enacted that 'all fencers, bearwards, common players of enterludes, and minstrels, wandering abroad; all juglers, tinkers, pedlars &c. shall be adjudged and deemed *rogues, vagabonds,* and *sturdy beggars.*'

You should be feasted in *Apolloes* hall;   260
But (Lords) the chaps of wide-pancht gluttonie
Have wasted all the dainties of the land.
Servant *Philarchus*, what, no maske too night?
   Phil. A Play, a Maske, a Banquet, weele have all.   264

Enter STEWARD

   Stew. My Lord, the Players now are growne so proud,
Ten pound a play, or ¹ no point Comedy.   [*Exit.*
   Mavo. What, insolent with glib prosperity?
Faith Gentlemen; no Players will appeare: 268
Gallants, to your Maske.
   Phil. How soone they can remember to forget,
Their undeserved Fortunes and esteeme.
Blush not the peasants at their pedigree?   272
Suckt pale with lust. What bladders swolne with pride,
To strout in shreds of nitty brogetie!
   Mavo. Well, though the penny raisd them to the pound,
Just *Envie* causelesse Pride doth still confound.   276
   Phil. Well, let them blase, ther's none so blind but sees
Prydes fall is still frost-bit with miseries.

Enter a Maske

What, come they in so blunt, without devise?
   Fill. The night is dead before the sport be borne.   280
   Mavo. Cease Musick there! Prepare to banquet, sirs.
   Phi. Ceres and *Bacchus* tickled, *Venus* stirres.
   Mavo. Gallants unmaske, and fall to banquetting.

   ¹ No point. See *Love's Labour's Lost*, II. i. 190, & V. ii. 277.

A health about: carowse shall feede carowse.¹

Phil. The first is pledg'd, and heere begins a fresh.

Mavo. This royall health of welcome greetes you all.

Vouch. Bacchus begins to reel with going round.

Phil. The grape begins to fume.

Mavo. Why let it fret.—Not pledge a Nobleman?

Champ. I like this Jewell, Ile have his fellow.

Bell. How? you? what! fellow it? gip, Velvet gards!

Champ. Insolent, for-beare!

Mavo. A petty-foggers whoodded wife so pearcht?

Champ. Why not, proud Lord? then bid your mincks come downe.

Vouch. Dishonourable Lord, I say thou li'st.

Mavo. I challenge thee on that disgracefull word.

Vouch. Here answer I thy challenge in this wine.

Mavo. I will confirme thy pledge, and meete thee too.

They speake and fall asleepe on the Stage. Sound Musicke. Enter ENVY *alone to all the Actors sleeping on the Stage: the musicke sounding: she breaths amongst them.*

Envy. Downe climbing *Pride* to *Stygian Tartarie!*
The breath of *Envy* fils the empty world:
Envy whose nature is to worke alone,
As hating any Agent but her selfe.
Turne, turne, thou Lackey to the winged Tyme!
I envie thee in that thou art so slow,
And I so swift to mischiefe. So, now stand.

¹ Compare with *Hamlet*, V. ii. 300. "The queen *carouses* to thy fortune, Hamlet."

Peace, Plenty, Pryde, had their competitors,
But I enjoy my Soveraignty alone.
Now shall proud Noblesse, Law, and Merchandize   308
Each swell at other, as their veines would breake.
Fat Ignorance, and rammish Barbarisme
Shall spit and drivell in sweete Learnings face :
Whilst he, half starv'd in Envie of their power,   312
Shall eate his marrow, and him-selfe devoure.
Awake yee Brawne-fed Epicures; looke up!
And when you thinke your clearest eyes to finde,
Be all their Organs strooke with *Envie* blind.   [*Exit.* 316
      They all awake, and begin the following Acte.

ACTUS 4.   SCÆNA 1

  Mavo. O, pallid Envie, how thou suck'st my bloud!
And wastes my vitall spirits : I could rave,
Runne madde with anguish for my slight respect.
O wher's the honour to my high borne bloud!   4
When every peasant, each Plebeian,
Sits in the throne of undeserv'd repute;
When every Pedlers-French is term'd Monsignuer;
When broad-cloathd trades-man, and what-lack-you-sir   8
Is wrapt in riche habiliments of silke,
Whil'st urgent need makes Princes bend their knee
As servile as the ignobilitie,
To crouch for coyne, whilst slaves tye fast our Lands   12
In Statute Staple, or these Marchants bands.
  Bellu. Wan ghostlike *Envie* spungeth up my bloud

Whil'st I behold yon halfe-fac'd Minion,
The daughter of some Cloves and Cinamon,
To equall me in rich accoustrements.
O, wher's the outward difference of our birth!
When each odde-mincing mistresse Citty-Dame
Shall dare to be as sumptuously adorn'd,
With Jewels, chaines and richest ornaments,
As wee from whom their Fathers held their land
In bond-slaves Tenure, and base villianage.

    Vouch. Why should yon bubble of Nobility,
Yon shade of Man, appropriate *Epithetes*
Of noble, and right honorable sir,
To the blind Fortune of his happy birth?
Why should this reeling world (drunke with the juice
Of *Plenties* bounty,) give such attribute
Of soveraigne title, place and dignity,
To that same swolne up Lord, whom blinded chance
Above his vertues merite doth advance
To high exalted state, whilst all repine
To see our sweate rewarded, and our paine
Guerdond but with a single fee, an Angels gaine?

    Champ. God for his mercy! how yon Lady jetts
And swoopes along in Persian royalty.
O I could pine with *Envie*, and consume
My heart in fowle disdaine, that she should strout
And swell in ostentation of her birth,
Decking the curled tresses of her haire
With glittering ornaments, whilst I am pent
In nice respect of civil modesty.

Ile not indure it. Lawyers wives shall shine 44
Spight of the lawe, and all that dare repine.
 Vel. Drops of cold sweat hang on my fretting brow.
O, I could gnash my teeth, and whip myselfe,
Parboyle my liver in this envious heate 48
Of deepe repining Malice! I am vext,
Stung with a Viperous impatience,
That yon Nobility, yon *John-a-Stile,*
Should sole possesse the throne of dignity, 52
Whilst wee fat Burgomasters of the state,
Rich treasuries of gold, full stuft up trunkes,
With all the fattest marrow of the land
Should be debarr'd from types Majesticall, 56
And live like *Æsops* Asse: whilst our meane birth
Curbes our aspiring humours from the seate
Of honours mounted state; I cannot sleepe,
My entrailes burne with scorne, that Merchandize 60
Should stand and lick the pavement with his knee,
Bare-head, and crouching to Nobility.
Though forfeited to us be all their state
Yet *Envie* (still) my heart doth macerate. 64
 Perp. Gip, Mistresse, Madam! and French-hood intaild
Unto a *Habeas Corpus:* Jesu God!
How proud they jet it: and must I give wall,
And bend my body to their Mistresse-ships? 68
O husband, I am sick, my cheeke is pale
With——
 Vel. With what my sweete?
 Perp. With *Envie;* which no Physick can prevent. 72

Shall I still stand an abject in the eye
Of faire respect; not mounted to the height,
To the top-gallant of o're-peering state,
That with Elated lookes of Majestie 76
I may out face the proud pild Eminence
Of this same gilded Madam *Bellula*,
And yon same *Jone-a-Noke*, chain'd Champertie?

   Vel. Content thee wife. The tide of Royalty 80
Shall onely flow into our Merchandize.
The gulphe of our Ambition shall devoure
All the supports of honour, lands and plate,
Rich minerall Jewels, sumptuous pallaces, 84
All shall be swallow'd by the yawning mouth
Of hungry Avarice. Thus I plotted it.
You see *Mavortius* stormie brow portends
Tempestuous whirle-winds of tumultuous armes; 88
Now when the breath of warre is once denounc'd,
Then troupe the gallants to our wealthy shops
To take up rich apparrell, pawne their land,
To puffe up *Prides* swolne bulke with plumy showes. 92
Then, when the Actions expectation flags,
And fills not up the mouth of gaping hope,
To us returns the mal-contented youth,
And for the furnishment of one suite more 96
All, all, is ours, Jewells, plate and Lands,
All take cariere into the Marchants hands.
Then come, withdraw, and coole thy envious heate:
My pollicy shall make thy hopes repleate. 100

                   [*Exeunt* VELU. *and* PERPETU.

Camp. And shall I still (deere Vourcher) sit below,
Give place to Madams and these citty dames?
O how my Envy at their glory flames!
Vour. Be patient but a while (sweete Campertie)   104
And I will make the world do fealty
To thy exalted state. The Law shall stand
Like to a waxen nose or *Lesbian* rule,
A diall *Gnomon*, or a wethercocke   108
Turn'd with the breath of greatnesse every way;
On whose incertaintie our certaine ground
Of towring hight shall stand invincible.
The Dubious Law shall nurse dissention,   112
Which being pamper'd with our feeding helpes
Wee'le swell in greatnesse, and our pallace Towers
Shall pricke the ribs of Heaven with proud height:
Then let thy *Envy* cease, since thy high fate   116
Shall not discerne a fortune more Elate.
                              [*Exeunt* VOUR *and* CHAMP.
Bel. Se with what slight respect they passe from us,
Not giving to our births their due saluts.
O, Deerest Lord! shall high borne *Bellula*   120
Be sunke, and thus obscur'd by the proud shine
Of yon sophisticate base *Alcumie*,
Yon bullion stuffe: O noble blouds repine,
That durt usurpes the orbe where you should shine!   124
Mavo. Content thee, sweet, the lightning of my armes
Shall purge the aire of these grosse foggy clouds,
That doe obscure our births bright radiance.
When Iron *Mars* mounts up his plumy Crest   128

The Law and Merchandize in rust may rest:
Then *Envy* cease; for e're the Sonne shall set
Ile buckle on *Mavortius* burganet.

[*Exeunt* MAVO. *and* BELL.

Enter CHRISOGANUS *solus.*

Chri. Summa petit livor, perflant altissima venti.[1]   132
Then, poor Chrisoganus, who'll envy thee,
Whose dusky fortune hath no shining gloss
That Envys breath can blast? Oh, I could curse
This idiot world, this ill-nurst age of Peace,   136
That foster[s] all save virtue; comforts all
Saving industrious art, the souls bright gemme;
That crusheth down the sprouting stems of Art;
Blasts forward wits with frosty cold contempt;   140
Crowning dull clods of earth with honours wreath;
Gilding the rotten face of barbarism,
With the unworthy shine of Eminence—
O, I could wish myself consum'd in air,   144
When I behold these huge fat lumps of flesh,
These big-bulkt painted posts that senseless stand,
To have their backes pasted with dignity,
Quite choking up all passage to respect—   148
These huge Colossi, that roll up and down,

[1] Compare Macilente's opening speech in Act i. Sc. 1, of *Every man out of his humour*. Like this, it begins with a line of latin. The general tone and purpose of the two speeches are identical, though Jonson's is infinitely the better. Marston flattered Jonson, and may have written this to curry favour with him. Jonson says of Carlo-Buffone 'no honourable or reverend personage whatsoever can come within the reach of his eye, but is turned into all manner of variety by his adulterate similies.'

And fill up all the seat of man with froth
Of outward semblance, whilst pale Artizans
Pine in the shades of gloomy Academes   152
Faint in pursuit of virtue, and quite tired
For want of liberal food for liberal art,
Give up the goal to sluggish Ignorance!
O whether doth my passion carry me?   156
Poor fool, leave prating.   Envy not their shine
Who still will flourish, though great *Fate* repine.   [*Exit.*

Enter BELCH, GULSH, GUT *and* CLOUT, *with an* INGLE.

Gul. Jack of the Clock-house, where's master Post-hast?

Bel. In my book for Slow-pace; twelve-pence on's pate for staying so late.   160

Gut. Prologue begin (*rehearse &c.*)

'Gentlemen, in this envious age we bring Bayard for Bucephalus. If mired, bogg'd, draw him forth with your favours. So, promising that we never meane to perform, our Prologue peaceth.'   164

Gul. 'Peaceth'? What peaking Pageanter penned that?

Bel. Who but Master Post-hast?

Gut. It is as dangerous [1] to read his name at a play door
As a printed bill on a plague door.   168

Gul. [*Clout*] You wear the handsomst compact hilt I've seen.

Ingle. Doth this fashion like my friend so well?

Bel. [*Clout*] So well I mean to wear it for your sake.

Ingle. I can deny thee nothing, if I would.   172

Gul. Fie, how this Ingling troubles our rehearsal. Say on.

Gut. Fellow Belch, you have found a haunt at my house:

---

[1] Posthast's name unpopular.

You must belch and breathe your spirits somewhere else.
Bel. Jealous of me, with your seat for Master John? 176
Gut. When the door's shut the sign's in Capricorn.
Clou. Then you might heave the latch up with your horn.
Gul. This cuckoldy coil hinders our rehearsal.
Gut. ' I'll tear their turret tops 180
' I'll beat their bulwarks down,
' I'll rend such rascals from their rags,
' And whip them out of town.
Bel. ' Patience, my lord, your fury strays too far.' 184
Gul. Stay, sirs, rehearse no further than you are,
For here be huffing parts in this new book.
Gut. Have I e'er a good humour in my part?
Gul. Thou hast never a good one out of thy part. 188
Bel. I'll play the conquering king, that likes me best.
Gut. Thou play the cowardly knave—Thou dost but jest.
Clowt. Half a share, half a shirt. A Comedian,
A whole share or turn Camelion.[1] 192
Gul. Well sirs, the gentlemen see into our trade,
We cannot gull them with brown-paper stuff,
And the best poets grown so envious,
They'll starve rather than we get store of money. 196
Gut. Since dearth of poets lets not players live by wit,
To spite them let's to wars, and learn to use a spit.
Clout. O excellent ill—a spit to roast a rhyme!
Gut. 'Twill serve you to remember dinner time. 200
Bel. That's true, 'tis time, let's away. [*Exeunt.*

---

[1] Cuthbert Cony-catcher, Defence of Cony-catching, 1592. Greene said ' as they were comedians to art, so the actions of their lives were chamelion-like.'

ACTUS QUINTUS.

Enter WARRE, AMBITION, FURY, HORROR, RUINE

War. Rule fier-eied *Warre !* revell in blood and flames:
Envy, whose breath hath poysoned all estates
Hath now resigned her spightfull throne to us.
Stand forth *Ambition*. Fly through the land, 4
And enter every brest of noble blood.
Infect their honored mindes with factious thoughts,
And make them glister in opposed armes:
Let unjust force, and scarlet *Tyranny*, 8
Wait on their Actions till their ulcers breake,
Or else be launced by the hand of *Warre*,
Which cannot be without a lasting scarre.
  Amb. Ambition like a Pestilence doth fly 12
To poyson Honour and Nobility. *Exit* AMBITION.
  War. Fury, thy turne is next. Goe now and fill
The trunck of Peasants with thy dangerous breath,
Inspire them with the spirit of Mutiny, 16
Rage, and rebellion; make them desperate,
Hurry them headlong unto every ill,
Like dust rais'd with a whirlwind; let their eyes
Be ever fixt upon the brused prints, 20
Made in their state by wilde oppression;
And (after all) possesse them with this fire:
That onely Warre must purchase their desire.
  Fury. Fury shall shine amongst this multitude, 24

Like a bright Meteor in the darkest cloud.   [*Exit* FURY.
   War. Horror shall greet the bosome of greene youth;
The melting liver of pied gallantry;
The wrinckled vizard of Devotion;   28
The cheverell¹ conscience of corrupted law;
And frozen heart of gowty Merchandize.
Horror wound these, strike palsies in their limmes,
And as thou stalk'st (in thy prodigious shape,)   32
And meet'st a fellow swolne with mounted place,
Shake him with glaunses of thy hollow eyes,
And let thy vigour live as his heart dies!
   Horr. Ynough, ere long the ayre shall ring with shrikes,   36
And sad lament of those whom *Horror* strikes.   [*Exit* HORROR.
   War. Horror, adiew!
These three are Ushers to our Deity,
Onely vast Ruine heere attends on us,   40
And is a follower of our high designes:
Ruine, thou faythful servant to grimme Warre,
Now teach thy murdring shot to teare mens limm's,
Thy brazen Cannons how to make a breach   44
In a fayre Citties bozome; teach thy fiers
To climbe the toppes of houses; and thy mines
To blow up Churches in th' offended skye.
Consume whole groves and standing fields of Corne,   48
In thy wild rage, and make the proud earth groane
Under the weight of thy confusion.
   Ruine. This and much more shall *Ruine* execute.

¹ Fr. *chevreuil*, roebuck. Easily-giving, or stretching leather. See *Romeo & Juliet*, II. iv. 87: *Hen. VIII.*, II. iii. 32: *Twelfth Night*, III. i. 13.—F.

War. Meanewhile weele steepe our sinowie feet in blood, 52
And daunce unto the Musicke of the field;
Trumpets for trebbles, bases, bellowing drummes.
Broyles Envy bred, but Warre shall end those brawles,
Deafe warre, that will not heare a word of Peace: 56
Sharpe pikes shall serve for subtle lawiers pens;
The Marchants silkes shall turne to shining steele;
In steed of false yard stickes, large horsemens staves,
Shall measure out true patterns of their graves. [*Exeunt.*

Enter BELSH *setting up bills. Enter to him a* CAPTAIN.

Capt. Sirrah, what set you up there?
Bel. Text-bills for plays.
Capt. What? Plays in time of warrs? Hold Sirrah!
There's a new plot. 64
Bel. How many mean you shall come in for this?
Capt. Player, 'tis press money.
Bel. Press-money, press-money? alas, sir, press me?
I am no fit actor for the action. 68
Capt. Text-bills must now be turned to iron bills.

[*Exit* CAPTAIN.

Bel. And please you, let them be dagger pies.

Enter an OFFICER, POSTHASTE, GULSH, GUT, *and* CLOUT.

Off. Sir Oliver's men? The last players took the towns reward
like honest men. 72
Gulsh. Those were a couple of coney-catchers that
Cousen mayors, and have no consort but themselves.
But we are a full company, and our credit

With our master known.

 Off. Meanwhile there's press-money for your reward.

 Clout. No (I thank your worship) we mean not to trouble your town at this time.

 Off. Well masters, you that are master-sharers Must provide you upon your own purses.

 Gut. Alas, sir, we players are privileged:
Tis our audience must fight in the field for us,
And we upon the stage for them.

 Post. Sir, as concerning half a score angels,
Or such a matter, for a man in my place—

 Off. Those days are out of date.

 Bel. The more's the pity, Sir.   [*Exit* OFFICER.

 Gul. Well, I've a brewer to my Ingle:
He'll furnish me with a horse great enough.

 Post. Faith, I'll e'en paste all my ballads together,
And make a coat to hold out pistol-proof.

 Clout. I marvel what use I should make of my Ingle,
The hobby-horse seller.

 Gut. Faith, make him sell a whole troop of horse
To buy thee one.

 Bel. Sirs, if these soldiers light upon our playing 'parell
They'll strut it in the field, and flaunt it out.

 Post. Well, sirs, I have no stomach to these wars.

 Gut. Faith, I've a better stomach to my breakfast.

 Clout. A shrewd mornings work for players!

 Omnes. Let's be gone.   [*Exeunt*

Enter Mavortius *and* Larius *on one side,* Philarchus *and* Hiletus *on the other with weapons Drawne:* Chrisoganus *betweene them.* Ambition *breathing amongst them.*

Chri. Have patience, worthy Lords, and calme your spirits.
Mavo. Peace, prating Scholler! Bid the Sea be still, 104
When powerfull windes doe tosse the raging waves;
Or stay the winged lightning in his course:
When thou doost this, thy words shall charm me too;
Till then preserve thy breath. 108
  Phil. Mavortius, dar'st thou maintaine thy words?
  Mavo. How? dare *Philarchus?* yes, I dare doe more,
In bloud or fire; or where thou darst not come,
In the numme fingers of cold death I dare. 112
  Phi. Swallow those words, or thou shalt eate my sword.
  Lar. He is no Estrich, sir, he loves no yron.
  Hil. And yet me thinkes he should be by his plume.
  Mavo. What are you playing with my feather too? 116
  They all runne one at another, Chrysog: *steps betweene them.*
  Chris. O stay your rages!
Let not Ambition captivate your blood:
Make not your hates objects for vulgar eyes.
  Mavo. A pox upon this linguist, take him hence. 120
Philarchus, I defie thee, and in scorne
Spit on thy bozome; vowing heere by heaven
If either sword or fire or strength of men,
Or any other steeled violence, 124
Can bring to swift confusion what is thine

Upon this grateful soyle, it shall be done.
  Phi. And when 'tis done, I will restore my wrongs
Out of thy Forts, thy Castles, and thy lands.   128
  Mavo. My lands?
  Phi. I, factious Lord, till then adiew:
Weele shine like Commets in next enter-view.
                        [*Exeunt* PHI. *and* HILE.
  Mavor. My soule is bigge in travaile with revenge,   132
And I could rip her wombe up with a stabbe
To free th' imprisoned issue of my thought.
                        [*Exeunt. Manet* CHRISOGANUS
  Chri. O, how this vulture (vile Ambition)
Tyers on the heart of greatnesse, and devoures   136
Their bleeding honours; whil'st their empty names
Lye chain'd unto the hill of infamie:
Now is the time wherein a melting eye
May spend itself in teares, and with salt drops   140
Write woe and desolation in the dust,
Upon the frighted bosome of our land.
Pitty and Piety are both exilde,
Religion buried with our Fathers bones,   144
In the cold earth, and nothing but her face
Left to adorne these grosse and impious times.   [*Stand aside*

A noise within, crying Liberty, liberty. Enter a sort of Russetinys
    and Mechanicalls, (FURY *leading them*) *and crying confusedly*

  Omnes. Liberty! liberty! liberty!
  1. Nay but stay, stay my Masters; we have not insulted yet who
shall be our Captaine.   149

2. Masse, that's true: faith, let's all be Captaines.

3. Content, so wee shall bee sure to have no equalitie amongst us. 152

4. O, it's best, for (for mine owne part) I scorne to have an equall.

1. Well then: what exploit shall we do first?

2. Marry Ile tell you: Lets pluck down the Church, and set up an Ale-house. 157

Omnes. O excellent, excellent, excellent; a rare exploit, a rare exploite.

1. Good: this is for exploite: but then there's a thing cal'd Action. 161

3. O, that's going to Sea; that we have nothing to do withall.

4. No, we are all for the land, wee.

2. Land, I: weele pluck downe all the noble houses in the land, e're we have done. 165

1. It were a most noble service, and most worthy of the Chronicle.

2. Slid, these Lords are growne so proud: Nay, weele have a fling at the Lawyers too. 168

3. O, I, first of all at the Lawyers.

4. True, that we may have the law in our owne hands.

1. O, then we may take up what we will of the Marchants.

2. I, and forfet our bonds at pleasure, nobody can sue us. 172

3. O, 'twill be rare: I wonder how much Velvet will apparell me and my horse.

4. Talke not of that man, weele have inough: All shall be common.

1. Wives and all: what, *Helter, skelter!* 176

2. Slid, we are men as well as they are.

3. And we came all of our Father *Adam*.
2. Goe to then, why should we be their slaves?
Omnes. Liberty, liberty, liberty! [*Exeunt*
Chri. See, see, this common beast the multitude 181
(Transported thus with fury) how it raves,
Threatning all states with ruine, to englut
Their bestiall and more brutish appetites. 184
O you auspicious and divinest powers,
(That in your wisdomes suffer such dread plagues
To flow and cover a rebellious land)
Give end unto their furies! And drive back 188
The roaring torrent on the Authors heads
That (in their pride of Rage) all eyes may see
Justice hath whips to scourge impiety! [*Exit.*

Enter LYON-RASH *to* FOURCHIER *sitting in his study at one end of the stage: At the other end enter* VOURCHER *to* VELURE *in his shop.*

Lyon. Good morrow, maister *Fourcher*. 192
Four. Maister Lyon-rash, you are welcome:
How fare you, sir, in these prodigious times?
Lyon. Troth, like a man growne wilde and desperate,
E'ene spent with horror of their strange effects. 196
Four. I feare they will be much more stranger yet.
Lyon. And you have cause to feare, sir.
Four. So have you: if wealth may make a man suspect his state.
What newes heare you, sir? sit downe I pray you. 200
They sit and whisper, whilst the other two speake.
Vour. I wonder how you dare keepe open shoppe,

Considering the tumults are abroad.
They say the Nobles all are up in armes,
And the rude commons in disseverd troupes
Have gathered dangerous head, and make such spoyle
As would strike dead a true reporters tongue.
  Vel. Faith I am ignorant what course to take,
Wee i'th Citty heere are so distracted,
As if our spirits were all earth and ayre,
I know not how: each houre heere comes fresh newes
And nothing certaine.
        The other two againe.
  Four. Well, if this be true,
The issue cannot be but dangerous.
  Lyon. O they have made the violent'st attempts
That ere were heard of: ruin'd Churches, Townes,
Burn't goodly Manours, and indeed lay'd wast
All the whole Country, as they passe along.
        The other.
  Vour. Ther's no prevention if they once come heere,
But that our Citty must endure the sack.
  Vel. I feare it, Sir.
  Vour. Faith, we are sure to feele
The fury of the tempest when it comes.
The Law and Merchandize may both go begge.

        Enter CHAMPERTY *to her husband, and* LYON-RASH.

  Cham. Where are you, husband, do you heere the newes?
  Four. What newes, on God's name?
  Cham. O the enimies!

Four. What of the enemies?
Cham. They are entred into the citty 228
Lyon. Adiew, good maister *Fourcher.*
Fou. Lord have mercy upon us!
Cham. O, good Maister *Lyon-rash*, goe pray.
[*Exeunt* FOUR. LYON. CHAM.

Vel. How now, what noyse is this? 232
Vou. They cry, arme! arme! me thinkes. [*Enter* PERPETUANA
Perp. O, sweet heart, the Spaniards [1] are come!
We shall all be kild they say.
Maister Vourcher, what shall we doe? O Lord! 236

Enter a sort of fellowes with armour and weapons, and crosse the stage, crying arme! arme! arme!

Omn. Arme! Arme! Arme! [*Exeunt.*

Enter a Captain with Soldiers, the Soldiers having most of the players apparel, and bringing out the players amongst them.

Sol. Come on, players; now we are the sharers,
And you the hired men. Nay, you must take patience.
Slid, how do you march! 240
Sirrah, is this you would rend and [2] tear the cat
Upon a stage, and now march like a drown'd rat.
Look up and play the *Tamburlaine*,[3] you rogue you. [*Exeunt*

---

[1] The Spaniards: a contrary terror to that of the insurgent boors: this a portion of the earlier play.

[2] Compare Bottom's "part to tear a cat in": *Mid. Night's Dream*, I. ii. 31.—G.

[3] Tamburlaine—an early allusion: points to 1590.

Enter all the factions of Noblemen, Peasants and Cittizens fighting: The ruder sorte drive in the rest, and cry " a sacke! a sacke! Havoke, havocke! Burne the Lawiers bookes! Teare the Silkes out of the shops!" In that confusion, the Scholler scaping from among them, they all go out and leave him upon the Stage.[1]

Chri. Thus Heaven (in spite of fury) can preserve   244
The trustfull innocent and guiltlesse soule.
O, what a thing is man, that thus forgets
The end of his creation; and each houre
Strikes at the glory of his maker thus?   248
What brazen vizage, or black yron soule
Hath strength to Justifie so Godlesse deeds?
Hee that is most infeoft to *Tyrannie,*
The man whose Jawes burne most with thirst of bloud,   252
What coulours or thin cobweb can he weave
To cover so abhor'd iniquities?
If then there be no shadow, no pretext,
To vaile their loathed bodies; what should make   256
Men so inamour'd on this strumpet warre,
To doate upon her forme? when (in her selfe)
Shee's made of nothing but infectious plagues?
Witnesse the present *Chaos* of our Sceane,   260
Where every streete is chain'd with linckes of spoile.
Heere proud *Ambition* rides; there *Furie* flies;
Heere *Horror*, and there ruthlesse *Murder* stalkes,

[1] This scene belongs to the new play. After Essex's rebellion, intestine faction was more to be dreaded than external invasion.

Led on by *Ruine*, and in steele and fire,
That now on toppes of houses, now in vaults,
Now in the sacred Temples, heere and there
Runnes wilde.   [*Exit*

    Allarmes in severall places, that brake him off thus: After a retreat sounded, the Musicke playes and POVERTY *enters.*

ACTUS SEXTUS. SCÆNA 1.

Enter POVERTY, FAMINE, SICKNESSE, BONDAGE *and* SLUTTISHNESSE.

  Pover. Raigne, *Poverty*, in spite of tragick warre,
And triumph over glittering vanitie!
Though want be never voide of bitter woes,
Yet slow pac'd remedy, true patience, showes!
See worldling worlds of Vertue lin'd within,
Though sinners all, yet least repleat with sinne.
I scorne a scoffing foole about my Throne,
An artlesse Ideot, that (like *Esops Dawe*[1]
Plumes fairer fether'd birds: no, *Poverty*
Will dignifie her chaire with deepe Divines:
Philosophers and Schollers feast with me,
As well as Martialists in misery.
First change the houre from five to fatall sixe,
Then ring forth knells of heavie discontent,
With sighes and groans whil'st I have government.
  Fam. Thin *Famine* needs must follow *Poverty*.

---

[1] Poverty scorns the " upstart crowe decked with others plumes."

My bones lye open, like a withered tree
By stormes disbarkt of her defending skinne,
So neere the heart the weather beates within.

   Sick. O, end thy Age, that we may end our dayes!   20
Once Objects, now all Abjects to the world;
For after feeble Sicknesse death ensues,
And endeth griefe that happy joye renews.

   Bond. Then Bondage shall unbolt those cruell barres   24
That thralls faire honour in obscure reproach,
And savage-like yoakes up humanity,
To bind in chaines true-borne civillity.

   Slut. Though *Sluttishnesse* be loathsome to herselfe,   28
Penurious time must be obscene and base;
Who hates the rich must dwell with Poverty,
Since rule in any thing is Soveraignty.

   Pov. Were *Poverty* a word more miserable   32
Then Mans austere invention could propound,
Yet is poore Honesty rich Honors ground:
Whose eyes unvail'd, like to th' unhoodded Hawke,
Looke straight on high, and in the end aspire   36
To feele the warmth of Princes holy fire.
Yet Honor, Wealth, Lands, and who wins the prize,
Obtaines but Vanity of Vanities.
Come follow me, my never failing friend.   [*Exeunt*

   Enter MAVORTIUS *and* PHILARCHUS *at severall doores.*

   Mavo. The broyles of warre wherein I gloried more   41
Then *Priams Hector*, who by burning walls
Was traild along (dread victories deepe fall),

So from these gates myselfe, in meane disgrace, 44
Am banisht forth, pinch't through with poverty,
Who tels us all 'tis true that shee hath sed
Poore flyes will tickle Lyons being[1] *dead.*

Phil. The thirst of Honour call'd me to the warres, 48
Where I have drunke a health (too deepe a draught)
My full-mouthd bags may now be fild with ayre,
The Divell and Ambition taught it me.

Mavo. Is that Philarchus that complaines? 'Tis so. 52

Phil. See how Mavortius turnes away his face;
To seeke to friends 'tis holden for disgrace.

Mavo. Time was, I could have din'd amongst my friends;
Now stands at every door a Jack and Apes, 56
And tels me 'tis too late, his Lord hath din'd.

Phil. This miserable world would make one mad.
I stept unto a Vintner at the Barre,
And offered him my Rapier for a pawne; 60
The sawcie slave tooke it in such a scorne,
And flung it in the streets, replying thus;
Meere want brings weapons out of use with us.

Mavo. See poore *Philarchus* powring out his plaints 64
To unrelenting walls, relentlesse men.

Phil. Are wounds rewards for Souldiers in the field?
What? sell our lands? are these the fruits of *Warre?*
Then dye, *Philarchus,* let not shame survive 68
Thy fainting honour, dead and yet alive.

Mavo. Heere come our wives, how wretchedly they looke.

[1] This adage perhaps alluded to by Nash.

Enter PERPETUANA *and* BELLULA

Bell. My Jewels pawnd, my rings are gone to wrack,
The greedy Usurer hath gotten all. 72
Perp. I am a prey to wretched *Poverty;*
Ill featur'd *Famine* will devoure us up,
Whose wrinckled face is like pale deaths aspect.
Phil. Behold my wife, like Winters parramour, 76
Rob'd and bereav'd of nuptiall Ornaments
' *Hide thee* Philarchus *lower then the grave;*
' *The Earth will cover though it cannot save.*
Perp. If men lament, whose wonted yron-hearts 80
Were harder then the Armour they have worne,
And waile the Agent of a woman's voyce,
What shall weake women and poor Ladies doe?
Fall to those teares, that we were borne unto. [*Exeunt*
Mavo. Could I but learne (with *Crœsus*) to endure 85
The falling sicknesse of sad *Poverty*,
Who lost a rich commanding Emperie,
Patience would proove a tutor to my grieves. 88
Chri. Thou want's a *Solon* to consort with thee,
To prove affliction is the perfect way
That leads to Joves tribunall dignity.
Il hast thou govern'd thy prosperity, 92
That canst not smile in meere adversity.
Looke uppon me (the poorest slave in shew
That ever fortune buried in mishappe :)
Yet this is Natures richest Jewell-house, 96

And teacheth me to weepe at all your wants.

Phil. Why thou art farre more wretcheder then wee :
How canst thou teach us then tranquillity ?

Chris. See'st thou this poore and naked bozome heere ?
Dost thou behold this scorn'd uncovered head ?
When thou wast rich and Peerelesse in thy pride,
Content did never harbour in thy brest,
Nor ere had love her residence in thee ;
(I meane the love of perfect happinesse)
But skillesse grudging from a haughty spirit
Did blind thy senses with a slender merit ;
Whil'st I (poore man) not subject to such thought,
Gave entertaine to those sweet blessed babes
Which Sapience brought from Wisedomes holy brest,
And thought me rich to have their company.
By nursing them in Peace I shun'd all Sloth ;
Nor yet did *Plenty* make me prodigall :
Pride I abhor'd, and term'd the Beggers shield ;
Nor ever did base *Envie* touch my heart ;
Yet alwayes loov'd to beare (as *Solon* sed)
A Turtles eye within an Aspickes head :
Nor could the ratling fury of fierce warre
Astonish me more than the mid-night clock,
The Trumpetter to Contemplation :
For *Poverty*, I shake her by the hand,
As welcome Lady to this wofull Land.

Mav. How might we tread the path's to happy ends,
Since foes to Learning are not Vertues friends ?

Chris. First entertaine submission in your soules,

To frame true concord in one unity.
Behold the faire proportion of a man,
Whome heavens have created so compleate; 128
Yet if the arme make warre against the head,
Or that the heart rebell against the braine,
This elementall bodie (thus compact)
Is but a scattred *Chaos* of revenge. 132
Your lawes appoincted to be positive
(By *Warre* confounded) must be brought againe:
For law is that which Love and Peace maintaine.

   Phili. Thou Sonne of knowledge (richer then a man) 136
We censure thy advice as oracles.

   Chri. Follow, and Ile instruct you what I can.

   Ma. " We followed beasts before, but now a man.   [*Exeunt*

       Enter FOURCHER, VOURCHER, LYON-RASH *and* VELURE

   Four. O Heavens! powring high-pryzd favours forth, 140
Like to the honny dew that sweetes the Leaves,
Once send us *Peace*, that fairest Palme-crownd Queene.

   Vour. Ruine and *Warre*, the precedents of Wrath,
That crop't the fifty Sonnes of *Hecuba*, 144
Have rid their circuit through this fertile soyle,
And quite transform'd it to a Wildernesse.

   Vel. Come let us sit and mourne with sad laments
The heavy burdens of our discontents. 148

   Lyon. To waile our want let speaking slacke the paine,
For words of griefe divide the griefe in twaine.

   Vel. Our Shops (sometimes) were stuft with cloath of gold,
But *Warre* hath emptied them, and Spyders build 152

Their Cob-web-tents, weaving foule dusty lawne
For poore woe-working *Poverty* to weare.

Four. O woes! behold our poore distressed wives.

Enter PERPETUANA *and* FILISELLA.

Perp. From *Poverty* to *Famine*, worse and worse. 156
Fili. The scurge of *Pride*, and Heavens detested curse.
Perp. Wher's that excesse consum'd upon the back?
Fili. Sunke down to Hell, whil'st hunger feeles the lacke.
Perp. Who now will pity us, that scorn'd the poore? 160
Fili. Pitty is past when *Peace* is out of doore.
Perp. Drincke thou my teares and I will drinke up thine,
For nought but teares is miseries salt wine.
Fil. We that have scornd to dresse our meate our selves, 164
Now would be glad if we had meate to dresse.
Perp. And if Lament were remedie for want,
Their cates were course that in Lament were scant.
Lyon. Comfort, sweete wife, ill lasts not alwaies so; 168
And good (sometimes) makes end of lingring woe.
Perp. My griefe is thine.
Lyon. And mine is most for thee.
Per. My care is thine. 172
Lyon. Be mine for thee and me.   [*Exeunt.*

Enter Country serving-men.

1. Faith, *Poverty* hath paid my wife on the petticoate.
2. From[1] these devowring woormes, eate men alive,
And swollow up whole Mannours at a bit; 176

[1] Query, For.

The whil'st our hungry bodies die for lacke,
And honest husbandry must goe to wracke.

    1. Pray, sirs, for *Peace*, that best may please us all.
From citties *Pryde* the Country takes his fall.   180

    2. Tis Time, for plough-shares (now) are turned to bills;
Cart-horses prest to carry Cavalliers;
True laboring servants counted Souldiours slaves.

    1. Though *Famine* hungerstarve, yet heaven saves.   184

    Omn. Then let us pray to heaven all for *Peace*,
For thence comes comfort, plenty, and increase.   [*Exeunt*

Enter POSTHAST, *with his Hostesse.*

Host. Post me no posting, pay me the shot.
You live by wit, but we must live by money.   188

    Post. Goody Sharp, be not so short.
I'll pay you, when I give you money.

    Host. When you give me money! Go to, I'll bear no longer.

    Post. What, and be under fifty?   192

Enter CONSTABLE.

Host. Master Constable, ho! these players will not pay their shot.

    Post. Faith, sir, war hath so pinch'd us we must pawn.

    Const. Alas, poor players! Hostess, what comes it to?

    Host. The Sharers dinners sixpence a piece. The hirelings—
    pence.   196

    Post. What, sixpence an egg, and two and two at an egg?

    Host. Faith, famine affords no more.

    Post. Fellows, bring out the hamper. Choose somewhat out
    o'th' stock.

Enter the players.

What, will you have this cloak to pawn? What think you it's
   worth?   200
Host. Some fower groats.
Omn. The pox is in this age: here's a brave world fellows!
Post. You may see what it is to laugh at the audience.   203
Host. Well, it shall serve for a pawn.   [*Exit Hostess.*
Const. Soft, sirs, I must talk with you for tax-money,
To relieve the poor; not a penny paid yet.
Post. Sir, at few words: we shared but fifteen pence last week.
Const. But 'tis well known that each maintains his punk, 208
And taverns it with drunken suppers still.
Omn. Alas, they are our wives.
Const. Ye are not all married.
Post. Who are not are glad to bring such as they can get? 212
Bel. Before I'll give such a precedent, I'll leave playing.
Gul. Faith, and I too: I'll rather fall to work.
Post. Fall to work after playing? unpossible!
Const. Sirs, will you hear the truth?   216
Gut. Sir, you may choose.
Const. But you must all choose whether you'll be shipped, and
set a shore no man knows where, as the Romans did, or play for
the maintenance of the poor, and yourselves kept like honest
men.
Omn. We choose neither.
Post. Saving your sad tale, will you take a pot or two?
Const. The dearth of malt denies it.
Clout. It's a hard world if the constable despise it.   224

Gul. Must we be shipp'd in earnest, or do you make us sheep in jest?

Const. Ecce signum.

Post. Constable, do you know what you do?

Const. Aye, banish idle fellows out o'th' land. 228

Belch. Why, Constable, do you know what you see?

Const. Aye, I see a Madge-howlet, and she sees not me.[1]

Post. Know you our credit with Sir Oliver?

Const. True, but your boasting hath cracked it, (I fear). 232

Gut. Faith, I must fall to making fiddle strings again.

Bel. And I to curl horse-tails to make fools beards.

Post. I'll boldly fall to ballading again.

Const. Sirs, those provisos will not serve the turn. 236
What ho! sailors! ship away these players.

Enter sailors.

Sail. The wind blows fair, and we are ready, sir.

Const. No matter where it blows, away with them. 239

Post. It's an ill wind blows a man thus clean out of ballading.

[*Exeunt.*

Enter PEACE, BACCHUS, CERES *and* PLENTY, *bearing the* Cornu copiæ, *at the one doore. At the other* POVERTY *with her attendants; who, beholding* PEACE *approach, vanish.*

Peace. Bondage, wan *Sicknesse,* and bare *Poverty,*
Vanish like clowds before the Easterne light,
Now *Peace* appeares. Hence all to endlesse night!
And you dejected spirits, crusht with want, 244

[1] 'See' in original: evidently should be 'me.'—G.

HISTRIO-MASTIX, Act VI.

Mount up your mindes unto the fairest hope,
Neede hath nurst *Peace* within your *Horoscope*,
The warme reflexion of whose cheering beames
Makes you as rich as bright *Pactolus* streames. 248
Shine plentuous Bountie, crowne the naked world
With odourous wreaths of thy aboundant sweetes.
Laborious *Artizanes*, now bustle up
Your drouping spirits with alacritie;
Peace gives your toyling sweat a due regard,
Crowning your labour with a rich reward.
Ceres be lavish, *Bacchus* swell to brimme,
And all to *Peace* sing a propitious himne. 256

They begin to sing, and presently cease.

A Song.

*With Lawrell shall our Altars flame,
In honour of thy sacred name.*

Enter ASTRÆA *ushered by* FAME, *supported by* FORTITUDE *and*
RELIGION, *followed by* VIRGINITY *and* ARTES.

Peace. No more[1]:
Be dumbe in husht observance at this sight: 260
Heere comes *Amazements* object, wonders height,
Peaces patronesse, *Heavens* miracle,
Vertues honour, *Earths* admiration,
Chastities Crowne, *Justice* perfection, 264
Whose traine is unpolute *Virginity*,
Whose *Diadem* of bright immortall *Fame*

---

[1] These lines are quite in another style from any of the rest: but see further on where the old style recurs.

Is burnisht with unvalued respect,
Ineffable wonder of remotest lands;   268
Still sway thy gratious Scepter! I resigne;
What I am is by Thee, my selfe am thine!

    Q. Eliza.[1]   Astræa *mounts unto the throne.*

Mount, Emperesse, whose praise for Peace shall mount,
Whose glory, which thy solid vertues wonne,   272
Shall honour *Europe* whilst there shines a Sunne!
Crown'd with Heavens inward beauties, worlds applause;
Thron'd and reposd within the loving feare
Of thy adoring Subjects: live as long   276
As Time hath life, and *Fame* a worthy tongue!
Still breath our glory, the worlds *Empresse,*
Religions Gardian, *Peaces* patronesse!
Now flourish Arts, the Queene of *Peace* doth raigne;   280
Vertue triumph, now shee doth sway the stemme,
Who gives to *Vertue* honours Diadem.
All sing *Pæans* to her sacred worth,
Which none but Angels tongues can warble forth: 284
Yet sing, for though we cannot light the Sunne,
Yet utmost might hath kinde acceptance wonne.

                Song.

        Religion, Arts and Merchandise   288
           triumph, triumph:
        Astræa rules, whose gracious eyes
           triumph, triumph.

---

[1] This '*Q. Eliza*' is in the margin of the original, and so is quite an exceptional feature in the printing.—G.

  O're *Vices* conquest whose desires   292
   triumph, triumph :
  Whose all to chiefest good aspires,
   then all triumph.

In the end of the play.   296

PLENTY
PRIDE
ENVY   To enter and resigne their severall Scepters to
WARRE *and*   PEACE, sitting in Maiestie.[1]
POVERTY   300
                   301

FINIS.

NOTES TO HISTRIO-MASTIX.

1. The plan of this play is not original. Clement Marot, in a letter to the Duchess Marguerite in Oct. 1521 from the Camp in Hainault, says—' Minfant bears witness in his comedy of *Fatal Destiny*, saying

   " Peace begets Prosperity :
   Prosperity breeds Wealth :
   Of Wealth come Pride and Luxury :
   Pride with Contention swell'th :
   Contention looks to War for health :
   War begets Poverty :
   Poverty breeds Humility :

[1] This is an alternative end to the play—the older finale probably.

>   Humility brings Peace again:
>   So turn our deeds in endless chain."
>
>   (*Clement Marot*, by Henry Morley. Vol. i. p. 131.)

So Lodge, *A Fig for Momus*, 1595. F4 verso. Satire 5.

>   Briefly, the greatest gifts whereof we boast
>   Are those which do attempt and tire us most.
>   Peace brings in pleasure; pleasure breeds excess;
>   Excess procureth want; want works distress;
>   Distress contempt, &c.

Puttenham (p. 217 Arber's reprint) quotes *Ihean de Mehune*, the French Poet—

>   Peace makes plenty, plenty makes pride;
>   Pride brings quarrel, and quarrel brings war;
>   War brings spoil, and spoil poverty,
>   Poverty patience, and patience peace:
>   So peace brings war, and war brings peace.

Simon Harward—Solace for the soldier and sailor, 1592. B3 verso—

'Peace hath increased plenty, plenty hath wrought pride, pride hath hatched disdain, and disdain hath brought forth such strifes and debates, such suits of law, such quarrellings and contentions, as never were heard of in any age before us.'

2. *The Play within the Play of Histrio-Mastix* (pp. 32, 39).— There is the precedent of the *Midsummer Night's Dream* for the play as rehearsed not corresponding with the play as played. But no precedent for putting *Troilus and Cressida* into the middle of

The Prodigal Child. Was the *Midsummer Night's Dream* the provocative of the *Histrio-Mastix*? Who was the author of the *Pyramus and Thisbe* there parodied, or rather caricatured?

3. [*Characteristics of Post-hast* (pp. 33, 37).—The theory that Posthast is meant for Shakspere is very well borne out by the limning of the character—due allowance being made for the fact that the limner of Posthast draws in enmity to Shakspere. Post-hast is represented as being—In manners a gentleman (by comparison with his rude fellows) but an 'upstart' in reality, and somewhat of a *bon-vivant*. In capacity he is shown as of ready and comprehensive wit, with great aptness for leading and persuading others. And in his literary style we are told there is—

'no new luxury of blandishment,
But plenty of Old England's mothers words.'

All which, allowance being made for the writer's adverse bias, comes very near to what we otherwise know Shakspere to have been.—G.]

Comedy of the Prodigal Son,

IN WHICH DESPAIR AND HOPE ARE VERY ARTIFICIALLY
INTRODUCED.

Comedy of the Prodigal Son.[1]

PERSONS.

Father of the PRODIGAL SON.
PRODIGAL SON.
Brother of the PRODIGAL SON.
Host.
Hostess or Wife.

Daughter of Host.
DESPAIR.
HOPE.
Citizen.
[Servant].

ACT I.

Enter the Father, an old grey-headed man, with a staff in his hand. The PRODIGAL SON *has a young horsemans switch [or perhaps a childs cockhorse, or staff to ride on] and is jolly. Afterwards the Brother, a simple plain man, who goes his own gate.*

Father. Ah my beloved son, wilt thou then so hastily depart from me? It gives me real pain and grief. With great and mighty toil and care have I brought thee up, that thou art come to thy years of discretion, and now wilt thou leave me, and forsake me in my old age? Prythee bethink thee well, dear son, and stay with me.

Son. My dearest father, I have told you often enough, it cannot be. I must make my essay in the world. For this cause give me my Patrimony. It cannot be otherwise; I must from hence.

Fath. Ah my beloved son, be entreated, and go not hence. Thou seest that I, this earthly and corruptible[2] being, have now

---

[1] For account of this play, and how and why it appears in this work, see Introduction to *Histrio-Mastix*, pp. 11—15.

[2] The text says incorruptible, but it is manifestly wrong.

past by the greater part of my days. Forsake me not now in mine old age, and stay with me till you see out mine end.

Son. Dearest father, once more I say, it cannot but be so; I must from hence. No prayers can remedy it. Dearest father, I ask, what is he for a man, who always lies there at home like a wolf in his den, and never comes from his mothers apron-string? Me thinketh he is a very stupid and wretched creature, he has no notion of suiting with others humours (mores), never has he been any where, or come anywhere, he has seen nothing, heard nothing, learnt nothing. In a word he knows nothing, and is a notorious Geck and Gull (ein alber Geck und Narr) No, I have no liking that way;[1] it is not in my desires; No, I will cast the world about my ears, and I will learn its various manners and tongues. And so when I come home again, I shall fill my friends ears with (God's my life) the wonders I have seen. Yes, every man will gladly have me by him; every one will show me great honour, will make legs to me, skink beer in the glass, and ever do the *baseles manus* before me. But God grant, dearest father, that I may find you once more in life and good health. But if not, as God would part me hence, so my brother is here, whom you will always have by you. He, without me, will see you honestly committed to the earth.

Fa. Yea, my dearest son, it is a fine thing for a young man who goes to essay the world, to travel and see much. But such essay is of two kinds. One man will go forth and take not a penny

[1] This may be the German equivalent for poetry like that of Arviragus in *Cymbeline* (Act III. iii. 37)—

How
In this our pinching cave, shall we discourse
The freezing hours away? We have seen nothing.
We are beastly. Subtle as the fox for prey,
Like warlike as the wolf for what we eat, &c.

or a mite of his family's own. He fears God, takes service with honest people, and so sees much good, and makes his essay in the world with vast profit. He sees and experiences much, learns meanwhile liberal sciences, and studies to be virtuous. Others go forth taking a great fortune with them, and then they rely on it. But these for the most part lightly go forth to their own loss and ruin, for they have not God before their eyes, and keep not his commandments. They live day and night in a din, and live a wild and godless life. They lose the bloom of their youth with good-for-nothing companions, or even with whores and ingles; they study every vice till they have spent all their fortune; and after all they have learnt nothing in their youth, they cannot take service in good houses, nay, Gods judgment comes down upon them. At last they fall to beggary, and perish in starvation and misery. And so, since my prayers will not now avail to make thee stay with me, but thou wilt from hence and see the world, thou may'st even go whither thou wilt. But now I go in to fetch thee the portion of thy goods that belongeth to thee. [*Exit.*

Son. Now may I be joyful, that my father is gone to fetch my Patrimony, with which I go into the world, and make myself jolly and frolic, and am my own master. Here will I not longer bide;— I could not—For here, if I were with my companions, with pretty women and girls, and did not think any one in the whole town would know it; Well, the moment I came home, my father knew it, there went old scolding, I warrant I was well plagued. If I said to my father, I am young, and fond of the world—he always gave me answer, yea my Son, but it costs much money. It may cost what it likes, I must have company. I am so jolly that I know not what to do for joy. Ho, hollah, courage! ho, hollah, courage!

[*Dance and Sing*]. But my dearest brother, tell me, how comes it you stand so troubled? Have you the Cornelium?

Brother. Yes in truth I have the Cornelium, but it is for you, because you are so saucy and wild. I am the elder brother and you the younger. You can't have learnt your wild life from me; you have never seen me pass a single night outside my fathers house, as you often do, but I abide at home, and do my fathers business, and see that his land is well sown and weeded. But now you demand your inheritance, and will go away with it. So I know well you will straight take to this wild life yet more, as soon as you have gone, and you will find yourself a beggar. Therefore bethink you well, leave your portion here, and bide at home, for here you have it always more secure, and may enjoy it with pleasure. But to carry it forth among strangers, you will certainly lose it, and find yourself in poverty.

Son. What! brother, will you too preach me a long sermon? No indeed, let be; you should rather mount the pulpit if you want to preach, and leave me unmolested. I have been already plagued quite enough. I know there are many such foolish Gecks to be found, like you, who like always to lie in their dens like wolves, and never to move from one spot. Do you think that I too will be such a fool? No indeed, I will have a scuffle (Schloff) in the world, and hunt for joy and health. Now my dear brother, be at peace; we will see which of us twain gathers fruit the best—I with my going forth, or you with your lying still. I know indeed, when I come back again, you will have to stand at the table, and wait on me like a Lord, when I begin to talk of this and that place, of all the wondrous things I've seen, and where the best and prettiest damsels be; then will you stand, mouth shut, eyes fixed, and spit upon yourself that you have never made the like essay. But now there comes my Father, bringing me a heap of money.

Father. See here, my dearest son, thou hast thy portion. But first observe my words, and ever hold my exhortations, which I now will utter, fast in thine heart. First, have God for ever before thine eyes; pray him each night and morn to be thy Guide, and not to let thy foot glide from the right way, lest thou comest to the way of sinners and perdition. Be a foe to tippling and unchastity, for where these two wickednesses be, out of that heart shall God the Holy Ghost be driven. For unchastity drives out the Holy Ghost, who maketh no abode in our hearts with us, like as when we chase away the bees with smoke. And then when one has driven out the pure and holy Spirit, straight there comes the wicked unclean Spirit, makes his dwelling there again, takes the heart and so possesses it that it must act according to his will, to wit, he drives and irritates it all to shame and crime, but keeps it off from God, and his holy word, and so, when he has got it wholly in his leash, he makes it serve him, and dishonour the creator of the heavens and the earth. Beware thee too of wicked women, of dicing and of playing. So thou dost according to my exhortations thou shalt be indeed an honest man, to me and to my friends an honour and a joy.

Son. My dearest Father I will ever learn to practise your advice while I remain in life, as far as shall be possible. And, now dear Father thus I take my way; Adieu, adieu, God have you in his keeping!

Father. O dearest son, our Lord God be thy Guide; may he conduct and lead thee that thy foot thou dash not 'gainst a stone! Once more, beware of wicked and lascivious company. And now, so, go in peace.

SCENE IV.

Son. Adieu, Adieu, dear brother; now I go, and do commit thee to the custody of the Angel of God!

Brother. Behave thyself, my dearest brother, well, follow thy Fathers love, and so with fruit and profit travel forth. God ever prosper thee in thy journey, and in all thou dost or leavest undone.

[*Exeunt Father and Elder brother*

Son. Now have I a stately sack full of money; with it I will live gloriously, like a nobleman. Ho! be merry now, ye pretty maidens! rejoice with me, for I have money enough to live upon a long time. My old father made me a deal of preaching and exhortation, how I must do to get happiness on my travels. But, indeed, I dont remember a word he preached to me, for I gave no heed to it; When I saw him bringing the money I thought of this, in what lands I might find the best girls. I have in this an odd turn of mind, that it is a vexation to me when a man stands and makes many ceremonies, and gives me advice. But now I must arise and go forth on my journey. Hollah! hollah! my man.

SCENE V.

Servant. Dear master, what will you?

Son. Do you hear, have you made all ready for my journey? Are the horses groomed and saddled?

Servant. Yes, the horses are ready saddled, and all finely prepared.

Son. Good. Now let us go hence

Farewell—into the world I ride,
How, where I like, I do and bide—

Father, mother, brother dear
May stay at home and serve God here.
[*Exeunt. Now the trumpets sound, and they ride away.*

ACT II.

Enter SON *and Servant*

Son. This beautiful happy and lordly town pleases me so extraordinarily well, that I would altogether choose to abide here always —But, do you hear, go in quickly and find out where is the best Hostelry in the whole town, and especially where there are pretty girls in the house, and command everything to be prepared handsomely, and then bring me word back anon; meanwhile I will go walk here.

Servant. Yes Master, I go, and order such a lodging after your hearts desire and pleasure [*goes a step or two from him*] Now I go for it, to look out a lodging for my master; but I know not where to find it—ah, there goes a man yonder, him will I speak to, and ask whether he cannot direct me to an Inn. Good day Sir.

Host. It is no help to me for you to say good day. Don't speak to me now, for I am so worried in my foolish head, that I scarce know what I shall do.

Servant. I, my dear, be not so peevish. I only wanted to ask you a little question—but now I see you are not good to be spoken to. I must go farther [*going away*]

Host. Go not away, tell me what wilt thou?

Servant. Tell me first, why you are so worried and foolish in your head?

Host. You must know that I entertain guests, and thereby

maintain myself with my wife and children. But now for a long while I have had no guests, whereupon I have come to be quite mad, for my purse is quite empty, and I know not what will soon become of me; and thus am I clean grown (gremen) a fool, and so you must know how I come to have the Cornelium, to walk by myself so sulkily.

Serv. Now is that the reason? You must know that I have come to you only to ask where the best Inn is, for I have this day come into the Town with my master, and as we are unknown here, we have as yet no lodging.

Host. O my good friend, do you want an Inn? At my house you shall have as good as you can find in the whole town. But tell me, is your Master a man of worship, and has he much money with him?

Serv. Has he not money! Methinks if he could eat it, he would have. For precious stones, gold, silver and small change he has plenty and store. In the Inns where we have lately been he has truly paid all double of his own free will, so that all the days of my life I have seen no Lord or Count more free and liberal than my master.

Host. My good friend, that would be a right guest for me. I pray you heartily bring him here to me in the Inn, and then the profits I make of him you shall enjoy with me.

Serv. Yes my good friend, may be he will lie at your lodgings; but on condition, you must have pretty girls with you in the house. For he rests in no Inn wherein there are none such.

Host. Ho, ho, thereof have I no lack; only see what a beautiful daughter and wife I have. Hollah! Hollah! dear wife and daughter, come out to me anon.

Enter Wife and Daughter. She has a green bunch of grapes (Hering? Herling) *in her hand.*

Wife. What wilt thou, husband? pray tell us anon.

Host. My dearest daughter and wife, now be glad with me. This man here will bring (foriren) us his master to lodge. He is a rich gentleman, and pays double; Go to and bid him welcome.

Wife. Dear husband, this were mortal good for us [*goes to the Servant*] O, your Master shall be heartily welcome to me.

Servant. I thank you, virtuous lady.

[*Wife speaks aside to Host.*

Daughter. You strangers are Godly welcome to me.

Servant. I thank you heartily, fair maid. Methinks if my master saw you, you would be mortally agreeable to him.

Daugh. Young fellow, prithee tell me, is your master young and handsome, and has he plenty of money?

Serv. Fair maiden, he is such a paragon of young and handsome fellows, that if a girl do but see him, he must be held in great love and renown. For gold and goods think not he lacks, he has plenty and store.

Daug. Ah, my fine young fellow, prithee let him not shy off to any other place for lodging, but bring him here to us.

Wife. Listen, young fellow; you said your Master would like to have maidens with him; he shall have no lack, for here is my daughter; herself shall be his body servant, and you my young fellow, would you have one too? you shall always get one, and every night you sleep with me. Wherefore I pray, let not your Master enter any other place, but bring him to us.

Servant. Hostess, well said; only hold me as you have told me, and we will pass our time in joy and pleasure. No indeed, to no other Inn than this will I bring my master, where a man can have pretty women and maidens—So now I go to bring my Master to his Inn. [*goes a step or two forward*] But were may he be now? I believe I must spend half a day looking for him. No see where he comes as wanton as a Village Parson.

Son. How comes it, my man, that you have been so long. I have been anxiously waiting for you.

Serv. O, my dear Master, I have found the best Inn in the whole town, where you pay really nothing, and, what will please your heart. There is in the same house a superb maiden so beautiful that in my life I have never seen a prettier, and the Hostess has told me that she shall wait on you, and I shall always have the Hostess when I will.

Son. O, my faithful servant, you have lighted on a marvellous good lodging. Is then the concubine I am to have so beautiful? I am in extraordinary luck. But come straight and show me where this house is, for the beautiful report you give of it makes it impossible for me to wait here longer.

Serv. Yes, my dear Master, follow me now, I will bring you to it. [*Goes back with him: Host, Hostess, and Daughter are standing together, speaking aside*] See here, Master, there they stand together talking. The Man is the Host, the Woman the Hostess, the maiden their daughter.

Son. Indeed a more beautiful person than this maiden have I never seen. The longer I stand and look even at this distance, the more and more I fall in love with her. O now if I am quite to satisfy my heart, then will I take my whole joy and pleasure with the beautiful maiden. But I know not how it may come to pass, that my heart beats and trembles so. Truly I have not courage to dare to go up to a maid and speak to her.

[*Meanwhile the others are talking secretly together—The Host sees him ; The son goes on walking.*]

Host. See dear wife and daughter, this is our guest walking yonder. He is indeed a splendid gentleman; methinks he has plenty of money. But daughter, do you hear, you must go to him straight, and fetch him in friendly wise to the house.

Daugh. Ah, dearest father, I dare not go to him. I fetch my breath so short that I cannot speak—My heart flutters in my bosom; I am afraid.

Mother. But look you, daughter, how you serve us. You must go to him. Why is it afraid? What does your heart beat for? Why cant you speak to him? I advise you take care not to be so fearful. See what a handsome youth and splendid fellow it is. No, you shall go, and you must bring us in a rare prize, or our business will be nought.

Host. Dont stay till we compel you—Go. [*takes her by the arm*] Potz Valentine, that you should stand like a stuck pig—See, s'blood, how the man stands like a shamefaced virgin—You have been a whore nigh three years; run forth, be quick [*goes to him*]

Daug. Fair young sir, you shall be Godly welcome to me.

Son. Beauteous maiden, I thank you heartily, and specially for coming out here to me.

Dau. Fair young sir, I have heard that you are on your travels to make trial of the World. Prithee tell me how many tongues you know.

Son. 'Tis true fair maiden, I travel to see all beauteous girls, and to gain experience of the World. But for the tongues, I only know two, my mothers, and Latin. Pray tell me what you can speak in that way.

Daug. My fair young sir, I only speak Italian perfectly, and no other. But pray come with me into my Fathers house, there will we make better acquaintance, and discourse together. [*takes him by the hand; leads him to the Host and Hostess.*]

Host. Dear gentleman, you shall have Gods welcome.

Hostess. O, the gentleman shall be a welcome guest to us.

Son. Thanks, dear Host and Hostess.

Hostess. Dear daughter, take the gentlemans hand, and go with him into the house.

Dau. Fair young sir, pray come in with me.

Son. Fair maiden, I go with you, and where you be, there I abide also. But, dear Host and Hostess, pray make ready quickly a grand feast and dainty banquet, at which your fair daughter yourself and mine host shall be my guests. Let there be lack of nothing, and provide nobly, for I will pay well and double it.

Hostess. My dear gentleman, I will do so; I pray you, only turn in, and play with my daughter, for she only likes you.

[*Exeunt.*

ACT III.

Enter the hostess, to cover the table.

Hostess. Dear Waiter come, let us cover the table straight, for your master wants to have a grand banquet.

Serv. Yes, my master is a liberal fellow. He is no screw, but orders fresh and lordly feasts. The happier and friskier he is, the better I like him. Give me here one end of the table-cloth.

Hos. You are a good fellow, that is a fact. Go in anon, and fetch us the wine and the comfits.

Serv. I go.

Hostess. Yes, in truth, our guest is a free-handed Cavalier, that I see plainly. And in truth I will reckon all double, for he has bid me himself. Such openhanded fellows are not often to be found. So we must fasten on him, till we have stolen and vexed him out of all he has. See, you are quick back with the wine and comfits. You are an active fellow I must say that of you.

Serv. Hoho! am I active? if I have to fetch anything for a pretty girl I am a deal more active. And so I gain their favour, and they praise me, and that feels so soft.

Hostess. Yes I believe it well, good fellow; but now we must deck this table supremely handsomely. Only go in and tell your master to come, for all is ready presently.

Serv. I go and tell him.

[*Hostess meanwhile pours the wine into the Rummers, and puts the sugar on the shives* (*slices*)]

Hostess. Now it's all ready. And see, here they come all together.

Enter SON, *has the Concubine by the hand, Host, and Servant*

Son. O my dear Hostess, how stands it, or how is it with you. I see you have just made all ready.

Hostess. Dear Gentleman, It is all right with me. All is now ready here. You can be seated when you please.

Son. Pray, fair damsel, come and sit by me.

Dau. Yes, fair young Sir, as you like it [*They go and sit by one another*]

Son. Prithee, mine Host and Hostess, sit you down with us, for today we must show ourselves merry and joyful.

Host. Yes, my dear gentleman, we will sit [*Host and Hostess sit*]

Son. Nay, prithee, let us be merry and glad, and you musicians fiddle away, and make your Citherns twang—

[*the players fiddle—The Son drinks to the daughter, and so goes round twice. They eat the comfits—The* PRODIGAL SON *has the Daughter in his arms and kisses her*].

Son. Yooks, holla, lusty, rusty, frisky and frolic. [*The players leave off*] Sir Host, drink round, and make yourself jolly with me.

Host. My dear gentleman, I am jolly—I beg to present you with this glass of wine.

Son. Thanks, mine Host—Prithee more glasses; Drawer, skink away—My beautiful girl, be but a little jolly.

Dau. O my fair young sir, I am merry and in good mettle.

Son. Mine Hostess, be you merry too, and drink to me once more.

Hostess. O my dear gentleman, I am more merry and frolic than ever I was in my life. But I will drink this glass to you.

Son. God bless you, Hostess. Now Musicians, make merry, twang your strings again—[*The players begin again, fiddling very piano so that the actors may speak at the same time. The* PRODIGAL SON *kisses the girl; they whisper together*]

Daug. Dearest young fellow, I would ask a favour of you if I knew you would not deny me.

Son. O my dearest girl, will I deny you? no truly; whatever you shall require of me, so far as I have, shall be yours.

Daug. Sweetheart, I was going to ask you to give me the gold chain which you wear round your neck, that I may be always reminded of you, as if you were with me.

Son. Yes, sweetheart, this is but a slight and small thing. I thought you would bid somewhat higher. And this chain, though it came to me from a lover's hand, and she herself, so she regarded me, was promised that it should never leave me, but that I would always wear it for her sake.—Yet as you ask for it, I will not regard or keep my vow. There, take it and wear it for my sake. [*He hangs it about her neck*]

Dau. Sweetheart, I am deeply grateful to you.

Son. These thanks are not needed; but now hold out straight the fingers of both your hands. I will present you with these [*he sticks all her fingers full of rings*]

Dau. O, sweetheart, you give me too much. I am most deeply and earnestly grateful to you [*he pushes her hat off, kisses her, &c*]

Son. Yooks! hollah! jolly gay, frisky, frolic and no mistake (denial). Mine Host, what are we to do to pass the time; shall we not play some game at cards?

Host. Tho' I can't play much, yet I will not deny you, and will wager with you as long as I have a penny in my purse.

Son. Good mine Host. Youngster, quick, the cards. [*The Youth gives cards*] Now mine Host, say, what shall we play at?

Host. Indeed I don't know, believe me; let us play 'beggar my neighbour,' (arm mach reich)

Son. It is all the same to me; what you will; play on.

Host. My dear gentleman, we will first have a glass or two, to get courage to play; what say you?

Son. All is good to me, mine Host, that liketh you; drink away. [*They pledge one another once or twice; the Host never drinks more than half his glass*]

Host. So, now we will begin; I'll deal the cards. How high shall we play?

Son. I'll lay 50 crowns. Will you play as high?

Host. I'll lay always the same as you [*They play; the Host wins.*] See here, dear gentleman, this is mine, I have won it.

Son. That is nothing. Away once more; I'll lay the same again, lay you against me. [*They wager again. They begin to play*] The wine has made me drunk. Sweetheart, help me play, and look to it.

Host. See, this too is mine; there are the cards.

Son. Sweetheart, I'm so drunk, that I can't see any more. Look at the cards and tell me, has he won?

Dau. O yes, sweetheart, he has won this fairly.

Son. Go your ways then. There, take you the rest of the money, and play with him for it, for I am sleepy—Then we two will go to sleep.

Dau. With all my heart, sweetheart. Father, deal the cards, I'm playing now for my paramour [*he wins*]

Host. Daughter, I've won this of you

Dau. Now, Father, I may well say this day you have had Fortune and Luck.

Son. Truly I'm very drunk, and have no more desires to play. We will now leave off and go to bed. Sweetheart, come with me.

Daug. With pleasure, dearest, as you wish. [*Exeunt ambo, to bed*]

Host. See here, Wife, what a booty I have here. It was easy to spoil the Churl, for he took no care of his play. If I had as much more I should soon be a rich man.

Hostess. Dear husband, what a heap of money you have here. Now you must let me have a gown all of velvet.

Host. Yes wife, you shall have it; but we must still look to it well that we get all his silver, gold and stones from him. Have you instructed your daughter what to do at night?

Hostess. Yes, I'll see to that. My daughter I have taught well how to do—When he has fallen asleep by her side, she is secretly to rise, and to take his purse out of his hose—There is still a great treasure left in it.

Host. My dear wife, you have taught her well and rightly. Tis thus the feathers of young prodigals must be plucked. Come, we will go in.

ACT IV.

Enter the SON *holding the daughters hand, with a nightcap on his head. She has his purse, which she has stolen in the night, and gives it secretly to her Mother, who rejoices over it; she again gives it to her husband, who goes away with it and hides it.*

Son. Good morning, Hostess.

Hostess. Thanks, dear gentleman. Tell me, did you sleep well?

Son. My Hostess, not quite well; for there was a nightingale near me, that always prevented my sleeping. Guess what this nightingale was, and I will give you 40 crowns.

Hostess. Dear gentleman, it is a hard nut, and I cannot so lightly guess. But if I knew that you would really pay me the 40 crowns down I would puzzle my brains a bit over it, and perhaps guess it after long speculation.

Son. See, Hostess, dont you believe me now? What the devil do I care for 40 crowns? [*The Host now makes away with the purse*] As soon as you can guess right I will give you the money.

Hostess. Give me a little respite [*respiration*] that I may ponder on it.

Son. You may take it. But you, Sweetheart, tell me with what jollity shall we pass the time to-day.

Dau. I know not—If you like, I would play at tables with you. You shall wager the clothes you have on, and I my petticoat that I wear, and he that loses shall straight strip himself, and give it to the winner.

Son. O my fair maiden, and sweet love, you have found out a wonderful play: Truly my greatest joy is to play with pretty maids for their clothes, and to make them strip before me.

Hostess. Gentleman, methinks I can read your nightingale. Is it not my daughter that prevented your sleeping?

Son. Yes, you have guessed, and for her I have not closed my eyes all night, so sweetly and joyously did she sing to me.

Hostess. So now I have won the 40 crowns. Prithee give them to me now.

Son. Yes, Hostess, you have won them honestly, and I will give them you soon. But first listen. Once more prepare a splendid and lordly banquet, much more lordly and splendid than yesterday's, for I am going to bid and have a heap of pretty maidens at this feast. Tarts, fine large marchpanes, Sugarbread—In a word, the best you can find in the Town of game fishes and birds—the best drink you can light upon, fetch it, as the best Valteline [Reinfall] Hungarian and Rhenish, the best Malvoisy to be had, that it may be like a Prince's table, for I have lots of money and I can well pay for it. And when it is out, I will get more, though gold and money had daily to be coined for it. Theres no help for it; I cannot bear solitude and dump, my humour is always fresh and frolic. Methinks if I were not frolic in the World I must die. Yooks! Holla! frisk, courage, allegro! we will first make ourselves right jolly.

Hostess. Yes, dear gentlemen, you have well said; be frisky, and not like so many other hermitlike fools. They are not really men. I must praise you for being always so merry and freeh, even so early in the morning. But dear, gentleman, give me now my 40 crowns, and some gold besides to provide this banquet as you have always done before, when I have got any thing for you.

Son. Yes mine Hostess, come here, I will give it you [*Goes to the table, looks for his purse in his pocket; can't find it; is much astonished, runs to the daughter*] Ah, sweetheart, you have my purse, and have taken it from me in play to vex me a little. Prithee give it me back.

Dau. Sweetheart, why do you come upon me, as if I had taken your purse? No indeed, think not so; know that I have it not.

Son. Ah now, why do you vex me? I know it is your way. Give it here, you certainly have it; I know you are so rogueish.

Dau. What the devil do you mean, or what do you imagine, as though I had used you like a thief? Truly I have it not, so I swear.

Son. Ah, my dear Hostess, if you have taken it in joke give it me again.

Hostess. Why do you talk so to me? Indeed I have not taken it.

Enter Host.

Son. Ah my dear Host, my purse is gone, have you not found it?

Host. What the devil do I know of your purse? did you give it me to keep. I ask you not to speak to me so audaciously.

Son. I gave it not you to keep; but I must have lost it here, and I only ask, have you not found it?

Host. Truly I have found no purse. Who knows where you lost it? If you had lost it here, I have such honest servants that they will give it you again. All my life I have lodged here many great men, and when they lost anything in my House it was always honourably restored to them. Therefore hold in such words, for we are such honest folk that we covet nothing unrightly.

[*Host and Hostess stand and speak together;* SON *is very discontented; goes and sits by the table, lays his head in his hands*]

Son. O, covet or not, my purse or gold is gone all the same. [*sits troubled and sighs*]

Dau. Sweetheart, be at peace, and be not so troubled. Who knows but the purse may come back again.

Son. O call me no more Sweetheart, for love and joy have an end, and great sorrow has befallen my heart. O how should I get it again when it is stolen; the Thief will keep it and never bring it back. Shall I not therefore be sorrowful? Ay me what shall I do now? For not a farthing more do I possess. All my gold silver and jewels were in my purse, which is now stolen from me.

Dau. Hoho! no more money; that is a bad look-out [*des siehet übel auss*] [*goes to Father*] Dear Father, he sits, and has the Cornelium vehemently. He says, and bemoans himself that he has no more money.

Host. Has he no more money. I cant digest that. So now he is no longer of any use here [*goes to him*] Do you hear, what did you say? Have you no more money?

Son. No, not a farthing have I more. Some I have soon spent. The rest I had some thief has stolen from me.

Host. Yes yes; no more money, so I am not to be satisfied, it is stolen or taken from you. What care I for that? you shall pay me.

COMEDY OF THE PRODIGAL SON, ACT IV.

Hostess. And, do you hear, you must pay me too, you know that to give me nothing for my pains would not be at all good.

Dau. Here listen too, you poor prodigal, who is to pay me? you know what you have gelobet and promised me

Son. Why do you torture me? You know, Host, that I have paid you double for everything, and you too Hostess. You have got enough by me, methinks, and moreover likewise my purse full of gold is stolen away. Therefore leave me at peace, and molest me no more, for you are all paid double, and more than double, and I do not owe you a farthing.

Host. What the devil bring you in question? are we double paid? No indeed, with all I have not enough. I will be paid more, and so I will take whatever I can get, your horses your trunks with your clothes, and everything you have. Wife and daughter, take hold of him, and strip off all his clothes, and then hunt him out of the house.

Dau. Do you hear rascally knave—if we can't be paid otherwise we take what we can get. Here strip me off straight your hose and doublet [*He resists. She tries to strip him*]

Hostess. You cheating knave, the doublet I must have. The hose belong to my daughter [*They fasten on*]

Son. What will you do to me? Will you put me to shame? [*he resists*]

Hostess. See husband, he will not let himself be stripped.

Host. Do you hear, cheating rogue and knave, make no resistance, and let yourself be stripped willingly, or I will so dress you with my sword that your guts shall hang at your feet, and you shall never depart alive.

Son. Ay me, is there no pity? [*they strip him, search him, and*

take his keys and all that he has about him, and then beat him. *Enter the servant.*]

Servant. Early this morning my master bad me fetch the fiddlers, who are coming presently. To day we shall make ourselves right merry. But what the devil are they about? Hoho! now I know what that betokens. No, here I bide not, but I go too. I will run the best I know how. [*Runs away. They have now stript off the doublet.*]

Son. Ah pity! and give me an old doublet, that I go not quite naked.

Dau. No, we will give you nothing, but hunt you out in your skin.

Host. Yes, this old one will I give you [*Chucks him old hose and doublet*] Don 'em quick, and then drive you the beggar out of the house. [*Hostess and daughter each take a great rod, flog him violently, and hunt him out of the house*]

Dau. You blackguard knave! go, run: the longer here the more beating you get, and there pull me off your hose.

Son. O smite me not so sore! I run. [*hunt him out*]

ACT V.

Enter the SON *in his beggars clothes.*

Son. Ay me! why has my luck so turned? Ah, now I must starve. O my true Father! if I had followed your precepts I had never come to such misery. O God pity me, be gracious to me a Sinner! Let thy great wrath be somewhat assuaged, and forgive me my sins. I can scarce stir for hunger, for these three days I have not seen a piece of bread, much less eaten. O how palpably

I now see God's justice! If I might but have the bread which I have in my day thrown under foot, or dropped under the table, I could now feast upon it. But now I cannot get a crumb. Dire necessity now constrains me to ask good folks to give me a little bread. Here will I go to this door and beg. Ah, my good kind gentleman, I pray you pity me, and give me an alms, wherewith I may ward off my grievous hunger.

[*A voice behind the hangings answers him*] I can give thee nothing; myself have hardly enough to share with my wife and children their daily bread. There is now a great famine in the land. Therefore go farther; God help thee.

Son. Ay me—Miserable man! what am I to do now, with such rebuffs? I will try once more, and go to another door. Take pity upon a famishing man, who must soon lose his life for hunger.

[*A voice answers him*] God comfort thee, thou poor man, gladly would I give thee, if I only had anything—but with all my bitter sweat I can scarce get enough to shield my own from hunger. Therefore go farther, and beg there.

Son. Alas, poor troubled wretch! what shall I do now? No man will take pity on me and give me a little bread. O thou Almighty and all-sufficient God, have mercy on me, and take me to thy grace again! O I know not what now to do, whether to go farther and beg, for they likewise may rebuff me. But necessity compels me, if I would not starve and perish with hunger. Ah, pity me a poor miserable man, and divide with me some small alms, that I perish not with hunger. Almighty God will reward you double.

[*One answers him*] Why do you beg here at my door? Pack off! I have nothing to give you; I have scarcely my own daily bread.

For there is such great dearth in the whole country as none alive remembers; go therefore from my door, and beg of other folk.

Son. Ay me, ay me, what now shall I try? Now I must die of hunger, if thou almighty God dost not have mercy on me. Oh, I am too faint to stand. [*He falls on the ground*]

Enter SATAN *to him, with a drawn sword, and speaks to him.*

Despair. See, poor lost wretch, how thou liest, for every man to spit upon and spurn. Thou hast been rich, and now art a poor beggar. Thou knowest thou wast not obedient to thy father; thou madest him give thee thy patrimony, wherewith thou wentest forth into a far country, didst waste and consume it in a twinkling, with harlots and wanton companions. In a word, thou art a great sinner, and thy sins can never be forgiven thee. The Judgment of God is now upon thee, and thou shalt never more come into His grace, but must be damned eternally. Thou shalt now utterly perish with hunger, and it would be an eternal shame if any man saw thee who knew thee heretofore. Therefore thou must now fall into Despair. Take this sword and cut short thy life.

Son. Ah how full of anguish is my heart! Tell me, what is thy name?

Despair. My name's Despair.

Son. 'Tis time. I am a great sinner—

As he begins to speak, enter HOPE *running in haste*

Hope. In this poor man shalt thou have no part. Begone! hence, straightway, Satan, with thy poison. [*wrenches the sword out of his hand, with which he drives him out, and throws the sword after him*] Be not led astray, miserable man. Though Satan showed thee all thy sins; repent and mourn th m; have hearty ruth and sorrow for them; pray God earnestly and fervently to forgive them, and take thee back to grace. Then, though thy sins were as many as the sand of the sea, if thou only hast sorrow and hatest them in thy soul, and hast a believing and penitent heart, God will indeed forgive them. Bear now thy Cross with patience, and doubt not of God's grace. And though He may turn away from thee a little while, yet hope surely that it will not be long, but that he will relieve thy hunger.

Son. O tell me, what is thy name?

Hope. My name is Hope.

Son. O Hope! thy sayings I will believe, for thou makest not ashamed. But though the devil violently revisits me, and reproaches my sins to me, and tells me that I shall never more be received to grace, since I am so great a sinner, yet will I not doubt of Gods goodness, but fight valiantly against Satan, and hope firmly that God will forgive my great and manifold sins, mitigate this cross and famishing, and take me back to grace!

Hope. Do so. Hold thee fast to his grace, and fight like a good soldier; for know the devil will not yet yield with his poison, but seek to hold thee tighter. [*Goes away. The* SON *remains lying in great tribulation. Enter a common citizen*]

Cit. I am a citizen of mean condition; I am just come out of the town and am going to my farm. But what do I see lying here? a poor miserable man. Do you hear! why lie you here so wretchedly?

Son. Ah, dear Sir, I am a poor miserable man; for three days I have not seen bread, much less eaten any. I have begged for alms, but no man would give me any. And here I lie for weakness, and here I must die unless some one has pity upon me, and gives me bread to stay my hunger.

Cit. I well believe you. But can you not betake yourself to some one for whom you work?

Son. Oh sir, how cheerfully would I work if I could find a Master. I pray thee take pity on me, and take me for a servant! Day and night will I work with you if I only gain just enough to still this crying hunger.

Cit. I know not; I wanted no servant. Moreover, there is at this time so vehement a dearth that a man can scarce maintain himself. But I will take pity on thee, so follow me now, and go with me to my walled yard, there will I give you something to do.

Son. I thank you. Our God will reward you that you took me in my need, that I should not die of hunger. I will serve you diligently and truly.

ACTUS SEXTUS.

Enter the PRODIGAL SON *with a basket on his arm and a staff in his hand*

Son. Alas for the poor miserable woeful dearth; the longer it is, the worse for poor me. Now has my master sent me into the fields to feed his swine. But I am so famished that I can scarce stir; the famine is so sore that my master himself has no bread. O how fain would I now eat with the swine their food of husks, but I cannot get it. For the swine themselves have none, and I must tend them here, where they may grub for roots. O Lord and Father of heaven and earth, how grievously have I sinned against thee! my sins and transgressions are many, I come now with penitent heart before thee, and beweep my sins bitterly. O! Almighty God, this my punishment have I well deserved; but with heart crushed and broken, contrite and believing I come to thee and pray, be merciful to me a poor sinner, and think no more of my great sins, for I am a bitter foe to them, and am heartily sorry for them. O Lord! I renounce them; I hope firmly thou wilt help me. O, my dearest father, had I followed your precepts which you rehearsed to me, and gave me as the best viaticum (zehrppenning) for my journey, alack, it would never have come to this pass with me. But I was wanton and petulant, and would not even listen to advice from him. O, dearest father, how many hired servants hast thou who have their fill of bread, while I perish here with hunger.

[*sighs violently, weeps bitterly. Despair comes to him*]

Despair. Poor miserable wretch, lo, where thou liest, there must thou likewise perish of hunger. Thou sayest that if thou hast a penitent heart God will be merciful to you; but it is quite otherwise. Thy sins are too great to be forgiven. Thou seest now plain enough how God hath forsaken thee, and will no longer help thee; thou art undone for ever. Only take this sword, and take thy life.

Hope. Thou shameless devil, how darest thou be so bold, as again to tempt such a penitent? No thou shalt never get this man into thy claws. His Faith and Hope are too great. Therefore take yourself off to the abyss of hell, and pack hence, for thou shalt have no part in him. [HOPE *takes the sword, and drives away* DESPAIR *with it.*] Thou miserable man, abide constant in hope, rise up, and go to thy father, and say to him, Father, I have sinned against heaven and before thee, and am henceforth no more worthy to be called thy son. Make me as one of thy hired servants.

Son. O Hope, thou quickenest me mightily! thou still dwellest in my heart. Thy counsel will I at last follow, and I will straight arise to journey to my Father.

Hope. Follow me. I will show thee the way which thou must go.
[Exeunt.

Enter the Father of the PRODIGAL SON.

Father. O how sore is my heart troubled that I know not where my younger son may be, whether living or dead. I am alas certified that he must be fallen into great poverty, and has run through all his wealth quite unprofitably. But I would not care or bestow a thought on this if I could but see him alive. [*sits at the table, puts his hands under his head. Enter the* PRODIGAL SON]

Son. O there I see my fathers house; and do I see aright? Is that my father himself so malcontent? Oh I am so fearful; I know not what to do.

Father. [*Sees him afar off, arises and runs to him*] O how highly am I rejoiced; thou art my dear son; you touch my heart; welcome art thou to me [*falls on his neck; kisses him;* SON *falls on his knees before him*]

Son. O heart-loved father, I have sinned against heaven and before thee, and henceforth I am not worthy to be called thy son!

Father. Arise, beloved son [*he rises*] Hollah! hollah! boy, come here.

Servant. Here am I, master. O whom see I here; welcome home, welcome.

Son. Lo, do I find thee here? when did you come?

Serv. O, I have been long here, I left you when I saw the two harlots stripping off your clothes.

Father. Do you hear, boy, go in straight, and fetch my son forth the best clothes, and put them on him; and give him a finger ring for his hand, and shoes on his feet, and bring here a fatted calf and kill it. We will eat and be merry, for this my son was dead and is alive again, he was lost and is found. Now, dear son, follow me into the house. We will be merry. [*Exeunt.*

Enter the brother; he has a rake in his hand, and a fishermans coat on (*Seejuch*).

Broth. I come straight from my fathers field which I have sown. Now will I go home and tell my father how much I have sown today. [*goes a step or two; stood still*] But what in Gods name is the matter, with this noise and preparation in the house! They are so jovial, I cannot tell what it means. [*Servant comes running out as if he had message to do.*] Hollah! boy, dont run over me. Stay still and be questionable. Tell me what means the clapping and business in my fathers house—why are they so merry?

Serv. Your brother is come, and the father has slain a fatted Calf, because he has him back safe and sound, and therefore they are so jovial. I have to make ready, and carry in these benches and stools, for a great company is to be entertained today. If you had not come, your Father told me to run to the field to you and fetch you to the house.

Bro. It discontents me grievously; I am so angry I cannot tell what to do; shall I go home and be merry because my whoremaster brother is come back? No truly, that is not my mind. Go in straight and tell my father that I do not wish to come home.

Serv. Yes, I will go and tell him.

Bro. Do I not well to be angry? I have worked all on for my father like an ass, and have never had a feast made for me. But this my brother, who has wasted all his living with wanton and dishonest companions, and now comes back home as a poor beggar—for him we must be merry and joyful. Me seemeth it is gross injustice; were I my father I would have welcomed you with the stick. But here comes my father himself.

Fath. Ah, dear son, I beseech thee come in with me. Why standest thou here outside? For what cause wilt thou not enter?

Bro. Dearest father, do you think that it angers me not? You know how many years I have served you truly and worked like a horse in the ropes. Yes, all your land have I yearly helped to ear. In a word, you never had to blame me that I had transgressed your commandment, yet you have never given me a goat to make merry with my friends. But now this thy son is come, who has flung away his living on harlots, you have killed a fatted calf, and will be merry with your friends and neighbours, only because he has come home in a whole skin.

Fa. My dearest son, prithee be not so displeased with thy brother, and with our joy. Dearest son, thou art always with me, and all that is mine is thine. Yet consider my dear son, this thy brother was dead and is alive again, was lost and is found. O have not so stony a heart. Rejoice with me, for thy brother was in the devils claws, but now has he come to his right mind, and is converted, and is come to us with penitent heart, and now he is heir with us of eternal life and Paradise. Therefore be joyful with us, dearest son.

Bro. Dearest father, you have rightly corrected me, I am heartily glad that my brother is converted, that he with us may inherit God's kingdom. Now I will go in with you and be merry.

[END.]

NOTES TO *PRODIGAL SON*.

THE treatment of the story is the same as in Greene's *Mourning Garment*, where Philador the Prodigal is conducted by Greene into a Hostelry, where he is fleeced, like the Prodigal in this play, by the Host and his family. It is quite as probable that Greene stole his ideas from this play as that the writer of this play stole his from Greene: *Mancillia*, Greene's first tale, was probably taken from a play of the same name, performed at Court by the E. of Leicester's servants in 1573.

In the *Prodigal Son* it is easy to see that the German translator has imported all the ceremonious words and sentences. Where the English writer put *my Son*, or *mine* Host, the German has *Mein hertz lieber Sohn*, or *mein lieber Herr Wirth*. Some of the dialogue is a mere bandying of such compliments, without any other content. The English must have been quite embowelled here.

The poetry is all lost; and where comparisons are introduced they are rather German than English. The English would not understand 'to stay at home like a Wolf.'

The Scripture texts and allusions are well preserved. This gives the last act of the play a simplicity and grandeur which perhaps retains some flavour of the original.

Greene in one place flouts Shakspere as a theological poet (Pref. to *Never too late*); says also that clerks wrote stuff which they made public under his name; perhaps referring to a piece like this, which is pretty conclusively shown to be Shakspere's by the play *Histrio-mastix*.

For other notes upon the *Prodigal Son* see Introduction to *Histrio-mastix*, ante, p. 3.

[STORY OF THE PLAY.]

THE story of the play is simply that of the New Testament parable, the scene being changed, apparently, to Germany, as the residence of the Prodigal's father, and Italy (see p. 101, l. 4), as the chief locality of the Prodigal's 'riotous living.' A man has two sons, the elder industrious and contented, who lives with his father and attends well to his father's and the family's affairs generally, in the old patriarchal fashion; the younger son idle, discontented, and possessed by an insatiable liking for being 'jolly,' and for roaming forth in the world, and enjoying the pleasures of gay company. That the younger son may indulge his likings without stint, he demands of his father his patrimony, and tells the old man frankly that it is to furnish him with the means for going forth to see and enjoy the world, as he cannot longer bide at home to be, as he expresses it, in somewhat of the language of Arviragus in *Cymbeline* (p. 91, l. 5), like a wolf, only acquainted with his own den. The father tries to dissuade him, and gives him much good advice. But the Prodigal is so bent upon enjoying himself in his own 'jolly' way, that he will not give any heed to his father; and presently the brother, giving like good advice, is as unsuccessful as the father. The father then gives his younger son his fortune, and with it, and much more good counsel, and the old man's blessing, the Prodigal goes forth. The 'riotous living' shewn is rather sparingly confined to a few scenes only, all enacted in a single inn, and that, seemingly, a very poor one. The only participators, too, in the way of company, are the Innkeeper and his wife and daughter. These three feast and play cards with the Prodigal, of course at his expense, and they cheat at cards, and otherwise fleece him without stint. The craving of the Prodigal for 'pretty girls and women' is met by the host and hostess at once giving up their daughter to him; and the daughter, being at one with her parents in the desire to make money out of the Prodigal, readily assents to the arrangement. After several feasting bouts, the daughter robs her paramour of his purse, and gives it to her father. The purse being missed, and the Prodigal announcing that he has now no more money, host, hostess, and daughter all set upon him and strip him for alleged unsatisfied debts; and then they turn him out of doors in rags. Starving, and begging from door to door, the Prodigal becomes repentant, and calls upon God for forgiveness, and for mercy. Despair, otherwise the Devil, then comes, and suggests suicide; but Hope drives the Devil off, and persuades the Prodigal to repent. The Prodigal then takes service with a poor citizen, whose swine he tends and feeds with. Despair again tempts him, and is again driven off by Hope, who then counsels the Prodigal to return to his father. The return is a very close rendering of the parable, including the jealousy of the elder brother at the rejoicing over the Prodigal's return, and the final overcoming of that jealousy by the father.—G.

IACKE DRVMS
Entertainement,

Or

THE COMEDIE
OF Pasqvil AND

Katherine.

As it hath beene sundry times plaid by the Children of Powles.

Newly corrected.

London,
Printed by *W. Stansby*, for *Philip Knight*, and are to be sold at his shop in Chancery-Lane, ouer against the Roles.
1 6 1 6.

[THE STORY OF THE PLAY.]

[THIS play is a comedy of character and intrigue, whose scene is laid in the London suburb of High-gate. The second title—the Comedie of Pasquil and Katherine—describes the principal story of the play, Jack Drum's doings being quite subordinate. Sir Edward Fortune has two daughters. The eldest, Camelia, is wooed by Brabant junior, a Court gallant, and John Ellis, a doltish, rich yeoman. She is fickle, and turns from one to the other, and then from both to Planet, a good-natured cynic, and friend to Brabant junior. Katherine, the younger daughter, is as constant as her sister is fickle. Two of her suitors are Pasquil, a romantic youth, and Mamon, an old usurer. Mamon, being rejected, hires a Frenchman to murder his rival, Pasquil. The Frenchman discloses the plot to Pasquil, who lies down and feigns death. Katherine, thinking her lover dead, leaves home in despair. After a time, Pasquil finds her; but Mamon now determines to deprive Pasquil of the love he cannot win for himself by destroying Katherine. He throws 'oile of Toades' over her, upon which she warns Pasquil away from her as from a doomed woman. Pasquil then tears up Mamon's 'indentures and bonds,' and so sends that usurer mad, and into 'Bedlame,' and then goes mad himself. Meanwhile, Camelia, having jilted Brabant junior and John Ellis, fancies she is in love with Planet. Brabant junior, hearing an assignation planned between Camelia and Planet, thinks Camelia false to him. He orders his page to shoot Planet; and the deed being done, as he thinks, takes Planet's place at the meeting with Camelia, where, disguised as his friend, he learns that the latter has only met Camelia to chide her for her treatment of himself (Brabant). Brabant's remorse now leads him to attempt suicide, but he is arrested in the act; and, Planet presently coming in, a reconciliation follows. At this point Katherine reappears cured; and Pasquil also appearing, and becoming cured of his madness through the recovery of his mistress, the hands of the lovers are joined by Sir Edward. Camelia now goes successively to Brabant junior, John Ellis, and Planet, who each refuse her, and so punish her 'light inconstancie.' The more broadly-humorous second plot concerns chiefly Jack Drum, Sir Edward's man; Winifride, his daughter's maid; and the caricature of a Frenchman, John fo de King. Drum is in love with Winifride, but she plays the Frenchman off against him. She persuades Drum to get into a sack to be conveyed to her chamber, and so contrives that the Frenchman shall carry off the sack, thinking she is in it. When the sack is opened, the Frenchman, instead of embracing Winifride, gets a beating from Jack Drum. Several scenes are taken up with wit-combats between the two Brabants, Planet, and M. Puffe, an exquisite in the use of euphuistical language. Brabant senior, besides being, as he thinks, a great wit and critic, is a great practical joker. A joke he plays upon the Frenchman, who is very lascivious, and always looking out for 'a vench,' is to introduce him to his own wife as a courtezan. Brabant believes his wife will repulse the Frenchman, but she does not; and, in the end of the play, the arch-censurer and gull-maker is crowned with horns as a self-made cuckold.—G.]

INTRODUCTION.

No anonymous play can bear more satisfactory evidence, either of its date or its author, than '*Jack Drums Entertainement, or the Comedie of Pasquil and Katherine. As it hath been sundry times plaid by the Children of Powles.* London, Richard Olive, 1601. Another edition purports to be *newly corrected.* London, Printed by W. Stansby for Philip Knight . . . . . 1616.' It was written in the time of Elizabeth, after Kemp's Morris had been danced, while 'Peace with Spain' was the burden of every one's discourse, and in a 'women's year,' i. e. leap year, which must have been 1600. As for the author, the vocabulary of the play betrays him. In the *Poetaster*, written by Jonson against Marston and Dekker in 1601, the poetry and vocabulary of the former are satirized in the following verses :—

> 'Ramp up thy genius, be not retrograde,
> But boldly nominate a spade a spade.
> What, shall thy lubrical and glibbery muse
> Live as she were defunct, like punk in stews?
> . . . .
> No, teach thy members to poetize,
> And throw abroad thy spurious snotteries
> Upon that puft-up lump of barmy froth,
> Or clumsy chilblain'd judgment; that with oath

> Magnificates his merit, and bespawls
> The conscious time with humorous foam and brawls,
> As if his organons of sense would crack
> The sinews of my patience' . . . . .

Jonson afterwards administers a pill to Crispinus, and makes him vomit out these new terms, peculiar to his poetry—glibbery, chilblain'd, clumsy, barmy froth, puff, and others. It will be seen that these, and other equally characteristic Marstonian words, abound in the following play, and that the very series of words of one of the above lines—'clumsy, chilblain'd, judgment'—is found there, p. 156, l. 136.

> 'Let *clumsie judgements, chilblain'd* gowtie wits'.

So we have *bespawle*, p. 146, l. 302; *barmie froth*, p. 136, l. 35. Polyphemian *puffes*, p. 139, l. 124; *glibbery*, p. 139, l. 127.

> 'Cracke not the sinewes of my patience,' 175, l. 238.

Besides the words of the play, some of its sentences are ridiculed in the *Poetaster*. Thus in *Jack Drum* young Brabant is evidently Marston himself; now, p. 143, l. 227, he is described as

> 'a proper man,
> And yet his legs are somewhat of the least.'

In the *Poetaster*, Cloe says to Rufus Crispinus (Marston), 'Your legs do sufficiently show you are a gentleman born; for a man borne upon little legs is always a gentleman born.' Dekker, in the Gull's Horn-book, remembered this flirt at his friend by one who had 'brought either your feather, or your red beard (Rufus), or your little legs on the stage.' And as in *Jack Drum* Winifred persuades Camelia that a wise woman always weds a fool, in order to be her own mistress, so Cytheris tells Cloe in the *Poetaster* that 'wise women choose not husbands for the eye, merit, or birth, but wealth and sovereignty.'

At p. 172, l. 157, we have

'Some Evenuch'd vicarage, or some fellowship.'

A similar phrase is common in Marston's works—e. g. *Scourge of Villany*, ii., Sat. v. :

'What though pale Maurus paid huge Simonies
For his half dozen gelded vicaries.'

It is also found in the *Return from Parnassus*, which throughout is written in imitation of Marston's style.

The comic business of the play, which largely consists in the ridiculous euphuistic compliments of the gallants to one another, is in this respect exactly similar to much of Jonson's *Cynthia's Revels*, a play of the same date, and written against Marston and Dekker, who figure in it as Hedon and Anaides.

The likeness of the induction to Jonson's inductions will be manifest to all readers.

The play is one of the series which relate to the quarrel of Jonson with Marston and Dekker. In it young Brabant is Marston himself; while old Brabant, who was first of all intended for a witless patron of wit, a rich gull who spends his wealth in giving suppers to poets, insensibly becomes transformed to the great critic and scourge of the times, and is at last said to be one of those

'bombast wits
That are puff'd up with arrogant conceit

Of their own worth, as if Omnipotence
Had hoised them to such unequall'd height
That they surveyed our spirits with an eye
Only create to censure from above ;
When, good souls, they do nothing but reprove.'—p. 193, l. 317.

This phase of Brabant senior, is clearly meant for Jonson; in his character of a rich gull, and in the punishment which overtakes him in the end of the play, he could hardly be meant for Jonson, even in those days of reckless misstatement, when the satirist did not attempt a likeness, however caricatured, but thought himself most successful when he heaped together the foulest abuse.

In his Jonsonese character of a critic, who held himself immeasurably above all his contemporaries, Brabant the elder is made to pronounce two pieces of criticism, one on the children of Paul's, who seem to have been set up as rivals to the children of the Queen's Revels who acted in the Blackfriars theatre, and from thence, chiefly under the guidance of Jonson, 'berattled the common stages,' and drew the chief audience from the men actors. The Paul's boys, says Brabant,

'produce
Such musty fopperies of antiquity,
As do not suit the humorous age's back
With clothes in fashion.'—p. 199, ll. 111-14.

This seems to have been Marston's feeling also, in spite of his rebuke to Brabant—'you will be censuring still.' For in the induction to this play he

—'vows not to torment your listening ears
With mouldy fopperies of stale poetry.'—p. 134, l. 24.

In another place (p. 183, l. 37) Brabant gives his opinion of 'our modern wits.' First, the 'new poet Mellidus, (Marston, author of *Antonio and Mellida*,) is

'A slight, bubbling spirit, a cork, a husk.'

Next, Musus (either Chapman, who, as Chettle says, 'finished sad Musœus' gracious song,' or Daniel, whom Drayton, in *Endimion and Phœbe*, 1594, calls 'the sweet Musœus of these times') is 'as blunt as Pauls.' This criticism fits Daniel best, whose style, as Bolton says, is more prosaic than poetical, and whom Jonson thought 'a good honest man but no poet,' whereas he thought highly of Chapman.

Next, instead of commending the 'good, cordial, sappy style' of Decius (Drayton), Brabant calls him 'a surrein'd jaded wit—but a' rubs on.' And then in a collective judgment he says of them, 'they are all apes and gulls, vile imitating spirits, dry heathy turfs.'

Whether any of the other characters in the play were meant for living persons is not easy to decide. There is nothing very characteristic in Pasquil, though the name would suggest Nash. Dr Nicholson suggests that, as Nash was just dead, Marston, like Nicholas Breton, might usurp his literary name in order to profit by its popularity. Planet, to whom the sceptre of criticism seems to be tacitly conceded, one hopes may have been meant for Shakspere.

[*From the end of the play, in the original.*]

The names of all the Men and Women, that Act this Play.

THE MEN.

1. *Sir Edward Fortune.*
2. *Brabant Signior, and his Page.*
3. *Brabant Iunior, and his Page.*
4. *Planet.*
5. *Puffe, and his Page.*
6. *Iohn Ellis.*
7. *Mammon the Vsurer, with a great nose.*
8. *Flawne his Page.*
9. *Timothy Twedle.*
10. *Iacke Drum.*
11. *Pasquil.*
12. *Mounsieur.*

THE WOMEN.

1. *Katherine.*
2. *Camelia.*
3. *Winifride.*
4. *Market Woman.*

IACKE DRVMS
Entertainement,

OR
The Comedie of PASQVIL, and
KATHERINE.[1]

The Introduction.

Enter the Tyer-man.

I*N good faith, Gentlemen, I thinke we shall be forced to giue you right* Iacke Drums entertainement,[2] *for he that composde the Booke, we should present, hath done vs very vehement wrong, he hath snatched it from vs, vpon the very instance of entrance, and with violence keepes the boyes from comming on the stage. So, God helpe me, if we wrong your delights, 'tis infinitely against our endeuours, vnlesse we should make a tumult in the Tyring-house.* Exit Tyer-man.

Enter one of the Children.

You much mistake his Action, Tyer-man ;
His violence proceedes not from a minde
That grudgeth pleasure to this generous presence;

[1] & [2] See p. 140, l. 155.

But doth protest all due respect and loue, 12
Vnto this choise selected influence.
He vowes, if he could draw the musick from the Spheares,
To entertayne this presence with delight,
Or could distill the quintessence of heauen 16
In rare composed Scenes, and sprinkle them
Among your eares, his industrie should sweat
To sweeten your delights : but he was loth,
Wanting a *Prologue*, and our selues not perfect, 20
To rush vpon your eyes without respect :
Yet if youle pardon his defects and ours,
Hee'le giue vs passage, and you pleasing scenes,
And vowes not to torment your listning eares 24
With mouldie fopperies of stale Poetrie,
Vnpossible drie mustie fictions :
And for our parts, to gratifie your fauour,
Weele studie till our cheekes looke wan with care, 28
That you our pleasures, we your loues may share. *Exit.*

Actvs Primvs.

Enter Iacke Drum, *and* Timothy Twedle, *with a Taber and a Pipe.*

Drum. Come *Timothy Twedle*, tickle thy Pipe on the Greene, as I haue tippled the pot in the celler, and the hey for the honor of *High-gate!* you old *Troian*.

Twedle. And a heigh for the honor of *Hygate!* Hem. By my holy dam, tho I say it, that shuld not say it, I thinke I am as perfect in my Pipe, as Officers in poling, Courtiers in flatterie, or Wenches in falling : Why, looke you, *Iacke Drum*, 'tis euen as naturall to me, as bawdrie to a Somner, knauerie to a Promoter, or damnation to an Vsurer. But is *Holloway* Morrice prancing vp the hill? 9

Drum. I, I; and *Sir Edward*, and the yellow tooth'd, sunck-eyde, gowtie shankt Vsurer, *Mamon*, my young Mistresses, and all are comming to the Greene. Lay cushions, lay the cushions ! ha, the Wenches ! 12

Twed. The wenches, ha ! When I was a young man and could tickle the Minikin, and made them crie " thanks, sweet *Timothy*," I had the best stroke, the sweetest touch, but now (I may sigh to say it) I am falne from the Fiddle, and betooke me to thee. 16

He playes on his Pipe.

Enter Sir Edward Fortune, M. Mamon, Camelia, Katherine, and Winifride, Camelias maide.

Sir Ed. Sit, *M. Mamon.* Ha, here's a goodly day nigh !
Mam. I thanke you, sir, and faith, what newes at court ?
Sir Ed. What newes at Court ? Ha, ha ! Now Iesu God !
Fetch me some *Burdeux* wine. What newes at Court ? 20
Reprobate fashion, when each ragged clowt,
Each Coblers spawne, and yestie, bowzing bench,
Reekes in the face of sacred maiestie
His stinking breath of censure ! Out-vpon't !   *He drinks.*
Why, by this *Burdeux* iuyce, 'tis now become 25
The shewing-horne of Bezelers discourse,
The common foode of prate : " what newes at court ? "
But in these stiffe neckt times, when euery Iade 28
Huffes his vpreared crest, the zealous bent

Of Councellors solide cares is trampled on
By euery hacknies heeles: Oh, I could burst
At the coniectures, feares, preuentions,   32
And restles tumbling of our tossed braines:
Yee shall haue me an emptie caske that's furd
With nought but barmie froth, that ne're traueld
Beyond the confines of his Mistris lips,   36
Discourse as confident of peace with *Spaine*,
As if the *Genius* of quicke *Michiauel*
Vsher'd his speech!
   Mam. Oh forbeare, you are too sharpe with me.   40
   S. Ed. Nay, *M. Mamon*, misinterpret not,
I onely burne the bauen heath of youth,
That cannot court the presence of faire time
With ought but with, "what newes at Court, sweet sir?"   44
I had rather that *Kemps* Morice were their chat;
For of foolish actions, may be theyle talke wisely, but of
Wise intendments, most part talke like fooles.
The summe is this, beare onely this good thought,   48
The Counsell-chamber is the Phœnix[1] nest,
Who wastes it selfe, to giue vs peace and rest.
        The Taber and Pipe strike vp a Morrice.
        A shoute within.
        A Lord, a Lord, a Lord, who!
   Ed. Oh, a Morrice is come, obserue our country sport.
'Tis Whitson-tyde, and we must frolick it.   52

        [1] See note 2, p. 208.

Enter the Morrice.

The Song.

Skip it, and trip it, nimbly, nimbly, tickle it, tickle it, lustily,
Strike vp the Taber, for the wenches fauour, tickle it, tickle it lustily:
Let vs be seene, on Hygate-Greene, to dance for the honour of Holloway.
Since we are come hither, let's spare for no leather, 56
To dance for the honour of Holloway.

Ed. Well said, my boyes, I must haue my Lords liuory. What is't, a May-pole? Troth, 'twere a good body for a courtiers imprezza, if it had but this life, *Frustra florescit.* Hold Cousin, hold. 60

He giues the Foole money.

Foole. Thankes, Cousin, when the Lord my Fathers *Audit* comes, wee'l repay you againe. Your beneuolence too, sir.

Mam. What, a Lords sonne become a begger?

Foole. Why not, when beggers are become Lords sons? Come, 'tis but a small trifle. 65

Mam. Oh, sir, many a small make a great.

Foole. No, sir, a few great make a many small. Come, my Lords, poore and neede hath no law. 68

S. Ed. Nor necessitie no right, *Drum,* downe with them into the Celler. Rest content, rest content, one bout more, and then away.

Foole. Speak like a true hart. I kisse thy foot sweet knight. 72

The Morrice sing and dance, and Exeunt.

Mam. Sir *Edward Fortune,* you keepe too great a house.
I am your friend, in hope your sonne in law,

And from my loue I speake. You keepe too great a house.
Goe to, you doe. Yon same drie throated huskes 76
Will sucke you vp; and you are ignorant
What frostie fortunes may benumme your age:
Pouertie, the Princes frowne, a ciuill warre, or—

   S. Ed. Or what? Tush, tush, your life hath lost his taste. 80
Oh, madnesse! still to sweat in hot pursuit
Of cold abhorred sluttish niggardise:
To exile ones fortunes from their natiue vse:
To entertaine a present pouertie, 84
A willing want, for Infidell mistrust
Of gracious prouidence: Oh Lunacie!
I haue two thousand pound a yeere, and but two girles:
I owe nothing: liue in all mens loue: 88
Why should I now goe make my selfe a slaue
Vnto the god of fooles? Put worst: then, here's my rest—
I had rather liue rich to die poore, then liue poore to die rich. 91

   Mam. Oh, but so great a masse of coyne might mount from wholsome thrift, that after your decease your issue might swell out your name with pompe.

   S. Ed. Ha. I was not borne to be my cradles drudge:
To choke and stifle vp my pleasures breath: 96
To poyson with the venomd cares of thrift
My priuate sweet of life: onely to scrape
A heape of muck: to fatten and manure
The barren vertues of my progenie, 100
And make them sprowt, spight of their want of worth:
No, I doe loue my Girles should wish me liue,
Which few doe wish that haue a greedie Syre:

But still expect and gape with hungrie lip,
When hee'le giue vp his gowtie stewardship.
　Mam. You touch the quick of sense, but then I wonder
You not aspire vnto the eminence
And height of pleasing life : To Court! To Court!
There burnish; there spread; there stick in pompe,
Like a bright Diamond in a Ladies brow;
There plant your fortunes in the flowring spring,
And get the Sunne before you of respect:
There trench your selfe within the peoples loue,
And glitter in the eye of glorious grace.
What's wealth without respect and mounted place?
　S. Ed. Worse and worse. I am not yet distraught.
I long not to be squeas'd with mine owne waight :
Nor hoise vp all my sailes to catch the winde
Of the drunke reeling Commons : I labour not
To haue an awfull presence, nor be fear'd
(Since who is fear'd, still feares to be so fear'd)
I care not to be like the *Horeb* Calfe,
One day ador'd, and next pasht all in peeces :
Nor doe I enuie *Polyphemian* puffes,
Swizars slopt greatnesse : I adore the Sunne,
Yet loue to liue within a temperate zone :
Let who will climbe ambitions glibbery rounds,
And leane vpon the vulgars rotten loue,
I'le not corriuall him : The Sunne will giue
As great a shaddow to my trunck as his :
And after death like *Chesmen* hauing stood
In play for Bishops, some for Knights, and Pawnes,

We all together shall be tumbled vp, into one bagge.
Let hush'd calme quiet, rock my life asleepe:
And being dead, my owne ground presse my bones,
Whilest some old Beldame hobbling ore my graue,   136
May mumble thus: *Here lyes a Knight, whose money
Was his slaue.* Now *Iacke*, what newes?

Enter Iacke Drum.

Drum. And please your worship, the Morrice haue tane their liquor.   140

Sir Ed. Hath not the liquor tane them?

Drum. Tript vp their heeles, or so? One of them hath vndertaken to dance the Morrice from *Hyygate* to *Holloway*, on his heeles, with his hands vpwards.   144

S. Ed. That's nothing hard.

Drum. Yes, sir. 'Tis easier for him to dance on his head then his heeles, for indeede his heeles are turn'd ranck rebels, they will not obey, but they are tumbling downe the hill a-pace.   148

Mam. And I must after them. Farewell, my soules delight: Sweet *Katherine*, adieu! *Camelia*, good night.

S. Ed. Nay, not to *London*, sir, to night, Ifaith, at least stay supper.   152

Drum. Harke you, sir. There's but two Lambs, a dozen Capons, halfe a score couple of rabbets, three tartes, and foure tansies, for supper, and therefore I beseech you giue him *Iacke Drums* intertainment: Let the *Iebusite* depart in peace.   156

Sir Edw. Why, *Iacke* is not that sufficient!

Drum. I, for any Christian, but for a yawning Vsurer, 'tis but a bit, a morsell. If you table him, heele deuoure your whole Lordship.

He is a Quick-sand; a *Goodwin;* a Gulfe: As hungrie as the jawes of
a Iayle. Hee will waste more substance then *Ireland* Souldiers: A
Dye, a Drabbe, and a Paunch-swolne-Vsurer, deuoure whole Monarchies: Let him passe, sweet Knight, let him passe.

Sir Edw. Peace, knaue, peace! 164
Daughter, lay your expresse commandement vpon the stay
of Master *Mamon.* What, 'tis womens yeere!
Dian doth rule, and you must domineere.

Mam. No, sheele not wish my stay. Oh, I am curst 168
With her inexorable swiftnesse! By her loue,
Which dotes me more then new coin'd glowing gold,
The vtmost bent of my affection
Shoots all my fortunes to obtaine her loue; 172
And yet I cannot praise, but still am loth'd,
My presence hated: therefore, *Mamon,* downe,
Farewell, Sir *Edward*, farewell beauties Crowne.

Sir. Edw. Faith, as it please you for going, and her for wooing,
I will inforce neyther. 177

Kath. With your pardon, sir, I shal sooner hate my selfe,
Then loue him.

Sir Edw. Nay, be free, my daughters, in election. 180
Oh, how my soule abhors inforced yokes,
Chiefly in loue, where the affections bent
Should wholy sway the fathers kind consent.
'Fore God, when I was batcheler, had a friend, 184
Nay, had my father wisht me to a-wife,
That might haue lik'd me, yet their verie wish
Made me mistrust my Loue had not true course,
But had some sway from dutie, which might hold 188

For some slight space: but ô, when time shall search
The strength of loue, then vertue, and your eye,
Must knit his sinewes: I chusde my selfe a wife,
Poore, but of good discent, and wee did liue 192
Till death diuorc'd vs, as a man would wish:
I made a woman; now, wenches, make a man:
Choose one either of valour, wit, honestie, or wealth,
So he be gentle, and you haue my heart, 196
Ifaith you haue: What! I haue land for you both;
You haue loue for your selues. Heeres master *Mamon* now.

Drum. A Club-fisted Vsurer.

Sir Edw. A wealthie, carefull, thriuing Citizen. 200

Mam. Carefull, I. I let nothing without good blacke and white,
I warrant you.

Drum. Yes, sir.

Mam. No, sir. 204

Drum. A little backe wind, sauing your VVor. sir.

Mam. I am scoft at, where's my man there? Ho!

Came. Sir, you need not take the pepper in the nose,
Your nose is firie enough. 208

Mam. What *Flawne!* what *Christopher!* 'Hart where's the knaue
become? Hold, sirrah, carrie my cloake.

Enter Flawne.

Kath. It seemes he can scarce carrie himselfe.

Drum. He's ouer the shooes, yet heele hold out water, for I haue
liquor'd him soundly. 212

Mam. Why cannot you come where headie liquor is, but you
must needs bouze?

What! a man may lead a horse to the water, but heele chuse to
drinke.   215
  Flawn. True, but I am no horse, for I cannot chuse but drinke.
  Mam. A pale weake stripling, yet contend with Ale?
  Flawn. Why, the weakest goe to the pot still.   218
  Mam. That jest shall saue him. Sir *Edward*, now good day.
Exit.

  Sir Edw. Nay, sir, weele bring you a little of the way.
  Drum. Rely on me, *Christopher*, I will be thy staffe;
And thy Masters nose shalbe thy lanthorne & candlelight.   222
      Exeunt all. Manent Camelia and Winifride.
  Wini. Mistris *Camelia*, me thinkes, your eye
Sparkles not spirit as 't was wont to doe.
  Came. My mind is dull, and yet my thoughts are fixt
Vpon a pleasing obiect, *Brabants* loue.   226
  Wini. Indeed young *Brabant* is a proper man;
And yet his legs are somewhat of the least:
And, faith, a chittie, well complexion'd face;
And yet it wants a beard: A good, sweet youth;   230
And yet some say, he hath a valiant breath;
Of a good haire, but oh, his eyes, his eyes!
  Came. Last day thy praise extold him to the skies.   233
  Wini. Indeed, hee weares good clothes, and throwes his cloake
With good discretion vnder his left arme:
He curles his boot with judgement, and takes a whiffe
With gracefull fashion: sweares a valorous othe;
But, ô the deuil! hath a hateful fault, he is a yonger brother! 238
  Came. A younger brother? ô intolerable!
  Wini. No, Mistris, no: but there's Master *Iohn*,

Master *Iohn Ellis:* there's a lad, yfaith.
Ha, for a vertuous honest good youth! 242
   Came. Tut, hee is good because hee knowes not how to be bad,
Nor wherefore he is good.
   Wini I know not, mee thinkes, not to bee bad, is good inough
in these dayes. 246
   Came. Nay, he is a foole, a perfect ideot.
   Wini. Why, all the better. And I'le tell you this :
The greatest ladie in the land affects him,
Nay, doates vpon him, I, and lyes with him. 250
   Cam. What ladie, good sweet *Winifride*, what ladie, say? Faith
there bee some good partes about the foole, which I perceiue not,
yet another may: what ladie, good sweet *Winifride ?* say, quicke,
good wench. 254
   Wini. The ladie *Fortune*.
   Came. Why, my nam's *Fortune*, too.
   Wini. Then you must needs fauour him ;
For *Fortune* fauours fooles. 258
   Came. Oh, but to hugge a foole is odious.
   Wini. Foule water quencheth fire well enough ;
And with more liuely pallat, you shall taste
The juice of pleasures fount, at priuate times : 262
Pish ! by my maiden head, were I to match,
I would elect a wealthie foole 'fore all.
Then may one hurrie in her chariot,
Shine in rich purpled Tissue, haue hundred loues, 266
Rule all, pay all, take all, without checke or snib.
When being married to a wise man (O the Lord !)
You are made a foole, a ward, curb'd and controll'd, and

(O) out vpon't! 270

Came. Beleeue me wench, thy words haue fired me.
I'le lay me downe vpon a banke of Pinkes,
And dreame vpon't. Sweet foole, I, tis most cleere, 273
A foolish bed-mate, why he hath no peere. *Exit Camelia.*

Wini. Ha, ha! Her loue is as vncertaine as an Almanacke; as vnconstant as the fashion; just like a whiffe of Tabacco, no sooner in at the mouth, but out at the nose: I thinke in my heart I could make her enamoured on *Timothy Twedle.* Well, he that fees me best, speeds best. 279
For as it pleas'd my bribed lips to blowe,
So turnes her feath'rie fancie to and fro. *Exit.*

*Enter Brabant Iunior at one doore, Ned Planet
at the other.*

Bra. Good speed thee, my good sweet *Planet:* 282
How doost thou Chuck?

Pla. How now, *Brabant,* where haue you liu'd these three or for[1] foure daies?

Bra. Ho! at the glittering Court, my *Pytheas.* 286

Pla. Plague on ye, *Pytheas!* What haue you done there?

Bra. Why, lane in my Ladies lap; eat, drinke and sleep.

Pla. So hath thy Ladies dogge done. What, art in loue VVith yon *Hygate* Mammet still? 290

Bra. Still, I still, and still: I, in eternitie.

Pla. It shalbe chronicled next after the death of *Bankes* his horse I wonder why thou lou'st her?

Bra. Loue hath no reason. 294

---

[1] for in text, but redundant.—G.

Pla. Then is loue a beast.

Bra. O my *Camelia* is loue it selfe.

Pla. The deuill shee is : Hart, her lips looke like a dride Neatstoung : her face as richly yellow as the skin of a cold Custard, & her mind as setled as the feet of bald pated Time.   299

Bra. Plague on your hatefull humour, out vpon't !
Why should your stomacke be so queasie now,
As to bespawle the pleasures of the world ?
VVhy should you runne an Idle counter-course
Thwart to the path of fashion ?   Come, your reason ?   304
O you are buried in Philosophie,
And there intomb'd in supernaturals.
You are dead to natiue pleasures life.

Pla. Let me busse thy cheeke, sweet Pugge,   308
Now I am perfect hate.   I lou'd but three things in the world ; Philosophie, Thrift, and my selfe. Thou hast made me hate Philosophie. A Vsurers greasie Codpiece made me lothe Thrift : but if all the Brewers jades in the Towne can drugge me from loue of my selfe, they shall doe more then e're the seuen wise men of *Greece* could : Come, come, now I'le be as sociable as *Timon* of *Athens*.   314

Bra. Along with me then, you droming *Sagbut*.
I'le bring thee to a Crew.

Pla. Of Fooles wilt not ?   317

Bra. Faith, if you haue any weight of judgement, you may easily sound what depth of wits they draw. There's first my elder brother.

Pla. Oh, the Prince of fooles ; Vnequal'd Ideot :   320
He that makes costly suppers to trie wits :
And will not sticke to spend some twentie pound

To grope a gull: that same perpetuall grin,
That leades his corkie jests, to make them sinke 324
Into the eares of his deriders, with his owne applause.

Bra. Indeed, his jests are like *Indian* beefe, they will not last, & yet he pouders them soundly with his own laughter. Then there's the *Gotish French*-man, *Mounsieur Iohn fo de King*, know'st thou him? 329

Pla. Oh, I, to a haire, for I knew him when he had neuer a haire on his head.

Bra. Hee is a faithfull, pure Rogue.

Pla. I, I, as pure as the gold that hath beene seuen times tryed in the fire. 334

Bra. Then theres *Iohn Ellis*; and profound toung'd Master *Puffe*, hee that hath a perpetuitie of complement, hee whose phrases are as neatly deckt as my Lord Majors hensmen, hee whose throat squeakes like a treble Organ, and speakes as smal and shril, as the Irish-men crie pip, fine pip. And when his period comes not roundly off, takes tole of the tenth haire of his *Bourbon* locke: as thus. "Sweet, sir, repute me as a (*Puffe*) *selected spirit borne to bee the admirer of your neuer inough admired* (*Puffe.*)" 342

Pla. Oh, we shall bee ouer-whelm'd with an invndation of laughter! Come, where are they?

Bra. Here, at this tauerne.

Pla. In, in, in, in! I long to burst my sides, and tyre my spleene with laughter. *Exeunt.*

Enter two Pages, the one laughing, the other crying.

Page 1. Why do'st thou crie? 348

2. Why do'st thou laugh?

1. I laugh to see thee crie.

2. And I crie to see thee laugh.

Peace be to vs.   Heres our Masters. 352

*Enter Brabant Signior, Planet, Brabant Iunior, Iohn Ellis,
Master Puffe, and Monsieur Iohn fo de King.*

Bra. Sig. You shall see his humour. I pray you bee familiar with this gentleman, Master *Puffe*, hee is a man of a well growne spirit, richly worth your. I assure you, ha, ha, ha!

Puff. Sir, I enrowle you in the Legend of my (*Puffe*) intimates. I shall bee infinitely proud if you will deigne to value me worthie the imbracement of your (*Puffe*) better affection. 358

Pla. Speake you from your thought, sir?

Puffe. I, or would my silke stocke should lose his glosse else. I shall triumph as much in the purchase of your (*Puffe*) loue, as if I had obtained the great *Elixar:* Let vs incorporate our affections, I pray you : let mee be forward in your fauour.

Pla. Sir, I pray you let me beg you for a foole. 364

Puff. I affect no rudenesse, gentlemen. The heauens stand Propitious to your faire designes :
Assoone as next the Sunne shall 'gin to shine,
I will salute the eyes of *Katherine*. 368

Bra. Sig. Of *Katherine !* Master *Planet* obserue the next :
Master *Iohn*, what makes you so melancholy?

Ellis. I doe not vse to answere questions.

Bra. Iu. What are you thinking on now? 372

Ellis. I doe not vse to thinke.

Bra. Sig. Hee lookes as demurely, as if hee were asking his father blessing.

Ellis. I doe not vse to aske my father blessing. 376

Bra. Iu. 'Hart, how chance he is out of his similies?

Pla. I haue followed Ordinaries this twelue-moneth, onely to find a foole that had lands, or a fellow that would talke treason, that I might beg him. *Iohn*, be my Ward, *Iohn*, faith, I'le giue thee two coates a yeere and be my foole.

Bra. Sig. Hee shall bee your foole, and you shall bee his Coxcombe. Ha, ha! I haue a simple wit, ha, ha!

Pla. I shall crow o're him then. 384

Enter Winifride.

Wini. Is there not one Master *Iohn Ellis* here?

Page. There sits the thing so call'd,

Winifride and Ellis talke.

Br. Sig. Now to the last course: *Monsieur Iohn fo de King*, I will helpe you to a wench *Mounsieur*. 388

Moun. No point, a burne childe feere de fire.

Ellis. As a hungrie dog waiteth for a mutton bone, or as a tatter'd foot-boy for a cast sute, euen so will I attend on my Mistris.

Enter Winifride.

Moun. O my *Vinifride!* pree you awe, by gor, me ang de for her.

Bra. Sig. Nay, stay, stay, I will helpe you to a delicate plumplipt-wench. 394

Moun. Toh, phi, phi, your proffer ware stinke. Stay *Vinifride*, or by gor die, me die, me die by gor, me ang so desirous, adiew goot sir.

Bra. Sig. Oh, stay *Mounsieur*, how doe you pronounce *Demurra?* Ha, ha! I'le plague him. 399

Moun. Grand Sot, my vench is gone, and me brule, and me brule, like one mad bule. Me goe into de vater to coole my reine, ang my back made de vater hize againe: dus so brule. Me burst vor a vench, and yet, grand poc on you all, pree you adiew. 403

Ellis. As the Iigge is cal'd for when the Play is done, euen so let *Mounsieur* goe.

Moun. He, me teach you much French vor dis. I goe to *Hygate*, adiew grand Sots. *Exit Mounsieur.*

Ellis. As sore eies cannot indure the Sunne, nor scab'd hands abide salt water, so must I leaue all, and see my Mistris: And as faire Ladies doe vse foule foiles, euen so doe I bid you farewell.

Exit Ellis.

Bra. Sig. Why, this is sport Imperiall, by my Gentrie! I would spend fortie Crownes, for such another feast of fooles. Ha, ha! 413

Bra. Iu. I wonder who would be the foole then?

Bra. Sig. Why, 'tis the recreation of my intellect. I think I speake as significant, ha, ha! These are my zanyes: I fill their paunches, they feed my pleasures: I vse them as my fooles, faith, ha, ha! 418

Pla. 'Tis a generous honour[1].

Bra. Sig. Troth, I thinke you haue a good wit, ha! Pray you sup with me. I loue good wits, because mine owne is not vnfortunate: Pray you sup with me. 422

Pla. I'le giue God thankes, sir, that hath sent a foole to feed me.

[1] Perhaps should be humour.—G.

Bra. Sig. Come along then. Ye shall haue a Capon, a Tansie, and some kick-showes of my wits, ha, ha! some toies of my spirit.

Exit Bra. Sig. and Bra. Iunior.

Pla. I will eate his meate, and spend's monie, that's all the spight I can doe him: but if I can get a Pattent for concealed Sots, that Daw shall troupe among my Ideots. *Exit.*

Actvs Secvndvs.

Enter M. Puffe with his Page.

Puff. BOy, what's a clocke?
Page. Past three, and a faire morning.

Puff. Burnes not that light within the sacred shrine? I meane the chamber of bright *Katherine*. 4

Page. I. Should appeare by these presence, that it doth.

Puff. I wonder that the light is vp so soone.

Page. O, mistris Snuffe was wearie with sleeping in the socket, and therefore hath newly put on her stammell petticoate, and taken her pewter state, to giue light to things are in darknesse. 9

Puff. I see that women of grauitie and sweetnesse are soone vp.

Page. And I know that women of leuitie and lightnesse are soone downe. 12

Puff. Boy cleere thy throte, and mount thy sweetest notes
Vpon the bosome of this sleeke-cheekt aire:
That it may gently breathe them in the eare
Of my adored Mistris: Come begin. 16

The Song.

DElicious *beautie that doth lye*
Wrapt in a skin of Iuorie,
Lye still, lye still vpon thy backe :
And, Fancie, let no sweet dreames lacke 20
To tickle her, to tickle her with pleasing thoughts.
But if thy eyes are open full,
Then daine to view an honest gull,
That stands, that stands, expecting still, 24
When that thy casement open will,
And blesse his eyes, and blesse his eyes, with one kind glance.

The Casement opens, and Katherine appeares.

Puff. All happinesse and vnconceiu'd delight
Waite on the loue of sweet fac'de *Katherine!* 28

Kathe. Good youth, Amen : I doe returne your wish
With ample interest of beatitude.

Puff. I doe protest, with ceremonious (puffe) lips,
The purest bloud of my affection 32
Is euen fatally predestinate
To consecrate it selfe vnto your (puffe) loue.

Kath. Vnto my loue? Oh, sir, you bind me to you :
Faire Gentleman, I haue a thankefull heart, 36
Tho not a glorious speech to sweet my thankes.

Puff. Reward my loue, then, with your kinder loue.

Kath. With my loue, sir? I relish not your speech.

Puff. I, with your loue, in pleasing marriage. 40

Kath. Alas, sir, cannot be : my Loues a man,
Who hardly can requite the deare protests

Of kind affection, which you seeme to vow
Vnto his fortunes. Kind youth, you did wish 44
All happinesse to wait vpon my loue:
Well he shall know it when we next doe meet,
And thanke you kindly: now good morrow, sweet.
  Puff. You take my, my, my meaning (puffe.) 48
  Pag. Nay, if he be puffing once, the fire of his wit is out.
  Puff. Why, shee is gone. 'Hart, did I rise for this?
  Page. She cannot indure puffing. O, you puft her away!
  Puff. Let's slinke along vnseene: 'tis yet scarce day. 52
                                                      Exeunt.

  *Enter Mamon with Flawne, bearing a light
                before Mamon.*

Flawn. Now, me thinkes I hold the candle to the Deuil.
Mam. Put out the light, the day begins to breake.
Flawn. Would the day and thy necke were broke together.
Mam. Oh, how the gowt and loue doe tire me! 56
Flawn. Why, sir, loue is nothing but the verie gowt.
Mam. As how, *Flawne?* as how?
Flawn Thus, sir: gowt and loue, both come with idlenesse; both incurable; both humorous; onely this difference: the gowt causeth a great tumour in a mans legs, and loue a great swelling in a womans belly. 62

Mam. VVhy, then O Loue, O Gowt, O gowtie Loue! how thou tormentst old *Mamon.* Good morrow to the sweet-lipt *Katherine.* Eternall spring vnto thy beauties loue!

  Kath. Alas, good aged sir, what make you vp? 66
In faith, I pittie you, good soule to bed.
Troth, soone youle crie, Oh God, my head, my head.

Mam. No, *Katherine*, the wrinkling print of Time
Err'd when it seal'd my forehead vp with age : 70
I haue as warme an arme to entertaine
And hugge thy presence in a nuptiall bed
As those that haue a cheeke more liuely red :
And tho my voice be rude, yet *Flawne* can sing 74
Peans of beautie, and of *Katherine*.
List to the Musicke that corrupts the gods,
Subverts euen destinie, and thus it shogs.

The Song.

Hunck, chunck, chunck, chunck, his bags doe ring, 78
A merrie note with chuncks to sing :
Those that are farre more yong and wittie
Are wide from singing such a Dittie
As Chunck, chunck chunck.
There's Chunck, that makes the Lawyer prate, 82
There's Chunck, that makes a foole of Fate :
There's Chunck, that if you will be his,
Shall make you liue in all hearts blisse.
With Chunck, chunck, chunck.

Kat. 'Tis wel sung, good old man. Hence with your gold. 86
Leaue the greene fields, 'tis dewie, youle take cold.

Mam. The casements shut. Well, here Ile lurke and stay,
To see who beares the glorie of the day.
Hence, hence, to *London*, *Flawne*, let me alone. 90

Flawn I can hardly leaue him alone, for the Deuill and double
Duckats still associate him : but I am gone. *Exit.*

Enter Pasquill.

Pas. The glooming morne with shining armes hath chaste
The siluer Ensigne of the grimme-cheekt night, 94
And forc'd the sacred troupes of sparkling stars
Into their priuate Tents; yet calme-husht sleepe
Strikes dumbe the snoring world: yet frolicke youth,
That's lately matcht vnto a wel shapte Lasse, 98
Clips his sweet Mistris with a pleasing arme;
Whil'st the great power of Imperious Loue
Summons my dutie to salute the shine
Of my Loues beauties.   Vnequald *Katherine!* 102
I bring no Musicke, to prepare thy thoughts
To entertaine an amorous discourse:
More Musick's in thy name, and sweet dispose,
Then in *Apollos* Lyre, or *Orpheus* Close. 106
I'le chaunt thy name, and so inchaunt each eare
That *Katherina's* happie name shall heare.
My *Katherine*, my life, my *Katherine!*
  Kath. My *Ned*, my *Pasquil!* sweet, I come, I come, 110
Euen with like swiftnesse, tho not with like heart:
As the fierce Fawlcon stoupes to rising fowle,
I hurrie to thee: doe not goe away,
The place is priuate, and 'tis yet scarce day. 114
  Pas. Oh, these kind words imparadize my thoughts.
  Ma. Ha, ha! young *Pasquil*, haue I found you out?
Ist you must bore my nose? I'le bore your heart:
Why, this same boy's as bare as naked truth. 118
A low-eb'd gallant, yet sheele match with him:

Ile match him. If his skinne be ponyard proofe,
He may scape the force of gold and murder. If not,
As you returne, sir, I will pepper you.   *Exit.*

    Enter Katherine to Pasquill.

And art thou come, deere heart, first fee be this,
This kind imbrace, and next this modest kisse.
 Pas. This is no kisse, but an *Ambrosian* bowle,
The *Nectar* dew of thy delicious sowle :
Let me sucke one kisse more, and with a nimble lip,
Nibble vpon those Rosie bankes, more soft and cleere
Then is the jewell'd tip of *Venus* eare.
Oh, how a kisse inflames a louers thought !
With such a fewell let me burne and dye,
And like to *Hercules* so mount the skie.
 Kath. Come, you grow wanton. Oh, you bite my lip !
 Pas. In faith you jest, I did but softly sip
The Roseall juice of your reuiuing breath :
Let clumsie judgements, chilblain'd gowtie wits
Bung vp their chiefe content within the hoopes
Of a stuft drie-Fatt : and repose their hopes
Of happinesse, and hearts tranquillitie
Vpon increase of durt : but let me liue
Clipt in the cincture of a faithfull arme,
Luld in contented joy, being made diuine
With the most precious loue of *Katherine.*
 Kath. Let the vnsanctified spirit of ambition
Entice the choice of muddie-minded dames
To yoke themselues to swine, and, for vaine hope

Of gay rich trappings, be still spurd and prickt
With pining discontent for nuptiall sweets ; 148
But let me liue lou'd in my husbands eyes,
Whose thoughts with mine, may sweetly simpathize.
    Pas. The heauens shall melt, the sun shall cease to shine,
Before I leaue the loue of *Katherine*. 152
    Kath. Nay, when heauens melted, & the sun strook dead,
Euen then my loue shall not be vanquished.
    Pasq. When I turne fickle, vertue shall be vice.
    Kath. When I proue false, Hell shall be Paradise. 156
    Pasq. My life shall be maintain'd by thy kinde breath.
    Kath. Thy loue shall be my life, thy hate my death.
    Pasq. Oh, when I die, let me imbrace thy waste!
    Kath. In death let me be counted thine and chaste! 160
    Pasq. Heauens graunt, being dead, my soule may liue nie thee.
    Kath. One kisse shall giue thee mine eternally.
    Pasq. In faire exchange vouchsafe my heart to take.
    Kath. With all my mind. Weare this, *Ned*, for my sake. 164
But now no more, bright day malings our loue.
Farewell, yet stay! But 'tis no matter too.
My father knowes, I thinke, what must ensue.
Adieu! Yet harke! Nay, faith, adieu, adieu! 168
    Pasq. Peace to thy passions, till next enterview! *Exeunt.*

Enter Mamon, and Monsieur Iohn for the King.

    Mam. Now *Monsieur*, be but confident and hold. [? bold]
There is the price of bloud. This way he comes.
Strike home, bold arme, and thou shalt want no crownes. 172

Moun. Feare you noting, when he is die me bring you word.

Exit Mamon.

Hee! by gor braue crowne, braue monney!
Mee haue here a patent to take vp, one, two, treescore
Vench: fine crowne, fine vench, vnreasonably fine,   176
Dis monney is my baude. Mee send a French crowne
To fetch a fine vench, de French crowne fetch de
Fine vench, de fine vench take de French crowne,
And giue me de French poc. He! excellent. You see   180
Mee kill a man, you see mee hang like de *Burgullian*.
Hee no poine: Hee by Gor, mee haue much vitt,
Ang me much bald, and me ang much bald wit.
Here come de Gentleman metre *Pasquil*.   184

Enter Pasquil.

Pasquil. Is't possible, that sisters should so thwart
In natiue humours? One's as kind and faire,
As constant, vertuous, and as debonaire,
As is the heart of goodnesse: The other, proud,   188
Inconstant, fantasticke, and as vaine in loues
As trauellers in lyes: Blest *Katherine*,
Camelia's not thy sister, if shee bee,
Shee's bastard to the sweets that shine in thee.   192

Moun. Boniour Metre *Pasquil, sance Iest,* mee am hired to kill
you. *Mounsieur Mamon, Mestier:* Iounck, iounck, giue mee money
to stab you; but mee know there is a God that hate bloud, derfore,
me no kill. Me know dere is a vench that loue Crowne, derefore
me keepe de money.   197

Pasq. Vnhallowed villaine, that with gold and bloud,

Thinkes that almightie loue can be withstood!
Hold, *Mounsieur!* There are more Crownes, onely doe this: returne to *Mamon*, tell him the deede is done, and bring him hither, that hee may vainely triumph in my bloud. I haue some painting, which I found by chaunce in loose *Camelias* chamber. With that I'le staine my brest. Goe, and returne with speed. 204

   Moun. He! by gor, I smell a rat. Me flie, me flie, by gor.

                                                     Exit Mounsieur.

   Pasq. Lewd miscreant! that through the throat of hell,
Wouldst mount to heauen, and enioy loue,
Invaluably precious: No, rancke churle, 208
Thou wast not made to slauer her faire lips
With thy dead rewmy chops, nor clip her waste
With thy shrunke bloudlesse arme. I heare him come.
Now, *Pasquil*, faigne. ô thou eternall light, 212
Mourne, that thy creatures should in bloud delight!

                    He lies downe, and faines himselfe dead.

            Enter Mamon, and Mounsieur.

   Mam. Now, smug-fac'd boy, now nibble on her lips.
Now sippe the dew of her delicious breath.
Stinke, rot, damne, bake in thy cluttered bloud: 216
Snakes, Toades, and Earwigs, make thy skull their nest:
Ingendring dew-wormes, cling ore-thwart thy brest!

   Moun. Hush, hush, leaue praying for dead. 'Tis no good *Caluianisme, Puritanisme.* Dissemble, here are company.   *Exit Moun.*

            Enter Brab. Sig. and Planet.

   Brab. Sig. Good morrow, sir. Who lies there murdred? 221

Mam. Oh, Gentlemen! The kindest, vertuous youth
That e're adorned *London.* Damned theeues,
To spoile such hopes. The last words that he spake   224
Sticks still within the hollow of mine eare.
Katherine, quoth he, hold *M. Mamon* deare.
I know not what he meant, but so he said.
If that you passe to *Hygate*, tell the Knight   228
Pasquil is sunke into eternall night.

Plan. Faith, 'twas a good youth. Come *Brabant*, come away.
                    Exeunt Brabant and Planet.

Mam. Dead *Kate*, dead *Kate*, dead is the boy,
That kept rich *Mamon* from his ioy!   232
            Mamon sings, Lantara, &c. Pasquil riseth, and
                        striketh him.

Mam. Oh, the Deuill! The ghost of *Pasquil!* I am dead! If you haue any curtesie in you, beleeue it. I beleeu'd you when you faign'd, beleeue me now, for I am almost dead, numb'd vp with feare. Giue faith, sweet gentle youth!   236

Pasq. Old wretch, amend thy thoughts, purge, purge, repent! I'le hide thy vlcer, be but penitent.   *Exit.*

Mam. Ha, I thinke 'twas but his ghost that swept along.   239

            Enter Monsieur singing.

Grand sot Mamon, *Pho, phy, phy, phy! a foutra pour vos chunck chunck!* Iohn fo de King, *teach you a ding*, Iohn fo de King *grand sot, sot, sot!*   *Exit Monsieur.*

Mam. Death, plague, and hel, how is curst *Mamon* vext!   243
Scourg'd with the whip of sharpe derision :
I'le home, and starue. This crosse, this peeuish hap,

Strikes dead my spirits like a thunder-clap. *Exit Mamon.*

Enter Brabant Iunior, and Planet.

Brab. Gods precious! I forgot to bring my Page, 247
To breathe some Dittie in my Mistris eare.

Plan. Wouldst haue a Ballet to salute her with?

Brab. No, but a song. How wouldst thou court thy Mistris?

Plan. Why, with the World, the Flesh, and the Deuill. 251

Brab. Right dog! Well thoult sweare, that I am blest
Beyond infinitie of happinesse,
When thou beholdest admired *Camelia*. 254

Plan. And God would blesse mee with three such Mistresses,
I would giue two of them to the Deuill, that hee would take the
third.

Brab. Oh, when shee clips, and clings about my necke,
And sucks my soule forth with a melting kisse— 258

Plan. Doth shee vse thee so kindly then, ha?

Brab. O, I; and calls me "deare, deare *Brabant*," and (ô Iesu
  God!)
I cannot expresse her sweets of entertaine.
Shee'le so insinuate with chaste amorous speech, 262
And play the wanton with such prettie grace,
And vowes loue to me: Oh, I'le make thee mad
To see how gracious *Brabant's* in her eye.
Here is her window; marke but when I call, 266
How swift shee comes, and with what kind salutes
Shee welcomes me. What, ho, *Camelia*!
Faith youle be tane vp: what in bed so late?

Winifride lookes from aboue.

Plan. And you take her vp, *Brabāt*, sheele take you down. 270

Brab. Hart! they heare not: My *Camelia*, wake!

Wini. What harsh, vnciuill tongue keeps such a coyle?

Brab. Winifride, 'tis I. Tell my sweet *Duck* I am here.
Now marke, *Ned Planet,* now obserue her well. 274

Wini. Shee wonders at your rudenesse, that intrudes
Vpon the quiet of her mornings rest;
And shee's amaz'd, that with such impudence
You dare presume to intimate some loue to her; 278
As if shee knew you more then for a youth,
A yonger brother, and a stipendarie.

Enter Iohn Ellis.

Plan. Now marke, *Ned Planet,* now obserue her kindnes.
Good morrow, *M. Iohn.* 282

Ellis. As the Countrey maid crieth to her Cow to milke her; or as the Trauailer knocketh with his Hostesse for a reckning; euen so doe I call to thee, ô Mistris.

Camelia, from her window.

Came. Sweet *Iohn,* my loue, here's thy *Camelia:* 286
Hold, weare this fauour, with this kisse vpon't.

Brab. Flesh and bloud cannot beare such disgrace!

Brabant beates Ellis.

Ellis. Helpe, helpe, helpe, helpe! Hee boxes mee, that hee doth.
Helpe, helpe! 290

Enter Sir Edward, Katherine, Drum, and Twedle.

Sir Ed. What outrage haue we here so early vp?
Sir, you doe wrong the quiet of my house.

Enter Camelia.

Ifaith you doe, and 'tis but rudely done,
Goe too, 'tis not. Is this a place to brawle? 294
  Plan. And please thee, knight, Ile tell thee faith & troth.
  Cam. What, did he strike thee, sweet?
  Ellis. I, in good deed, law, and a my conscience, I thinke he hath made my nose bleede. 298
  Cam. And would not you draw your weapon out, and to it lustily, as long as you could stand?
  Ellis. I doe not vse to draw.
  Cam. Did he giue thee a boxe on the eare, and wouldst thou take it? 303
  Ellis. And he be such a foole to giue it me, why should not I be so wise as to take it?
  Cam. Pure honestie! Kinde Ducke! Kisse me, sweet *Iohn*. 306
  Brab. Iu. Hart! Sir *Edward*, will you suffer this?
Now on my life, shee is enamour'd on the fooles bable.
  Sir Ed. Goe too, sir boy, forbeare, you wrong my loue;
And you forget your selfe to vse such iests, 310
Such nastie ribauldrie, vpon my daughter:
I tell you *M. Brabant*, shee doth loue[1]
Any that meriteth the name of man!
  Bra. Iu. Why, he's no man, but a very———— 314
  Sir Ed. Wel, wel, no more; my house, my selfe, my loue,
Opens their hearts with liberall imbrace,
To entertaine your presence: I, or any mans,
So they'le be ciuill, modest, not prophane; 318

---

[1] doth shee—*orig.*

Not like to those that make it their chiefe grace
To be quite graceles.

Plan. Well said, honest Knight.
We haue had bloud enough to day alreadie: 322
Ned Pasquil's slaine by bloudie murdering Rogues.

Sir Ed. Speake softly! God forbid, my daughter heares:
Tell me the circumstance, I pray you, Sir.

Kath. Eternall death vnto my happinesse! 326
My *Pasquil* slaine? Oh God, oh God, oh God!

Exit Katherine, tearing her haire.

Plan. I, and I thinke the Vsurer made a Tent
Euen of his nose, it was so red and neere.

Sir Ed. God for his mercy, what mischance is here! 330
A good youth, a vertuous modest youth,
Ifaith, he was. And I can tell you, sir,
My daughter *Katherine*—Where is shee now?
Whither's shee gone? *Drum,* call her hither, strait. 334

Drum. Your *Drum* will sound a call, sir, presently.

Exit Drum.

Sir Ed. And as I told you, sir, my daughter *Katherine*
Affected him right dearly: by my peace of soule,
If he had liu'd, I could haue heartily wisht 338
He had beene my sonne-in-law, Ifaith I could:
But see the will of God. How now, *Drum,*
Where's my daughter?

Drum. Sir, shee is either inuisible, or deafe, for I can neither see
her, nor shee heare me. 343

Sir Ed. Body of mee, my heart misgiues me now!
Looke, call, search, run all about.

ACT II.]   *OF PASQVIL AND KATHERINE.*   165

My daughter gone? Goe all and search her out.   346
Here's *Pasquil,* ha? Is this the man that's dead?

Enter Pasquil.

Pasq. Let me intreat this fauour, doe not search
Or be inquisitiue why I fain'de:
Repute me worthy your better censure: and thus thinke   350
My cause was vrgent; the rest lye buried.
  S. Ed. Well, I would you had not fainde.
  Pasq. Why, would you haue had me dead indeede?
  S. Ed. Oh no, but I haue lost my child, I feare,   354
By your strange fayning. Shee no sooner heard
The tydings of your death, but gone shee was,
And God knowes whither. Ha! what newes now?

Enter Drum.

Drum. 'Tis easier to finde wit in Ballating, honestie in   358
Brokers, Virginitie in *Shordich,* then to heare of my Mistris.
  S. Ed. Broch me a fresh butt of *Canary* sacke,
Let's sing, drinke, sleepe, for that's the best reliefe
To drowne all care, and ouer-whelme all griefe.   362
Powre wine, sound musicke, let our blouds not freeze.
Drinke Dutch, like gallants, let's drinke vpsey freeze.
  Exeunt S. Edward, Planet, Brabant, Drum and Twedle.
  Came. Seruant, youle goe in too, and stay dinner?
  Ellis. I, in truth, for as the itch is augmented   366
By scratching, so is my loue by seeing my Mistris.
            Exeunt Camelia and Ellis.
  Pasq. How's this, how's this, My *Katherine* gone hence?

Senses awake! And thou amazed soule
Vnwinde thy selfe from out the Labyrinth   370
Of gaping wonder, and astonishment.
My *Katherine* departed? how? which way?
Foole, foole, stand not debating, but pursue:
Haste to her comfort, for from thee doth spring   374
(Wretch that thou art) her cause of sorrowing!   *Exit.*

ACTVS TERTIVS.

Enter a Page, solus.

Page. HA, ha, ha! tipsie, tipsie, tipsie! all turn'd whirlegig! *Iohn fo de King, Drum,* and *Timothy Twedle,* are rare fine, ha! for the heauens, Ifaith: *Drums* Lyon drunke, and hee dings the pots about, cracks the glasses, swaggers with his owne shaddow. Honest *Tymothy,* is *Mawdelin* drunke, and he weepes for kindnesse, and kisses the hilts of *Iacke Drums* dagger. *Mounsieur's* Goat drunke, and he shrugs, and skrubs, and hee's it for a wench. Here they come reeling. I must packe, or wee shall swagger; for they hauing a cracke in their heads, and I a fault in my hands. Wee shall ne're agree.   10
                                                         Exit.

Enter Drum, Mounsieur, and Twedle.

Drum. A seruing-man, quoth you? Hart! and if I serue any that's flesh and bloud, would I might ne're taste my liquor more: Stand bare whilst he makes water, out vpon't! I'le to *Ireland,* and there I'le Tan, ran, ty, ry, dan; Sa, sa, sa, sa: Nay, 'tis the onely life.   15

Twed. Nay, good Thewte[1] hart: good kind *Iacke*, stay. If you would loue me as I loue you, wee would liue and die together: And please God, would I were dead, and[2] you are gone. And here's *M. Iohn fo de King*, a very honest man too. 19

Drum. I, I, hee's a very good honest man: for there's not a haire betwixt him and heauen.

Twed. Heele liue with vs now, and teach vs French. 22

Moun. I, by my trott, ang you helpe me to a vench now, me teach you French, fiue towsand, towsand yeere. ô, your secke is hote, and make me brule, and brule, and burne, for a (*hee*) by gor your secke is hote. 26

Enter Winifride.

Drum. Welcome, *Basilisco*, thou wilt carrie leuell, and knock ones braines out with thy pricking wit. Kisse mee, sweet wench, kisse me. 29

Moun. Hee! my *Vinifride*, by gor you are come, in te verie nick to pleasure mee. Pree you kisse mee, clip mee, loue me, or by gor me ang die, certaine.

Drum. Out, you French dogge! touch my Loue, and I'le——— 34

Moun. Touch her! by gor me touch her, and touch her, and touch her!

Drum. I'le touch you, I'le flash you, I'le vench yee!

Wini. Put vp, put vp, for the passion of God, put vp! or if youle needs too it, sheathe both your weapons in me first!

Drum. Hart! touch my loue, touch my *Winifride!* 40

Winif. Harke you, *Iack*. Come to my chamber an houre hence, and you shall haue what you will aske, and I can graunt.

[1] Sweet-heart (?)—G. [2] And=an, if.—G.

Drum. Why, then my choller's downe. *Iohn fo de King,*   43
Foutra for you.   *Exit Drum.*

Moun. Foutra for mee! Futtra, futtra, futtra, fiue towsand futtra's for you!   46

Twed. Stay, friend *Iacke,* I'le reele along with you, if youle not swagger.   *Exit Twedle.*

Winif. Sweet, sweet *Monsieur!* Hang yon slaues, I loue you infinitely.   50

Moun. By gor, mee teach you French foure towsand yeere dan!

Winif. Well, *Mounsieur,* I'le giue you pleasure.

Moun. But will you presently? quickly, for by gor me am a hot shot.   54

Winif. I, so they say, I heard you were vnder the *Torred zone* last day.

Moun. Pish! 'tis no matter, me am like a Tabacco pipe, de more me am burne, de cleaner me am.   58

Winif. Well then, two houres hence come to my chamber, and *Timothy Twedle* shall giue you me in a sacke.

Moun. In a sacke? Ha, very well.   61

Winif. And you shall carrie mee to my Masters house at *Holloway,* for in the house wee cannot be priuate without suspect. Till then, farewell.   *Exit Winifride.*

Moun. By my trot, vnreasonably good! I carrie de vench on my backe, and de vench carrie mee on her (hee!) Fine backe, fine vench, fine *Mounsieur,* fine, fine, fine Knight, all fine, vnreasonably fine. Mee sing vor ioy! By gor mee sing la, liro, liro, la, lilo!   *Exit.*

Enter Brabant Signior, Brabant Iunior, and Planet.

Bra. Sig. Gentlemen, as e're you lou'd wench, obserue *M. Puffe*, and me. 70

Bra. Iun. What shall we obserue you for ?

Bra. Sig. Oh, for our complement.

Planet. Complement, what's that ?

Bra. Sig. Complement, is as much as (what call you it) 'tis deriued of the Greeke word—a pox on't. 75

Plan. Complement, is as much as—what call you it; 'tis deriued of the Greeke word—a pox on't.

Enter Puffe.

Bra. Sig. You shall see *M. Puffe* and mee tosse it. Ifaith, marke with what grace I encounter him. 79

Plan. Hart! Thy brother's like the instrument the Merchants sent ouer to the great *Turke*: You need not play vpon him, hee'le make musicke of himselfe, and hee bee once set going. 82

Bra. Sig. M. Puffe, I long to doe faire seruice to your loue.

Puffe. Most accomplisht wit, exquisitely accoutred (*Puffe*) Iudgement. I could wish my abilitie worthy your seruice, and my seruice worthy your abilitie. 86

Plan. By the Lord, fustian, now I vnderstand it: complement is as much as fustian.

Bra. Sig. I protest, your abilities are infinite, your perfections matchlesse, your matchlesse perfection infinite in abilitie, and your infinite abilitie matchlesse in perfection. 91

Plan. Good againe! Reioyce *Brabant*, thy brother will not liue long, he talkes idlely alreadie.

Puffe. Delicious spirit, disparage not your courtesie. Stand not bare to him that was borne to honor you. 95

Bra. Sig. Let vs presse our haires then, with an vniforme consent.

Puffe. The pressure of my haires, or the puncture of my heart, stands at the seruice of your sollide perfections: My life is bound to your loue, your loue being my life: Tho my life bee not worthy your loue, your perfection is the center to which all the paralells of my affection are drawne: Your loue my life, your perfection my affection, being—————— 103

Plan. Your Asse, my Foole!

Puffe. Being chain'd by the mightie coplet of ineuitable destiny. Who seeth the Sunne, but hee must adore it? Who seeth beautie, but hee must honour it? Who vieweth gold, but he must couet it? Then (O then!) who can behold your sun-like beauteous golden beauties, but he must more then adore, much more then honour, and most infinitely loue to be out—out—out— 110

Bra. Iu. Out, he is indeed.

Plan. He's at a stand, like a resty Iade, or a Fidler, when he hath crackt his Minikin.

Puffe. Outragiously addicted to the worthy pursuit of such matchlesse worth. 115

Bra. Sig. Sir, I can rest but truely thankefull for your more then good conceit of my no lesse then little worth. And now, sir, for the consequent houres of the day, how stands your intention for imployment? 119

Puffe. I ha' tane my leaue of *Sir Edward;* bid adieu to loue; my Mistris is gone; my humour is spent; my ioyes are at an end, and therefore, Gentlemen, I leaue loue, and fall to the (*puffe*) Law. I

ACT III.]   *OF PASQVIL AND KATHERINE.*   171

will interre my selfe in *Ploydens* coffin, and take an eternall *Conge* of the world. And so, sweet gallants, farewell.   *Exit.*

Bra. Sig. Nay, I'le follow you to your graue. Gentlemen, youle not accompanie the coarse?   *Exit.*

Plan. No, no. Looke, *Ned Brabant*, yon's a pleasing obiect for thy eyes.   128

Enter Camelia, Ellis, and Winifride.

Bra. Iu. My Mistris is turn'd *Bucephalus:* no body must ride her but *Alexander:* no bodie kisse her, but *Iohn Ellis*. Now stand and list, good *Planet*.

Cam. Come sweetest loue, let's giue time pleasing wing,   132
What shall we make, some purposes, or sing?

Ellis. I will sing, so you will beare my burthen.

Cam. Come, lay thy head then in my Virgin lap,
And with a soft sleeke hand I'le clap thy cheeke,   136
And wring thy fingers with an ardent gripe:
I'le breathe amours, and euen intrance thy spirit,
And sweetly in the shade lie dallying.

The Song.

Now dally, sport, and play, this merry month of May,   140
This is the merry, merry month, Sweet time for dallying:
The Birds sit chirping, chirping; the Doues sit billing, billing,
Philip is treading is treading, is treading, is treading, is treading.
    All are to pleasures willing.   144
You that are faire and wittie, Obserue this easie Dittie,
And leaue not Natures, Natures blisse; Doe not refuse to kisse.
The Birds sit chirping, chirping; the Doues sit billing, billing,
Philip is treading, is treading, &c.   148

Bra. Iun. Death! I can holder: Life of loue,

Amazing beautie! Let not me seeme rude,
Tho thus I seeme to square with modestie—
   Ellis. Pray you let me goe, for hee'le begin to square: 152
And euen as some doe weare Muffes for warmth, some for wantonnesse, some for pride, some for neither, but to hide gowtie fingers, so will I get your Fathers consent, and marrie you. Fare you well.
Exit.

   Cam. Sir, it were good you got a benefice,   156
Some Evenuch'd Vicaridge, or some Fellowship,
To prop vp your weake yonger brothership.
Match with your equalls, dare not to aspire
My seate of loue: I wisse, Sir, I looke higher.   160
   Bra. Iun. Astonishment of Nature, be not proud
Of *Fortunes* bounties: *Brabant* is a man,
Tho not so clog'd with durt as others are:
I doe confesse my yonger brothership;   164
Yet therein lay no such disparagement
As your high scorne imputes vnto my worth.
Coach-Iades, and Dogs, are coupled still together
Only for outward likenesse, growth and strength,   168
But the bright modells of eternitie
Are ioyn'd together for affection,
Which in the soule is form'd. Oh, let this moue.—
Loue should make marriage, and not marriage Loue.   172
   Pla. Woo her no more, *Brabant:* thou'lt make her proud.
You *Dutch* Ancient, why should you looke higher?
His birth's as good as yours; and so's his face—
Put off your Iengle-Iangles, and be not as faire, (and¹)   176

    ¹ 'And not' in original.—G.

He shall renounce it, 'for this Audience—
Put off your clothes, and you are like a *Banbery* cheese,
Nothing but paring: Why should you be proud,
And looke on none but Weather-cocks, forsooth?   180
O, you shall haue a thousand pound a yeere!
B'ar Ladie, that's a bumming sound.   But, harke!
Wilt therefore be a slaue, vnto a slaue,
One that's a bound Rogue vnto Ignorance?   184
Well, thou'lt serue to make him gellide broaths,
And scratch his head, and may be, now and then
Heele slauer thee a kisse.   Plague on such marriages!

  Cam. Rude, vnciuill Clowne!   188

  Pla. Tut, raile not at me! turn your eie vpon the leprosie of your owne iudgement. Lothe it, hate it, scorne it, and loue this yong Gentleman; who is a Foole in nothing, but in louing thee: mad in nothing, but affecting thee: and curst in eternitie, if he marry thee.   193

  Cam. Sir, you ha' spoke exceeding pleasingly;
For which I loue you, as I loue a dull dead eye.
Brabant, I doe coniure thee, court not me.   196
Doe not presume to loue or fancie me.

  Bra. Iu. How, not presume to loue or fancie you?
Hart! I will loue you, by this light I will,
Whether you will or no, I'le loue you still.   200
Spight of your teeth I will your loue pursue,
I will, by heauen! and so, sweet soule adieu.   *Exit Bra. Iun.*

  Cam. Farewell, & neuer view my face againe.   *Exit Cam.*

  Plan. Harke you, faire *Winifride*, sweet gentle maid.   204
I haue but fained with you all this while,

I dote vpon the sweet *Camelia*;
And if your fauour will but second me,
I vow, when I shall wed *Camelia*, 208
To indow you with a hundred pound a yeere;
And what I haue shall stand at your command.

   Win. Sir, I will vndertake to forward your faire loue,
So you'le remember what you here doe vow. 212

   Plan. If I forget it, heauen forget me:
Doe you but praise me. Let not her once know
I loue, or doe affect her, for the world.

   Win. Well, feare no rubs. Farewell, faire bounteous sir.

Exit Winifride.

   Plan. It workes, it workes, magnificent delight! 217
Laughter, triumph! for e're the Sunne goe downe,
Thy forehead shall be wreath'd with pleasures crowne.

Exit Planet.

Enter Pasquil at one doore, and his Page at the other.

   Pas. Now my kind Page, canst thou not heare, nor see, 220
Which way my *Katherine* hath bent her steps?

   Page. Sir, I can.

   Pas. What, canst thou, my sweet Page?
What, canst thou boy? 224
Oh how my soule doth burne in longing hope,
And hangs vpon thy lips for pleasing newes!

   Page. Sir, I can tell ye.

   Pas. What? O! how my heart doth quake and throb with
feare. 229

   Page. Sir, I can tell you nothing of her, in good faith.

Pas. Oh, thou hast tortur'd me with lingring hope.
Goe, haste away. Flie from the pestilence 232
Of my contagious griefe; it will infect thee, boy,
Murder thy youth, and poison thy lifes ioy.
Runne, search out *Katherine*, in her eies dwell
Heauens of joy: but in *Pasquil* hell! 236
Oh thou omnipotent infinitie!
Cracke not the sinewes of my patience
With racking torment: Insist not thus to scourge
My tender youth with sharpe affliction: 240
If I doe loue that glorie of thy hand,
That rich *Idea* of perfection,
With any lustfull or prophane intent,
Crost be my loue, murdred be all my hopes: 244
But if with chaste and vertuous arme I clip
The rarest modell of thy workemanship,
Be then propitious, O eternall light,
And blesse my fortunes, maugre hellish spight! 248

Enter Katherine in a petticoate.

Kat. Blacke sorrow, nurse of plaints, of teares and grones,
Euaporate my spirit with a sigh,
That it may hurrie after his sweet breath,
Who made thee dote on life, now hunt for death! 252

Pas. What soule is that, that with her teare-full eies
Seemes to lament with me in miseries?

Kath. Here seemes to be the pressure of his truncke:
Deare earth confirme my doubt. Was this the place 256
Which the faire bodie of my *Pasquil* prest,

When he lay murdred? See, the drooping grasse
Hangs downe his mourning head, and seemes to say,
This was the fatall place, where *Pasquil* lay. 260
Oh, thou sweet print, stampt by the fairest limbes,
The richest Coffin of the purest soule
That euer prest the bosome of the earth,
First, drinke my teares, and next sucke vp my bloud. 264
Now thou immortall spirit of my Loue,
Thou precious soule of *Pasquil*, view this Knife
Which once thou gauest me, and prepare thy arme
To clip the spirit of thy constant Loue! 268
Deare *Ned*, I come, by death I will be thine,
Since life denies it to poore *Katherine*.
   She offers to stabbe her selfe.
 Pas. Hold! hold! thou miracle of constancie.
First, let heauen perish, and the craz'de world runne 272
Into first *Chaos* of confusion,
Before such cruell violence be done
To heir faire brest, whose fame, by vertue wonne,
Shall honour women whil'st there shines a sunne. 276
 Kath. Thrice sacred spirit, why do'st thou forsake
Elizeum pleasures, to withhold the arme
Of wretched *Katherine?* Oh let me die!
Retire, sweet Ghost: doe not pollute thy hand 280
With touch of mortals.
 Pas. Amazement of thy Sex, *Pasquil* doth liue,
And liues to loue thee in eternitie.
Be not agast, recouer spirit, (Sweet) 284
'Tis *Pasquil* speakes, 'tis *Pasquil* clips thy waste,

'Tis *Pasquil* prints a kisse on thy faire hand.

   Kath. What, doe I dreame? or haue I drawne the sluce
Of life vp? and thorow streames of bloud
Vnfelt, haue set my prisoned soule at large?
Am I in heauen? or in *Pasquils* Armes?
I am in heauen, for my *Neds* imbrace
Is *Katherines* long wish'd celestiall place.

   Pas. Diuinitie of sweetnesse, I protest,
If these inferior Orbs were rowled vp,
And the Imperiall heauen bar'd to my view,
'Twere not so gracious, nor so much desir'd,
As my deare *Katherine* is to *Pasquils* sight.

   Kath. Heauen of Content, *Paphos* of my delight!

   Pas. Mirrour of Constancie, life-bloud of loue!

   Kath. Center to whom all my affections moue!

   Pas. Renowne of Virgins, whose fame shall ne're fleet!

   Kath. Oh, I am maz'd with ioy, I pree-thee, sweet,
Vnfold to me, what sad mischance it was,
Forc'd thy deaths rumour, and such woes disperc'de.
Sad sorrow past, delights to be rehearsed.

   Pas. It will be tedious, but, in briefe, thinke thus :—
Old *Mamons* malice was the venomb'd fome
That poisoned all the sweets of our content.

   Kath. Alas, deare heart, that loue should be so crost.
Now good *Ned* fetch my gowne, 'tis at yon house;
I would be loth to turne to *Hygate* thus.

   Pas. I am oblig'd, with infinite respect, to doe you seruice.
Oh, power diuine, was euer such a loue as *Katherine*?

   Ent. Ma. Look, *Mamon*, search, *Mamon*, this way she went;

Put on thy spectacles, this way she went:
Blest, blest, blest, be thy natiuitie! 316
Yonder she sits. I'le either haue her now,
Or none shall e're enioy her with content.
    Kath. How loue's impatient! when will *Ned* returne?
    Ma. Tut, 'tis no matter when: look where thy *Mamon* is. 320
    Kath. Good Deuill, for Gods sake do not vex my sight:
Did'st not thou plot the death of my deare Loue?
    Ma. Yes, yes, and would complot ten thousand deaths;
Euen damne my soule, for beauteous *Katherine*. 324
My ship shall kemb the Oceans curled backe
To furnish thee with braue Abiliaments;
Rucks of rich Pearle, and sparkling Diamonds
Shall fringe thy garments with Imbroadrie: 328
Thy head shall blaze as bright with Orient stone,
As did the world being burnt by *Phaeton*.
    Kath. You make me death, for pitties sake forbeare:
Oh, when will *Pasquil* come? Good sir, depart. 332
When wilt returne? I pray you sir, goe hence,
And troth, I will not hate you: nay, I'le speake
Against my heart and say, I lothe you not.
You vex my patience, gentle sir, forbeare, 336
I begge it on my knee, and with a teare!
    Mam. Tut! will you loue me, and detest yon boy?
    Kath. Heauen detest me first, and lothe my soule.
    Mam. Is it your finall resolution? 340
    Kath. God knowes it is. So, good sir, rest content.
    Mam. I, I will rest; and thou shalt rest thus blur'd;
Thus poison'd; venom'de with this oile of Toades.

If *Mamon* cannot get thee, none shall joy 344
Which he could not enjoy. I feare no Law;
Gold in the firmest conscience makes a flaw.
Rot like to *Helen*, *Spittle* hence, adiew;
Let *Pasquil* boast in your next interuiew. 348

   Kath. Be pittifull, and kill me, gentle sir!
Heauen, my heart is crackt with miserie:
Where shall I hide me? which way shall I clense
The eating poison of this venom'de oile? 352
Poore wretch (alas) see where thy *Pasquil* comes.

   Pas. Here Loue, put on your gowne. How now? good God!
Heauen giue me patience: Who hath vsd thee thus?

   Kath. The Deuill in the shape of *Mamon*. Sweet, 356
Touch me not. *Pasquil*, I conjure thee now,
By all the power of affection,
By that strickt bond of loue that linkes our hearts,
Leaue and abandon me eternally. 360
I merit now no loue, yet prethee, sweet,
Vouchsafe to giue me leaue to loue thee still.
But I doe binde thee by thy sacred vow,
Of our once happie, and thrice blessed loue, 364
Follow not *Katherine*: Good *Ned*, doe not grieue:
In time iust heauen may our woes releeue.

                                  Exit Katherine.

   Pas. Furens. O *dira fata, sæua, miseranda, horrida,*
Quis hic Locus? quæ Regio? quæ Mundi plaga? 368
Vbi sum? Katherina, Katherina, Eheu Katherina.

Enter Mamon.

Mam. My spectacles will betraie me. Looke, *Mamon*, search *Mamon;* hereabouts they fell.

Pas. Welcome *Erra Pater,* you that make Prognostications for euer. Where's you Almanacke? 373

Puls his Indentures out of Mamons bosome.

Mam. Lord blesse my Obligations! Lord blesse my bonds! Lord blesse my Obligations! Alas, alas, alas!

Pas. Let me see, sir; now when will true valour be at the full? Oh, there's an opposition. 'Tis eclipsed: *Venus,* I *Venus* is mounted. Where's the Goat now? Kemb'd, fine kem'd. Oh, heere are Dogge daies. Out vpon't! Dogge daies, Dog daies, Dogge daies, out-vpon't! 380

He teares the papers.

Mam. Alas, my Obligations! my Bonds! my Obligations! my Bonds! Alas, alas, alas!

Pas. Katherina, Katherina, Eheu Katherina.

Exit Pasquil.

Mam. Obligations! Obligations! Alas, my Obligations! 384 I am vndone, vndone, vndone!

Enter Flawne.

Flawn. Sir, sir, sir!

Mam. What "sir" you for, you Dogge, you Hound, you Crust! What's best newes with you now? Out-alas my Obligations! my Bonds! I am vndone, vndone! 389

Flawn. Sir, the best newes is, your ship (the Hope-well) hath hapt ill, returning from *Barbarie.* 'Tis but sunke, or so: not a scrap of goods sau'de. 392

Mam. Villaines, Rogues, Iewes, Turkes, Infidels! My nose will rot off with griefe! O the Gowt, the Gowt, the Gowt! I shall runne mad, runne mad, runne mad! 395

Flawn. Amen, amen, amen! But there's other newes to comfort you withall, sir.

Mam. Let's heare them, good *Flawne*. My ship, my bonds, my bonds, my ship! I shall runne madde vnlesse thy good newes reclaime me. Let's heare thy newes. 400

Flawn. Your house with all the furniture is burnt; not a ragge left. The people stand warming their hands at the fire, and laugh at your miserie. 403

Mam. I defie heauen, earth and hell! renounce my nose! plague, pestilence, confusion, famine, sword and fire, devoure all! devoure me, devoure *Flawne*, devoure all! Bonds, house, and ship, ship, house, and bonds! Despaire, Damnation, Hell! I come, I come, so roome for *Mamon*, roome for Vsurie, roome for thirtie in the hundred! I come, I come, I come! 409

Exit Mamon.

Flawn. Why, me thinkes this is right now. I'le euen lay him vp in *Bedlame*: commit him to the mercie of the whip, the entertainment of bread and water, and the sting of a Vsurers Conscience for euer. *Exit Flawne.*

ACTVS QVARTVS.

Enter Drum and Winifride.

Drum. TRuely, mistris *Winifride*, as I would bee willing to be thankefull, and thankefull to find you willing to prostrate your faire parts to my pleasure, so I hope you wil remember your promise, and promise what you now remember. If you haue forgot, I would bee glad to put you in mind of it. 5

Wini. Truely, friend *Iohn*, as I would bee loth to breake my promise, so I would be vnwilling to keepe my word to the dishonesting of my virginitie. Marie for a nights lodgeing or so, I will not be strait lac'd to my friend. Therefore thus it must be. To night I must lye at the Farme at *Holloway*. Thither shall you be conueied in this Sacke, and laid in my chamber, from whence you shall haue free accesse to the pleasures of my priuate bed. 13

Drum. VVell then, bee constant, *Winifride*, and you shall find mee faithfull *Iacke Drum :* And so, taking leaue of your lips, I betake me to the tuition of the Sacke. 16

Enter Twedle. *Exit Drum.*

Twe. Winifride, my mistris *Camelia* staies for you to attend her to the Greene. I must goe and clap my Tabers cheekes there, for the heauens, Ifaith. 19

Wini. Stay a little here, and if *Iohn fo de King* come, giue him that Sack. Oh, I could crack my Whalebones, break my Buske, to thinke what laughter may arise from this! 22

Enter Mounsieur. *Exit Winifride.*

Moun. By my trot, dis loue is a most cleanly Ientleman. He is very ful of shift. De fine vench can invent ten towsand towsand trick to kisse a men (*he!*) See, by gor, she ha keep her word! Shee is in de secke alreadie, hee. Braue, by gor! My bloud das sparkle in my veine for ioy! Metre *Timotty*, you must giue me dat secke dere. 28

Timo. Owy da, *Mounsieur.* That is well pronounced, is it not?

Moun. Ritt, ritt, ritt, excellan: excellan: adiew *Timothy.* Me am almost burst for ioy! *Exit Mounsieur.*

Twe. Well, I know what the wenches on the Greene are saying now, as well as if I were in their bellies: When will *Timothy* come: When will honest *Timothy* approch. When will good *Timothy* draw neere? Wel wenches, now reioyce, for *Timothy Twedle* doth come. *Exit Twedle.*

Enter Pla. Bra. Sig. and Bra. Iunior.

Bra. Iu. Brother, how like you of our moderne wits? 37
How like you the new Poet *Mellidus?*

Bra. Sig. A slight bubling spirit, a Corke, a Huske.

Pla. How like you *Musus* fashion in his carriage? 40

Bra. Sig. O filthilie, he is as blunt as *Paules.*

Bra. Iu. What thinke you of the lines of *Decius?* Writes he not a good cordiall sappie stile?

Bra. Sig. A surreinde Iaded wit, but a rubbes on. 44

Pla. Brabant, thou art like a paire of ballance, Thou wayest all sauing thy selfe.

Bra. Sig. Good faith, troth is, they are all apes and guls, Vile imitating spirits, drie heathie Turffes. 48

Bra. Iu. Nay brother, now I think your iudgement erres.

Pla. Erre, hee cannot erre, man, for children and fooles speake truth alwaies.

Enter Mounsieur with a Sacke, and Iacke Drum in it.

Bra. Sig. See who comes yonder sweating with a packe. 52

Pla. Mounsieur, what doe you beare there, ha?

Moun. Pree you away; you breake my glasses der. Ieshu! Now me know not what to doe: Zot dat I was to come dis way widd dem. 56

Pla. Glasses, you salt rheume. Come what ha you there?

Moun. Trike no more for Ieshu sake! By gor mee haue brittle vare, if you knocke it it will breake presant. Pre you adiew.

Bra. Iu. We must know what's in the bag, Ifaith. 60

Moun. By my trot, mee tell you true: will you no trike me, den?

Bra. Iu. No, faith, but see you tell vs true, or else—

Moun. Or else, or else, by gor! Doe wat you please wid me. Sweet *Vinifride*, my verie art dus vurst, he, by gor. Mee did not dinke to vrong yow dus: come out sweet *Vinifride;* me much discredit yow. 66

He, *Iacke Drum!* Iesu, vat made you dere?

Drum. Gentlemen, my M. desires you to come sup with him. I was sent to inuite you, and this itching Goate, would needes ease my legges and carrie me: I hope you'le come, and so I take my leaue. I, I am guld, but if I quit her not, well— 71

Exit Drum.

Bra. Sig. Come, there's some knot of knauerie in this tricke.

Pla. His culler is not currant: well, let passe.

Bra. Sig. Come *Mounsieur*, come, I'le helpe you to a Wench. Goe downe the hill before, I'le follow you. 75

Moun. Mee dank you: Mor deu, he mon a mee, me ame trooke dead wit griefe: de cock of my humore is downe, and me may hang my selfe vor a Vench. *Exit Moun.*

Bra. Sig. Gentlemen, will you laugh hartily now?

Pla. I, and if thou wilt play the foole kindly now. 80

Bra. Sig. I will strait frame the strongest eternall iest

ACT IV.] *OF PASQVIL AND KATHERINE.*

That e're was builded by inuention:
My wife lies verie priuate in the Towne:
I'le bring the *French* man to her presently, 84
As to a loose lasciuious Curtezan.
Nor he, nor you, nor she, shall know the rest,
But it shall be immortall for a iest. *Exit Bra. Sig.*

   Bra. Iu. Farewell brother, we shall meet at *Hygate* soone. 88
   Pla. The wicked iest be turnde on his owne head:
Pray God he may be kindly Cuckoled. *Exeunt both.*

Enter Camelia and Winifride.

   Came. Carrie this fauour to my *Ellis* straight,
I long to see him, prethee: bid him come. 92
   Wini. I would be loth to nourish your defame,
And therefore, Mistris, pray you pardon me.
   Came. What, is thy iudgement of my *Ellis* changde?
   Wini. No, that is firme: but your estate is changde. 96
You know your sister's strangely vanished,
And now the hope and reuenue of all
Cals you his sole and faire apparant heire:
Now, therefore, would I haue you change your loue. 100
Indeed, I yeeld, 'tis moderne policie,
To kisse euen durt that plaisters vp our wants.
I'le not denie, 'tis worthie wits applause,
For women on whom lowring Fortune squints, 104
And casts but halfe an eie of due respect,
To pinne some amorous Idiot to their eies,
And vse him as they vse their Looking-glasse,
See how to adorne their beauties by his wealth, 108

And then case vp the foole and lay him by.
But for such Ladies as your selfe is now,
Whose fortunes are sustain'd by all the props
That gracious Fortune can aduance you with,   112
For such a one to yoke her free sweet youth
Vnto a Lowne, a Turke-like barbarous Sot,
A gilden Trunchion, fie! 'tis slauish vile.
Oh, what is richer then content in loue?   116
And will you now hauing so huge a Ruck
Of heap'd vp fortunes, goe and chaine your selfe
To a dull post, whose verie eyes will blaze
His base-bred spirit, where so e're he comes,   120
And shame you with the verie name of wife?
No, Mistris, no: I haue found out a man
That merits you, if man can merit you.

  Came. Lord, what a tide of hate comes creeping on   124
Vpon my former iudgement! Come, the man?

  Wini. The man? (oh God) the man is such a man,
That he is matchlesse! Oh, I shall prophane
His name with vnrespected vtterance.   128

  Came. Oh, thou tormentest me, deare *Winifride*, the man?

  Wini. By the sweet pleasures of an amorous bed,
I thinke you will be deified by him.
O God, the most accomplish'd man that breathes,   132
And *Planet* is the man.

  Came. Out on the, Deuill! There's a man indeed!

  Wini. Nay, looke you now: you'le straight oreshoote your selfe.
You'le say hee's sowre and vnsociable: 136
Tush you know him not, that humour's forc'd:

But in his natiue spirit hee's as kind
As is the life of loue. And, then, the clearest skinne,
The whitest hand, the cleanest, well shap'd legge: 140
The quickest eye: Fie, fie! I shall but blurre
And sulley his bright worth with my rude speech.

Came Well, if he court me, I'le not be much coy. 143

Wini. Court you? nay, you must court him, for ought I know:
You must not thinke, forsooth, that I am fee'd
To vrge you thus. I solemnely protest 146
I motion this out of my pure vowed loue,
Which wisheth all aduancement and content
To attend the glorie of your beautious youth.

Came. O, I am *Planet* stricken, *Winifride!* 150
How shall I intimate my loue to him?

Wini. I saw him comming vp the hill euen now;
Send him a fauour, and I'le beare it to him,
And tell him you desire to speake with him. 154

Exit Winifride.

Came. Do, do, deare *Winifride;* sweet wench, make haste!

*Enter Sir Edward Fortune, and Iohn Ellis with
a Paper in his hand.*

Ellis. Sir, I haue her good will; and please you now to giue me your consent. And looke you, sir, here I haue item'd forth what I am worth. 158

Sir Edw. Tush, shew mee no items! And shee loue you, a Gods name, I'le not bee curst by my daughter for forcing her to clip a oath'd, abhorred match. And see how fortunate we are. Looke where she stands. 162

Came. Sweet *Planet*, thou onely gouern'st me.

Sir. Ed. Daughter, giue mee your hand. With your consent I giue you to this gentleman.

Came. Marie, phoh! Will you match me to a foole? 166

Sir. Ed. God pardon me, not I! Why M. *Ellis*, ha! Had you her consent? Speake freely, man.

Ellis. Indeed, law, now: I thought so: By my troth You sed you lou'd me, that you did, indeed. 170

Came. I, as my foole, my Ideot; to make sport.

Sir Ed. Fie daughter! You are too plaine with him. Alas, my sonne, *Simily* is out of countenance.

Ellis. Truely as a Mill-horse is not a Horse-Mill, and as a Cart-Iade is not a Iade-Cart, euen so will I goe hang my selfe. 175

Sir Ed. Marie, God forbid! What frolicke, frolicke, man. Weele haue a Cup of Sacke and Sugar soone, shall quite expell these mustie humours of stale melancholy.

Enter Pasquil and a Countrey Wench, with a Basket of Egges.

Pas. Is this the Egge where *Castor* and *Pollux* bred? I'le cracke the Bastard in the verie shell. 180

Coun. Mayd. Alas, my markets! my markets are cleane spoilde!
Exit Wench.

Pas. Vbi Hellena, Vbi Troia? ist not true my *Ganimede?* When shall olde *Saturne* mount his Throne againe? See, see, alas! how bleake *Religion* stands! 184
Katherina Katherina! You damned *Titanoies*, Why pricke you heauens ribs with blasphemie? *Python* yet breathes, olde gray hair'd pietie.

ACT IV.]   OF PASQVIL AND KATHERINE.

Sir Ed. Alas, kind youth, how came he thus distraught?   188
Page. I left him in pursuit of *Katherine*,
And found him in this strange distemperature.
Pas. O sir, ist you that stampe on litrature?
You are inspired, you, with Prophesie.   192
Ellis. Not I, as I shall be sau'd.   I am M. *Iohn Ellis*, I.
Sir Edw. Come, come, let's intice him by some good meanes:
I'le labour to reclaime him to his wits.
O, now my daughter *Katherine* remembers me!   196
Where art thou girle?   Heauen giue me patience!
Pas. Poore, poore *Astrea!* who blurres thy orient shine?
Come, yons the Capitoll of *Iupiter*.
Let's whip the Senate, els they will not leaue   200
To haue their Iustice blasted with abuse
Of flattering *Sycophants.*   Come, let's mount the stars.
Reuerend antiquitie goe you in first———
Dotage will follow.   Then comes pale-fac'de lust———   204
Next *Sodome;* then *Gomorha.*   Next poore I.
By heauen my heart is burst with miserie!   *Exit Pas.*

Enter Brabant Signior, Mounsieur and the Page.

Moun. I ha tell yow de verie trote of the lagge[1] iest.   By gor, your England Damosels are so feere, so vittie, so kit! by my trote, shee tosse mee wish vey shee please der: but pre yow were is de Vench?   Is dis de house?   Ha, is dis de house, pre yow tell me, ha?
Bra. Sig. It is, it is, and she is in the inner Chamber: Boy call her forth.   *Exit Page.*

[1] ? bagge; in reference to the sack trick Mounsieur has just been subjected to.—G.

Moun. Sings. *By gor, den, me must needs now sing.*
Ding, ding, ading, Dinga, dinga, ding, 214
For me am now at pleasures spring.
Dinga, ding, ding, dinga, dinga, dinga, ding,
And a hee da vench, da vench, da vench,
Which must my bruling humour quench. Coma, coma, com. 218

Enter Mistris Brabant.

Mist. Bra. Now sweet, you kept your promise well last night.
Moun. By gor, she giue him much kind word alreadie.
Bra. Sig. Wel, to make thee amends, boy, fetch vs a quart of *Canarie* Sacke. Pre-thee, *Mall*, entertaine this *French* Gentleman.
Mist. Bra. Sir, you are verie welcome to my lodging. 223
Moun. Me danck you. And first me kisse your fingre: next me busse your lip: and last me clip your vaste. And now foutra for de *Vinifride!*
Page. Sir *Edwards* Caterer passed by, sir. You will'd mee to remember Lemmons. 228
Bra. Sig. Gods precious, 'tis true! Boy, goe with mee to Billingsgate. *Mall,* I'le returne straight.

Exit Bra. Sig. and his Page.

Moun. Will yow no Vin, sir, he! He is gone purposely, by my trote, most kind Gentleman. Faire Madame, pree you pittie me. By Gor, me languish for your loue. Mee am a pouera *French* Ientleman. Pree shew mee your bed-Chambre. 234
Mist. Bra. What meane you, sir, by this strange passion?
Moun. Nay, noting. By Gor, damosell, you bee so faer, so admirably feer, flesh and bloud cannot indure your countenance. Mee brule, ang mee brule, ang yow ha no compassion: by gor, mee

ang quite languish. Last night mee goe to bedde, and mee put de candle behinde mee, and, by my trote, me see cleane torough me, me ang so drie. Mee put a cold plattre at my backe, and my backe melt de plattre quite; doe so burne. Pree you shew me your bed Chambre. Me will bee secret, constant. I loue you vnreasonably vell, vnreasonably vell, by gor! 244

Mist. Bra. In faith, you make mee blush. What should I say?

Moun. Say no, ang take it: Or, arke you one ting. Say neder yea nor no, but take it, ang say noting.

Mist. Bra. You will be close and secret? 248

Moun. Secred, by gor, as secred as your sowle! mee will tell noting, possible!

Mist. Bra. Well, sir, if it please you to see my Chamber, 'tis at your seruice. *Exit Mist. Brabant.*

Moun. He! now me ang braue *Mounsieur!* By gor, ang mee had know dis, me woode haue eate some Potatos, or Ringoe: but vell: he! Me will tanck Metre *Brabant* vor dis. By gor me am caught in heauen blisse! *Exit Mounsieur.*

Enter Camelia and Winifride, hanging on Planets armes.

Came. Oh, too vnkind! why do'st thou scorne my loue? 257
Shee that with all the vehemence of speech
Hath beene pursued, and kneeled to for loue,
Prostrates her selfe, and all her choicest hopes,
As lowe as to thy feet. Disdaine me not:
To scorne a Virgin is mans odious blot. 262

Pla. To scorne a man is Virgins odious blot.
Wert thou as rich as is the Oceans wombe,

As beautious as the glorious frame of heauen,
Yet would I lothe thee worse then varnisht skuls, 266
Whose riuels are daub'd vp with plaistering paint.
   Came. O Rockie spirit!
   Plan. Breathe not in vaine. I hate thy flatterings,
Detest thy purest elegance of speech, 270
Worse then I doe the Croking of a Toade.
   Winif. Sweet Gentleman!
   Plan. Peace! you Rebato-pinner, Poting-sticke.
You bribde corrupters of affection, 274
I hate you both. By heauen I hate her more
Then I doe loue my selfe. Hence, packe away!
I'le sooner dote vpon a bleare-eide Witch,
A saplesse Beldame, then I'le flatter thee. 278
   Cam. Be not too cruell, sweet *Planet*, deare relent,
Compassionate my amorous languishment!
   Plan. Ha, ha! I pree thee kneele, beg, blubber, crie,
Whilst I behold thee with a lothing eie, 282
And laugh to see thee weepe!
   Cam. Looke, on my knees I creepe,
Be not impenetrable, beautious youth!
But smile vpon me, and I'le make the aire 286
Court thy choice eare with soft delicious sounds.
Bring forth the Violls: each one play his part,
Musick's the quiuer of young *Cupids* dart. 289
      The Song with the Violls.
   Plan. Out, *Syren!* Peace, scritch-owle! Hence, chattering Pie!
The blacke-beakt night-Crow, or the howling Dog,
Shall be more gracious then thy squeaking voice:

ACT IV.]   *OF PASQVIL AND KATHERINE.*   193

Goe sing to *M. Iohn.* I shall be blunt
If thou depart not. Hence, goe mourne and die :   294
I am the scourge of light inconstancie.   *Exit Cam. & Winif.*
Thus my deare *Brabant,* am I thy reuenge,
And whip her for the peeuish scorne shee bare
To thy weake yonger birth : ô, that the soules of men   298
Were temperate like mine ! Then Natures paint
Should not triumph o're our infirmities.
I doe adore, with infinite respect,
Women whose merit issues from their worth   302
Of inward graces; but these rotten posts
That are but gilt with outward garnishment,
O, how my soule abhorres them ! Yon's my friend.

Enter Brabant Iunior.

I will conceale what I for him haue wrought :   306
Nice iealousie mistakes a friendly part.
Now, *Brabant,* where's thy elder brother, ha?
What, hath he built the iest with *Mounsieur* yet ?   309
   Bra. Iu. Faith, I know not, but I heard he left the Frenchman with his wife.
   Planet. Knew shee thy brothers meaning ?
   Bra. Iu. Not a whit. Shee's a meere stranger to this merriment.
   Plan. Hit, and be luckie ! ô, that 'twere lawfull, now,   314
To pray to God that he were Cuckoled.
Deare *Brabant,* I doe hate these bumbaste wits,
That are puft vp with arrogant conceit
Of their owne worth; as if *Omnipotence*   318
Had hoised them to such vnequald height,

That they suruai'd our spirits with an eye
Onely create to censure from aboue;
When good soules they doe nothing but reproue. 322
See where a Shallop comes.   How now, what newes?

Enter Winifride, and whispers with Planet.

Bra. Iu. What might this meane, that *Winifride* salutes
The blunt tongu'd *Planet*, with such priuate speech?
See with what vehemence shee seemes to vrge 326
Some priuate matter.   *Planet* is my friend,
And yet the strongest linke of friendship's strain'd,
When female loue puts to her mightie strength.
Marke, marke, shee offers him *Camelias* scarfe: 330
Now on my life 'tis so : *Planet* supplants my Loue!

Plan. Friend, I must leaue thee, preethee pardon me;
Weele meet at supper soone with the good knight.

Exeunt Plan. and Winifride.

Bra. Iu. I, I, content : O hell to my delight! 334
My friend will murder me: Thin Cob-web Lawne
Burst with each little breath of tempting sweets!

Winifride speakes from within.

Shee intreats you, *M. Planet*, to meet
Her at the Crosse stile. 338

Bra. Iu. Ha, at the crosse stile! Well, I'le meet him there.
He that's perfidious to me in my loue,
Confusion take him, and his bloud be spilt, 341
Without confusion to the murderer.   *Exit Brabant.*

Actvs Qvintvs.

*Enter Bra. Iu. and his Page, charging
a Pistoll.*

Bra. Iu. SO; lode it soundly. Murder's great with me.
Goe, Boy, discharge it, euen in *Planets* brest.
Shoot him quite through, and through; thou canst not sin
To murder him, that murdered his deare friend 4
With damned breach of friendship. When he is slaine
Bring me his Cloke and Hat. Here I will stay,
To be imbrac'd in stead of *Planet:* Goe: Away! *Exit Boy.*
I had rather die with bloud vpon my head, 8
Shame and reproch clogging my heauie houre,
Then t'haue my friend still wounding of my soule
With reprobate *Apostacisme* in loue.
O, this *Sophisticate* friendship, that dissolues 12
With euery heate of Fancie: let it melt
Euen in Hels Forge! Harke, the Pistoll is discharg'd;
The Act of gorie murder is perform'd.
Haue mercy, heauen: ô, my soule is rent 16

Enter the Page.

With *Planets* wound! Come, Boy, the Hat and Cloke.
Goe poste to *Scotland:* there are crownes for thee.
Leaue *Brabant* vnto death and obloquie. *Exit Page.*
Why, now the vlcerous swelling of my hate 20
Is broken forth: Oh, that these womens beauties,
This Natures witchcraft, should inchaunt our soules

So infinitely vnrecouerable!
That hell, death, shame, eternall infamie, 24
Cannot reclaime our desperate resolues!
But we will on spight of damnation.

Enter Camelia and Winifride.

Come yee poore garments of my murdered friend,
Mourne that you are compeld to hide his limbs 28
That slue you[r] Master. See, *Camelia* comes.
I'le stand thus muffled and deceiue her sight:
When loue makes head friendship is put to flight.

Cam. Persist not still, ô thou relentlesse youth, 32
To scorne my loue! What tho I scorn'd thy friend,
Doe not vpbraid me still with hating him;
Doe not still view me with a lothing eie.
For *Brabants* sake doe you but loue me, sweet, 36
And I'le not scorne him. Why shouldst be so nice
In keeping lawes of friendship? Didst thou e're heare
Of any soule that held a friend more deare
Then a faire woman? 40

Bra. Iu. O, the sting of death! How hath *Brabant* err'd?
Hence thou vile wombe of my damnation!
Oh, thou wrong'd spirit of my murdred friend,
Thou guiltlesse, spotlesse, pure, immaculate: 44
Behold, this arme thrusting swift vengeance
Into the trunck of a curst damn'd wretch!

He drawes his Rapier.

Winif. Heele spoile himselfe: Let's run and call for helpe!
Exit Camel. and Wini.

Bra. Iu. Now haue I roome for murder: This vast place, 48
Hush'd silence, and dumbe solitude are fit
To be obseruers of my Tragedie.
Planet, accept the smoke of reeking bloud
To expiate thy murder. Friend, I come: 52
Weele troope together to *Elizium!*

*Enter Sir Edward, Camelia, Winifride, Ellis, Brabant Sig.
Twedle, Drum, and others.*

Sir Ed. Hold, haire-brain'd youth! what mischiefe mads thy thoughts?

Bra. Iu. Forbeare, good knight. You neuer sinn'd so deep 56
As in detayning this iust vengeance
To light vpon me. But know I will die.
I haue infring'd the lawes of God and Man,
In shedding of my *Planets* guiltlesse bloud, 60
Who I supposde corriuald me in loue
Of that *Camelia*, but iniuriously:
And therefore, gentle Knight, let mine owne hand
Be mine owne hang-man. 64

Bra. Sig. Brother, I'le get you pardon, feare it not.

Bra. Iun. You'le get my pardon, brother? Pardon me,
You shall not; for I'le die in spight of thee.

Sir Ed. I am turn'd wilde in wonder of this act! 68

Enter Planet, and the Page.

Plan. Come, *Brabant*, come, giue me my Cloke and Hat:
The euening's raw and danke; I shall take cold.
How now? turn'd mad! Why star'st thou on me thus?

Giue me my Cloke.   Hart! is the youth distraught?   72

 Bra. Iu. Ha, doest thou breathe! Let's see where is thy wound?

 Plan. Doest breathe, my wound? what doest thou meane by this?

 Page. Gentlemen, I can direct you forth   76
This Labyrinth of intricate misdoubts.
My Master will'd me kill that Gentleman.
Now, I thought he was mad in putting me
To such an enterprise; and therefore sooth'd him vp   80
With I sir, yes sir, and so sir, at each word,
Whilst he would shew me how to hold the Dagge,
To draw the Cock, to charge, and set the flint.
Meane time I had the wit to thinke him mad;   84
And therefore went, and as he will'd me shoot,
Which he, God knowes, thought pearc'd his deare friends heart;
Then went and borrowed that same hat and cloke
Of *M. Planet;* brought them to my Master;   88
And so—

 Plan. No more, no more, Knight, I will make thee smile
When I discourse how much my friend hath err'd.

 Sir Ed. I will dissolue and melt my soule to night   92
In influent laughter.   Come, my Iocund spirit
Presageth some vnhop't-for happinesse:
Wee'le crowne this euening with triumphant ioy.
I'le sup vpon this Greene.   Here's roome enough   96
To draw a liberall breath, and laugh aloud:
Drum, fetch the Table: *Twedle,* scoure your Pipe,
For my old bones will haue a round to night.

Now, by my troth, and I had thought on't, too, 100
I would haue had a play : Ifaith, I would.
I saw the Children of *Powles* last night,
And troth they pleas'd me prettie, prettie well :
The Apes in time will doe it handsomely. 104

 Plan. Ifaith, I like the audience that frequenteth there
With much applause : A man shall not be chokte
With the stench of Garlick ; nor be pasted
To the barmie Iacket of a Beer-brewer. 108

 Bra. Iu. 'Tis a good, gentle audience, & I hope the boies
Will come one day into the Court of requests.

 Bra. Sig. I, and they had good Plaies. But they produce
Such mustie fopperies of antiquitie, 112
And doe not sute the humorous ages backs,
With clothes in fashion.

 Plan. Well, *Brabant*, well, you will be censuring still.
There lies a iest in steep. Will, whip you for't. 116

 Sir Ed. Gallants, I haue no iudgement in these things,
But will it please you sit ? *Camelia*,
Call these same Gentlemen vnto thee, wench :
O there with thee my *Katherine* was wont 120
To sit with gracefull presence. Well, let't passe :
Fetch me a cup of Sacke. Come, Gallants, sit.
M. Brabant, M. Planet, I pray you sit.
Young *M. Brabant,* and, Gods precious ! *M. Iohn,* 124
Sit all, and consecrate this night to mirth.
Here is old *Neds* place : Come, sound Musicke there,
What, Gallants, haue you ne're a Page can entertaine
This pleasing time with some French brawle, or Song ? 128

What shall we haue, a Galliard? troth, 'tis well.
            A Galliard.
Good Boy! Ifaith, I would thou hadst more roome.

            Enter Katherine.

Kath. Once more the gracious heauens haue renew'd
My wasted hopes: Once more a blessed chance   132
Hath fetcht againe my spirit from the sownd
And languishing despaire of happinesse.
A skilfull Beldame, with the iuyce of hearbs,
Hath cur'd my face, and kild the venoms power.   136
And now if *Pasquil* liue and loue me still
Heauen is bounteous to poore *Katherine.*
Yon suppes my Father; but my *Ned's* not there.
I feare; and yet I know not what I feare.   140

    Sir Ed. Gallants, I drinke this to *Ned Pasquils* health.
    Plan. Ifaith, I'le pledge him. Would he had his wits.
    Sir Ed. And I my daughter. Fill me one cup more:
No griefe so potent, but neat sparkling wine   144
Can conquer him: Oh, this is iuyce diuine.
    Kath. Would he had his wits? Oh, what a numming feare
Strikes a cold palsey through my trembling bloud!

            Enter Pasquil, mad.

    Pasq. Vertue shall burst ope the Iron gates of hell: 148
I'le not be coop'd vp. Roome for *Phaeton!*
Lame Policy, how canst thou goe vpright?
O lust, staine not sweet Loue! Fie, be not lost
Vpon the surge of vulgar humours. You Idiot!   152
Riuet my Armour, and Caparison

A mightie Centaure; for I'le run at Tilt,
And tumble downe yon Giant in the dust.
Sit, gentle Iudges of great *Radamant:* 156
Let not *Proserpine* rule thee. Oh, shee's dead.
Now, thou art right *Eacus:* I appeale to thee:
Haue pittie on a wretches miserie!

    Sir Ed. I am quite sunck with griefe. What shall we doe 160
To get recouerie of his wits againe?

    Bra. Iu. Let Musicke sound; for I haue often heard
It hath such sweet agreement with our soules,
That it corrects vaine humours, and recalls 164
His straggling fancies to faire vnion.

    Plan. Why, the soule of man is nought but simphonies—
A sound of disagreeing parts—yet faire vnite
By heauens hand, diuine by reasons light. 168

    Sir Ed. Sound Musicke, then. Pray God it take effect.
        The Musicke sounds, and Pasquils eye is fixt vpon
                        Katherine.

    Bra. Iu. Marke with what passion he sucks vp the sweets
Of this same delicate harmonious breath.

    Plan. Obserue him well. Me thinks his eye is fixt 172
Vpon some obiect, that seemes to attract
His very soule forth with astonishment.
Marke with what vehemence his thoughts doe speake,
Euen in his eyes. Some creature stands farre off, 176
That hath intranc't him with a pleasing sight.

    Pasq. Amazement, wonder, stiffe astonishment
Stare and stand gazing on this miracle!
Perfection of what e're a humane thought 180

Can reach with his discoursiue faculties,
Thou whose sweet presence purifies my sence
And do'st create a second soule in me!
Deare *Katherine*, the life of *Pasquils* hopes! 184

 Kath. Deare *Pasquil*, the life of *Katherines* hopes!

 Pas. Once more let mee imbrace the constant'st one
That e're was tearmde her Sex perfection.

 Kath. Once more let me be valued worth his loue, 188
In decking of whose soule the graces stroue.

 Pas. Spight hath out-spent it selfe, and thus, at last,
     Both speake.
We clip with ioyfull arme each others wast.

 Sir Edw. O, pardon me, thou dread omnipotence, 192
I thought thou could'st not thus haue blessed me!
O, thou hast deaw'd my gray haires with thy loue,
And made my olde heart sprout with fertill ioy.

 Kath. Forget, deare father, that my act hath wrong'd 196
The quiet of your age.

 S. Ed. No more, no more! I know what thou would'st say.
Daughter, there's nothing but saluation
Could come vnto my heart more gracious 200
Then is the sight of my deare *Katherine*.
Sonne *Pasquil*, now, for thou shalt be my sonne,
What! frolicke! gentle youth.

 Pas. Is *Mamon* heere? 204

 Drum. Oh sir, M. *Mamon* is in a Citie of *Iurie*, called *Bethlem*, *alias*, plaine *Bedlame:* The price of whips is mightily risen, since his braine was pittifully ouertumbled: they are so fast spent vpon his shoulders. 208

Pas. Oh sacred heauens, how iust is thy reuenge!

Sir Ed. Why? did he cast you in the labyrinth
Of these strange crosses?

Pasq. Yes, honor'd Knight; which in more priuate place,
And fitter time, I will disclose at large.

Came. Faith, sister, as I am your elder borne,
So will I match before, or with you, sure.
Young *M. Brabant*.

Bra. By this light, not I.

Cam. Honest *M. Ellis*.

Ellis. No indeed, law, not I. I doe not vse to marrie.
For euen as blacke patches are worne,
Some for pride, some to stay the Rhewme, and
Some to hide the scab, euen so *Iohn Ellis*
Scorne her, that hath scorned him.

Came. Vertuous Master *Planet*.

Plan. Errant wandring starre, we shall ne're agree!

Came. M. Brabant, M. Planet, M. Ellis, faith, I'le haue any!

Sir Ed. But no body will haue thee: This is the plague of light inconstancie.

Goe *Twedle*, bid the Butler broch fresh wine:
Set vp waxe lights, and furnish new the boords:
Knocke downe a score of Beefes:
Inuite my neighbours straight,
And make my dressers grone with waight of meat.
M. Ellis, pray you let vs heare your high Dutch song,
You are admired for it: Good, let's heare it.

Ellis. I doe not vse to sing: and yet euen as when the skie falls

we shall haue Larkes, euen so, when my voice riseth you shall
haue a song. 237

He singeth, holding a Bowle of drinke in his hand.

The Song.

Giue vs once a drinke, for an the blacke Bowle.
    Sing, gentle Butler, balley moy ;
For an the blacke bowle. Sing gentle Butler, balley moy. 240
Giue vs once some drinke, for an the pinte Pot.
Sing, gentle Butler, balley moy, the pinte pot ;
For an the blacke bowle. Sing, gentle Butler, balley moy.
Giue vs once a drinke, for an the quart Pot. 244
Sing, gentle Butler, balley moy, the quart, the pinte pot;
For an the blacke bowle. Sing, gentle Butler, balley moy.
Giue vs once some drinke, for an the pottle pot.
Sing, gentle Butler, balley moy, the pottle, the quart, the pint pot; 248
For an the blacke bowle. Sing, gentle Butler, balley moy.
Giue vs once a drinke, for an the gallon pot.
Sing, gentle Butler, balley moy, the gallon, the pottle, the quart,
    the pint pot; For an the blacke bowle. 252
Sing, gentle Butler, balley moy.
Giue vs once a drinke, for an the Firkin.
Sing, gentle Butler, balley moy, the firkin, the gallon, the pottle,
    the quart, the pinte pot ; For an the blacke bowle. 256
Sing, gentle Butler, balley moy.
Giue vs once a drinke, for an the Kilderkin.
Sing, gentle Butler, balley moy, the Kilderkin, the firkin, the gal-
    lon, the pottle, the quart, the pinte pot ; 260
For an the blacke bowle. Sing, gentle Butler, balley moy.

Giue vs once some drinke, for an the Barrell.
Sing, gentle Butler, balley moy, the barrell, the kilderkin, the firkin, the gallon, the pottle, the quart, the pinte pot ;   264
For an the blacke bowle. Sing, gentle Butler, balley moy.
Giue vs once some drinke, for an the Hogshead.
Sing, gentle Butler, balley moy, the hogshead, the barrell, the kilderkin, the firkin, the gallon, the pottle, the quart, the pinte pot ;
For an the blacke bowle. Sing, gentle Butler, balley moy.   269
Giue vs once a drinke, for an the But.
Sing, gentle Butler, balley moy, the Butt, the hogshead, the barrell, the kilderkin, the firkin, the gallon, the pottle, the quart, the pinte pot ; For an the blacke bowle.   273
Sing, gentle Butler, balley moy.
Giue vs once some drinke, for an the Pipe.
Sing, gentle Butler, balley moy, the Pipe, the butt, the hogshead, the barrell, the kilderkin, the firkin, the gallon, the pottle, the quart, the pinte pot ; For an the blacke bowle.   278
Sing, gentle Butler, balley moy.
Giue vs once some drinke, for an the Tunne.
Sing, gentle Butler, balley moy, the Tunne, the pipe, the butt, the hogshead, the barrell, the kilderkin, the firkin, the gallon, the pottle, the quart, the pinte pot ; For an the blacke bowle.
Sing, gentle Butler, balley moy.   284

   Sir Ed. Well done. Ifaith, 'twas chanted merrily :
What, my Gallants, ne're a tickling iest,
To make vs sowne with mirth, e're we goe in ?   287
   Bra. Sig. Faith, Gent. I ha' brewed such a strong headed iest,
Will make you drunke, and reele with laughter :

You know *Mounsieur Iohn fo de King?* 290

Sir Ed. Very well: he read French to my daughters.

Bra. Sig. I, to gull the Foole, haue brought him to my wife, as to a loose lasciuious Curtezan, shee being a meere stranger to the iest, and there, some three houres agoe, left him: But I am sure shee hath so cudgeld him with quicke sharpe iests, and so batter'd him with a volley of her wit, as indeed shee is exceeding wittie, and admirable chaste, that in my conscience heele neuer dare to court women more. Would to God he were return'd! 298

Enter Mounsieur.

Sir Ed. See, euen on your wish, he's come.

Moun. Iesu preserue you! sweet Metre *Brabant.* By gor, de most delicat, plumpe vench dat euer mee tuche: Mee am your slaue, your peasaunt; By gor, a votre seruice whil'ste I liue vor dis.

Bra. Sig. He would perswade you now, that hee toucht her with an immodest hand. Ha, ha, ha! 304

Moun. Tuch her? By gor, me tuch her, and tuch her, and me tuch her. Me ne're tuch such a venche. De fines foote, de cleanest legge, de sleekest skin: and me tell e sure token; she hath de finest little varte—you know veare: he! by gor, mee ne're tuch such a vench. 309

Sir Ed. Pray God hee haue not brew'd a headie iest indeede.

Bra. Sig. Why, faith, Gentlemen, I am Cuckold: by this light I am! 312

Moun. By gor, mee no know. You tell a mee 'twas a Curtezan. Pray you pardon me. By my trote, me teche you French to t'end of the vorlde.

Pla. Come, here's thy cap of Maintenance, the Coronet 316

Of Cuckolds.   Nay, you shall weare it, or weare
My Rapier in your guts : by heauen !
Why, doest thou not well deserue to be thus vs'd ?
Why should'st thou take felicitie to gull
Good honest soules ? And in thy arrogance,
And glorious ostentation of thy wit,
Thinke God infused all perfection
Into thy soule alone, and made the rest
For thee to laugh at ? Now, you Censurer,
Be the ridiculous subiect of our mirth.
Why Foole, the power of Creation
Is still Omnipotent : And there's no man that breathes
So valiant, learned, wittie, or so wise,
But it can equall him out of the same mould
Wherein the first was form'd.   Then leaue proud scorne,
And, honest selfe-made Cuckold, weare the horne !

   Bra. Sig. Weare the horne ? I, spite of all your teeth,
I'le weare this Crowne, and triumph in this horne.

   Sir Ed. Why, faith 'tis valorously spoke, faire Sir :
Wee'le solemnize your Coronation
With royall pompe.   Now, Gentlemen, prepare
A liberall spirit to entertaine a iest,
Where free light Iocund mirth shall be enthron'd
With sumptuous state.   Now, Musicke, beat the aire :
Intrance our thoughts with your harmonious sounds,
Our *Fortune* laughes, and all content abounds.   *Exeunt omnes.*

FINIS.

[*The names of the Actors follow : see* p. 132.]

NOTES.

1. *Jack Drum's Entertainment* (p. 133, l. 2; p. 140, l. 156) was a kind of proverbial expression for ill-treatment. 'Not like the entertainment of *Jacke Drum*, who was best welcome when he went away.'—Thos. Coryate, ed. 1776, v. iii. sign. C c 3 : See *Nares*. See also *All's Well*, iii. 6. 1. 41.—F.

2. *Sacred maiestie*, p. 135, l. 23.—In the passage containing these words we have the exaggerated reverence for the ruling class so often indulged in by Shakspere, with its usual accompaniment of expressed disgust for such of the common folk as presume to discuss, even from their poor ale-house benches, ' affairs of State.'—G.

3. *The Counsell-chamber is the Phœnix nest, who wastes it selfe to give us peace and rest*, p. 136, l. 49.—*Jack Drum's Entertainment* contains no flattery of the sovereign; but, in the above and accompanying lines, we have a passage which may be taken as rather warmly complimentary of what we should in these days call ' the ministry.' In politics, therefore—and Mr Simpson has always insisted upon the political character and connexions of the Elizabethan plays—*Jack Drum* may be classed as ' ministerial.'—G.

4. *Let the Jebusite depart in peace*, p. 140, l. 156.—By Jebusite, or native of Jerusalem, *Jack Drum* makes *Mamon* a Jew. Compare this with the next speech, beginning,—' I, for any Christian,' and with the three facts that (1) *Mamon* is a usurer, who lends at 'thirty in the hundred' (p. 181, l. 409): (2) He is expressly endowed 'with a great nose' (see list of characters, p. 132, and the text, p. 142, l. 208; p. 181, l. 393); and (3) In the treatment he gets at the hands of the dramatist there is a likeness to that meted out to Shylock in the *Merchant of Venice*, more particularly at p. 180, l. 381, *et seq.*, and the intention seems strengthened. *Mamon's* scenes, with *Pasquil* first, and *Flawne* afterwards, at p. 180, l. 373, *et seq.*, are, in their plan and mode of treatment, very like that of Shylock's outcry over the loss of his daughter and his ducats (as told by Salanio), and that between Shylock and Tubal: *Merchant of Venice*, II. 8, l. 41, and III. 1. Perhaps the stage popularity of Shakspere's Shylock (1596 or 1597) induced the writer, or writers, of *Jack Drum* (1601) thus to make *Mamon* a sort of Shylock.—G.

A Warning for Faire Women,

containing

The most Tragicall and Lamentable Murther of
Master George Sanders, of London,
Marchant, nigh Shooters Hill; consented
unto by his owne wife,
acted by M. Browne, Mistris Drewry and Trusty
Roger, agents therin: with
thier seuerall ends. As it hath beene
lately diuerse times acted by the right Honorable
the Lord Chamberlaine his
Seruantes.

Printed at London
by Valentine Sims for William Aspley.
1599.

[THE STORY OF THE PLAY BRIEFLY TOLD.]

[THIS play is a rendering of a popular London murder of 1573—arrests, trials, executions, confessions and all complete—done for the stage in a (generally) very servile following of the contemporary accounts by Stowe and others, as given at p. 217, *et seq.* Captain Browne, a young Irish officer and London gallant, on a visit at the house of Mr George Sanders, a wealthy city merchant living near Billingsgate, falls in love with his host's pretty wife. He importunes Mrs Drury, a widow friend of the Sanderses, to help him plead his love; which Mrs Drury agrees to do, on promise of an ample reward. Mrs Drury claims 'surgery' as her 'profession,' but avows that she gets her 'best living' by fortune-telling; and she commences to inveigle Mrs Sanders by 'reading her hand,' and telling her, as the result, (1) That she will soon be a widow; (2) That she will thereupon marry a gentleman—'a gallant fellow,' of 'great estates,' &c.; and (3) That the gentleman destined to be her second husband is the Captain Browne she has met at her own table once, and seen but once since. Mrs Sanders is at first very sorry to hear this; but after a time she views it as her destiny. The interviews thereupon procured for Browne by the woman Drury lead the wife further astray, till she loves Browne as he loves her. Browne is now seized with the wish to remove Sanders from his and his love's path; and he plots with Mrs Drury, and her equally unscrupulous man, Roger, the murder of the merchant. Twice Browne waylays Sanders, but is prevented from striking the blow by the intrusion of company. His third attempt results in the death of the merchant, and the mortal wounding of John Beane, an attendant. Browne sends a handkerchief dipped in Sanders's blood to Ann Sanders as a token that the merchant has been killed. But, coming immediately after to his mistress, he finds her already filled with remorse; and is repulsed by her. Browne then flies the hue-and-cry, being furnished with money belonging in part to Mrs Sanders and in part to Mrs Drury. Arrested at Rochester, he is recognized as the murderer by the dying John Beane, and is then tried and condemned. He repents, confesses, and implicates Drury and her man Roger; but, through love, seeks to save Ann Sanders by declaring her innocent. And so he is hanged. Then follow the trials, confessions, and executions of Mrs Drury, Mrs Sanders, and Roger. At various points in the course of the play, *Tragedy* appears as a species of *Chorus*, and with the aid of 'Dumb shows,' in which figure *Murther*, *Lust*, *Chastity*, and other personifications, as well as the chief actors in the drama, indicates the working of such parts of the plot as are not otherwise set forth.—G.]

INTRODUCTION.

THIS anonymous play was published by Valentine Sims for William Aspley, in 1599. It was one of the plays acted by the Lord Chamberlain's Company. It is perhaps the most noteworthy of a whole class of plays, those, namely, which dramatized murders which for any special reason attracted great interest. Two plays of this class have been attributed to Shakspere. The *Yorkshire Tragedy* was printed with his name on the title-page in 1608, and *Arden of Faversham*, printed in 1592, was reprinted by Edward Jacob, a Faversham man, in 1770, and by him attributed to Shakspere. The present play has thus much in common with *Arden*, that it represents a murder committed many years before the date of the drama, and that its materials were taken either from the Chronicles, or from the contemporary accounts upon which the Chronicles were founded. Holinshed and Stowe give an identical relation, drawn, with slight corrections, from a contemporary account written either by Clearke or Nowell, the two ministers who prepared the murderers for their execution. Other plays of the kind, like the *Yorkshire Tragedy* and *Page of Plymouth*, represented the event while it was still fresh in memory.

The title of the play, *A warning for fair women*, has much in common with the *Alarum for London*, and testifies to the didactic and educational intention which the Lord Chamberlain's company wished to be supposed to underlie their efforts to amuse the public.

The writers or printers of ballads had set this example long before. Thus we find on the registers of the Stationers' Company in 1564,

> 'A warning to wanton wives,
> To flee from folly the length of their lives.'

In 1565,

> 'A warning to all maids that brews their own bane,'

and,

> 'A warning for widows that aged be;
> How lusty young youth and age can agree.'

The didactic intention of the play assumes quite a controversial form in the conversation between Master James, Master Barnes, and the Mayor of Rochester about the effect of plays upon the conscience of the guilty. The stories are introduced by the head and shoulders, but they have this point of interest: that one of them is evidently a story, which found a place in the *Hamlet* of 1589, where Hamlet, instead of his vague reference,

> 'I have heard
> That guilty creatures sitting at a play
> Have, by the very cunning of the scene,
> Been struck so to the soul, that, presently,
> They have proclaim'd their malefactions;
> For murder, though it have no tongue, will speak
> With most miraculous organ.'

The story told by Hamlet to Horatio in the play of 1589 is as follows:—

'There was a pretty casus in Germany, near Strasburg. A wife had murdered her husband by piercing him through the heart with a shoemaker's awl; and then, with the help of her paramour, buried him under the doorstep. So matters stood for as long as nine years: when certain actors came that way, and acted a tragedy containing a similar incident. The wife, who was sitting with her paramour at the play, was so touched in her conscience, and began to cry aloud and to shriek, " Woe is me! that touches me! So it was that I killed my husband." She tore her hair, ran out of the theatre to the judge, confessed of her own accord the murder, and, as this was found to be true, she, in deep repentance for her crime, received the consolations of a priest, and in true contrition gave up her body to the executioner, and commended her soul to heaven.'

This I suppose to be meant for the third example, the one related by Master James in the following play (p. 310, l. 1060). It is the same incident as the first of the three related by Heywood in his *Apology for Actors* (Shaks. Society's reprint, pp. 57—60) in much greater detail. Heywood, writing in 1612, tells it as 'a domestic and home-born truth, which within these few years happened. At Lin, in Norfolk, the then Earl of Sussex' players acting the old History of Friar Francis, and presenting a woman, who insatiately doting on a young gentleman, the more securely to enjoy his affection, mischievously and secretly murdered her husband, whose ghost haunted her; and at divers times, in her most solitary and private contemplations, in most horrid and fearful shapes appeared and stood before her. As this was acted, a towns-woman, till then of good estimation and report, finding her conscience at this presentment extremely troubled, suddenly skritched and cried out, " Oh my husband, my husband! I see the ghost of my husband fiercely threatening and menacing me!" At which shrill and unexpected outcry the people about her, moved to a strange amazement, inquired the reason of her clamour, when presently, unurged, she told them that, seven years ago, she, to be possessed of such a gentleman, meaning him, had poisoned her husband, whose fearful image presented itself in the shape of that ghost. Whereupon the murdresse was apprehended, before the justices further examined, and by her voluntary confession after condemned. That this is true, as well by the report of the actors as the records of the town, there are many eye-witnesses of this accident yet living vocally to confirm it.'

It appears by Henslowe's diary that the Earl of Sussex' men acted *Friar Francis* at the Rose in 1593. The predecessor of the then Earl had been Lord Chamberlain; and perhaps the successor kept up a connection with the company of actors, who may have occasionally appeared under his patronage, as his men. At any rate the complimentary references made to them in the text of the following play lead to the conclusion that there was at least an identity of interest, if not of persons, between the Lord Chamberlain's men of 1599 and the Earl of Sussex' men of 1593, and perhaps five years earlier.

The first of the stories, the one told by the Mayor of Rochester, may be identified with Heywood's third story (pp. 58—60) by the incident of the nail in the temples. 'Another of the like wonder happened at Amsterdam, in Holland. A company of our English Comedians (well known) travelling those countries, as they were before the burgers and other the chief inhabitants acting the last part of the *Four Sons of Aymon*, towards the last part of the history, where penitent Rinaldo, like a common labourer, lived in disguise, vowing, as his last penance, to labour and carry burdens to the structure of a goodly church, then to be erected; whose diligence the labourers envying, since, by reason of his stature and strength, he did usually perfect more work in a day than a dozen of the best—he working for his conscience, they for their lucres—whereupon, by reason his industry had so much disparaged their living, conspired among themselves to kill him, waiting some opportunity to find him asleep, which they might easily do, since the sorest labourers are the soundest sleepers, and industry is the best preparative to rest. Having spy'd their opportunity, they drave a nail into his temples, of which wound immediately he died. As the actors handled this, the audience might on a sodaine understand an out-cry and loud shrike in a remote gallery; and pressing about the place, they might perceive a woman of great gravity strangely amazed, who with a distracted and troubled brain oft sighed out these words, "Oh my husband, my husband!" The play, without further interruption, proceeded; the woman was to her own house conducted, without any apparent suspicion; everyone conjecturing as their fancies led them. In this agony she some few days languished. And on a time, as certain of her well-disposed neighbours came to comfort her, one amongst the rest being church-warden; to him the sexton posts, to tell him of a strange thing happening to him in the ripping up of a grave: "See here," quoth he, "what I have found": and shows them a fair skull, with a great nail pierced quite through the brain-pan: "But we cannot conjecture to whom it should belong, nor how long it hath lain in the earth, the grave being confused, and the flesh consumed." At the report of this accident the woman out of the trouble of her afflicted conscience discovered a former murder; for twelve years ago, by driving that nail into that skull, being the head of her husband, she had treacherously slain him. This being publicly confessed, she was arraigned, condemned, adjudged, and burned.'

It was in the year 1602 that Robert Shawe was engaged in writing the *Four Sons of Aymon*, and the play was revived in 1624. Unless there was an earlier play on the same subject, the mention of the story in the *Warning for Fair Women*, printed in 1599, shows Heywood's circumstantial details to be mere fudge. It is evident, however, that these stories were common places of the advocates of the stage from 1589, when one of them appears in *Hamlet*, to 1612, when Heywood wrote. It is interesting, also, to observe that the story of *Friar Francis*, the play which produced the incident related in the early *Hamlet*, is itself related to the story of Hamlet by means of the ghost of the murdered man.

The induction to the *Warning* is notable also in that it contains what is apparently a fling at Shakspere's *Richard III*, *Henry V*, *Macbeth* and *Hamlet*, in Comedy's speech beginning— 'How some damned tyrant to obtain a crown'—It may cause surprise that such open mockery of the method, if not of the very plays, of Shakspere should have been allowed on his own stage. Perhaps it testifies to the large-heartedness of the man, who was tolerant of criticism because he felt how little it touched him. If we could be sure that Jonson's prologue to *Every man in his humour* was ever pronounced on the boards of Shakspere's theatre, it would be another case in point. But that prologue is not in the original quartos of the play. A second supposition is that in 1599 Shakspere was travelling, perhaps in Scotland, and that in his absence he was considered to be fair game. Anyhow, for one reason or another, there can be little doubt that in the induction to the following play a fling at the great Dramatist, on whose shoulders the fortunes of the Lord Chamberlain's men chiefly rested, was permitted to be pronounced at his own theatre and by his fellow-actors.

ACCOUNT OF THE MURDER OF MR SANDERS FROM STOWE,

CHRON. A.D. 1573, p. 674 (ed. Howes, 1615).

"THE 25 of March, being Wednesday in Easter week, and the feast of the Annunciation of our Lady, George Browne cruelly murdered two honest men near unto Shooters Hill in Kent, the one of them was a wealthy merchant of London named George Sanders, the other John Beane of Woolwich; which murder was committed in manner as followeth.

On Tuesday in Easter week (the four and twentieth of March) the said George Browne receiving secret intelligence by letter from Mistress Anne Drury that Master Sanders should lodge the same night at the house of one Master Barnes in Woolwich, and from thence go on foot to St. Mary Cray the next morning, lay in wait for him by the way, a little from Shooters hill, and there slew both him and John Beane, servant to Master Barnes: but John Beane having 10 or 11 wounds, and being left for dead, by Gods providence revived again, and creeping away on all four, was found by an old man and his maiden, and conveyed to Woolwich, where he gave evident marks of the murderer.

Immediately upon the deed doing Browne sent Mistress Drury word thereof by Roger Clement (among them called trusty Roger) he himself repaired forthwith to the Court at Greenwich, and anon after him came thither the report of the murder also. Then departed he thence unto London, and came to the house of Mistress Drury, where though he spake not personally with her, after conference had with her servant trusty Roger, she provided him twenty pounds that same day, for the which she laid certain plate of her own and of Mistress Sanders to gage. On the next morrow, being Thursday (having intelligence that Browne was sought for) they sent him six pounds more by the same Roger, warning him to shift for himself by flight, which thing he foreslowed not to do: nevertheless the Lords of the Queens majesty's council caused so speedy and narrow search to be made for him that upon the eight and twentieth of the same month he was apprehended in a mans house of his own name at Rochester, and being brought back again to the Court was examined by the Council, to whom he confessed the deed as you have heard, and that he had oftentimes before pretended and sought to do the same, by the instigation of the said Mistress Drury, who had promised to make a marriage between him and Mistress Sanders (whom he seemed to love excessively) nevertheless he protested (though untruly) that Mistress Sanders was not privy nor consenting thereunto. Upon his confession he was arraigned at the Kings Bench in Westminster Hall the 18 of April, where he acknowledged himself guilty, and was condemned as principal of the murder, according to which sentence he had judgment, and was executed in Smithfield on Monday the 20 of April, at which time also untruly (as she herself confessed afterward) he laboured by all means to clear Mistress Sanders of committing evil of her body with him, as also of procuring or consenting to the murder of her husband, and then beginning to sing a psalm, O Lord turn not away thy face &c., he flung himself besides the ladder, and so shortened his own life; he was after hanged up in chains near unto the place where he had done the fact.

In the mean time Mistress Drury and her man being examined, as well by their own confessions as by falling out of the matter (and also by Brownes appeachment thought culpable) were committed to ward. And after Mistress Sanders being delivered of Child and churched (for at the time of her husbands death she looked presently to lie down) was upon Mistress Drury's mans confession and other great likelihoods likewise committed to the Tower, and on Wednesday the sixt of May arraigned with Mistress Drury at the Guildhall, the effect of whose indictment was, that they by a letter written had been procurers of the said murder, and knowing the murder done had by money and otherwise relieved the murderer. Whereunto they pleaded not guilty, howbeit they were both condemned as accessaries to Master Sanders death and executed in Smithfield the 13 of May, being Wednesday in Whitsun week, at which time they both confessed themselves guilty of the fact. Trustie Roger Mistress Drurys man was arraigned on Friday the 8 of May, and being there condemned as accessary, was executed with his Mistress at the time and place aforesaid. Not long after, Anthony Browne, brother to the forenamed George Browne was for notable felonies conveyed from Newgate to York, and there hanged."

OTHER ACCOUNTS.

THERE were probably ballads on the subject, but as the Stationers' register for the years 1571—1575 is lost, we are without the means of knowing what they were.

There is a book—

A briefe discourse

of the late murther of master George Saunders a worshipfull Citizen of London : and of the apprehension, arreignement, and execution of the principall & accessaries of the same.

¶ *Imprinted at London by* Henry Bynneman, *dwelling in Knightrider Streete, at the Signe of the Mermayde.* Anno 1573.

[Press Mark in Lambeth Library, 29. 9. 28.]

INTRODUCTION.

FOrasmuch as the late murther of Master Saunders, Citizen and Merchant taylor of this citie, ministreth great occasion of talk among al sorts of men, not onelie here in the Towne, but also farre abrode in the Countrie, and generally through the whole Realme: and the sequeles and accidents ensewing thereupon, breede muche diversitie of reports and opinions, while some do justly detest the horriblenesse of the ungratious facte, some lamente the greevous losse of their deare friends, some rejoice at the commendable execution of upright justice, the godlye bewayle the unmeasurable inclination of humane nature to extreame wickednesse, and therewith magnifie Gods infinite mercie in revoking of folorne sinners to finall repentance, many delight to heare and tell newes, without respect of the certentie of the truth, or regarde of dewe humanitie, every man debating of the matter as occasion or affection leades him, and few folke turning the advised consideration of God's open judgements, to the speedie reformation of their owne secrete faults: It is thought convenient (gentle reader) to give thee a playne declaration of the whole matter, according as the same is come to light by open triall of Justice, and voluntarie confession of the parties, that thou mayst knowe the truth to the satisfying of thy mind, and the avoyding of miscredite, and also use the example to the amendment of thy life. Notwithstanding thou shalt not look for a full discoverie of every particuler bymatter appendant to the presente case, whiche might serve to feede the fond humor of such curious appetites as are more inquisitive of other folkes offences than hastie to redresse their owne; for that were neyther expedient nor necessarie. And mens misdoings are to be prosecuted no further with open detestation, than till the parties be eyther reclaymed by reasonable and godly perswasion, or punished by orderly and lawfull execution, according to the qualitie of their offence. When lawe hath once passed upon them, and given them the wages of their wicked deserts; then christian charitie willeth men eyther to burie the faults with the offendours in perpetuall silence, or else so to speak of them, as the vices and not the parties themselves may seeme to be any more touched.

But hereof shall more be spoken (God willing) in the winding up of this matter. Nowe I will set downe, first the murthering of master Saunders by George Brown, with Browne's apprehension, triall and execution; then the trial and execution of Anne Saunders, the wife of the said George Saunders, of Anne Drewrie, Widowe, and of Roger Clement, called among them trustye Roger, the servant of the said Anne Dreurie; And lastlye a briefe rehearsall of certaine sayings and dealings of the parties convicted, betwene the tyme of their apprehensions and the tyme of their execution, whiche are not things propre and peculiar to the very bodie of the case, but yet incident, and therfore necessarie for the hearer, as wherby will appeare the verie originall cause, and first grounde of this ungodlye deede: And this rehearsall shall be shutte up and concluded with a horte Admonition howe we ought to deale in this and al other such cases.

The Tuisdaye in Easter weeke last past (which was the xxiiij day of March) the sayde George Browne receyving secrete intelligence by letter from mistresse Drewrie that master Saunders shoulde lodge the same nighte at the house of one Master Barnes in Woolwich and from thence go on foote to Sainte Marie Cray the nexte morning, met him by the way a little from Shooters hill, betwene seven and eight of the clocke in the forenoone, and there slew both him, and also one John Beane the servant of the said Master Barnes

Assoone as master Saunders felt himself to have his deathes wounde (for hee was striken quite and cleane through at the first blowe) he kneeled downe, and lifting up his handes and eyes unto heaven, sayd, God have mercie on mee, and forgive me my sinnes, and thee too, (speaking to Browne, whom in deede he knewe not, whatsoever report hath been made of former acquayntance betwixte them) and with that worde he gave up the Ghost. And Browne (as he himselfe confessed afterward) was thereat striken with suche a terrour and agonie of hart, as he wist not what to doo, but was at the point to have fainted even then and oftentimes else that day, and coulde brooke nother meate nor drinke that he receyved of all that day after. He was so abashed afterward at the sight of one of master Saunders little yoong children, as he had much adoo to forbeare from swownding in the street, a notable example of the secret working of Gods terrible wrath in a guiltie and bluddie conscience. But M. Barnesis man having ten or eleven deadly wounds, and being left for dead, did by Gods woonderfull providence revyve againe, and creeping a great waye on all foure, (fore hee could nother go nor stande) was found by an old man and his mayden that went that way to seeke their kine, and conveyed too Woolwich, when he gave evident tokens and markes of the murtherer, and so continewing still alive till he had bin apprehended and brought unto him, dyed the next Munday after. Immediatly upon the deede doing, Browne sent mistresse Drewrie woorde thereof by trustie Roger, he himself repayred forthwith to the Court at Greenwich, and anone after him came thither the report of the murther also. Then departed he thence unto London streightwayes, and came to the house of Mistresse Drewrie, howbeit he spake not personally with hir. But after conference had with him, by hir servant Roger, she provided him xx pounds the same day, for the which mistress Drewry layde certaine plate of hir owne and of mistresse Saunders to gage. And upon the next day beeing Thursday morning (havyng in the meane tyme had intelligence that Brown was sought for) they sent him sixe pounds more by the sayde Roger, and warned him to shifte for himselfe by flight, which he forslowed not to do. Neverthelesse the Lordes of the Queenes Majesties Counsell, caused so speedie and narow searche to be made for hym in all places, that upon the 28 of the same moneth he was apprehended in a mans house of his own name at Rochester, by the Mayor of the towne: and beeing broughte backe again to the Courte, was examined by the Counsell, unto whom he confessed the deede, as you have hearde, and that he had oftentymes before pretended and soughte to do the same, by the instigation of the said widowe Drewrie, who (as he says) had promised to make a mariage between him and mistresse Saunders, (whome he seemed to love excessively) the desire of which hope hasted him forwarde to dispatche the fact.

Nevertheles he protested, (howbeit untruly) y^t mistres Saunders was not privie nor consenting therunto. Upon this confession he was arreigned at ye Kings Bench in Westminster Hal on friday ye xvii of April, wher acknowledging himself guiltie, he was cōdemned as principall of the murther of Master Saunders, according to whiche sentence he was executed in Smithfield on monday the xx of the same moneth, at which tyme (thoughe untruely, as she hirself confessed afterwarde) he laboured by all meanes to clear mistress Saunders of committing evil of hir bodie with him: and afterward was hanged up in chaynes neare unto the place, where he hadde doone the facte.

Thus much concerning the very case of the murther itselfe, and

INTRODUCTION.

the punishment of the principall doer therof. As for the acknowledgement of the former wickednesse of his life, and the heartie repentance that he pretended for the same, even to his very death, I deferre them to the last part of this matter, to which place those things do more peculiarly pertain. In the mean time Mistress Drewrie and hir man beeing examined, and as well by their own confessions, as by the falling out of the matter in consequence, and also by Brownes appeachment, thought culpable, were committed to warde. And anone after Mistresse Saunders beeing delivered of childe & churched (for at the time of her husband's death she looked presently to lye downe) was upon Mistresse Drewries mans confession, and upon other great likelyhoodes and presumptions likewise committed to warde, and on Wednesday, the sixth of May, arreigned with Mistresse Dreurie at the Guildehall, the effecte of whose severall inditements is this: That they had by a letter written, been procurers of the sayd murther, and so accessaries before the fact: And knowing the murther done, had by money and otherwise, relieved and been ayding to the murtherer, and so accessaries also after the facte. Whereunto they both of them pleaded not giltie. And Mistresse Saunders, notwithstanding the avouchement of Mistresse Drewries man face to face, and the great probabilities of the evidence given in against hir by master Geffry the Queenes majesties Serjeant, stood so stoutly stil to the deniall of all things (in which stoute deniall she continued also a certain tyme after hyr condemnation) that some were brought in a blinde beliefe, that either she was not giltie at all, or else had but brought hir selfe in danger of lawe through ignorance, and not through pretenced malice. Howbeit forasmuch as bare deniall is no sufficient barre to discharge manifest matter, and apparent evidence: they were both condemned as accessaries to master Saunder's death, and executed in Smithfield the thirteenth of May, beeing the Wednesday in the Whitsonweeke, at whiche time they both of them, confessed themselves guiltie of the facte, for which they were condemned, and with very greate repentaunce and meakenesse, receyved the rewarde of their trespasse, in the presence of many personages of honor and worship, and of so great a number of people, as the like hathe not bene seene there togither in any mans remembraunce. For almoste the whole fielde, and all the way from Newgate, was as full of folke as coulde well stande one by another: and besides that, great companies were placed bothe in the chambers neere abouts (whose windowes & walles were in many places beaten down to looke out at) and also upon the gutters, sides, and toppes of the houses, and upon the battlements and steeple of S. Bartholmewes.

Mistresse Drewries man was arreigned at Newgate on Friday the viii of Maye, and beeing there condemned as accessarie, was executed with his mistresse, at the time and place aforesayd.

Thus have ye heard the murthering of master Saunders, with the apprehension, arreignement, condemnation, and execution of the principall and of the accessaries to the same. Now let us proceede to the incidents that hapned from the times of their apprehensions to the time of their deathes, and so to the admonition, which is the conclusion and fruite of this whole matter.

Whereas it was determined that mistresse Saunders & mistresse Drewrie should have suffered upon the nexte Saterday after their condemnation, whiche was Whitson even; the matter was stayde till the Wednesday in Whitson weeke, upon these occasions ensuing. The booke of maister Saunders accomptes and reckenings, wherupon depended the knowlege of his whole state, was myssing.

Certaine summes of money were sayde to be in the handes of parties unknowne, the intelligence whereof was desyred and sought for to the behoofe of master Saunders children. The parties convicted were to be reformed to Godwarde, and to be broughte to the willing confessing of the things for which they had bene justly condemned, and whiche as yet they obstinatly concealed.

And besides al this, one Mell, a minister that had heretofore ben suspended from his Ministerie, accompanying mistresse Saunders from hir condemnation to Newgate, and conferring with hir, as it had bene to give hir good counsell and comforte, was so blinded wyth hir solemne asseverations and protestations of innocencie, that notwithstanding he had heard hir inditement, with the exact and substantiall triall of hir case: yet notwithstanding, he perswaded himself that she was utterly cleere, and thereuppon falling in love wyth hir, dealte with mistresse Drewrie to take the whole guilt upon hir selfe, undertaking to sue for mistresse Saunders pardon. And so what by his terrifying of hir, with the horroure of mischarging and casting away of an innocent, what with his promising of certaine money to the mariage of hir daughter, and with other perswasions: she was so wholly woone that way, that as wel before certaine personages of honour, as also before the Deane of Paules & others, she utterly cleered mistresse Saunders of the facte, or of consent to the same, taking the whole blame thereof to hir self, and protesting to stande therin to the death, contrarie to hir former confession at the tyme of hir arreignement.

Mistresse Saunders also, after the laying of this platte, stoode so stoutely to hir tackling, that when the Deane of Paules gave hir godly exhortation for the clearing of hir conscience, and for the reconciling of hir self unto God, as the time and case most needefully

required, (as other had done before) he coulde obtayne nothing at
hir hande. By meanes whereof, he was fayne to leave hir that
time, which was the Friday, not without great griefe and indignation of mind to see hir stubborne unrepentauntnesse. In the
meane while, the sayd Mell discovering his purpose, and whole
platforme to an honest Gentleman, whom he unskilfully toke to
have bin a welwiller to obtayne the pardon of mistresse Saunders,
was partly by that meanes, and also by other follies of his owne,
cut off from his enterprise. For when he came to sue for hir pardon, which thing he did with such outrage of doting affection, that
he not only proffered summes of money, but also offered his owne,
body and life for the safety of the woman, whom he protested upon
his conscience to be unguilty. The Lordes of the Counsell, knowing
hir to be rightly condemned by good justice, and being privie to
the state of the case beforehand, and also finding him out by his
owne unwise dealings (whereof among other one was, that he intended to marie hir) not only frustrated his desire, but also adjudged
him to stand upon the pillorie, with apparant notes and significa-
tions of his lewde and foolishe demeanour. According to the
which appointment, he was set upon a pillorie by the place of
execution at the tyme of theyr suffering, with a paper pinned upon
hys breast, wherein were written certain wordes in great Letters
conteyning the effecte of his fact, to his open shame : videlicet,
For practising to colour the detestable factes of George Saunders wife
Which was a very good lesson to teache all persons to refrayne from
any devises or practises to deface or discredite the honorable pro-
ceedings of Counsellours, and publike and lawfull forme of trialles
and judgementes according to Justice, or to hinder the beneficiall
course of so good examples.

By this occasion Mistresse Sanders was utterly unprovided to die at that time, and therfore as well in respect of mercie, as for the considerations aforesaid, a further respite was given to them unwitting, and a reprivie was sent by M. Mackwilliams for a time if neede were. In the meane time, (that is to wit upon the saturday morning) the constant reporte goeth, that as certaine men came talking through Newgate, one happened to speake lowde of the gallowes that was set up, and of the greatnesse and strongnes of the same, saying it would hold them both and moe, the sounde of which wordes did so pierce into the watchfull eares of mistresse Saunders, who lay neare hand, that being striken to the heart with the horror of the present death which she loked for that day, she went immediatly to mistresse Drewrie, and telling hir that she knew certainly by the wordes which she had heard, that they should by all likelihode be executed that day, asked hir if she would stand to hir former promise. But mistresse Drewrie after better consideration of hirself, counselling hir to fall to playne and simple dealing: telling hir, that for hir owne parte she was fully determined not to dissemble any longer, nor to hazarde hir owne soule eternally for the safetie of another bodies temporall life. Then mistresse Saunders, who had determined to acknowledge nothing against hir selfe, so long as she might bee in any hope of life; howbeit that she always purposed to utter the truth, whensoever she should come to the instant of death, as she hir self confessed afterward; being striken both with feare and remorse, did by the advice of master Cole, (who laboured very earnestly with hir to bring hir to repentance, and was come to hir verye early that morning, because it was thought they should have bene executed presently) send for the Deane of Paules agayne, and bewayling her former stubburnes, declared unto him and master Cole, master Charke, and master Yong, that shee had given hir consent and procurement to hir husbands death, through unlawfull lust and liking that she had to Brown, confessing hir sinfulnesse of life committed with him: and humbly submitting hirselfe to her deserved punishment, besought them of spirituall comfort and councell, which thing they were glad to perceyve, and thereupon employed their travell to do them good: and laboured very painfully to instruct them aright: for (God wote) they founde all the three prisoners very rawe and ignorant in all things perteyning to God and to their soule health, yea and even in the very principles of the Christen religion. Neverthelesse through Gods good working with their labour, they recovered them out of Sathans kingdome unto Christ, insomuch that besides their voluntary acknowledging of their late heinous fact, they also detested the former sinfulnesse of their life, and willingly yelded to the death which they had shunned, uttering such certaine tokens of their unfayned repentance, by all kinde of modestie and meekenesse, as no greater could be devised., For Mistresse Saunders the same day sent for hir husbands brothers and their wives and kinsfolke that were in the towne, whiche came unto hir the day before hir death: in whose presence she kneeling mildely on hir knees, with abundance of sorrowful teares, desired them of forgivenesse for bereving them of their deare brother and friende: whereunto Master Saunders the Lawyer in the name of them al answered, that as they were very sorie both for the losse of theyr friend, and also for hir heinous fault, so they heartily forgave hir, and, in token thereof kneeled downe altogyther, praying to GOD wyth hir and for hir, that hee also woulde remitte hir sinne.

Besides this pitiful submission, she also bewayled hir offence towardes hir owne kinred, whome she had stayned by hir trespas, and towardes the whole worlde, whom she had offended by hir crime, but especially hir children, whome she had not onely berefte bothe of father and mother, but also lefte them a coarsie and shame. Wherfore, after exhortation given to such of them as were of any capacitie and discretion, that they shoulde feare God, and learne by hir fall to avoyde sinne, she gave eche of those a booke of maister Bradfordes meditations, wherin she desired the foresayd three preachers to write some admonition as they thought good. Whiche done, she subscribed them with these wordes, *Youre sorowfull mother Anne Saunders;* And so blessing them in the name of God and of our Saviour Jesus Christ, she sent them away out of hir sorrowfull sight, and gave hirselfe wholly to the settling of hir grieved heart, to the quiet receiving of the bitter cup, which she dranke of the next day, as hath bene tolde before. Howbeit, without doubt, to hir everlasting comforte.

And mistresse Drewrie, no lesse carefull of hir owne state, besides hir humble repentance in the prison, and hir earnest desiring of the people to pray for hir selfe, and the others with hir as they came toward execution, did upon the Carte not onely confesse hir giltinesse of the facte, as mistresse Saunders had don, but also with great lowlinesse and reverence, first kneeling downe towards the Earle of Bedforde and other noble men that were on horssbacke on the East side of the stage, tooke it upon hir death that whereas it had bin reported of hir that she had poysoned hir late husbande Master Drewrie, and dealt with witchcraft and sorcerie, and also appeached divers merchante mens wives of dissolute and unchast living, she had done none of all those things, but was utterlie cleare bothe to God and the worlde of all such manner of dealing. And then with like obeysance, turning hir self to the Earle of Darbie, who was in a chamber behind hir, she protested unto him before God, that whereas she had bene reported to have bene the cause of separation betwixte him and my Lady his wyfe; she neither procured nor consented to any suche thing. But otherwise, wheras in the time of hir service in his house, she had offended him, in neglecting or contemning hir duetie, she acknowledged hir fault, and besoughte him for Gods sake to forgive hir: who very honorably, and even with teares accepted hir submission, and openly protested himselfe to pray hartily to God for hir.

Hir servant also, having openly acknowledged his offence, kneeled meekly downe, praying severally with a preacher, as eche of them had done at their first comming to the place. Which done they were all put in a readinesse by the Executioner, and at one instant (by drawing away the Cart wheron they stoode) were sent togither out of this worlde unto God.

And Browne also, a good while afore, during the time of his imprisonment, comming to a better minde than he had bene of in time paste, confessed that he had not heeretofore frequented sermons, nor received the holy sacrament, nor used any calling upon God private or publike, nor given him self to reading of holy Scripture, or any bookes of godlynesse: but had altogither followed the appetites and lustes of his sinfull flesh, even with greedinesse and outragious contempt both of God and man. Neverthelesse God was so good unto him, and schooled him so well in that short time of imprisonment, as he cloased up his life with a marvellous apparance of heartie repentance, constant trust in Gods mercy through Jesus Christ, and willingnesse to forsake this miserable worlde.

Now remayneth to shewe what is to be gathered of this terrible example, and how we oughte to apply the same to our owne behoofe. First I note with S. Paule, that when men regarde not to knowe God, or not to honour him when they know him; God giveth them over to their own lustes, so as they runne on from sinne to sinne, and from mischiefe to mischiefe, to do suche things as are shamefull and odious, even in the sight of the worlde, to their owne unavoydable perils. And when the measure of their iniquitie is filled up, there is no way for them to escape the justice of God, which they have provoked. Insomuch that if they might eschue all bodily punishment, yet the very hell of their owne conscience would prosecute them, and the sting of their minde would be a continuall prison, torment and torture to them, wheresover they went. Agayne on the other side we must marke the infinite greatnesse of Gods wisdome and mercy, who perceyving the perverse wilfulnesse of mans frowarde nature to sinning, suffreth men sometimes to runne so long upon the bridle, till it seeme to themselves, that they may safely do what they liste, and to the worlde, that they be past recoverie unto goodnesse: and yet in the end catching them in their chiefe pride, he rayseth them by their overthrow, amendeth them by their wickednesse, and reviveth them by their death, in such wise blotting out the stayne of their former filthe, that their darknesse is turned into light, and their terrour to their comfort. Moreover, when God bringeth such matters upon the stage, unto ye open face of the world, it is not to the intent that men should gaze and wonder at the persons, as byrdes do at an Owle, not that they should delight themselves & others with the fond and peradventure sinister reporting of them, nor upbrayd the whole stocke and kinred with the fault of the offenders: no surely, God meaneth no such thing. His purpose is that the execution of his judgements, should by the terrour of the outward sight of the example, drive us to the inward consideration of ourselves. Beholde, wee bee all made of the same moulde, printed with the same stampe, and indued with the same nature that the offenders are. We be the impes of the old Adam, and the venim of sinne whiche he received from the olde serpent, is shedde into us all, and woorketh effectually in us all. Suche as the roote is, such are the braunches, and the twiggs of a thorne or bramble can beare no grapes. That we stande it is the benefite of Gods grace, and not the goodnesse of our nature, nor the strengthe of oure owne will. That they are falne, it was of frayltie: wherfrom we be no more priviledged than they: and that shoulde we oversoone perceive by experience, if we wer left to our selves. He that looketh severely into other mennes faultes, is lightly blynd in his owne: and he that either upbraydeth the repentant that hath receyved punishment, or reprocheth the kinred or ofspring with the fault of the auncestor or alye, how greate so ever the same hath ben; sheweth himselfe not to have any remorse of his owne sinnes, nor to remember that he himselfe also is a man: but (which thyng he woulde little thinke) he fully matcheth the crime of the misdoer, if he do not surmount it by his presumptuousnesse.

When it was tolde oure Saviour Chryst that Pylate had mingled the blood of certain men with their owne sacrifise, what answere made hee? Did he detest the offenders? did he declame against their dooings? Did he exaggerate the fault of the one, or the crueltie of the other? No. But framing and applying the example too the reformation of the hearer, suppose ye (sayd he) that those Galileans wer greater sinners than all the other Galileans, bycause they suffered such punishment? I tell you nay: but except ye repente, ye shall all likewise perish. Or think ye that those eightene upon whom the toure in Silo fell, and slew them, were sinners above all y^t dwelt in Hierusalem? I tel you nay: but except ye repent, ye shall all perishe likewise. Let us applie this to our presente purpose. Were those whom we saw justly executed in Smithfield greater sinners than al other English people? were they greater sinners than all Londoners? Were they greater sinners than all that looked upon them? No verily: but except their example leade us to repentance, we shall all of us come to as sore punishment in this worlde, or else to sorer in the worlde to come. Their faults came into the open Theater, & therefore seemed the greater to our eyes, and surely they were great in deede: neyther are ours the lesse, bicause they lye hidden in the covert of oure hearte. God the searcher of all secrets seeth them, and if he list he can also discover them. He hath shewed in some, what al of us deserve, to provoke us al to repentance, that al of us might have mercie at his hand, and shewe mercie one to an other, & with one mouthe, and one hearte glorifie his goodnesse. It is sayde by the Prophete Samuel, that disobedience is as the sinne of Witchcrafte. Lette every of us looke into himselfe (but first lette him put on the spectacles of Gods lawe, and carie the lighte of Gods worde with him) and he shall see suche a gulfe of disobedience in himselfe, as he maye well thinke there is none offender but himselfe. I say not this as a cloaker of offences, that white should not be called white, & blacke, blacke; or as a patrone of misdoers, that they should not have their deserved hyre: but to represse our hastie judgementes and uncharitable speeches, that we myght both detest wickednesse with perfect hatred, and rue the persons with christen modestie:

knowing that with what measure we met unto others, with the same shall it be moten to us agayne.

Finally, let al folkes both maried & unmaried, learne hereby to possesse & keepe their vessell in honestie and cleannesse. For if the knot betwene man and wife (whiche ought to be inseparable) be once broken, it is seldome or never knit again. And though it be, yet is not the wound so thoroughly healed, but there appeereth some skarre ever after. But if the sore rancle & fester inwardly (as commonly it doth except the more grace of God be) in the end it bursteth forth to the destruction or hurt of both parties, not lightly without great harme to others also besides themselves, as we see by this example. For when the body which was dedicated to God to be his temple and the tabernacle of his holy spirite is become the sinke of sinne & cage of uncleannesse, the divill ceasseth not to drive the parties still headlong unto naughtinesse, till they be falne eyther into open shame and daunger of temporall law: or into damnable destruction both of body and soule, according as Salomon in his Proverbes sayth, that the steps of a harlot leade downe unto death, and hir feete perce even unto hell. Therefore good reader, so heare and reade this present example, as the same may turne to the bettering of thy state, and not to occasion of slaunder, nor to the hurt of thine owne conscience, nor to the offence of thy Christian brethren. *Fare well.*

Anne Saunders confession as she spake it at the place of execution.

Good people, I am come hither to die the deathe, whereunto I am adjuged as worthely & as deservedly as ever died any; I had a good husband, by whom I had manie children, with whom I lived in wealth, & might have done stil, had not the devill kindled in my hearte, first the hellish firebrand of unlawfull lust & afterward a murtherous intent to procure my saide husbande to be bereved of his life, which was also by my wicked meanes accomplished, as to the world is known. And as I woulde if he coulde heare me, if it might be, prostrate upon the ground, at my husbands feete, aske mercy with plentiful teares of him, so that which I may & I oughte to doe, I aske mercye of God, I aske mercie of all men and women, of the world, whom by my deede & example I have offended: and especiallye I bewaile my husband, and aske mercie of my children whom I have bred of so good a father. I aske mercy of his kindred and frendes whom I have hurt, & of all my frends & kindred, of whom I am abashed and ashamed: as beyng of my selfe unworthy of pittie, yet I besech them all, & you all, & all the whole worlde of the same, even for Gods sake, and for our Saviour Christs sake. And I thank God with my whole hart, he hathe not suffered me to have the reigne and bridle of sinning gyven me at my will, to the daunger of my eternall damnation, but that he hath founde out my sin, and brought me to punishment in this world, by his fatherly correction, to amend, to spare, and save me in the world to come; & I beseche him graunte me his heavenly grace, that all who do behold or shall heare of my death, may by the example therof be frayed from like sinning. And I besech you all to pray for me and with me.

The Prayer whiche was said by Anne Saunders at the place of execution, the copie wherof, she delivered unto the right honourable the Earle of Bedforde.

As I doe confesse wyth great sorrow (O deare father) that I have grievously, and oftentimes sinned against heaven and against thee,

& am unworthy to be called thy daughter, so (O deare Father) I acknowledge thy mercy, thy grace & love towards me, most wretched sinner, offred me in my Lord & saviour Jesus Christe, in whom thou givest me an heart to repent. And by repentance hast put away my sinnes and throwne them into the bottome of the Sea, O deare Father encrease and continue this grace untill the ende, and in the ende. I testifie this day (O Lord my God) thy love, O Lorde, thy saving health is life everlasting, and joy without end: and bicause thou hast touched my sinfull heart with the displeasure of my sinne, and with a desire of thy kingdome, O deare Father, for thy Christes sake, as I hope thou wilt, so I beseeche thee to finish that good worke in me. Suffer me not, mercifull & loving Father, to be troubled with death when it layeth hold on me: nor with the love of life when it shall be taken away. O Lorde nowe as thou hast, so still lifte up my soule as it were with an eagles wings unto Heaven, there to beholde thee. Lorde into thy hands I commit my body, that it be not troubled in death, and my soule that it see not damnation. Come Lord Jesu come assiste me with thy holy Spirite, a weake woman in a strong battell, come Lord Jesu, come quickly save thy handmaide that putteth hir trust in thee, beholde me in Christ, receive me in christ, in whose name I pray, saying, Our Father &c.

Anne Saunders dying to the world, and living to God.

After this she also said a godly Prayer out of the Service boke which is used to be said at the hour of death.

A note of a certaine saying which Master Saunders had lefte written with his owne hand in his studie.

Christ shalbe magnified in my body whither it be [Philip. i] thorough life or else death. For Christ is too me life, death is to me advantage. These words were M. Nowels Theame which he preached at the buriall of my brother Haddon upon Thursday being ye xxv day of Januarie Anno do. 1570, Anno Reginæ Elizabeth 13. Among other things which he preached this saying of his is to be had alwayes in remembrance, that is, that we must all (when we come to pray) first accuse and condemne ourselves for our sinnes committed against God before the seat of his Justice, and then after cleave unto him by faythe in the mercy and merites of our Savioure & Redeemer Jesus Christ whereby we are assured of eternall salvation.

There is also a notice of this murder in 'Sundry strange and inhuman murders lately committed.' London, Thos Scarlet. 1591. 4° bk letter, 8 leaves. A Copy at Lambeth. And in Munday's 'View of sundry examples,' [1581] p. 79 in the [Old] Shakespeare Society's reprint of 'John a Kent & John a Cumber.' It will be noticed that Charke (or Nowell) in the above account affirms that the ministers converted Browne before his death. This contradicts not only the account in the Chronicles, but the statement at p. 224, that Browne still untruly protested the innocence of Ann Saunders when he was on the scaffold. The prayers and speeches of the tract are all more or less fictitious composed rather for the edification of the pious than to engage the belief of the critical reader.

A Warning for Faire Women.

CHARACTERS IN THE INDUCTION.

TRAGEDY, HISTORY, COMEDY.

CHARACTERS IN THE DUMB SHOWS.

TRAGEDY. *Furies*—MURTHER, LUST, CHASTITY, *and the chief actors in the drama.* JUSTICE, MERCY, DILIGENCE.

CHARACTERS IN THE DRAMA.

GEORGE SANDERS, *a Merchant.*
ANNE SANDERS, *his wife.*
MISTRESS ANNE DRURY.
TRUSTY ROGER, *her servant.*
CAPTAIN GEORGE BROWNE.
SANDERS' *little son, and two other children of his.*
SANDERS' *man.*
A Draper.
A Milliner.
A gentleman, friend to Sanders, and his apprentice.
Another gentleman, attended by a man with a torch—a waterman.
MASTER BARNES, *of Woolwich.*
JOHN BEANE, *his man.*
OLD JOHN.
JOAN, *his maid, betrothed to John Beane.*
Yeoman of the buttery.
MASTER JAMES.
HARRY, *a schoolboy.*
Four Lords.
Two messengers.
Waterman.
Page.
BROWNE, *a butcher of Rochester.*
Mayor of Rochester, Pursuivant, Sergeants.
Lord Mayor.
Lord Chief Justice.
Clerk.
Sheriff, and his officers.
ANTHONY BROWNE, *brother of George.*
A Minister.
Two carpenters, TOM PEART *and* WILL CROW.
Keeper of Newgate.
Doctor—
Halberds, attendants, officers.

A Warning for Faire Women.

THE INDUCTION.

Enter at one door HYSTORIE *with Drum and Ensigne:* TRAGEDIE *at another, in her one hand a whip, in the other hand a knife.*

  Trag. Whither away so fast? Peace with that drum!
Down with that ensign, which disturbs our stage!
Out with this luggage, with this foppery!
This brawling sheepskin is intolerable.   4
  Hist. Indeed, no marvel though we should give place
Unto a common executioner!
Room room! for God's sake let us stand away.
Oh, we shall have some doughty stuff to day.   8

        Enter COMEDIE *at the other end.*

  Trag. What, yet more cats guts? oh, this filthy sound
Stifles mine ears. More cartwheels creaking yet?
A plague upon 't. I'll cut your fiddle strings
If you stand scraping thus to anger me!   12
  Com. Gup, mistress buskins, with a whirligig! are you so touchy?
Madam Melpomene, whose mare is dead,
That you are going to take off her skin?   16

Trag. A plague upon these filthy fiddling tricks, 1(
Able to poison any noble wit.
Avoid the stage, or I will whip you hence !
  Com. Indeed thou may'st, for thou art murther's Beadle;
The common hangman unto Tyranny. 2(
But History ! what, all three met at once ?
What wonder 's towards, that we are got together ?
  Hist. My meaning was to have been here to-day,
But meeting with my lady Tragedy 24
She scolds me off:
And, Comedy, except thou canst prevail
I think she means to banish us the stage.
  Com. Tut, tut, she cannot ; she may for a day 28
Or two, perhaps, be had in some request
But once a week if we do not appear,
She shall find few that will attend her here.
  Trag. I must confess you have some sparks of wit 32
Some odd ends of old jests scrap'd up together,
To tickle shallow unjudicial ears :
Perhaps some puling passion of a lover,
But slight and childish. What is this to me ? 36
I must have passions that must move the soul ;
Make the heart heavy and throb within the bosom,
Extorting tears out of the strictest eyes—
To rack a thought, and strain it to his form, 40
Until I rap the senses from their course.
This is my office.
  Com. How some damn'd tyrant to obtain a crown
Stabs, hangs, impoisons, smothers, cutteth throats : 44

And then a Chorus, too, comes howling in
And tells us of the worrying of a cat:
Then, too[1], a filthy whining ghost,
Lapt in some foul sheet, or a leather pilch,   48
Comes screaming like a pig half stick'd,
And cries, *Vindicta!*—Revenge, Revenge!
With that a little rosin flasheth forth,
Like smoke out of a tobacco pipe, or a boy's squib.   52
Then comes in two or three [more] like to drovers,
With tailors' bodkins, stabbing one another—
Is not this trim? Is not here goodly things,
That you should be so much accounted of?   56
I would not else—

  Hist. Now, before God, thou'lt make her mad anon;
Thy jests are like a whisp unto a scold.

  Com. Why, say I could, what care I, History?   60
Then shall we have a Tragedy indeed;
Pure purple buskin, blood and murther right.

  Trag. Thus, with your loose and idle similies,
You have abused me; but I'll whip you hence: [*she whips them.*
I'll scourge and lash you both from off the stage.
Tis you have kept the Theatres so long,
Painted in play-bills upon every post,
That I am scorned of the multitude,   68
My name profan'd. But now I'll reign as Queen.
In great Apollo's name, and all the Muses,
By virtue of whose Godhead I am sent,
I charge you to begone and leave this place!   72

[1] In the original, of.

Hist. Look, Comedy, I mark'd it not till now,
The stage is hung with black, and I perceive
The auditors prepar'd for Tragedy.

Com. Nay, then, I see she shall be entertain'd. 76
These ornaments beseem not thee and me.
Then Tragedy kill them to-day with sorrow,
We'll make them laugh with mirthful jests tomorrow.

Hist. And, Tragedy, although to-day thou reign, 80
Tomorrow here I'll domineer again. [*Exeunt.*

Trag. [*turning to the people.*]
Are you both gone so soon? Why then I see
All this fair circuit here is left to me.
All you spectators, turn your cheerful eye: 84
Give entertainment unto Tragedy.
My scene is London, native and your own.
I sigh to think my subject too well known.
I am not feigned[1]. Many now in this Round 88
Once to behold me in sad tears were drown'd.
Yet what I am I will not let you know,
Until my next ensuing scene shall show.

Enter SANDERS, ANNE SANDERS, DRURY, BROWNE, ROGER *and* MASTER SANDER'S *servant.*

Sand. Gentleman, here must we take our leave 92
Thanking you for your courteous company,
And for your good discourse of Ireland,
Whereas it seems you have been resident,
By your well noting the particulars. 96

---

[1] I, the tragedy or story to be presented, am not feigned, but true.—G.

Browne. True sir, I have been there familiar,
And am no better known in London here
Than I am there, unto the better sort;
Chiefly in Dublin, where, ye heard me say, 100
Are as great feasts as this we had to-day.
　Sand. So have I heard. The land gives good increase
Of every blessing for the use of man;
And 'tis great pity the inhabitants 104
Will not be civil, nor live under law.
　Browne. As civil in the English Pale as here,
And laws obeyed, and orders duly kept;
And all the rest may one day be reduc'd. 108
　Sand. God grant it so. I pray you what's your name?
　Br. My name's George Browne.
　San. God be with ye, good master Browne.
　Br. Many farewells, master Sanders, to your self, 112
And to these Gentlewomen: Ladies, God be with you!
　Anne Sand. God be with ye, sir.
　Dru. Thanks for your company;
I like your talk of Ireland so well 116
That I could wish time had not cut it off.
I pray ye, sir, if ye come near my house,
Call, and you shall be welcome, Master Browne.
　Br. I thank ye, mistress Drury—is't not so? 120
　Dru. My name is Anne Drury.
　Sand. Widow, come, will ye go?
　Dru. I'll wait upon you, sir.
　[*Exeunt* SANDERS. ANNE SANDERS *makes a courtesy and departs,
　　　　and all the rest, saving* ROGER, *whom* BROWNE *calls.*

Browne. Heark ye, my friend. 124
Are not you servant unto Mistress Drury?
    Rog. Yes, indeed, forsooth. For fault of a better,
I have served her, man and boy, this seven years.
    Br. I pray thee do me a piece of favour, then, 128
And I'll requite it.
    Rog.   Any thing I can.
    Bro. Entreat thy mistress, when she takes her leave
Of master Sanders and his wife, to make retire
Hither again, for I will speak with her. 132
Wilt thou do 't for me?
    Rog.   Yea, sir, that I will.
Where shall she find ye?
    Br.   I'll not stir from hence.
Say I entreat her but a word or two.
She shall not stay longer than likes herself. 136
    Rog. Nay sir, for that, as you two can agree.
I'll warrant you I'll bring her to ye straight.   [*Exit* ROGER.
    Br. Straight or crooked, I must needs speak with her;
For, by this light, my heart is not my own, 140
But taken prisoner at this frolic feast,
Entangled in a net of golden wire
Which Love had slily laid in her fair looks.
O, master Sanders, th' art a happy man, 144
To have so sweet a creature to thy wife—
Whom I must win, or I must lose my life.
But if she be as modest as she seems,
Thy heart may break, George Browne, ere thou obtain. 148
This Mistress Drury must be made the mean,

What e'er it cost, to compass my desire.
And I hope well she doth so soon retire.

[Enter ROGER *and* DRURIE.

Good mistress Drury, pardon this bold part
That I have play'd upon so small acquaintance,
To send for you. Let your good nature hide
The blame of my bad nurture for this once.

Dru. I take it for a favour, master Browne,
And no offence, a man of your fair parts
Will send for me, to stead him any-way.

Rog. Sir, ye shall find my mistress as courteous a gentlewoman
as any is in London, if ye have occasion to use her.

Br. So I presume, friend. Mistress, by your leave—

[take her aside

I would not that your man should hear our speech,
For it concerns me much it be concealed.

Dr. I hope it is no treason you will speak.

Br. No, by my faith, nor felony.

Dr. Nay, then,
Though my man Roger hear it, never care.
If it be love, or secrets due to that,
Roger is trusty, I dare pawn my life,
As any fellow within London walls.
But if you have some secret malady
That craves my help, to use my surgery,
Which, though I say 't, is pretty—he shall hence.
If not, be bold to speak, there 's no offence.

Br. I have no sore; but a new inward grief
Which by your physic may find some relief.

Dr. What, is 't a surfeit?
Br.   Aye, at this late feast.   176
Dr. Why *Aqua cælestis*, or the water of balm,
Or *Rosa solis*, or that of Doctor Steevens
Will help a surfeit. Now I remember me,
Mistress Sanders hath a sovereign thing   180
To help a sudden surfeit presently.
Br. I think she have. How shall I compass it?
Dr. I'll send my man for some on 't.
Br.   Pray ye, stay.
She 'll never send that which will do me good.   184
Dr. O say not so, for then ye know her not.
Br. I would I did so well as I could wish.   [*Aside*
Dr. She 's even as courteous a gentlewoman, sir,
As kind a peate as London can afford.   188
Not send it, quotha? yes, and bring 't herself,
If need require. A poor woman t' other day,
Her water-bearer's wife, had surfeited,
With eating beans (ye know 'tis windy meat)   192
And the poor creature 's subject to the stone:
She went herself, and gave her but a dram;
It holp her straight; in less than half an hour
She fell unto her business till she sweat,   196
And was as well as I am now.
Br. But that which helps a woman helps not me—
A woman's help will rather do me good.
Dr. I' faith, I ha found you! Are ye such [a] one? 200
Well, Master Browne, I warrant, let you alone!
Br. But Mistress Drury, leave me not yet alone,

For if ye do I never shall alone
Obtain the company that my soul desires.
Faith, tell me one thing—Can ye not do much
With Mistress Sanders.   Are you not inward with her?

   Dr. I dare presume to do as much with her
As any woman in this city can.

   Br. What's your opinion of her honesty?

   Dr. O, very honest : Very chaste, i' faith.
I will not wrong her for a thousand pound.

   Br. Then all your physic can not cure my wound.

   Dr. Your wound is love.   Is that your surfeit, sir?

   Br. Yea, and 'tis cureless without help of her.

   Dr. I am very sorry that I cannot ease ye.

   Br. Well, if ye can, i' faith, I will well please ye.

   Dr. You wear a pretty turkesse there, methinks.
I would I had the fellow on 't.

   Br.   Take ye this—
Upon condition to effect my bliss.

   Dr. Pardon me that, sir: No condition!
For that grief I am no physician.
How say'st thou Roger? Am I?

   Rog. Yea, forsooth, mistress, what?   What did ye ask?

   Dr. This gentleman's in love
With Mistress Sanders, and would have me speak
In his behalf.   How say'st thou, dare I do 't,
And she so honest, wise and virtuous?

   Br. What! mean ye mistress Drury to bewray
Unto your man what I in secret spake?

   Dr. Tush, fear not you; 'tis trusty Roger this :

I use his counsel in as deep affairs.
How sayst thou, Hodge? 232

Rog. Mistress, this say I. Though Mistress Sanders be very honest, as in my conscience she is, and her husband wise and subtle, and in all Billingsgate Ward not a kinder couple, yet if you would wrong her husband, your dear friend, methinks ye have such a sweet tongue as will supple a stone, and for my life, if ye list to labour, you'll win her. Sir, stick close to my mistress. She is studying the law: and if ye be not strait-laced ye know my mind. She'll do it for ye; and I'll play my part. 240

Br. Here Mistress Drury this same ring is yours,

[*gives her a ring*

Wear 't for my sake; and if ye do me good,
Command this chain, this hand, and this heart blood.
What say ye to me? speak a cheerful word. 244

Rog. Faith Mistress, do; he's a fine gentleman:
Pity he should languish for a little love.

Dr. Yea, but thou knowest they are both my friends;
He's very wise, she very circumspect, 248
Very respective of her honest name.

Rog. If ye list you can cover as great a blame.

Dr. If I should break it, and she take it ill?

Rog. Tut, you have cunning, pray ye use your skill. 252
To her Master Browne.

Br.   What say ye to me Lady?

Dr. This I say
I cannot make a man. To cast away
So goodly a creature as yourself were sin. 256
Second my onset, for I will begin

To break the ice, that you may pass the ford.
Do your good will; you shall have my good word.
   Br. But how shall I have opportunity?   260
   Dr. That must be watch'd; but very secretly.
   Br. How? at her house?
   Dr.   There ye may not enter.
   Br. How then?
   Dr.   By some other fine adventure:
Watch when her husband goes to the Exchange.   264
She'll sit at door: to her, though she be strange;
Spare not to speak, ye can but be denied:
Women love most, by whom they are most tried.
My man shall watch, and I will watch my turn: 268
I cannot see so fair a gallant mourn.
   Br. Ye bless my soul by showing me the way!
O Mistress Drury, if I do obtain
Do but imagine how I'll quit your pain.   272
But where's her house?
   Dr.   Against St. Dunstan's Church.
   Br. St. Dunstan's in Fleet street?
   Dr.   No, near Billingsgate,
St. Dunstans in the East. That's in the West.
Be bold to speak for I will do my best.   276
   Br. Thanks, Mistress Drury. Roger, drink you that;
And as I speed expect your recompence.
   Rog. I thank ye, sir; nay, I will gage my hand,
Few women can my mistress force withstand.   280
   Dr. Sir, this is all ye have to say?
   Br. For this time mistress Drury we will part;

Win mistress Sanders, and ye win my heart!
　Dr. Hope you the best; she shall have much ado　　284
To hold her own when I begin to woo.
Come Hodge.　　　　　　　　　　　　　　　[*Exit.*
　Rog. I trust sir when my mistress has obtained your suit
You 'll suit me in a cast suit of your apparell.　　288
　Br. Cast and uncast shall trusty Roger have,
If thou be secret, and an honest knave.　　[*Exeunt omnes*

　Enter ANNE SANDERS *with her little son, and sit at her door.*

　Boy. Pray ye mother when shall we go to supper?
　Anne. Why, when your father comes from the Exchange.　292
Ye are not hungry since ye came from school?
　Boy. Not hungry mother, but I would fain eat.
　Anne. Forbear awhile until your father come:
I sit here to expect his quick return.　　296
　Boy. Mother, shall not I have new bow and shafts
Against our school go a feasting?
　Anne.　　　　　　　　Yes, if ye learn:
And against Easter new apparel too.
　Boy. You 'll lend me all your scarfs, and all your rings,　300
And buy me a white feather for my velvet cap,
Will ye mother? Yea, say; pray ye say so!
　Anne. Go, prattling boy, go bid your sister see
My closet lockt when she takes out the fruit.　　304
　Boy. I will, forsooth, and take some for my pains.　[*Exit boy.*
　Anne. Well, sir sauce, does your master teach ye that?
I pray God bless thee, th'art a very wag.

Enter BROWNE.

Br. Yonder she sits to light this obscure street,
Like a bright diamond worn in some dark place:
Or like the moon, in a black winters night,
To comfort wandering travellers in their way.
But so demure, so modest are her looks,
So chaste her eyes, so virtuous her aspect
As do repulse loves false Artillery.
Yet must I speak, though checkt with scornful way;
Desire draws on, but Reason bids me stay.
My tutress, Drury, gave me charge to speak,
And speak I must, or else my heart will break.
God save ye, Mistress Sanders! All alone?
Sit ye to take the view of passengers?

Anne. No, in good sooth, sir, I give small regard
Who comes or goes. My husband I attend,
Whose coming will be speedy from th' Exchange.

Br. A good exchange made he for single life,
That join'd in marriage with so sweet a wife.

Anne. Come ye to speak with Master Sanders, sir?

Br. Why ask ye that?

Anne. Because ye make a stay
Here at his door.

Br. I stay in courtesy,
To give you thanks for your last company.
I hope my kind salute doth not offend?

Anne. No, sir, and yet such unexpected kindness

Is like herb John in broth.
  Br.   I pray ye how is that? 332
  Anne. 'T may e'en as well be laid aside as used.
If ye have business with my husband, sir,
Y'are welcome; otherwise, I'll take my leave.
  Br. Nay, gentle mistress, let not my access 336
Be means to drive you from your door so soon:
I would be loth to prejudice your pleasure.
For my good liking at the feast conceived,
If Master Sanders shall have cause to use 340
The favour of some noble personage,
Let him employ no other but George Browne
T'effect his suit, without a recompence— 343
I speak I know not what, my tongue and heart ⎫
Are so divided through the force of love.   ⎭ [*Aside.*
  Anne. I thank ye, sir; but if he have such cause,
I hope he's not so void of friends in court
But he may speed and never trouble you: 348
Yet I will do your errand, if ye please.
  Br. E'en as 't please you. I doubt I trouble ye?
  Anne. Resolve your doubt, and trouble me no more. 351
  Br. 'T will never be; I thought as much before. [*Aside.*
God be with you Mistress
  Anne.   Fare ye well, good sir.
  Br. I'll to Nan Drury yet, and talk with her. [*Exit.*
  Anne. These errand-making [1] gallants are good men,
hat cannot pass, and see a woman sit, 356
Of any sort, alone at any door,

[1] Gad-abouts.—G.

But they will find a 'scuse to stand and prate.
Fools that they are to bite at every bait!

Enter SANDERS.

Here he comes now, whom I have lookt for long. 360
    San. How now, sweet Nan, sit'st thou here all alone?
    Anne. Better alone, than have bad company.
    San. I trust there 's none but good resorts to thee!
    Anne. There shall not, sir, if I know what they be. 364
Ye have stay'd late sir at th' Exchange to-night.
    San. Upon occasion, Nan. Is supper ready?
    Anne. An hour ago.
    San.   And what good company?
None to sup with us? Send one for Nan Drury: 368
She 'll play the wag, tell tales, and make us merry.
    Anne. I think sh' as supt, but one shall run and look.
If you[re] meat be marr'd, blame yourself, not the cook.
    San. Howere it be, we 'll take it in good part, 372
For once, and use it not. Come, let's in, sweetheart. [*Exeunt.*

Enter ANNE DRURY *and* TRUSTY ROGER *her man. To them* BROWNE.

    Dr. Roger, come hither. Was there no messenger
This day from Master Browne, to speak with me?
    Rog. Mistress, not any; and that I marvel at. 376
But I can tell you, he must come and send,
And be no niggard of his purse beside,
Or else I know how it will go with him.
He must not think to anchor where he hopes, 380

Unless you be his pilot.

Dr.   Where is that?
The fellow talks and prates he knows not what.
I be his pilot? whither? canst thou tell?
The cause he doth frequent my house, thou see'st,   384
Is for the love he bears unto my daughter.

Rog. A very good cloak, Mistress, for the rain;
And therein I must needs commend your wit.
Close dealing is the safest. By that means   388
The world will be the less suspicious:
For whilst 'tis thought he doth affect your daughter,
Who can suspect his love to Mistress Sanders?

Dr. Why now thou art as I would have thee be   392
Conceited, and of quick capacity.
Some heavy drawlatch would have been this month
(Though hourly I had instructed him)
Before he could have found my policy.   396
But, Hodge, thou art my heart's interpreter:
And be thou secret still, as thou hast been,
And doubt not but we 'll all gain by the match.
George Browne, as thou knowest, is well reckoned of;   400
A proper man, and hath good store of coin;
And Mistress Sanders, she is young and fair,
And may be tempered easily like wax;
Especially by one that is familiar with her.   404

Rog. True, mistress: nor is she the first by many,
That you have won to stoop unto the lure.
It is your trade, your living. What needs more?
Drive you the bargain, I will keep the door.   408

ACT I.] *A WARNING FOR FAIRE WOMEN.*

Dr. Trusty Roger, thou well deservest thy name!
Rog. But, Mistress, shall I tell you what I think?
Dr. Yes, Hodge, what is 't?
Rog.   If you 'll be ruled by me,
Let them pay well for what you undertake.
Be not a spokeswoman, mistress, for none of them,
But be the better for it.   Times will change,
And there 's no trusting to uncertainties.
  Dr. Dost think I will? Then beg me for a fool!
The money I will finger 'twixt them twain
Shall make my daughter such a dowry
As I will match her better than with Browne;
To some rich Attorney, or Gentleman.
Let me alone.   If they enjoy their pleasure
My sweet shall be to feed upon their treasure.
  Rog. Hold you there mistress.   Here comes Master Browne.

Enter BROWNE.

  Br. Good morrow, Mistress Drury.
  Dr.   What, Master Browne?
Now, by my faith, you are the very last man
We talkt of.   Y'are welcome, sir; how do you?
And how speed you concerning that you wot of?
  Rog. Mistress, I'll void the place, if so you please,
And give you leave in private to confer.
  Br. Whither goes Roger? call him back again.
  Dr. Come hither, sirrah.   Master Browne will have you stay.
  Br. Why, how now Roger? will you shrink from me?
Because I saw you not, do you suppose

I make no reckoning of your company? 434
What, man! Thy trust it is I build upon.
  Rog. I thank you, sir: nay, pray you be not offended,
I would be loth to seem unmannerly.
  Br. Tut, a fig's end! Thy counsel will do well, 438
And we must use thee; therefore tarry here.
I have no other secret to reveal,
But only this, that I have broke the ice,
And made an entrance to my love's pursuit. 442
Sweet Mistress Sanders, that choice argument
Of all perfection, sitting at her door
Even now I did salute. Some words there pass'd,
But nothing to the purpose; neither time 446
Nor place consorted to my mind. Beside,
Recourse of servants and of passengers
Might have been jealous of our conference;
And therefore I refrain'd all large discourse. 450
Only thus much I gather'd by her speech;
That she is affable, not coy, nor scornful,
And may be won, would you but be entreated
To be a mediator for me, and persuade her. 454
  Rog. I pray you do so, Mistress; you do know
That Master Browne's an honest gentleman,
And I dare swear will recompense you well.
  Br. If she do mistrust me, there's my purse, 458
And in the same ten angels of good gold;
And when I can but have access to her,
And am in any possibility
To win her favour, challenge of me more— 462

A hundred pound in marriage with your daughter.

   Dr. Alas! how dare I, Master Browne? Her husband
Is one that I am much beholding to;
A man both loving, bountiful, and just;   466
And to his wife, in all this city, none
More kind, more loyal-hearted, or more firm:
What sin were it to do him, then, that wrong!

   Br. O speak not of his worth, but of her praise!   470
If he be firm, she's fair; if he bountiful
She's beautiful; if he loyal, she's lovely;
If he in all the city for a man
Be the most absolute, she in all the world   474
Is for a woman the most excellent.
O, earth hath seldom such a creature seen,
Nor subject been possessed with such a love!

   Rog. Mistress, can you hear this and not be mov'd?   478
I would it lay in me to help you, sir:
I' faith you should not need so many words.

   Br. I know that; thou hast always been my friend;
And though I never see Anne Sanders more,   482
Yet for my sake drink this. And, Mistress Drury,
England I must be forced to bid farewell,
Or shortly look to hear that I am dead,
Unless I may prevail to get her love.   486

   Rog. Good mistress, leave your dumps, and speak to him:
You need not study so, 'tis no such labour.
Alas! will you see a gentleman cast away?
All is but George, I pray you let be done.   490

   Dr. Well, Master Browne, not for your money's sake

So much, as in regard I love you well,
Am I content to be your orator.
Mistress Sanders shall be certified 494
How fervently you love her, and withal,
Some other words I'll use in your behalf,
As you shall have access to her at least.
 Br. I ask no more. When will you undertake it? 498
 Dr. This day: it shall no longer be deferr'd;
And in the evening you shall know an answer.
 Br. Here, at your house?
 Dr.   Yea, here, if so you please.
 Br. No better place: I rest upon your promise. 502
So farewell, mistress Drury. Till that hour
What sweet can earth afford will not seem sour?
 Dr. He's sped i' faith: come Roger, let us go:
Ill is the wind doth no man profit blow. 506
 Rog. I shall not be the worse for it, that I know. [*Exeunt.*

    Enter MASTER SANDERS *and his man.*

 San. Sirrah, what bills of debt are due to me?
 Man. All that were due, sir, as this day are paid.
 San. You have enough then to discharge the bond 510
Of master Ashmore's fifteen hundred pound,
That must be tendered on the Exchange to night?
 Man. With that which master Bishop owes, we have.
 San. When is his time to pay?
 Man.   This afternoon. 514
 San. He's a sure man: thou need'st not doubt of him.
In any case take heed unto my credit.

I do not use, thou know'st, to break my word,
Much less my bond: I prithee look unto it;   518
And whenas Master Bishop sends his money,
Bring the whole sum. I'll be upon the Burse,
Or, if I be not, thou canst take a quittance.

  Man. What shall I say unto my mistress, Sir?   522
She bade me tell out thirty pounds e'en now
She meant to have bestowed in linen cloth.

  San. She must defer her market till to-morrow:
I know no other shift. My great affairs   526
Must not be hinder'd by such trifling wares.

  Man. She told me Sir the Draper would be here;
And George the Milliner with other things,
Which she appointed should be brought her home.   530

  San. All 's one for that; another time shall serve.
Nor is there any such necessity,
But she may very well forbear awhile.

  Man. She will not so be answered at my hand.   534
  San. Tell her I did command it should be so.   [*Exit.*
  Man. Your pleasure shall be done, sir, though, thereby,
'Tis I am like to bear the blame away.

  Enter ANNE SANDERS, MISTRESS DRURY, *and Draper and a Milliner.*

  Anne. Come near, I pray you. I do like your linen, and you shall have your price. But you, my friend. The gloves you showed me and the Italian purse are both well made, and I do like the fashion; but trust me, the perfume I am afraid will not continue; yet upon your word I'll have them too. Sirra, where is your Master?

Man. Forsooth, he's gone to th' Exchange, even now.

Anne. Have you the money ready which I call'd for?

Man. No, if it please you: my master gave me charge
I should deliver none.

 Anne. How's that, sir knave?   546
Your master charged you should deliver none!
Go to, despatch, and fetch me thirty pound,
Or I will send my fingers to your lips!

 Dr. Good fortune! Thus incensed against her husband: ⎫
I shall the better break with her for Browne.   ⎬ [*Aside.*
                          ⎭

 Man. I pray you, Mistress, pacify yourself;   552
I dare not do it.

 Anne. You dare not; and why so?

 Man. Because there's money to be paid to night   554
Upon an obligation.

 Anne. What of that?
Therefore I may not have to serve my turn?

 Man. Indeed, forsooth, there is not in the house,
As yet, sufficient to discharge that debt.   558

 Anne. 'Tis well that I must stand at your reversion;
Entreat my prentice, curtesy to my man,
And he must be purse-bearer when I need!
This was not wont to be your master's order.   562

 Dr. No, I'll be sworn of that. I never knew
But that you had at all times, Mistress Sanders,
A greater sum than that at a command.
Marry, perhaps the world may now be changed.   566

 Man. Feed not my Mistress' anger, Mistress Drury;
You do not well. Tomorrow, if she list

It is not twice so much but she may have it.
  Anne. So that my breach of credit in the while   570
Is not regarded. I have brought these men
To have their money for such necessaries
As I have bought, and they have honestly
Delivered to my hands. And now, forsooth,   574
I must be thought so bare and beggarly
As they must be put off until tomorrow.
  1. Good Mistress Sanders, trouble not yourself;
If that be all your word shall be sufficient   578
Were it for thrice the value of my ware.
  2. And trust me, Mistress, you shall do me wrong
If otherwise you do conceit of me.
Be it for a week, a fortnight, or a month,   582
Or when you will, I never would desire
Better security for all I am worth.
  Anne. I thank you for your gentleness, my friends,
But I have never used to go on credit.   586
There is two crowns betwixt you for your pains.
Sirrah, deliver them their stuff again,
And make them drink a cup of wine. Farewell.
  1. Good Mistress Sanders, let me leave the cloth: 590
I shall be chidden when I do come home.
  2. And I; therefore I pray you be persuaded.
  Anne. No, no, I will excuse you to your masters;
So, if you love me, use no more intreaty.   [*Exeunt.*
I am a woman, and in that respect .   595
Am well content my husband shall control me.
But that my man should overawe me too,

And in the sight of strangers, Mistress Drury, 598
I tell you true, does grieve me to the heart.
   Dr. Your husband was to blame, to say the troth,
That gave his servant such authority.
What signifies it, but he doth repose 602
More trust in a vild boy than in his wife?
   Anne. Nay, give me leave to think the best of him.
It was my destiny, and not his malice.
Sure I did know as well when I did rise 606
This morning, that I should be chafed ere noon
As where I stand.
   Dr.   By what, good mistress Sanders?
   An. Why by these yellow spots upon my fingers.
They never come to me but I am sure 610
To hear of anger ere I go to bed.
   Dr. 'Tis like enough. I pray you let me see.
Good sooth! they are as manifest as day.
And let me tell you, too, I see decyphered 614
Within this palm of yours, to quit that evil,
Fair signs of better fortune to ensue.
Cheer up your heart! you shortly shall be free
From all your troubles. See you this character, 618
Directly fixed to the line of life?
It signifies a dissolution.
You must be, mistress Anne, a widow shortly.
   Anne. No, God forbid! I hope you do but jest. 622
   Dr. It is most certain: You must bury George.
   Anne. Have you such knowledge then in palmestry?
   Dr. More than in surgery. Though I do make

That my profession, this is my best living.
And where I cure one sickness, or disease,
I tell a hundred fortunes in a year.
What makes my house so haunted as it is
With merchants wives, bachelors, and young maids,
But for my matchless skill in palmestry?
Lend me your hand again, I'll tell you more.
A widow, said I? Yea, and make a change,
Not for the worse, but for the better far.
A gentleman, my girl, must be the next,
A gallant fellow, one that is beloved,
Of great estates. 'Tis plainly figured here,
And this is called, the Ladder of Promotion.

   Anne. I do not wish to be promoted so.
My George is gentle and belov'd beside;
And I have e'en as good a husband of him
As any wench in London hath beside.

   Dr. True, he is good, but not too good for God.
He's kind, but can his love dispense with death?
He's wealthy, and an handsome man beside,
But will his grave be satisfied with that?
He keeps you well, who says the contrary?
Yet better's better. Now you are arrayed
After a civil manner, but the next
Shall keep you in your hood and gown of silk,
And when you stir abroad ride in your coach,
And have your dozen men all in a livery,
To wait upon you. This is somewhat like.

   Anne. Yet had I rather be as now I am;

If God were pleased that it should be so.

Dr. Aye marry, now you speak like a good Christian—
'If God were pleased.' O, but he hath decreed
It shall be otherwise; and to repine 658
Against his providence, you know 'tis sin.

Anne. Your words do make me think I know not what;
And burden me with fear as well as doubt.

Dr. Tut! I could tell ye for a need, his name 662
That is ordained to be your next husband.
But for a testimony of my former speeches
Let it suffice I find it in your hand
That you already are acquainted with him. 666
And let me see, this crooked line derived
From your ring-finger shows me, not long since
You had some speech[es] with him in the street,
Or near about your door I am sure it was. 670

Anne. I know of none more than that gentleman
That supt with us; they call him Captain Browne,
And he, I must confess, against my will,
Came to my door as I was sitting there, 674
And used some idle chat, might a been spared,
And more, I wis, than I had pleasure in.

Dr. I cannot tell—If Captain Browne it were
Then Captain Browne is he must marry you. 678
His name is George I take it; yea, 'tis so:
My rules of palmestry declare no less.

An. Tis very strange how ye should know so much.

Dr. Nay, I can make rehearsal of the words 682
Did pass betwixt you, if I were disposed;

Yet I protest I never saw the man
Since, nor before the night he supt with us.
Briefly, it is your fortune, Mistress Sanders;
And there's no remedy but you must have[1] him.
I counsel you to no immodesty:
Tis lawful, one deceased, to take another.
In the mean space I would not have you coy;
But if he come unto your house, or so,
To use him courteously; as one for whom
You were created in your birth a wife.

  An. If it be so, I must submit myself
To that which God and Destiny sets down.
But yet I can assure you, Mistress Drury,
I do not find me any way inclined
To change off new affection, nor, God willing,
Will I be false to Sanders whilst I live.
By this time he's return'd from the Exchange:
Come you shall sup with us.   [*Exit.*

  Dr.   I'll follow you.
Why this is well; I never could have found
A fitter way to compass Browne's desire,
Nor in her woman's breast kindled love's fire:
For this will hammer so within her head,
As for the new she'll wish the old were dead.
When in the neck of this I will devise
Some stratagem to close up Sanders' eyes.

[1] *Orig.*, leave him.—G.

ACT II.

Enter TRAGEDY *with a bowl of blood in her hand.*

Tr. Till now you have but sitten to behold
The fatal entrance to our bloody scene;
And by gradations seen how we have grown
Into the main stream of our tragedy. 4
All we have done hath only been in words:
But now we come unto the dismal act,
And in these sable curtains shut we up
The comic entrance to our direful play. 8
This deadly banquet is prepar'd at hand,
Where Ebon tapers are brought up from hell
To lead black Murther to this damned deed.
The ugly Screech-owl, and the night-Raven, 12
With flaggy wings, and hideous croaking noise,
Do beat the casements of this fatal house,
Whilst I do bring my dreadful furies forth
To spread the table to this bloody feast. [*They come to cover.*
[*The while they cover*]
Come forth and cover, for the time draws on.
Dispatch, I say, for now I must employ ye
To be the ushers to this damned train.
Bring forth the banquet, and that lustful wine 20
Which in pale mazors, made of dead mens skulls,
They shall carouse to their destruction.
By this they 're entered to this fatal door.

Hark! how the ghastly fearful chimes of night   24
Do ring them in: and with a doleful peal   *Here some strange*
Do fill the roof with sounds of tragedy :   *solemn   music,   like*
Dispatch, I say, and be their ushers in.   *bells, is heard within.*
The furies go the door and meet them. First the Furies enter before
  leading them, dancing a soft dance to the solemn music. Next comes
  LUST, *before* BROWNE, *leading* MISTRESS SANDERS *covered with a*
  black veil; CHASTITY *all in white pulling her back softly by the*
  arm. Then DRURY, *thrusting away* CHASTITY; ROGER *following.*
  They march about, and then sit to the table. The Furies fill wine.
  LUST *drinks to* BROWNE; *he to* MISTRESS SANDERS; *she pledgeth*
  him. LUST *embraceth her; she thrusteth* CHASTITY *from her;*
  CHASTITY *wrings her hands and departs.* DRURY *and* ROGER
  embrace one another. The Furies leap and embrace one another.
  Whilst they sit down TRAGEDY *speaks.*
Here is the Masque unto this damned murther.   28
The furies first, the devil leads the dance;
Next lawless Lust conducteth cruel Browne,
He doth seduce this poor deluded soul,
Attended by unspotted innocence,   32
As yet unguilty of her husbands death.
Next follows on that instrument of hell,
That wicked Drury, the accursed fiend
That thrusts her forward to destruction.   36
And last of all is Roger, Drury's man,
A villain expert in all treachery,
One conversant in all her damned drifts,
And a base broker in this murderous act.   40
Here they prepare them to these lustful feasts;

And here they sit, all wicked murther's guests.
     [TRAGEDY *standing to behold them awhile till*
     the show be done, again turning to the people.
Thus sin prevails! She drinks that poisoned draught,
With which base thoughts henceforth infects her soul,   44
And wins her free consent to this foul deed.
Now blood and Lust doth conquer and subdue,
And Chastity is quite abandoned.
Here enters Murther into all their hearts,   48
And doth possess them with the hellish thirst
Of guiltless blood. Now will I wake my chime,
And lay this charming rod upon their eyes,
To make them sleep in their security.   [*They sleep.*
Thus sits this poor soul, innocent of late,
Amongst these devils at this damned feast,
Won and betrayed to their detested sin,
And thus with blood their hands shall be imbrued.   56
   [MURTHER *sets down her blood, and rubs their hands.*
Thy hands shall both be touched, for they alone
Are the foul actors of this impious deed.   [*To* BROWNE.
And thine and thine: for thou didst lay this plot,
And thou didst work this damned witch devise;   [*To* DRURY *and*
Your hands are both as deep in blood as his.   ROGER.
Only thou diptst a finger in the same,
And here it is. Awake now when you will,   [*To* ANNE.
For now is the time wherein to work your ill.   64
  [*Here* BROWNE *starts up, draws his sword, and runs out.*
Thus he is gone whilst they are all secure,
Resolved to put these desperate thoughts in ure;

They follow him. And them will I attend,
Until I bring them all unto their end. 68

Enter SANDERS, *and one or two with him.*

San. You see sir, still I am a daily guest;
But with so true friends as I hold yourself
I had rather be too rude than too precise.
  Gent. Sir, this house is yours; you come but to your own; 72
And what else I call mine is wholly yours,
So much I do endear your love, sweet Master Sanders.
A light, ho, there!
  San. Well, sir, at this time I'll rather be unmannerly than cere-
    monious. 76
I'll leave you, sir, to recommend my thanks .
Unto your kind respective wife.
  Gent. Sir, for your kind patience, she 's much beholding to you;
And I beseech you remember me to Mistress Sanders. 80
  San. Sir, I thank you for her.
  Gent. Sirrah, ho! who 's within there?
  Prentice. Sir?
  Gent. Light a torch there, and wait and[1] M. Sanders home.
  San. If[2] shall not need, sir, it is light enough; 84
Let it alone.
  Gent.   Nay, I pray ye, Sir.
  San. I' faith, Sir, at this time it shall not need:
Tis very light, the streets are full of people,
And I have some occasion by the way, that may detain me. 88
  Gent. Sir, I am sorry that you go alone; 'tis somewhat late.

---

[1] Should be 'on'.—G.   [2] Probably should be 'I'.—G.

Sand. 'Tis well, sir.   God send you happy rest!

Gent. God bless you, Sir!   Passion of me, I had forgot one thing;
I am glad I thought of it before we parted:
Your patience, Sir, a little.   92

Here enters BROWNE *speaking, in casting one side of his cloak under
his arm.   While* MASTER SANDERS *and he*[1] *are in busy talk one
to the other,* BROWNE *steps to a corner.*

Browne. This way he should come, and a fitter place
The town affords not.   'Tis his nearest way;
And 'tis so late, he will not go about.
Then stand close, George, and with a lucky arm   96
Sluice out his life, the hinderer of thy love
Oh sable night, sit on the eye of heaven,
That it discern not this black deed of darkness![2]
My guilty soul, burnt with lust's hateful fire,   100
Must wade through blood t' obtain my vile desire.
Be then my coverture, thick ugly night:
The light hates me, and I do hate the light.

Sand. Good night, sir.

Gent. Good night, good master Sanders;   104
Sir, I shall see you on the Exchange to-morrow?

Sand. You shall, God willing, Sir.   Good night.

Brow. I hear him coming fair unto my stand—
Murther and death sit on my fatal hand!   108

---

[1] 'he' seems to be the 'Gent.'—G.   [2] Cf. *Macbeth*, I. v. 1, 51, *etc.*—G.

Enters a Gentleman with a man with a torch before. BROWNE *draws
to strike.*

   Gent. Who's there?
   Sand.   A friend
   Gent. Master Sanders? well met.
   Sand. Good even gentle Sir, so are you.
   Gent. Where have you been so late Sir?
   Bro. A plague upon 't, a light and company   112
E'en as I was about to do the deed.   [*Aside.*
See how the devil stumbles in the nick.
   San. Sir, here at a friend's of mine in Lumberd Street
At supper; where I promise you   116
Our cheer and entertainment was so great
That we have passed our hour.
Believe me, Sir, the evening's stolen away.
I see 'tis later than I took it for.   120
   Gent. Sirrah, turn there at the corner: since 'tis late
I will go home with master Sanders.
   Sand. No, I pray you sir, trouble not yourself,
Sir, I beseech you.   124
   Gent. Sir, pardon me: Sirrah, go on now where we are
My way lies just with yours.
   Sand. I am beholding to you.   [*Exeunt.*

BROWNE *cometh out alone.*

   Bro. Except by miracle, thou art deliver'd as was never man.
My sword unsheathed, and with the piercing steel   129
Ready to broach his bosom, and my purpose

Thwarted by some malignant enuious star!
Night, I could stab thee! I could stab myself, 132
I am so mad that he scaped my hands.
How like a fatal comet did that light
With this portentous vision fright mine eyes!
A masque of devils walk along with thee 136
And thou the torch-bearer unto them all!
Thou fatal brand, ne'er may'st thou be extinct
Till thou hast set that damned house on fire
Where he is lodged that brought thee to this place. 140
Sanders, this hand doth hold that death alone
And bears the seal of thy destruction.
[1] Some other time shall serve till thou be dead.
My fortunes yet are nere accomplished. [*Exit.*

[*Scene,* Woolwich.]

Enter MASTER BARNES *and* JOHN BEANE *his man.*

John Beane. Must I go first to Greenwich, sir? 145
Bar. What else?
Beane. I cannot go by water, for it ebbs;
The Wind's at West, and both are strong against us.
Bar. My meaning is that you shall go by land, 148
And come by water; though the tide be late,
Fail not to be at home again this night,
With answer of those letters which ye have.

---

[1] Either near, or ne'er—in one case the lines read as above; the other they run thus:

    Some other time shall serve. Till thou be dead
    My fortunes yet are ne'er accomplished.

ACT II.] *A WARNING FOR FAIRE WOMEN.* 275

This letter give to Master Cofferer. 152
If he be not at Court when ye come there,
Leave 't at his chamber in any case.
Pray Master Sanders to be here next week,
About the matter at S. Mary Cray. 156
 Beane. Methinks, sir, under your correction,
Next week is ill appointed.
 Barnes.   Why, I pray ye?
 Beane. 'Tis Easter week, and every holiday
Are Sermons at the Spittle.
 Bar.   What of that? 160
 Bean. Can Master Sanders then be spared to come?
 Bar. Well said, John fool. I hope at afternoon
A pair of oars may bring him down to Woolwich:
Tell him he must come down in any wise. 164
 Bean. What shall I bring from London?
 Bar. A fool's head.
 Bea. A calf's head 's better meat.
'Tis Maunday Thursday, sir, and every butcher
Now keeps open shop.
 Bar. Well get ye gone, and hie ye home. How now? 168
         [*Beane stumbles twice.*
What, art thou drunk, cans't thou not stand?
 Bea.   Yes, sir:
I did but stumble; God send me good luck,
I was not wont to stumble on plain ground.
 Bar. Look better to your feet then. [*Exit* BARNES.
 Bea.   Yes, for sooth. 172
And yet I do not like it. At my setting forth,

They say, it does betoken some mischance.
I fear not drowning, if the boat be good.
There is no danger in so short a cut. 176
Betwixt Blackwall and Woolwich is the worst,
And if the watermen will watch the anchors
I'll watch the catches and the hoyes myself.
Well I must go. Christ's cross, God be my speed! 180

Enter OLD JOHN *and* JOAN *his maid.*

Who comes there, a God's name? This woody way
Doth harbour many a false knave they say.

Old John. False knaves, ha? Where be they? let me see them.
Mass, as old as I am, and have little skill, I'll hamper a false knave
yet in my hedging bill. Stand! Thief or true man? 185

Joan. Master, it is John Beane.

John. Jesu! John Beane, why, whither away by land?
What make you wandering this woody way? 188
Walk ye to Greenwich, or walk ye to Cray?

Bean. To Greenwich, father John. Good morrow, good morrow.
Good morrow Joan, good morrow, sweet, to thee.

Joan. A thousand good morrows, gentle John Beane. I am glad
I met ye, for now I have my dream. I have been so troubled with
ye all this night, that I could not rest for sleeping and dreaming.
Methought you were grown taller and fairer, and that ye were in
your shirt; and methought it should not be you, and yet it was
you: and that ye were all in white, and went into a garden, and
there was the umberst sort of flowers that ever I see: and methought
you lay down upon a green bank, and I pinned gilliflowers in your
ruff, and then methought your nose bled, and as I ran to my chest

to fetch ye a handkercher, methought I stumbled and so waked. What does it betoken? 202

Bean. Nay, I cannot tell. But I like neither thy dream nor my own, for I was troubled with green meadows [1], and bulls fighting and goring one another, and one of them methought ran at me, and I ran away, that I sweat in my sleep for fear. 206

Old John. Tut, fear nothing, John Beane. Dreams are but fancies. I dream'd myself, last night, that I heard the bells of Barking as plain to our town of Woolwich as if I had lain in the steeple; and that I should be married, and to whom, trowest thou? but to the fine gentlewoman of London that was at your masters the last summer! 212

Bea. Who, Mistress Sanders? I shall see her anon, for I have an errand to her husband: Shall I tell her ye dreamed of her?

Old J. Gods forbod! no, she 'll laugh at me, and call me old fool. Art thou going to London? 216

Bea. Yea, when I have been at the Court at Greenwich. Whither go you, and your maid Joan?

Old J. To stop a gap in my fence, and to drive home a cow and a calf that is in my close at Shooters' hill foot. 220

Bea. 'Tis well done. Mass, I am merry since I met you two, I would your journey lay along with mine.

Joan. So would I with all my heart, John. Pray ye bestow a groat, or sixpence, of Carnation ribbin to tie my smock sleeves; they flap about my hands too bad; and I'll give you your money again.

Bea. That I will, i' faith. Will you have nothing, father John?

Old J. No, God-a-mercy, son John; but I would thou hadst my

---

[1] Green meadows :—So Falstaff's babbling 'of green fields' (*Hen. V.* II. iii. l. 17) may have been (in Quickly's mind) an omen of his death.—G.

Aqua vitæ bottle, to fill at the Black Bull by Battle Bridge.   228

   Bea. So would I. Well, here our ways part; you must that way, and I this.

   Old J. Why, John Beane, canst part with thy love without a kiss?

   Bea. Ye say true, father John. My business puts kissing out of my mind. Farewell, sweet Joan.   [*Kiss* JOAN.

   Joan. Farewell, sweet John: I pray ye have a care of yourself for my dream; and bless ye out of swaggerers company; and walk not too late. My master and I will pray for ye.   236

   Old J. That we will, i' faith, John Beane.

   Bea. God be with ye both. I could e'en weep to see how kind they are unto me. There's a wench! Well, if I live I'll make her amends.   [*Exeunt.*

             Enter BROWNE *and* DRURY.

   Bro. Nay, speak your conscience: Was't not strange fortune
That at the instant when my sword was drawn,
And I had thought to have nail'd him to a post,
A light should come, and so prevent my purpose?   244

   Dru. It was so, Master Browne. But let it pass;
Another time shall serve. Never give o'er
Till you have quite remov'd him out your way.

   Bro. And if I do, let me be held a coward,   248
And no more worthy to obtain her bed
Than a foul Negro to embrace a Queen.

   Dru. You need not quail for doubt of your reward.
You know already she is won to this,   252
What by my persuasion and your own suit,
That you may have her company when you will;
And she herself is thoroughly resolv'd

None but George Browne must be her second husband.

Bro. The hope of that makes me a nights to dream
Of nothing but the death of wretched Sanders,
Which I have vow'd in secret to my soul
Shall not be long before that be determin'd.
But I do marvel that our scout returns not,
Trusty Roger, whom we sent to dog him.

Dru. The knave's so careful, Master Browne, of you
As he will rather die than come again,
Before he find fit place to do the deed.

Bro. I am beholding both to you and him;
And, Mistress Drury, I'll requite your loves.

Enter ROGER.

Dru. By the mass, see where the whorson comes,
Puffing and blowing, almost out of breath.

Bro. Roger, how now, where hast thou been all day?

Rog. Where have I been? where I have had a jaunt
Able to tire a horse.

Bro.   But dost thou bring
Any good news where I may strike the stroke
Shall make thyself and me amends for all?

Rog. That gather by the circumstance. First, know
That in the morning, till 'twas nine o'clock,
I watch'd at Sanders' door till he came forth;
Then follow'd him to Cornhill, where he stay'd
An hour talking in a merchant's warehouse.
From thence he went directly to the Burse,
And there he walked another hour at least,

And I at 's heels. By this it struck eleven.
Home then he comes to dinner. By the way
He chanced to meet a gentleman of the Court, 284
With whom as he was talking, I drew near,
And at his parting from him heard him say
That in the afternoon, without all fail,
He would be with him at the Court. This done, 288
I watcht him at his door till he had din'd;
Follow'd him to Lion quay; saw him take boat,
And in a pair of oars, as soon as he,
Landed at Greenwich. Where, ever since, 292
I traced him to and fro with no less care
Than I had done before, till at the last
I heard him call unto a waterman,
And bade he should be ready, for, by six, 296
He meant to be at London back again.
With that away came I to give you notice,
That as he lands at Lion quay this evening
You might despatch him, and escape unseen. 300

   Bro. Hodge, thou hast won my heart by this day's work.

   Dru. Beshrew me, but he hath taken mighty pains.

   Bro. Roger, come hither. There 's for thee to drink;
And one day I will do thee greater good. 304

   Rog. I thank you, sir. Hodge is at your command.

   Bro. Now, Mistress Drury, if you please, go home.
'Tis much upon the hour of his return.

   Rog. Nay, I am sure he will be here straightway. 308

   Dru. Well, I will leave you, for 'tis somewhat late.
God speed your hand; and so, Master Browne, good night.

Rog. Mistress, I pray you, spare me for this once;
I'll be so bold as stay with Master Browne.

Dru. Do. And Master Browne, if you prevail,
Come to my house; I'll have a bed for you. *Exit.*]

Bro. You shall have knowledge if I chance to speed,
But I'll not lodge in London for a while,
Until the rumour shall be somewhat past.
Come, Roger, where is 't best to take our standing?

Rog. Marry, at this corner, in my mind.

Bro. I like it well, 'tis dark and somewhat close,
By reason that the houses stand so near.
Beside, if he should land at Billingsgate
Yet are we still betwixt his house and him.

Rog. You say well, Master Browne, 'tis so indeed.

Bro. Peace, then. No more words, for being spied.

Enter ANNE SANDERS *and* JOHN BEANE.

Anne. I marvel, John, thou sawst him not at court,
He hath been there ever since one o'clock.

Bea. Indeed, Mistress Sanders, I heard not of him.

Anne. Pray God that Captain Browne hath not been mov'd,
By some ill motion to endanger him!
I greatly fear it, he 's so long away. [*Aside.*
But, tell me, John, must thou needs home to-night?

Bea. Yes, of necessity; for so my Master bade.

Anne. If it be possible, I prithee stay
Until my husband come.

Bea.   I dare not, trust me;

And I doubt that I have lost my tide already.   336
    Anne. Nay, that 's not so : come I'll bring thee to the quay.
I hope we shall meet my husband by the way.
    Rog. That should be Mistress Sanders, by her tongue.
    Bro. It is my love. O how the dusky night   340
Is by her coming forth made sheen and bright!
I'll know of her why she 's abroad so late.
    Rog. Take heed, Master Browne. See where Sanders comes.
    Bro. A plague upon it! now I am prevented.   344
She being by, how can I murther him?

              Enter SANDERS.

    San. Your fare 's but eighteen pence. Here 's half a crown.
    Waterman. I thank your worship. God give ye good night.
    San. Good night, with all my heart.
    Anne.   Oh, here he is now.   348
Husband, you're welcome home. Now Jesu, man,
That you will be so late upon the water!
    San. My business, sweetheart, was such I could not choose.
    Anne. Here 's M. Barnses man hath stay'd all day   352
To speak with you—
    San. John Beane, welcome. How is 't?
How doth thy master, and all our friends at Woolwich?
    Bea. All in good health, sir, when I came thence.
    San. And what's the news, John Beane?   356
    Sla. My Master, sir, requests you, that upon Tuesday next you
would take the pains to come down to Woolwich, about the matter
you wot of.
    San. Well John, to-morrow thou shalt know my mind.   360

John. Nay, sir, I must to Woolwich by this tide.
San. What, to-night? There is no such haste, I hope.
Bea. Yes, truly, with your pardon, it must be so. 363
San. Well then, if, John, you will be gone, commend me to your Master, and tell him, without fail, on Tuesday, sometime of the day, I'll see him; and so good night.
Anne. Commend me likewise to thy master, John.
Bea. I thank you, Mistress Sanders, for my cheer. 368
Your commendations shall be delivered. [*Exit.*
Bro. I would thyself and he were both sent hence,
To do a message to the devil of hell,
For interrupting this my solemn vow. 372
But, questionless, some power, or else prayer
Of some religious friend or other, guards him:
Or else my sword's unfortunate. 'Tis so
This metal was not made to kill a man. 376
Rog. Good master Browne, fret not yourself so much:
Have you forgot what the old proverb is:—
The third time pays for all? Did you not hear
That he sent word to Master Barnes of Woolwich, 380
He would be with him as on Tuesday next?
'Twixt that and then lie you in wait for him;
And though he have escaped your hand so oft
You may be sure to pay him home at last. 384
Bro. Fury had almost made me pass myself.
'Tis well remember'd. Hodge, it so shall be.
Some place will I pick out as he does pass,
Either in going or in coming back, 388
To end his hateful life. Come, let's away

And at thy mistress' house we'll spend this night
In consultation how it may be wrought. *[Exeunt.*

Tragedy. Twice, as you see, this sad distressed man, 392
The only mark whereat foul Murther shot,
Just in the loose of envious eager death,
By accidents strange and miraculous
Escap'd the arrow aim'd at his heart. 396
Suppose him on the water now, for Woolwich,
For secret business with his bosom friend;
From thence, as fatal destiny conducts him,
To Mary-Cray, by some occasion call'd; 400
Which by false Drury's means made known to Browne,
Lust, Gain, and Murther spur'd this villain on
Still to pursue this unsuspecting soul.
And now the dreadful hour of death is come, 404
The dismal morning when the destinies
Do sheer the labouring vital thread of life,
Whenas the lambe left in the woods of Kent
Unto this ravenous woolfe becoms a pray, 408
Now of his death the generall intent
Thus Tragedie doth to your eyes present.

The Musicke playing, enters LUST, *bringing forth* BROWNE *and* ROGER, *at one ende,* Mistres SANDERS *and Mistres* DRURIE *at the other, they offering cheerefully to meete and embrace. Suddenly riseth vp a great tree betweene them. Whereat amazedly they step backe. Wherupon* LUST *bringeth an axe to Mistres* SANDERS, *shewing signes that she should cut it doune; which she refuseth, albeit Mistres* DRURIE *offers to helpe her. Then* LUST *brings the Axe to* BROWNE, *and shews the like signes to him as before. Wherupon he roughlie and suddenly hewes downe the tree, and then they run togither and embrace. With that enters* CHASTITIE, *with her haire disheveled, and taking Mistres* SANDERS *by the hand, brings her to her husbands picture hanging on the wall, and, pointing to the tree, seemes to tell her, that that is the tree so rashly cut downe. Wherevpon she, wringing her hands, in tears departes.* BROWNE, DRURIE, ROGER *and* LUST *whispering, he drawes his sword, and Roger followes him.* TRAGEDIE *expressing that now he goes to act the deed.*

LUST leades togither this adulterous route,
But, as you see, are hindred thus, before   412
They could attaine vnto their fowle desires.
The tree springs vp, whose bodie, whilest it stands,
Stil keepes them backe when they would fain embrace.
Whereat they start, for furie euermore   416
Is full repleat with feare and envie.
LUST giveth her the Axe to cut it downe,
To rid her husband whom it represents,
In which this damned woman would assist hir;   420
But though by them seduced to consent,
And had a finger in her husbands bloud,
Could not be woonne to murther him herselfe.
LUST brings the Axe to BROWNE, who suddenly   424
Doth giue the fatal stroke vnto the tree;
Which being done, they then embrace togither:
The act performde, now CHASTITIE appeares,
And pointing to the picture, and the tree,   428
Unto her guiltie conscience shewes her husband,

Even so cut off by that vile murtherer BROWNE:
She wrings her hands repenting of the fact,
Toucht with remorse, but now it is too late. 432
What's here exprest, in act is to be done.
The sword is drawne, the murtherer forth doth run:
LUST leades him on, he followes him with speede,
The onely actor in this damned deed. 436

Enter BROWNE *reading a Letter, and* ROGER.

Bro. Did I but waver, or were unresolv'd,
These lines were able to encourage me.
Sweete NAN I kist thy name, and for thy sake
What coward would not venture more than this? 440
Kil him? Yea, were his life ten thousand lives,
Not any sparke or cynder of the same
Should be vnquencht in bloud at thy request.
ROGER, thou art assurde heele come this way? 444
  Rog. Assurde, sir? why I heard him say so:
For hauing lodg'd at Wolwich al last night,
As soone as day appear'd, I got me vp,
And watcht aloofe at maister Barnses doore, 448
Til he and master Sanders both came forth.
  Bro. Til both came forth? what, are they both togither?
  Rog. No, sir; master Barnes himselfe went backe againe,
And left his man to beare him companie, 452
JOHN BEANE, you know him; he that was at London
When we laid wait for him at Billingsgate.
  Bro. Is it that stripling? wel, no more adoe.
ROGER, go thou unto the hedge corner, 456

At the hill foote: there stand and cast thine eie
Toward Greenwich parke.   See if Black Heath be cleare,
Least by some passenger we be descride.

   Roger. Shal ye not neede my help, sir? they are twaine.   460

   Brown. No; were they ten, mine arme is strong enough
Even of itselfe to buckle with them al;
And ere GEORGE SANDERS shal escape me now
I wil not recke what massacre I make.   464

   Rog. Wel, sir, Ile go and watch; and when I see
Any body comming, Ile whistle to you.

   Bro. Do so, I prethee: I would be alone,
My thoughts are studious and unsociable,   468
And so's my body, till this deede be done.
But, let me see, what time a day is't now?
It cannot be imagin'd by the sunne,
For why, I have not seene it shine to-day;   472
Yet as I gather by my comming forth,
Being then sixe, it cannot now be lesse
Than halfe an hower past seven; the aire is gloomy:
No matter, darknesse best fittes my intent.   476
Here wil I walke; and after shrowd my selfe
Within those bushes, when I see them come.

       Enter MAISTER SANDERS *and* JOHN BEANE.

   San. JOHN BEANE, this is the right way, is it not?
   Joh. I, sir, would to God we were past this wood.   480
   San. Why, art thou affraide?   See, yonder's company.
   Bro. They have espied me; I will slip aside.
   Joh. O God, sir, I am heavy at the heart!

Good Maister Sanders, let's returne backe to Wolwich, 484
Me thinkes I go this way against my wil.
  San. Why so, I prethee?
  Joh. Truly, I do not like
The man we saw; he slipt so soone away,
Behind the bushes.
  San. Trust me, John, nor I; 488
But yet, God willing, we wil keepe our way.
  Joh. I pray you, sir, let us go backe againe:
I do remember now a dreame was told me,
That, might I have the world, I cannot choose 492
But tremble every joint to thinke upon't.
  Sand. But we are men, let's not be so faint-hearted
As to affright our-selves with visions.
Come on, a God's name. 496

      [*Browne steps out and strikes up* JOHN'S *heeles.*
  John. Oh! we are vndone.
  Sand. What seeke you, sir?
  Bro. Thy bloud; which I will have.
  Sand. Oh, take my mony, and preserve my life.
  Bro. It is not millions that can ransome thee, 500
Nor this base drudge, for both of you must die.
  San. Heare me a word, you are a gentleman!
Soile not your hands with bloud of innocents.
  Bro. Thou speakest in vaine. 504
  San. Then God forgive my sinne!
Have mercie on me, and upon thee, too,
The bloudy author of my timelesse death!
  Bro. Now wil I dip my handkercher in his bloud, 508

And send it as a token to my love.
Looke how many wounds my hand hath given him:
So many holes Ile make within this cloth.
   San. Jesu, receive my soule into thy handes!
   Bro. What sound was that? It was not he that spake?
The breath is vanisht from his nostrils.
Was it the other? No, his wounds are such
As he is likewise past the use of speech.
Who was it then that thundred in mine eares
The name of Jesu? Doubtlesse 'twas my conscience:
And I am damn'd for this unhallowed deede.
O, sinne! how hast thou blinded me til now;
Promising me security and rest,
But givest me dreadful agony of soule!
What shal I do? or whither shal I fly?
The very bushes wil dis-cover me.
See how their wounds do gape unto the skies,
Calling for vengeance.
          Enter ROGER.
   Rog. How now, master Browne?
What! have you done? why so, let's away,
For I have spide come riding ore the heath
Some halfe a dozen in a company.
   Bro. Away! to London thou; Ile to the Court,
And shew my selfe, and after follow thee.
Give this to Mistris SANDERS. Bid her reade
Upon this bloudy handkercher the thing
As I did promise, and have now perform'd;—
But were it, ROGER, to be done againe,

I would not do it for a kingdomes gaine.

Rog. Tut, faint not now; come, let us haste away.

Bro. Oh! I must feare, whatever thou dost say:
My shadow, if nought else, will me betray. 540

> [*Exeunt.* BEANE, *left wounded and for dead,
> stirres and creepes.*

Beane. Dare I loke up, for feare he yet be neere,
That thus hath martirde me? Yea, the coast is cleere:
For all these deadly wounds, yet lives my heart.
Alacke, how loath poore life is from my limbes to part! 544
I cannot goe, ah no, I cannot stand:
O God! that some good body were neere hand,
To helpe me home to Wolwich ere I die;
To creep that way-ward whilst I live ile trye. 548
O could I crawle but from this cursed wood,
Before I drowne my selfe in my owne blood.

Enter OLD JOHN *and* JOANE.

Old John. Now, by my fathers saddle, *Joane*, I think we are bewitched. My beasts were never wont to breake out so often: Sure as death the harlotries are bespoken; but it is that heifer with the white backe that leades them al a gadding, a good lucke take her!

Joane. It is not dismal day, maister? did ye looke in the Amminicke? If it be not, then 'tis either long of the brended cow, that was nere wel in her wits since the butcher bought her calf; or long of my dreame; or of my nose bleeding this morning; for as I was washing my hands my nose bled three drops; then I thought of JOHN BEAN, God be with him, for I dream'd he was married,

ACT II.]   *A WARNING FOR FAIRE WOMEN.*   291

and that our white calfe was kild for his wedding dinner; God blesse them both, for I love them both well.   [*Beane creepes.*

Old John. Mary, amen, for I tel thee my heart is heavy; God send me good luck: my eyes dazel, and I could weepe. Lord blesse us! what sight is this? Looke, Jone, and crosse thy selfe.

Jone. O master, master, looke in my purse for a peece of ginger; I shall sweb, I shall swound; cut my lace, and cover my face, I die else; it is JOHN BEANE, killd, cutte, slaine! maister, and ye be a man, help!   569

Old John. JOHN BEANE? Now Gods forbod, alocke, alock! good John, how came ye in this pitteous plight? speake, good John; nay, groane not; speake! who has done this deede? thou has not fordone thy selfe, hast thou?   573

Beane. Ah no, no

Joane. Ah no, no, he neede not have done that, for God knowes I loved him as deerely as he loved me; speake, JOHN; who did it?   577

Beane. One in a white dublet and blew breeches: he has slaine another too, not farre off. O stoppe my woundes if ye can.

Old John. JOANE, take my napkin and thy apron, and bind up his wounds; and cows go where they wil til we have carried him home.   582

Joane. Wo worth him, John, that did this dismal deede; Heart-breake be his mirth, and hanging be his meede!

Old John. Ah, weladay! see where another lies, a hansome, comely, ancient gentleman: what an age live we in! when men have no mercy of men more than of dogges, bloudier than beasts! This is the deed of some swaggering, swearing, drunken, desperate Dicke. Call we them Cabbaleers? masse, they be Canniballes, that

have the stabbe readyer in their handes than a penny in their purse.
Shames death be their share! Jone, hast thou done? Come, lend
me a hand to lay this good man in some bush, from birds and from
beasts, till we carry home JOHN BEANE to his Maisters, and rayse
all Wolwich to fetch home this man, and make search: Lift there,
Jone: so, so. *They carry out* SANDERS.

Beane. Lord, comfort my soule, my body is past cure. 596

Old John. Now lets take up JOHN BEANE:
Softly, JONE, softly.

Jone. Ah, JOHN, little thought I to have carried thee thus within
this weeke; but my hope is aslope, and my joy is laide to sleepe.

[*Exeunt.*

Enter a yeoman of the Buttery, BROWNE, *and* MAYSTER JAMES.

Yeo. Welcome, maister Browne; what ist you'le drinke, ale or
beere?

Bro. Mary, ale, and if you please.
You see, sir, I am bold to trouble you.

Yeo. No trouble, sir, at all; the Queene, our Mistris, 604
Allowes this bounty to all commers, much more
To Gentlemen of your sort;—some ale there, ho!

Enter one with a Jacke and a court dish.

Yeo. Here, maister BROWNE, thus much to your health.

Bro. I thank you, sir; nay, prethee fill my cup. 608
Here, maister James, to you with all my heart.
How say you now, sir? was I not a-dry?

Yeo. Beleeve me, yes; wilt please ye mend your draught?

Bro. No more, sir, in this heate, it is not good. 612

M. James. It seemes, Maister BROWNE, that you have gone
  apace.
Came you from London that you made such haste?
But soft, what have I spide? your hose is bloudy.
  Bro. How, bloudy? where? Good-sooth, tis so indeede. 616
  Yeo. It seemes it is but newly done.
  Browne. No, more it is:
And now I do remember how it came:
Myselfe, and some two or three Gentlemen more,
Crossing the field, this morning, here, from Eltham, 620
Chaunc'd by the way to start a brace of hares,
One of the which we kild, the other 'scapt,
And pulling foorth the garbage, this befell;
But 'tis no matter; it wil out againe. 624
  Yeo. Yes, there's no doubt, with a little sope and water.
  M. James. I would I had beene with you at that sport.
  Bro. I would you had, sir, 'twas good sport indeede.
  Bro. Now, afore God, this bloud was ill espied. 628
But my excuse I hope wil serve the turne.   [*Aside.*
Gentlemen, I must to London this forenoone,
About some earnest busines doth concerne me;
Thankes for my ale, and your good companies. 632
  Both. Adieu, good maister BROWNE.
  Browne. Farewell unto you both.   [*Exit.*
  M. James. An honest proper Gentleman as lives.
God be with you, sir; Ile up into the Presence. 636
  Yeo. Y'are welcome, M. James; God be with ye, sir. [*Exeunt.*

Enter ANNE SANDERS, ANNE DREWRY, *and* ROGER: DREWRY *having the bloudy handkercher in her hand.*

Anne. Oh shew not me that ensigne of despaire,
But hide it, burne it, bury it in the earth,
It is a kalender of bloody letters, 640
Containing his, and yours, and all our shames!
   Dru. Good mistris Sanders, be not so outragious.
   Anne. What tell you me? Is not my husband slaine?
Are not we guiltie of his cruel death? 644
Oh! my deare husband, I wil follow thee!
Give me a knife, a sword, or any thing,
Wherewith I may do justice on my selfe:
Justice for murther, justice for the death 648
Of my deare husband, my betrothed love!
   Rog. These exclamations will bewray us all;
Good Mistress Sanders, peace!
   Dru.   I pray you, peace:
Your servants, or some neighbours else wil heare. 652
   Anne. Shall I feare more my servants, or the world,
Then God himselfe? He heard our trecherie,
And saw our complot and conspiracie.
Our hainous sinne cries in the eares of him, 656
Lowder then we can cry upon the earth.
A woman's sinne, a wives inconstancy:
Oh God, that I was borne to be so vile,
So monstrous and prodigious for my lust: 660
Fie on this pride of mine, this pamper'd flesh!

I will revenge me on these tising eyes,
And teare them out for being amourous.
Oh! Sanders, my deare husband! Give me leave, 664
Why do you hold me? are not my deeds ugly?
Let then my faults be written in my face.
    Dru. Oh do not offer violence to your selfe.
    Anne. Have I not done so already? Is not 668
The better part of me by me misdone?
My husband, is he not slaine? is he not dead?
But since you labour to prevent my griefe,
Ile hide me in some closet of my house, 672
And there weepe out mine eyes, or pine to death,
That have untimely stopt my husband's breath.
    Dru. What shall we doe, ROGER? go thou and watch
For master *Brownes* arrival from the Court; 676
And bring him hither, happily his presence
Wil be a meanes to drive her from this passion.
In the meane space I will go after her,
And do the best I can to comfort her. 680
    Rog. I will: take heede she do not kill her-selfe.
    Dru. For Gods sake haste thee, and be circumspect.

Enter SANDERS' YONG SONNE, *and another boy comming from schoole.*

    Yong San. Come, Harrie, shall we play a game?
    Har. At what? 684
    Yong San. Why, at crosse and pile.
    Har. You haue no Counters.
    Yong San. Yes, but I have as many as you.
    Har. Ile drop with you; and he that has most, take all. 688

Yong San. No, sir; if youle play a game, 'tis not yet twelve by halfe an houre, Ile set you like a gamster.

Har. Go to, where shall we play?

Yong San. Here, at our doore. 692

Har. What and if your father find us?

Yong San. No, hees at Woolwich, and will not come home to-night.

Har. Set me then; and here's a good. 696

Enter BROWN *and* ROGER.

Bro. Is she so out of pacience as thou saist?

Rog. Wonderfull, sir; I have not scene the like.

Bro. What does she meane by that? Nay, what meane I,
To aske the question? Has she not good cause? 700
Oh, yes; and we have every one of us just cause
To hate and be at variance with our selves.
But come; I long to see her. [*He spies the boy.*

Rog. How now, Captaine? 704
Why stop you on the sudden? why go you not?
What makes you looke so gastly towards the house?

Bro. Is not the formost of those prettie boyes
One of George Sanders sonnes? 708

Rog. Yes, 'tis is yongest.

Bro. Both yong'st and eld'st are now made fatherlesse,
By my unlucky hand. I prethee, go
And take him from the doore, the sight of him 712
Strikes such a terror to my guilty conscience,
As I have not the heart to looke that way,
Nor stirre my foote untill he be remoov'd.

Me thinkes in him I see his fathers wounds 716
Fresh bleeding in my sight; nay, he doth stand
Like to an Angel with a firy sworde,
To barre mine entrance at that fatall doore.
I prethee steppe, and take him quickly thence. 720
  Rog. Away, my prettie boy, your master comes,
And youle be taken playing in the street.
What, at unlawful games? away, be-gone.
'Tis dinner time, yong Sanders, youle be ierkt: 724
Your mother lookes for you before this time.
  Yong San. Gaffer, if you'le not tel my master of me,
Ile give you this new silke point.
  Rog. Go to, I will not. 728
  Har. Nor of me, and there's two counters: I have woonne no more.
  Rog. Of neither of you, so you wil be gone.
  Yong San. God be with you, ye shall see me no more.
  Har. Nor me; I meane playing at this doore. 732
  Rog. Now, captaine, if you please, you may come forward;
But see, where mistris SANDERS and my mistris
Are comming forth to meete you on the way?
  Dru. See where master BROWNE is, in him take comfort; 736
And learne to temper your excessive griefe.
  Anne. Ah, bid me feed on poyson and be fat;
Or looke upon the Basiliske and live;
Or surfet daily and be stil in health; 740
Or leape into the sea and not be drownde;
All these are even as possible as this,
That I should be recomforted by him
That is the authour of my whole lament. 744

Bro. Why, mistris ANNE, I love you dearly,
And but for your incomparable beauty
My soule had never dreamt of SANDERS death:
Then give me that which now I do deserve,   748
Your selfe, your love, and I will be to you
A husband so devote, as none more just,
Or more affectionate, shal treade this earth.

Anne. If you can crave it of me with a tongue   752
That hath not bin prophande with wicked vowes,
Or thinke it in a heart did never harbour
Pretence of murther, or put foorth a hand
As not contaminate with shedding bloud,   756
Then will I willingly graunt your request:
But oh! your hand, your heart, your tongue, and eye,
Are all presenters of my misery!

Bro. Talke not of that; but let us study now   760
How we may salve it, and conceale the fact.

Anne. Mountains will not suffice to cover it;
Cymerian darkenesse cannot shadow it;
Nor any pollicie wit hath in store   764
Cloake it so cunningly, but at the last,
If nothing else, yet will the very stones
That lie within the streetes cry out for vengeance,   767
And point at us to be the murderers.   [*Exeunt.*

Enter three Lords, MAISTER JAMES, *and two Messengers with their boxes, one Lord reading a letter.*

1 *Lo.* Fore God (my Lords) a very bloudy act:
                    This hath the letter.

2 Lo. Yea, and committed in eye of court,
Audatiously, as who should say, he durst
Attempt a murther in despite of Law.

3 Lo. Pray ye lets see your letter (good my Lord).
He takes and reades the letter.
Tenne wounds at least, and deadly ev'ry wound,
And yet he lives, and tels markes of the man.
Ev'n at the edge of Shooter's Hill, so neare.

1 Lo. We shal not need to send these Messengers,
For hew and cry may take the murtherers.

Enter a fourth Lord with a Water-man and a Page.

4 Lord. Nay, sirra, you shall tel this tale againe,
Before the Lords; come on: my Lords, what newes?

1 Lord. Bad newes, my Lord. A cruel murthers done,
Neere Shooters Hill, and here's a letter come
From Wolwich, from a gentleman of worth,
Noting the manner, and the marks of him,
(By likelihoode) that did that impious deede.

4 Lord. Tis noysd at London, that a marchant's slain,
One maister Sanders, dwelling neere Tames streete,
And that GEORGE BROWNE, a man whom we al know,
Is vehemently suspected for the fact,
And fled upon't, and this same Water-man,
That brought me downe, saies he row'd him up,
And that his hose were bloudy, which he hid
Stil with his hat, sitting bare-head in the boate,
And sigh'd and star'd as one that was afraide.
How saist thou, sirra, was't not so he did?

Wat. Yes, and 't please your Lordship, so it was. 796
Lord. What did he weare?
Water. A doublet of white satten,
And a large paire of breeches of blew silke.
　2 *Lord.* Was he so suted when you dranke with him, 800
Here in the buttery?
　M. Ja. Yea, my Lord, he was.
　3 *Lord.* And his hose bloudy?
　M. Ja. Just as he affirmes. 804
　3 *Lord.* Conferre the markes the wounded fellow telles with these
　　reports.
　1 *Lord.* The man that did the deede,　　　　　　　[*reades*
Was faire and fat, his doublet of white silke, 807
His hose of blew.　I am sory for GEORGE BROWNE.　[*lookes off*
Twas he, my Lords.
　4 *Lord.* The more accursed man.
Get warrants drawne: and messengers attend.
Cal al your fellowes: ride out every way: 812
Poste to the Ports: give charge that no man passe
Without our warrant.　One take boate to London;
Command the Sheriffes make wise and speedy search:
Descipher him by al the marks you can: 816
Let bloud be paid with bloud in any man.
　1 *Lord.* We were to blame els; come, my lords, let's in,
To signe our warrants, and to send them out.　　[*Exeunt omnes.*

　　　　　Enter DRURY *and* ROGER *with a bagge.*

　Dru. Roger, cans't thou get but twentie pound, 820
Of al the plate that thou hadst from us both?

Mine owne's worth twenty; what had'st thou of her?

 Rog. Two bolles and spoones: I know not what my selfe.
'Tis in a note; and I could get no more   824
But twenty pound.

 Dru.   Alas! 'twil do no good:
And he must thence, if he be tane he dies.
On his escape, thou knowest, our safety lies.

 Rog. That's true; alas, what wil ye have me do?   828

 Dru. Runne to Nan Sanders; bid her make some shift;
Try al her friends to helpe at this dead lift,
For al the mony that she can devise,
And send by thee with al the haste she may: 832
Tel her we die if Browne make any stay.

 Rog. I wil, I wil.   [*Exit* ROGER.

 Dru.   Thou wilt, thou wilt; alas,
That ere this dismal deede was brought to passe!   835
But now 'tis done, we must prevent the worst, *Enter* BROWNE
And here comes he that makes us al accurst.
How now, GEORGE BROWNE?

 Bro.   NAN DRURIE, now undone,
Undone by that, that thou hast made me doe.

 Dru. I make ye do it? your owne love made ye do it.   840

 Bro. Wel, done it is; what shal we now say too't?
Search is made for me, be I tane, I die;
And there are other as farre in as I.
I must beyond sea, money have I none,   844
Nor dare I looke for any of mine owne.

 Dru. Here's twenty pound, I borrowed of my plate,
And to your mistris I have sent for more.   *Enter* ROGER.

By Hodge, my man: Now, Roger, hast thou sped? 848
   Rog. Yea, of six pound; 'tis all that she can make;
She prayes ye tak't in worth,[1] and to be gone;
She heares the Shiriffes wil be there anone,
And at our house; a thousand commendations 852
She sends you, praying you to shift for your selfe.
   Bro. Even as I may. Roger, farewel to thee:
If I were richer, then thou should'st go with me,
But poverty partes company; farewel, Nan, 856
Commend me to my mistris, if you can.
   Dru. Step thither your selfe, I dare not come there;
Ile keep my house close, for I am in feare.
   Ro. God be with you, good Captaine.
   Browne.   Farewel, gentle Hodge.
Oh, master Sanders, wert thou now alive, 861
Al Londons wealth thy death should not contrive!
This heate of love and hasty climbing breeds,
God blesse all honest tall men from such deedes. 864

        Enter TRAGEDY *afore the shew.*

   Tragedy. Prevailing Sinne having by three degrees
Made his ascension to forbidden deedes,
As first, alluring their unwary mindes
To like what she proposde, then practising 868
To draw them to consent; and, last of all,
Ministring fit meanes and oportunity
To execute what she approved good;
Now she unvailes their sight, and lets them see 872

        [1] (?) Sterling.—G.

The horror of their foule immanity.[1]
And wrath, that al this while hath bin obscurde,
Steps forth before them in a thousand shapes
Of gastly thoughts, and loathing discontents: 876
So that the rest was promist now appeares
Unrest, and deep affliction of the soule,
Delight prooves danger, confidence dispaire,
As by this folowing shew shall more appeare. 880

Enter JUSTICE *and* MERCY, *when, having taken their seats* JUSTICE *falls into a slumber. Then enters wronged* CHASTITY, *and in dumbe action uttring her griefe to* MERCY, *is put away; whereon she wakens* JUSTICE, *who, listning her attentively, starts up, commanding his officers to attend her. Then go they with her, and fetch forth master* SANDERS *body, mistris* SANDERS, DRURY *and* ROGER, *led after it, and being shewne it, they al seeme very sorrowful, and so are led away. But* CHASTITY *shewes that the chiefe offender is not as yet taken, whereon* JUSTICE *dispatcheth his servant* DILIGENCE *to make further enquiry after the murderer, and so they depart the stage with* CHASTITY.

Tra. Thus lawles actions and prodigious crimes
Drinke not the bloud alone of them they hate,
But even their ministers, when they have done
Al that they can, must help to fil the Sceane, 884
And yeeld their guilty neckes unto the blocke.
For which intent, the wronged Chastity,
Prostrate before the sacred throne of Justice,

[1] Inhumanity.—G.

With wringing hands, and cheekes besprent with teares, 888
Pursues the murtherers. And, being heard
Of Mercy first, that in relenting wordes
Would faine perswade her to humility,
She turnes from her, and with her tender hand 892
Wakes slumbering Justice; when, her tale being told,
And the dead body brought for instance forth,
Strait inquisition and search is made,
And the offenders, as you did behold, 896
Discover'd where they thought to be unseene.
Then triall now remaines, as shall conclude,
Measure for measure, and lost bloud for bloud.

Enter GEORGE BROWNE, *and one* BROWNE, *a butcher in Rochester.*

But. 'Tis marvell, coosen BROWNE, we see you here, 900
And thus alone without all company:
You were not woont to visit Rochester,
But you had still some friend or other with you.
Bro. Such is th' occasion, coosin, at this time, 904
And, for the love I beare you, I am bold
To make my selfe your guest, rather then lie
In any publike Inne, because, indeed,
The house where I was woont to host is full 908
Of certaine Frenchmen and their followers.
But. Nay, coosin BROWNE, I would not have you thinke
I doe object thus much as one unwilling
To shew you any kindnesse that I can. 912
My house, though homely, yet such as it is,
And I myselfe will be at your commaund.

I love you for your name-sake, and trust me, sir,
Am proud that such a one as you will call me coosin,
Though I am sure we are no kin at all.

 Bro. Yes, coosin, we are kin; nor do I scorne
At any time to acknowledge as much,
Toward men of baser calling then your selfe.

 But. It may be so, sir; but to tell you truth,
It seemed somewhat strange to me at first,
And I was halfe afraid some ill had hapned,
That made you carefull whom you trusted to.

 Bro. Faith, coosin, none but this: I owe some money,
And one I am indebted to of late
Hath brought his action to an outlawry,
And seekes to do me all extremity.
But that I am not yet provided for him,
And that he shall not have his will of me,
I do absent me, till a friend of mine
Do see what order he may take with him.

 But. How now, whoe's this?

  Enter MAISTER MAYOR, MASTER JAMES, *with a purseuant and others.*

 Mayor. Where are you, neighbour Browne?

 But. Master Mayor, y'are welcome; what's the news, sir,
You come so guarded. Is there aught amisse?

 Bro. Heaven will have justice showne: it is even so!

 James. I can assure you 'tis the man we seeke,
Then doe your office, master Mayor.

 Mayor.   GEORGE BROWNE,

I doe arrest you, in her highnesse name, 94
As one suspected to have murdred
GEORGE SANDERS, Citizen of London.

Bro. Of murther, sir? there lives not in this land
Can touch me with the thought of murther. 94

Mayor. Pray God it be so; but you must along
Before their honors, there to answer it.
Here's a commission that commands it so.

Bro. Well, sir, I do obey, and do not doubt 94
But I shall prove me innocent therein.

James. Come, master Mayor, it is the Councels pleasure,
You must assist us till we come to Woolwich,
Where we have order to conferre at large 95
With master Barnes concerning this mishap.

Mayor. Withall my heart; farewell, good neighbor BROWN.

But. God keepe you, maister Mayor, and all the rest.
And, master Browne, beleeve me, I am sory 95
It was your fortune to have no more grace.

Bro. Coosin, grieve not for me, my case is cleare.
Suspected men may be, but need not feare. [*Exeun*

Enter JOHN BEANE, *brought in a chair, and* MASTER BARNES
and MASTER JAMES.

Barnes. Sir, how much I esteemd this gentleman, 96
And in how hie respect I held his love
My griefes can hardly utter.

M. James. It shall not neede, your love after his death expresse
 it. 96

Barnes. I would to God it could; and I am verie glad

My Lords of her most honourable Councel
Have made choice of your selfe, so grave a gentleman,
To see the maner of this cruell murther.

 M. James. Sir, the most unworthy, I, of many men,
But that in the hie bounty of your kindnes so you terme me.
But trust me, maister Barnes, amongst the rest
That was reported to them of the murther,
They hardly were induced to beleeve
That this poore soule, having so many wounds,
And all so mortall as they were reported,   [*Laying his hand*
With so much losse of blood, should possibly yet live; *upon him.*
Why, it is past beliefe.

 Barnes. Sir, it is so, your worthy selfe can witnes,
As strange to us, that looke upon the wretch,
As the report thereof unto their wisdoms.

 M. James. More fearful wounds, nor hurts more dangerous,
Upon my faith I have not seene.

 Beane. Hey, hoe, a little drinke: oh my head.

 Barnes. Good John, how doest thou?

 Beane. Whose that? Father John?

 Barnes. Nay, John, thy maister.

 Beane.   O Lord, my belly!

 M. Jam. He spends more breath that issues through his wounds,
Then through his lippes.

 Beane.   I am drie.

 Barnes.   John, doest thou know me?

 M. Jam. See where thy master is; look, dost thou know him?

 Barnes. Sir, he never had his perfit memory, since the first houre.

 M. Jam. Surely he cannot last.

Barnes. And yet, sir, to our seeming, I assure you
He sat not up so strongly, as you see him, 993
Since he was brought into this house, as now.
    M. James. 'Tis very strange.

Enter the Mayor of Rochester, with BROWNE *and Officers.*

Barnes. As I take it, Maister Mayor of Rochester. 996
    Mayor. The same, good master Barnes.
    Barnes. What happy fortune sent you here to Woolwich,
That yet your company may give us comfort in this sad time?
    Mayor. Beleeve me, sad indeed, and very sad; 1000
Sir, the Councel's warrant lately came to me
About the search for one Captain George Browne,
As it should seeme, suspected for this murther,
Whom in my search I hapt to apprehend. 1004
And hearing that the bodies of the murdred
Remained here, I thought it requisite
To make this in my way unto the Court,
Now going thither with the prisoner. 1008
    Barnes. Beleeve me, sir, ye have done right good service,
And shewne your selfe a painfull gentleman,
And shall no doubt deserve well of the state.
    M. James. No doubt you shall, and I durst assure you so:
The Councel wil accept well of the same. 1013
    Barnes. Good maister Mayor, this wretched man of mine
Is not yet dead; looke you where he sits;
But past all sense, and labouring to his end. 1016
    Mayor. Alas! poore wretch.
    Barnes. Is this that BROWNE that is suspected to have done

The murther? A goodly man, beleeve me:
Too faire a creature for so fowle an act. 1020
  Browne. My name is BROWNE, sir.
  M. James. I know you well; your fortunes have been
Faire as any gentlemans of your repute.
But, BROWNE, should you be guilty of this fact, 1024
As this your flight hath given shrewde suspition,
Oh BROWNE, your hands have done the bloodiest deed
That ever was committed.
  Bro. He doth not live dare charge me with it. 1028
  M. Ja. Pray God there be not.
  Mayor. Sergeants, bring him neare; see if this poore soule know
    him.
  Barnes. It cannot be; these two days space
He knew no creature.
  Bro.   Swounds, lives the villaine yet?   [*Aside.*
O how his very sight affrights my soule! 1033
His very eyes will speake had he no tongue,
And will accuse me.
  Barnes. See how his wounds break out afresh in bleeding.
  M. Ja. He stirs himselfe. 1037
  Mayor. He openeth his eyes.
  Barnes. See how he lookes upon him.
  Bro. I gave him fifteene wounds,   [*Aside*
Which now be fifteene mouthes that doe accuse me; 1041
In ev'ry wound there is a bloody tongue,
Which will all speake, although he hold his peace;
By a whole jury I shalbe accusde. 1044
  Barnes. John, dost thou heare? Knowest thou this man?

Beane. Yea, this is he that murdred me and M. Sanders.

[*He sinkes down.*

M. Ja. O, hold him up.

Mayor. John, comfort thy selfe.

M. Ja. Bow him; give him ayre.

Barnes. No; he is dead. 1048

Bro. Me-thinks he is so fearefull in my sight,
That were he now but where I saw him last,
For all this world I would not looke on him.

Barnes. The wondrous worke of God, that the poore creature, not speaking for two dayes, yet now should speake to accuse this man, and presently yeeld up his soule!

M. Ja. 'Tis very strange, and the report thereof
Can seeme no lesse unto the Lords. 1056

Mayor. Sergeants, away, prepare you for the court,
And I will follow you immediatly.

Barnes. Sure, the revealing of this murther's strange.

M. Ja. It is so, sir; but in the case of blood, 1060
Gods justice hath bin stil miraculous.

Mayor. I have heard it told, that digging up a grave,
Wherein a man had twenty yeeres bin buryed,
By finding of a naile knockt in the scalpe, 1064
By due enquiry who was buried there,
The murther yet at length did come to light.

Barnes. I have heard it told, that once a traveller,
Being in the hands of him that murdred him, 1068
Told him the fearne that then grew in the place,
If nothing else, yet that would sure reveale him.
And seven yeares after, being safe in London,

There came a sprigge of fearne, borne by the wind 1072
Into the roome whereas the murtherer was,
At sight whereof he sodainely start up,
And then reveald the murder.

M. Ja. Ile tell you, sir, one more to quite your tale. 1076
A woman that had made away her husband,
And sitting to behold a tragedy,
At Linne, a towne in Norfolke,
Acted by Players travelling that way,— 1080
Wherein a woman that had murtherd hers
Was ever haunted with her husband's ghost,
The passion written by a feeling pen,
And acted by a good tragedian,— 1084
She was so mooved with the sight thereof,
As she cryed out, ' the play was made by her,'
And openly confess her husband's murder.

Barnes. However theirs, God's name be praised for this: 1088
You, Mayor, I see, must to the Court,
I pray you do my duety to the Lords.

Mayor. That will I, sir.

M. Ja. Come, Ile go along with you.

[*Exeunt.*

Enter the Lords at the Court, and Messengers.

1 *Lord.* Where was Browne apprehended, Messenger? 1092

2 *Mess.* At Rochester, my Lord, in a Butcher's house of his owne name, from thence brought up to Wolwich.

4 *Lord.* And there the fellow he left for dead with all those wounds affirm'd that it was he. 1096

1 Mess. He did, my Lord, and with a constant voice, praid God forgive Browne, and receive his soule, and so departed.

1 Lord. 'Tis a wondrous thing,
But that the power of heaven sustain'd him, 1100
A man with nine or ten such mortal wounds
Not taking foode should live so many days,
And then at sight of BROWNE recover strength,
And speake so cheerely as they say he did. 1104

4 Lord. Aye, and soone after he avouch'd the fact
Unto Brownes face, then to give up the ghost.

2 Lord. 'Twas God's good wil it should be so, my Lord.
But what said Browne, did he deny the deede? 1108

1 Mess. Never, my Lord; but did with teares lament
(As seem'd to us) his hainous cruelty.

1 Lord. When wil they come?

1 Mess.   Immediately, my Lord;
For they have wind and tide, and boats do wait. 1112

Enter M. MAYOR, M. JAMES, &c.

M. James. My Lordes, the Mayor of Rochester is come with Browne.   [*Exit M. James.*

4 Lord. Let him come in. You, messenger,
Haste you to London to the Justices: 1116
Will them, from us, see an indictment drawne
Against GEORGE BROWNE for murdring of GEORGE SANDERS.

1 Lord. Welcome, good master Mayor of Rochester

Enter Mayor, BROWNE, *a Messenger, another, and* M. HUMPHERY.

Mayor. I humbly thanke your honours.

4 Lord.   We thank you,
For your great care and diligence in this,
And many other faithful services.
Now, maister Browne, I am sory it was your happe
To be so farre from grace and feare of God
As to commit so bloudy a murder.
What say ye? are ye not sory for it?
   Browne. Yes, my Lord, and were it now to do,
Al the world's wealth could not intice me too't.
   1 Lord. Was there any ancient quarrel, BROWNE,
Betwixt your selfe and Maister SANDERS?
   Browne. No.
   2 Lord. Was't for the mony that he had about him?
   Browne. No, my good Lord, I knew of none he had.
   4 Lord. No; I heard an inckling of the cause:
You did affect his wife, GEORGE BROWN, too much.
   Browne. I did, my Lord, and God forgive it me.
   3 Lord. Then she provok'd ye to dispatch him.
   Browne. No.
   4 Lord. Yes; and promised you should marry her.
   Browne. No, I wil take it upon my death.
   1 Lord. Some other were confederate in the fact;
Confesse then, BROWNE, discharge thy conscience.
   Browne. I wil, my Lord, at hower of my death.
   2 Lord. Nay, now, that they with thee may die for it.
              MAISTER JAMES *delivers a letter.*
   4 Lord. From whom is this letter?   [*Opens and reads it.*
   M. Jam. From the Sheriffes of London.
   4 Lord. I told ye mistris SANDERS hand was in.

The act's confessd by two, that she knew on't.

 Bro. They do her wrong, my Lords, upon my life.

 4 Lord. Why DRURY's wife and ROGER do affirme,   1148
Unto her face, that she did give consent.

 Bro. God pardon them, they wrong the innocent.
They both are guiltie and procurde the deed,
And gave me mony since the deede was done,   1152
Twenty-sixe pound to carry me away;
But mistris SANDERS, as I hope for heaven,
Is guiltlesse, ignorant how it was done;
But DRURY's wife did beare me stil in hand   1156
If he were dead she would effect the marriage;
And trusty ROGER, her base apple-squire,
Haunted me like a spright till it was done,
And now like divels accuse that harmlesse soule.   1160

 1 Lord. Well, M. Browne, w'are sory for your fall;
You were a man respected of us all,
And noted fit for many services;
And fie that wanton lust should overthrow   1164
Such gallant parts in any gentleman.
Now al our favors cannot do ye good,
The act's too odious to be spoken of,
Therefore we must dismisse ye to the Law.   1168

 4 Lord. Expect no life, but meditate of death;
And for the safe-gard of thy sinful soule,
Conceale no part of trueth for friend or foe.
And, maister Mayor, as you have taken paines,   1172
So finish it, and see him safe conveyd
To the Justices of the Bench at Westminster:

Wil them from us to try him speedily.
That gentleman shal go along with you,　　　　　　　　1176
And take in writing his confession.

 2 *Lo.* Farewel, GEORGE BROWNE, discharge thy conscience.
 Bro. I do, my Lord, that Sanders wife is cleere.　　[*Exeunt om.*

Enter some to prepare the judgement seat to the Lord Mayor, Lo. Justice, and the foure Lords, and one Clearke, and a Sheriff, who being set, commaund BROWNE *to be brought forth.*

 1 *Off.* Come, let's make haste, and we'l prepare this place. 1180
 2 *Off.* How well I pray you? what haste more then was wont.
 1 *Off.* Why divers lords are come from court to-day,
To see th' arraignment of this lusty Browne.
 2 *Off.* Lusty? how lusty? now hee's tame enough,　　　1184
And wilbe tamer.　Oh, a lusty youth!
Lustily fed, and lustily apparelled,
Lusty in looke, in gate, in gallant talke,
Lusty in wooing, in fight, and murthring,　　　　　　　1188
And lustily hangd, there's th'end of lusty Browne!
 1 *Off.* Hold your lusty peace, for here come the Lords.

Enter all as before.

 L. Mayor. Please it, your honors, place your selves, my lords.
 L. Justice. Bring forth the prisoner, and keepe silence there,
Prepare the Inditement that it may be read.　　　　　　1193
     Browne is brought in.
 Cleark.　To the barre, GEORGE BROWNE, and hold up thy hand. Thou art here indited by the name of GEORGE BROWNE, late of London, gentleman, for that thou, upon the xxv day of March, in

the xv yeare of the raigne of her Sacred Majesty, whom God long preserve, betweene the houres of vii and viii of the clocke in the forenoone of the same day, neere vnto Shooter's Hill, in the county of Kent, lying in wait of purpose and pretended malice, having no feare of God before thine eyes, the persons of George Sanders, gentleman, and John Bean, yeoman, then and there journeying in God's peace and the princes, feloniously did assault, and with one sword, price sixe shillings, mortally and wilfully, in many places diddest wound unto the death, against the peace, crown, and dignity of her majesty. How sayest thou to these fellonious murders, art thou guilty or not guilty?

 Bro. Guilty.

 Lo. Just. The Lord have mercy upon thee.   1208
Master Shiriff, ye shal not need to returne any Jury to passe upon him, for he hath pleaded guilty, and stands convict at the barre attending his iudgement. What canst thou say for thyselfe, Browne, why sentence of death should not bee pronounced against thee?

 Bro. Nothing, my Lord, but onely do beseech   1214
Those noble men assistants on that bench,
And you, my Lord, who are to justice sworne,
As you will answere at God's judgement seat,
To have a care to save the innocent,   1218
And (as my selfe) to let the guilty die,—
That's Drury's wife and her man trusty Roger.
But if Anne Sanders die, I do protest,
As a man dead in law, that she shall have   1222
The greatest wrong that ere had guiltlesse soule.

 Lo. Just. She shal have justice, and with favor, Browne.

ACT II.] *A WARNING FOR FAIRE WOMEN.* 317

 4 *Lo.* Assure yourselfe, Browne, she shal have no wrong.
 Bro. I humbly thanke your Lordships.
 2 *Lo.*   Hearke ye, Browne.
What countryman are ye borne?
 Bro.   Of Ireland, and in Dublin.
 Lo. Just. Have you not a brother calld Anthony Browne? 1228
 Bro. Yes, my Lord, whome, as I heare,
Your Lordship keepes close prisoner now in Newgate.
 Lo. Just. Wel, two bad brothers; God forgive ye both!
 Bro. Amen, my Lord, and you, and al the world.   1232
 Lo. Just. Attend your sentence.
 Bro.   Presently, my Lord;
But I have one petition first to make
Unto those noble men, which on my knees
I do beseech them may not be denyed.   1236
 4 *Lo.* What ist, GEORGE BROWNE?
 Browne.   I know the law
Condemnes a murtherer to be hangd in chaines.
O, good, my Lords, as you are noble men,
Let me be buried so soone as I am dead.   1240
 1 *Lo.* Thou shalt, thou shalt; let not that trouble thee,
But heare thy judgement.
 Lo. Just. Browne, thou art here by law condemned to die,
Which by thine owne confession thou deserv'st.   1244
Al men must die, although by divers meanes,
The maner how is of least moment, but
The matter why condemns or justifies.
But be of comfort; though the world condemne,   1248
Yea, though thy conscience sting thee for thy fact,

Yet God is greater than thy conscience,
And he can save whom al the world condemnes,
If true repentance turne thee to his grace. 1252
Thy time is short, therefore spend this thy time
In prayer and contemplation of thy end:
Labour to die better then thou hast liv'd:
God grant thou maist. Attend thy judgement now: 1256
Thou must go from hence to the place from whence thou camst,
From thence to th' appointed place of execution,
And there be hangd untill thou be dead,
And thy body after at the princes pleasure; 1260
And so the Lord have mercy upon thee, BROWNE.
Master Shiriff, see execution. And now take him hence,
And bring those other prisoners that you have.

   Bro. My Lords, forget not my petitions; 1264
Save poore Anne Sanders, for shee's innocent;
And, good my Lords, let me not hang in chaines.

  BROWNE *is led out, and* ANNE SANDERS *and* DRURY *brought in.*

   4 *Lor.* Farewel; let none of these things trouble thee.

   1 *Lor.* See how he labors to acquit Anne Sanders. 1268

   4 *Lor.* What hath his brother, that is in Newgate, done?

   Lo. Just. Notorious fellonies in Yorkeshire, my Lord.
Here come the prisoners; bring them to the barre;
Read their inditement; master Shiriffe, prepare 1272
Your jury ready. Command silence there!

      ANNE SANDERS *hath a white Rose in her bosome.*

   Cleark. Anne Sanders, and Anne Drury,
To the barre, and hold up your hands. 1275

ACT II.] *A WARNING FOR FAIRE WOMEN.* 319

You are here jointly and severally indited in forme following, vz. that you, ANNE SANDERS, and ANNE DRURY, late of London, spinsters, and thou, ROGER CLEMENT, late of the same, yeoman, and every of you jointly and severally, before and after the xxv day of March, last past, in the xv yeare of the reigne of her sacred Majesty, whom God long preserve, having not the fear of God before your eyes, did maliciously conspire and conclude with one GEORGE BROWN, gent., the death of GEORGE SANDERS, late husband to you, Anne Sanders, and did intice, animate, and procure the said George Browne to murder the said maister Sanders: And also after the said heinous murther committed, did with mony and other means aid, releeve, and abet the said Browne, knowing him to have done the deede, whereby you are all accessaries both before and after the fact, contrary to the peace, crowne, and dignity of our soveraigne Lady the Queene. How say ye, severally, are ye guilty, or not guilty, as accessaries both before and after to this felony and murther? 1292
  Anne. Not guilty.
  Drew. Not guilty.
  Clerk. How wil ye be tried? 1295
  Both. By God, and by the countrey.
  Lo. Just. Bring forth trusty ROGER, there.
Roger, what sayest thou to this letter?
Who gave it thee to carry unto Browne? 1299
  Rog. My mistris gave it me;
And she did write it on our Lady's eve.
  L. Just. Did Mistres SANDERS know thereof, or no?
  Rog. She read it twise before the same was seald. 1303
  Anne. Did I, thou wicked man!

This man is hirde to betray my life.

2 Lord. Fie, mistris SANDERS, you doe not wel
To use such speeches, when ye see the case   1307
Is too, too manifest.   But, I pray ye,
Why do you weare that white rose in your bosome?

Anne. In token of my spotlesse innocence:
As free from guilt as is this flower from staine.   1311

2 Lord. I feare it wil not fal out so.

L. Just. Roger, what mony carried you to Browne,
After the deede, to get him gone withall?

Roger. Twenty sixe pounds, which coine was borowed,   1315
Parte of my mistris plate, and some of mistris SANDERS.

L. Just. How say ye to that, mistris SANDERS?

Anne. Indeede, I grant, I misse some of my plate,
And now am glad I know the theefe that stole it.   1319

Roger. O God forgive ye! you did give it me;
And God forgive me, I did love ye al
Too wel, which now I deerely answer for.

1 Lord. Anne Drury, what say you? was not the plate   1323
Part of it yours, and the rest mistris Sanders,
According as your man hath here confessde,
With which she [1] borrowed twenty pound for Browne?

Dru. My Lord, it was.

2 Lord.   And you and she together   1328
Were privy of the letter which was sent.
Was it so, or no?   Why do you not speake?

Dru. It was, my Lord, and mistris Sanders knew
That Roger came the morning ere he went,   1332

[1] *read* he.—G.

ACT II.] *A WARNING FOR FAIRE WOMEN.*

And had a token from her to GEORGE BROWNE,
A handkercher, which after was sent backe,
Imbrude in Sanders bloud.

   L. Justice. Who brought that handkercher?
   Dru.   That did my man.
   1 *Lo.* To whom did you deliver it, sirra?
   Rog. To mistris SANDERS, at her house, my Lord.
   Anne. O God! My Lords, he openly belies me.
I kept my childbed chamber at that time,
Where 'twas not meete that he, or any man,
Should have accesse.
   L. Just.   Go to! Clog not your soule,
With new additions of more hainous sinne.
'Tis thought, beside conspiring of his death,
You wronged your husband with unchaste behaviour,
For which the justice of the righteous God
Meaning to strike you, yet reserves a place
Of gracious mercy, if you can repent;
And, therefore, bring your wickednesse to light,
That suffering for it in this world, you might,
Upon your hearty sorrow, be set free,
And feare no further judgement in the next;
But if you spurne at his affliction,
And beare his chasticement with grudging minds,
Your precious soule, as wel as here your bodies,
Are left in hazard of eternal death.
Be sorry, therefore, 'tis no petty sinne,
But murder, most unnatural of al,[1]

---

[1] Cf. *Hamlet* I. iv. 27.—'Murder most foul, strange, and unnatural.'—G.

Wherewith your hands are tainted, and in which,
Before and after the accursed fact, 1360
You stand as accessary. To be briefe,
You shal be carried backe unto the place
From whence you came, and so from thence, at last,
Unto the place of execution, where 1364
You shal al three be hang'd til you be dead.
And so the Lord have mercy on your soules!

Anne. Ah, good my Lords, be good unto ANNE SANDERS,
Or els you cast away an innocent! 1368

2 Lord. It should not seeme so by the rose you weare:
His colour now is of another hue.

Anne. So you wil have it; but my soule is stil
As free from murther as it was at first. 1372

Lo. Just. I think no less. Jailer, away with them.

Anne. Wel, wel, Anne Drury, I may curse the time
That e're I saw thee; thou broughtst me to this.

Rog. I will not curse, but God forgive ye both, 1376
For had I never knowne nor you, nor her,
I had not come unto this shameful death. [*Exeunt.*

Enter MAISTER BROWNE, *to execution, with the Sheriffe and Officers.*

Browne. Why do you stay me, in the way of death?
The peoples' eyes have fed them with my sight; 1380
The little babies in the mothers' armes
Have wept for those poore babies, seeing me,
That I by my murther have left fatherlesse,
And shreekt and started when I came along, 1384

ACT II.] *A WARNING FOR FAIRE WOMEN.*

And sadly sigh'd, as when their nurses use
To fright them with some monster when they cry.
 Sheriff. You have a brother, Browne, that for a murther
Is lately here committed unto Newgate,
And hath obtained he may speake with you.
 Browne. Have I a brother that hath done the like?
Is there another Browne hath kild a Sanders?
It is my other selfe hath done the deede:
I am a thousand, every murtherer is my owne selfe;
I am at one time in a thousand places,
And I have slaine a thousand Sanderses.
In every shire, each citty, and each towne
GEORGE SANDERS stil is murthered by GEORGE BROWNE.

BROWNE'S brother is brought forth.

 Brow. bro. Brother.
 Brow. Dost thou meane me?
Is there a man wil call me brother?
 Brownes bro. Yes, I wil cal thee so, and may do it,
That have a hand as deepe in bloud as thou.
 Brown. Brother, I know thee well. Of whence was thine?
 Brother. Of Yorke he was.
 Browne. SANDERS, of London, mine.
Then see I wel, Englands two greatest townes
Both fild with murders done by both the Brownes.
 Brother. Then may I rightly chalenge thee a brother:
Thow slewest one in the one, I one in th' other.
 Browne. When did'st thou thine?
 Brother. A month or five weekes' past.

Browne. Hardly to say, then, which was done the last.
Where shalt thou suffer?

Brother.   'Where I did the fact.   1412

Browne. And I here, brother, where I laid my act.
Then I see wel, that be it nere or further,
That heaven wil stil take due revenge on murther.

Brother. Brother, farewel, I see we both must die;   1416
At London, you, this weeke, next, at Yorke, I.

Browne. Two lucklesse brothers sent both at one hower,
The one from Newgate, thother from the Tower.   [*Exit* BROT.

Sheriffe. BROWNE, yet at last to satisfy the world,   1420
And for a true and certaine testimony
Of thy repentance for this deed committed,
Now, at the houre of death, as thou doest hope
To have thy sinnes forgiven at God's hands,   1424
Freely confesse what yet unto this houre
Against thy conscience, Browne, thou hast concealde,
Anne Sanders knowledge of her husband's death.

Bro. Have I not made a covenant with her   [*Aside.*
That, for the love that I ever bare to her,   1429
I will not sell her life by my confession?
And shall I now confesse it?   I am a villaine.
I will never do it.   Shall it be said BROWNE prov'd   1432
A recreant?   And yet I have a soule.
Well, God the rest reveale:
I will confesse my sinnes, but this conceale.
Upon my death shee's guiltlesse of the fact.   1436
Well, much ado I had to bring it out.   [*Aside.*
My conscience scarce would let me utter it:

I am glad 'tis past.

Shiriff. But, Browne, it is confest by Druries wife   1440
That she is guilty; which doth fully prove
Thou hast no true contrition, but conceal'st
Her wickednesse, the bawd unto her sinne.

Bro. Let her confesse what she thinkes good;   1444
Trouble me no more, good master Sheriff.

Shiriff. Browne, thy soule knowes.

Bro. Yea, yea, it does; pray you be quiet, sir.
Vile world, how like a monster come I soyld from thee!   1448
How have I wallowed in thy lothsome filth,
Drunke and besmear'd with al thy bestial sinne!
I never spake of God, unlesse when I
Have blasphemed his name with monstrous oathes;   1452
I never read the scriptures in my life,
But did esteem them worse then vanity;
I never came in church where God was taught,
Nor ever, to the comfort of my soule,   1456
Tooke benefite of sacrament or baptisme.
The Sabboth dayes I spent in common stewes,
Unthrifty gaming, and vile perjuries.
I held no man once worthy to be spoke of   1460
That went not in some strange disguisde attire,
Or had not fetcht some vile monstrous fashion
To bring in odious, detestable pride.
I hated any man that did not doe   1464
Some damned, or some hated, filthie deede,
That had been death for vertuous men to heare.
Of all the worst that live, I was the worst;

Of all the cursed, I the most accursed. 1468
All carelesse men, be warned by my end:
And, by my fall, your wicked lives amend. [*He leapes off.*¹

Enter a Messenger.

Messen. It is the Councel's pleasure, master Shiriff,
The body be convaide to Shooter's Hill, 1472
And there hung up in chaines.
Shiriff.   It shal be done.

Enter MASTER JAMES, *with the Minister.*²

M. Jam. Why, then you are perswaded, certainly,
That mistres Sanders is meere innocent?
Min. That am I, sir, even in my very soule. 1476
Compare but all the likelihoodes thereof:
First, hir most firme deniall of the fact;
Next, mistres Drury's flat confession,
That onely she and Roger did contrive 1480
The death of master Sanders; then your selfe
Cannot but be of mine opinion.
M. Jam. Then al you labour for
Is that I should procure her pardon. 1484
Min. To save an innocent
Is the most Christian worke that man can do;
Beside, if you performe it, sir, sound recompence
Shal quit your paines so well imployed herein. 1488

¹ See Note 2, p. 336.
² This Minister is Mell, of whom an account is given in Introduction, p. 227.—G.

M. Ja. Now, let me tell ye, that I am ashamde
A man of your profession should appeare
So far from grace, and touch of conscience,
As, making no respect of his owne soule, 1492
He should with such audaciousnes presume
To baffle Justice, and abuse the seate [1]
With your fond, over-weening, and slie fetch.
Thinke you the world discerneth not your drift? 1496
Do not I know, that if you could prevaile,
By this far-fetcht insinuation,
And mistris SANDERS pardon thus obtainde,
That your intent is then to marry her? 1500
And thus you have abused her poore soule,
In trusting to so weake and vaine a hope.
Well, sir, since you have so forgot yourselfe,
And (shamelesse) blush not at so bold offence, 1504
Upon their day of execution,
And at the selfe same place, upon a pillory,
There shall you stand, that al the world may see,
A just desert for such impiety.
Min. Good sir, hear me! 1508
M. Ja. I wil not heare thee; come, and get thee hence,
For such a fault too meane a recompence. [*Exeunt.*

Enter two Carpenters under Newgate.

Will. Tom Peart, my old companion? well met.
Tom. Good morrow, Wil Crow, good morrow; how dost? 1512
I have not seene thee a great while.

[1] State, perhaps.—G.

Will. Wel, I thank God; how dost thou? where hast thou bin this morning, so early?

Tom. Faith, I have bin up ever since three a clocke. 1516

Will. About what, man?

Tom. Why, to make worke for the hangman; I and another have bin setting up a gallowes.

Will. O, for Mistris Drewry; must she die to-day? 1520

Tom. Nay, I know not that; but when she does, I am sure there is a gallowes big enough to hold them both.

Will. Both whom? her man and her? 1523

Tom. Her man and her, and mistris Sanders too; 'tis a swinger yfayth. But come, Ile give thee a pot this morning, for I promise thee I am passing dry, after my worke.

Will. Content, Tom, and I have another for thee; and afterward Ile go see the execution. 1528

Tom. Do as thou wilt for that.

Will. But dost thou thinke it will be to-day?

Tom. I cannot tell; Smithfield is full of people, and the Shiriffes man, that set us a worke, told us it would be to-day. But come, shall we have this Beere? 1533

Will. With a good will; leade the way. [*Exeunt.*

Enter ANNE SANDERS, *and her keeper following her.*

Keeper. Cal'd you, mistres Sanders?

Anne. Keeper, I did: I prethee fetch up mistres Drury to me, 1536 I have a great desire to talke with her.

Keeper. She shall be brought unto you presently. [*Exit.*

Anne. Oh God! as I was standing at a grate

That lookes into the streete, I heard men talke, 1540
The execution should be done to-day;
And what a paire of gallows were set up,
Both strong and big enough to hold us all;
Which words have strucke such terror to my soule, 1544
As I cannot be quiet till I know
Whether Nan Drury be resolved still
To cleare me of the murder, as she promist:
And here she comes. I prethee, gentle keeper, 1548
Give us a little leave we may conferre
Of things that neerly do concerne our soules.
  Keeper. With al my hart, take time & scope enough. [*Exit.*
  Dru. Now, mistris Sanders, what's your wil with me? 1552
  Anne. Oh! mistris Drury, now the houre is come
To put your love unto the touch, to try
If it be currant, or but counterfait.
This day it is appointed we must die; 1556
How say you, then; are you stil purposed
To take the murder upon your selfe?
Or wil you now recant your former words?
  Dru. Anne Sanders, Anne, 'tis time to turne the leafe, 1560
And leave dissembling, being so neare my death.
The like I would advise your selfe to do.
We have bin both notorious vile transgressors,
And this is not the way to get remission, 1564
By joining sinne to sinne; nor doth't agree
With godly christians, but with reprobates,
And such as have no taste of any grace,
And, therefore, for my part, Ile cleere my conscience, 1568

And make the truth apparant to the world.
   Anne. Will you prove then inconstant to your friend?
   Dru. Should I, to purchase safety for anóther,
Or lengthen out anothers temporall life,
Hazard mine owne soule everlastingly,
And loose the endlesse joyes of heaven,
Preparde for such as wil confesse their sinnes?
No, mistris Sanders; yet there's a time of grace,
And yet we may obtaine forgivenes,
If we wil seeke it at our Saviour's hands.
But if we wilfully shut up our hearts
Against the holy spirit that knockes for entrance,
It is not this world's punishment shal serve,
Nor death of body, but our soules shal live
In endlesse torments of unquenched fire.
   Anne. Your words amaze me! and although ile vow
I never had intention to confesse
My hainous sinne, that so I might escape
The worlds reproach, yet God, I give him thanks!
Even at this instant I am strangely changed,
And wil no longer drive repentance off,
Nor cloake my guiltinesse before the world.
And in good time see where the Doctor commes,
By whome I have bin seriously instructed.
   Doct. Good morrow, mistris Sanders, and soules health
Unto you both; prepare yourselves for death.
The houre is nowe at hand, and, mistris Sanders,
At length acknowledge and confesse your fault,
That God may be propitioner to your soule.

Anne. Right reverend sir, not to delude the world,
Nor longer to abuse your patience,
Here I confesse I am a grievous sinner,
And have provok't the heavy wrath of God,
Not onely by consenting to the death
Of my late husband, but by wicked lust
And wilful sinne, denying of the fault;
But now I do repent, and hate myselfe,
Thinking the punishment preparde for me
Not halfe severe enough for my deserts.
  Doct. Done like a christian, and the childe of grace,
Pleasing to God, to angels, and to men;
And doubt not but your soule shall finde a place
In Abraham's bosome, though your body perish.
And, mistris DREWRY, shrinke not from your faith,
But valiantly prepare to drinke this cup
Of sowre affliction, 'twill raise up to you
A crowne of glory in another world.
  Dru. Good M. Doctor, I am bound to you;
My soule was ignorant, blind, and almost choak't
With this world's vanities; but by your councell
I am as well resolv'd to goe to death
As if I were invited to a banquet;
Nay, such assurance have I in the bloud
Of him that died for me, as neither fire,
Sword nor torment could retaine me from him.
  Doctor. Spoke like a champion of the holy Crosse.
Now, mistris Sanders, let me tell to you:
Your children, hearing this day was the last

They should behold their mother on the earth,
Are come to have your blessing e're you die, 1628
And take their sorrowful farewel of you.

Anne. A sorrowfull farewel 'twil be, indeede,
To them, poore wretches, whom I have deprivde
Of both the natural succours of their youth; 1632
But call them in, and, gentle keeper, bring me
Those bookes that lie within my chamber window.
Oh, maister Doctor, were my breast transparent,
That what is figurde there might be perceiv'd, 1636
Now should you see the very image of poore
And tottred ruines, and a slaine conscience.
Here, here, they come: be blind, mine eyes, with teares,
And soule and body now in sunder part. 1640

All. Oh! mother, mother!

Anne. Oh, my deare children!
I am unworthy of the name of Mother.

All. Turne not your face from us, but, e're you die,
Give us your blessing.

Anne. Kneele not unto me:[1] 1644
'Tis I that have deserv'd to kneele to you.
My trespas hath bereft you of a father,
A loving father, a kinde careful father;
And by that selfe same action, that foule deede, 1648
Your mother likewise is to go from you;
Leaving you, poore soules, by her offence,
A coresie and a scandall to the world.
But could my husband, and your father, heare me, 1652

[1] See Note 3, p. 336.

Thus humbly at his feete would I fal downe,
And plentifull in teares bewayle my fault.
Mercy I aske of God, of him, and you,
And of his kinred which I have abusde, 1656
And of my friends and kinred wheresoever,
Of whom I am ashamed and abasht,
And of al men and women in the world,
Whome by my foule example I have griev'd: 1660
Though I deserve no pity at their hands,
Yet I beseech them all to pardon me;
And God I thanke, that hath found out my sin,
And brought me to affliction in this world, 1664
Thereby to save me in the world to come.
Oh, children, learne; learne by your mother's fall,
To follow vertue, and beware of sinne,
Whose baites are sweete and pleasing to the eye, 1668
But, being tainted, more infect than poyson,
And are farre bitterer than gall it selfe.
And livd[1] in dayes where you have wealth at wil,
As once I had, and are well matcht beside, 1672
Content your selves, and surfet not on pride.

Enter Sheriffe bringing in TRUSTY ROGER *with holberds.*

Sheriffe. What, M. Doctor, have you made an ende?
The morning is far spent, 'tis time to go.
   Doct. Even when you wil, M. Sheriffe, we are ready. 1676
   Anne. Behold, my children, I wil not bequeath

[1] Query, living.—G.

Or gold or silver to you, you are left
Sufficiently provided in that point;
But here I give to each of you a booke 1680
Of holy meditations, BRADFORDS workes,
That vertuous chosen servant of the Lord.
Therein you shalbe richer than with gold;
Safer than in faire buildings; happier 1684
Than al the pleasures of this world can make you.
Sleepe not without them, when you go to bed,
And rise a mornings with them in your hands.
So God send downe his blessing on you al. 1688
Farewel, farewel, farewel, farewel, farewel!
 [*She kisses them one after another.*
Nay, stay not to disturbe me with your teares;
The time is come, sweete hearts, and we must part,
That way go you, this way my heavy heart. [*Exeunt.*

TRAGEDY *enters to conclude.*

Tra. Here are the launces that have sluic'd forth sinne, 1693
And ript the venom'd ulcer of foule lust,
Which being by due vengeance qualified,
Here TRAGEDY of force must needes conclude. 1696
Perhaps it may seeme strange unto you al,
That one hath not revengde another's death
After the observation of such course:
The reason is, that now of truth I sing, 1700
And should I adde, or else diminish aught,
Many of these spectators then could say,
I have committed error in my play.

Beare with this true and home-borne Tragedy,[1]
Yeelding so slender argument and scope
To build a matter of importance on,
And in such forme as, happly, you expected.
What now hath fail'd to-morrow you shall see
Perform'd by History or Comedy. [*Exit*

[1] See Note 4, p. 336.

Finis.

NOTES.

1. *This heate of love and hasty climbing breeds*, p. 302, l. 863. If 'such deedes' is not to be understood after 'breeds', perhaps the lines should read:—
   'This heate of love *an* hasty climbing breeds.
   God blesse all honest tall men from such deedes.';
'an hasty climbing' meaning a forced climbing of the gallows. The sentiment of the first line, too, is similar to that used in reference to another too ardent lover, Romeo (*Romeo and Juliet*, II. iii. 94), viz.,
   'Wisely and slow; they stumble that run fast.'—G.

2. *He leapes off*, p. 326, l. 1470. This stage-direction seems to point to the rare fact of an execution actually presented upon the stage.—G.

3. *Kneele not unto me*, p. 332, l. 1644. This is one of several passages which illustrate how servile a following the play often is of the original accounts of the murder of Mr Sanders. Compare with Introduction, pp. 230, etc.—G.

4. *This true and home-borne Tragedy*, p. 335, l. 1704. *Tragedy*, as *Chorus*, here apologizes for the poorness of the *Warning for Faire Women* as a play. From this it seems that the author (or one of the authors) was rather ashamed of his work, though circumstances (*i. e.* the popular craving for such things) having obliged 'that now of truth I sing,' he pleads for indulgence on the ground of
   'this true and home-borne Tragedy,
   Yeelding so slender argument and scope
   To build a matter of importance on;'
humbly winding up with—
   'What now hath fail'd to-morrow you shall see
   Perform'd by History or Comedy.'
In other words, 'We'll give you better stuff to-morrow.' Nevertheless, ignoble as was his theme, and distasteful to him as seems to have been its treatment, the playwright (or some one having a hand in the play) has contrived to give several touches to the chief character, Browne, which tend to the making of that character a hero of Tragedy rather than a mere malefactor—a process more completely—indeed, quite completely, and most sublimely—exemplified in the character of Macbeth.—G.

A PLEASANT COMEDIE

OF

FAIRE EM,

THE MILLER'S DAUGHTER OF MANCHESTER;

with the love of William the conqueror. As it was sundry times publiquely acted in the Honourable Citie of London by the right Honourable the Lord Strange his servants.

LONDON,
Printed for *Iohn Wright,* and are to be sold at his shop at the Signe of the Bible in Guilt-spur street without New-gate. 1631.

[THE STORY OF THE PLAY.]

[FAIRE EM is a love-comedy having two plots (p. 372-5 below), each of which works separately until the two sets of characters mingle in the last scene, as a means of giving a contrasted *finale* to the whole. In one plot William the Conqueror—when fast fixed upon the throne of England—falls in love with the portrait of Blanch, daughter of Sweyn, King of Denmark, which he sees blazoned upon the shield of the Danish Marquess Lubeck. Leaving Earl de March and Duke Dirot joint Regents in England, William assumes the name of Sir Robert of Windsor, and goes with Lubeck to woo Blanch at the Danish Court. At the first sight of Blanch, however, William's passion for that Princess disappears, and gives place to love for Mariana, a Swedish captive in the Court of King Sweyn, who loves and is loved by Lubeck. Blanch, having fallen in love with William, becomes jealous of Mariana, and quarrels with her. William and Lubeck also quarrel over Mariana; but Lubeck soon, out of friendship for William, abandons his suit to Mariana, and even pleads with her that she shall love his friend in his stead. But Mariana loves Lubeck too well to agree to this. Instead, she plots with Blanch that, after seeming to consent to sail for England with William, Blanch, masked, and pretending to be Mariana, shall be so carried off. Landed in England with his still masked prize, William is arrested by his own soldiers, who do not know him; and, his own identity established, he is at once called to the field, and away from his masked lady, to meet Sweyn, who has arrived with a warlike host in search of his daughter. Finding that Sir Robert of Windsor is no other than King William, Sweyn offers to abate his wrath in consideration of King William marrying his daughter. This, after a refusal, and some parley, due to the mortification felt by William at discovering that his masked lady is not Mariana, is agreed to; and William, taking Blanch, leaves Mariana to be taken by his friend Lubeck. In the other plot, Sir Thomas Goddard is living in hiding as the Miller of Manchester; and associated with him in the work of his mill are his daughter Em, and his man Trotter. Em is courted by Mandeville, a Manchester gentleman, and by Mountney and Valingford, friends and gentlemen of King William's Court, and by Trotter, her own serving-man. Mandeville is the favoured suitor; but, being jealous of Mountney and Valingford, he quarrels with Em, who, to drive off Mountney and Valingford, and to appease Mandeville's jealousy, assumes deafness and blindness. Before Mountney, Em pretends to be deaf; and before Valingford she pretends to be blind. Each of these two, however, suspects a trick, and suspects, moreover, that the trick has been suggested to Em by his friend; consequently the two quarrel. But Em's feigning, which fails to deceive her unwelcome wooers, really deceives Mandeville, the favoured wooer. From her simulated deafness and blindness, as acted before his rivals, Mandeville believes her to be really deaf and blind; and, abandoning her, makes love to Eleanor. Finally, Em and Eleanor appear before King William, each to claim Mandeville. When Mandeville finds that Em has feigned for his sake, he offers to renew his troth with her; but she rejects him with scorn. He then turns to Eleanor, who also refuses him. He then declares that he will abjure love; and is derided for being like the fox who could not reach the grapes. Em now consents to receive from King William the hand of the faithful and persevering Valingford; and at the same time the King restores her father, the miller, to his rightful place at Court as Sir Thomas Goddard.—G.]

INTRODUCTION.

(INCLUDING AN ACCOUNT OF ROBERT GREENE, HIS LIFE AND WORKS, AND HIS ATTACKS ON SHAKSPERE AND THE PLAYERS.[1])

A TRADITION current in the time of Charles II. caused the book-binder for the royal library to bind together the plays, *Faire Em*, *The Merry Devil of Edmonton*, and *Mucedorus*, and to label them SHAKESPEARE, VOL. I.[2] Another tradition assigned *Faire Em* to Robert Greene, this play and *Friar Bacon* being the only dramas which Edward Phillips[3] ascribes to his sole authorship.

Friar Bacon is Greene's; but *Faire Em* was a play which Greene himself mocked at, and attributed to the ignorant playwright, whom, after abusing for years, he at last named as *Shake-scene*, in 1592. The tradition, therefore, which attributed it to Shakspere dated from very early days. The truth seems to be that *Faire Em* is a satire upon Greene, and in a measure a parody of some of his works. This would account for the uncertainty of the tradition which attributed the play, sometimes to the one, sometimes to the other author.

Every student of Shakspere knows the attack made upon him by Greene in 1592, in the Epistle appended to the *Groatsworth of wit*. But no one has yet traced the earlier mutterings of the

---

[1] For a summary of this account of Greene, see the article Greene, R., in the Index.—G.

[2] See Boswell's Malone, vol. ii., p. 668. The vol. was in the Garrick Collection in the British Museum. It is now split up, and the plays separately bound.

[3] Theatrum Poetarum, 1675. Modern Poets, p. 161.

jealousy which then for the first time spoke out clearly. It may, I think, be shown, that the same actor-author who is abused in the Epistle, is also mocked at in the novel to which the Epistle is attached; that the same man is glanced at, in the same phrases, in the Epistle which Greene caused Nash to prefix to *Menaphon* in 1589; while in the novel of *Menaphon* itself, Greene criticizes the style of this 'Roscius' under the name of Doron. The same writer is also glanced at in Greene's *Never too Late*, and in his *Farewell to Folly;* which last contains the author's flout at the writer of *Faire Em*. If we wish to understand the birth and growth of this enmity, we must examine Greene's works in order.

Greene was some four years older than Shakspere. He was born about 1560, and took his degree of B.A. at Cambridge in 1578. His first recorded publication was the first part of his novel *Mamillia*,[1] registered in the Stationers' books, Oct. 3, 1580. The work seems to have incurred more criticism than Greene liked; but he showed due humility, and in March, 1581, registered a palinode in the shape of a ballad intituled, *Youth, seeing all his ways so troublesome, abandoning virtue and leaning to vice, recalleth his former follies with an inward repentance.* Neither this production nor the separate edition of the first part of *Mamillia* has survived. The second part of *Mamillia* was registered Sep. 6, 1583, the year that Greene became M.A., and was probably then published with the first part, and an epistle dated 'From my study in Clare-Hall the VII of July.' He had by this time repented of his repentance, and had learned to defy the criticism to which he had at first yielded. He now gave notice that he would not put up with

[1] This novel perhaps preserves the story of a drama of the same name, played at Court by the Earl of Leicester's servants in 1573.

censure. He wrote for the confiding admirer, not for the carping critic. 'Let Momus mock and Zoilus envy; let Parasites flatter and sycophants smile; yea, let the savage Satire himself, whose cynical censure is more than need, frown at his pleasure.' I imagine that the censure which vexed him was directed more against the inconsistency of his life and writings than against the writings by themselves. His novel was modest enough; but it was ridiculous to see the young libertine repenting of his novel, without changing his life. Unlike those free poets, who boasted that if their verse was liberal their lives were chaste, Greene was a modest writer and a loose liver; and he would ever and anon loudly bewail the venial sins of his pen, probably without much amendment of the grave faults of his conduct.

To the year 1584 belongs *Gwidonius*, registered April 11, and dedicated to the Earl of Oxford. In the address to the readers the author confesses that his critics had not attacked his style. 'I have before time rashly reached above my pitch, and yet your courtesy [is] such, as no man hath accused me.' Another production of the same year is *Arbasto*, registered Aug. 13, 1584, though the earliest extant edition is dated 1585. In the introduction Greene begs his readers, 'if some too curious carp at your courtesy that vouchsafe to take a view of this pamphlet,' to say 'though it be not excellent, yet it is a book,' as Alexander said of Hephæstion's charger. 'Though not Bucephalus, yet it is a horse.' The novel of *Arbasto* is concerned with the trials of the King of Denmark, who loves one daughter of the King of France, while she hates him; and hates the other daughter, who loves him. In time the hated maid dies of grief; when the other, relenting, offers her love, but is rejected, and dies. Arbasto is thereupon banished his kingdom. The story has some distant resemblance to that portion of *Faire Em* which concerns the loves of William the Conqueror. A third publication of this year is extant, the first part of *Morando*, which was not registered till it was reprinted in 1587. In the prefatory epistle Greene again attacks the 'savage satires and fleering sycophants,' the 'biting vipers, who seek to discredit all, having themselves no credit at all.'

In 1585, the year, as I have shown elsewhere,[1] when Shakspere began to write, or at least to touch up the writings of others for the stage, Greene's *Planetomachia* was both registered and published. It is remarkable as containing (sig. B4) 'a marvellous anatomy of the Saturnists,' and a Saturnine portrait of Valdracko, which appears to be Greene's first exercise in that school of abuse in which he afterwards became so great a proficient. It looks as if he was already stung and disappointed that an avaricious player, not content with his own province, should dare to intrude into the field of authorship, which ought to belong solely to the professed scholars. This intrusion he was pleased to treat as an injustice, and a breach of friendship. Those who act so, he describes as Saturnists, 'in friendship doubtful . . . hardly granting their right hand to any man . . . uncertain in sure matters, always knitting their brows, and looking down to the ground . . . which believe nothing but what they see, and as the Latin proverb saith, *nihil nisi quod Aristophanis et Cleanthis lucernam oleat emittentes*. In covetousness insatiable . . . changing all into gold . . . skilful artificers in resembling or dissembling . . .

---

[1] In an article on the 'Early Authorship of Shakespeare,' *North British Review*, vol. lii.; and *Notes and Queries*, 4th Series, viii. 1. [1585 was the year in which Shakspere's twins were born, and when he is generally supposed to have been in Stratford. He became 21 on or about April 23, 1585.—F.]

unthankful as swallows; haters of company . . . having many ears and many eyes; bearing a head without a tongue; at talk and company not uttering one word, and yet *Sardonio risu omnia condientes*; reaping that which other men sow; ignorant in that they chiefly know; answering all things in three words; fearing their own shadows, and starting at flies.' This character is embodied in Valdracko, an actor in 'Venus tragedy,' one of the tales of the book. Valdracko is 'stricken in age, melancholic, ruling after the crabbed forwardness of his doting will, not with justice and mercy; impartial, for he loved none but himself; politic, because experienced; familiar with none, except for his profit; in private and secret conspiracies he used no friend but himself; skilful in dissembling; trusting no one; silent, covetous, counting all things honest that were profitable.' Greene, perhaps, is here building up his ideal of the hateful character, ready to be attributed to any one he hated. But the men whom the libertine and spendthrift was most ready to hate, were they who succeeded where he failed, whom he could not help accusing of sucking his brains, stealing his ideas, refusing to make common property of their gains, and devoting themselves to self-love. It will be seen that the characteristics which he persistently attributes to the player-poet, who is almost the constant object of his envy, are mostly contained in this sketch of the Saturnist in *Planetomachia*.

There are no registrations of Greene's works for the year 1586, and no known printed editions of that date. Perhaps during this year he devoted himself with all his energies to writing for the stage; perhaps, on the other hand, he was for the second time on his travels; for he had seen too much of Europe to be easily comprehended in his Spanish and Italian voyage before 1583. However this may be, the next year, 1587, was singularly prolific, as if he was then giving out what he had gathered in during his year's silence. Besides a reprint of *Morando*, licensed Aug. 8, his *Farewell to Folly* was registered June 11, his *Penelope's Web* June 26; and, according to Herbert, his *Euphues Censure* and *Perimedes* in the course of the year. If his *Farewell to Folly* was published at this time, we shall also be obliged to suppose that his *Mourning Garment*, referred to in that work, was already printed. Now as the *Farewell to Folly* is the novel in which the reference to *Faire Em* occurs, it is important to fix its date, even at the cost of a somewhat tedious discussion.

Farewell to Folly was registered on June 11, 1587. In the epistle to the readers Greene tells us, 'I presented you alate with my *Mourning Garment*.' But the *Mourning Garment* was registered in 1590 (Herbert), and the earliest known edition of the *Farewell* is dated 1591. The question therefore occurs, was the *Mourning Garment*, though registered in 1590, published in 1587, and the *Farewell* printed in 1587, when it was registered; or was the publication of the *Farewell* postponed for four years, so as to come out in 1591? There is no difficulty in either supposition. The first editions of many of Greene's works are unknown; and if the *Mourning Garment* was registered in 1590, after having been printed in 1587, it is no more than we have seen in the case of *Morando*, which was printed in 1584 and registered in 1587. Moreover, of his eight known works before 1587, only three were registered previously to publication. We must look, therefore, for internal evidences of the dates. The dedication of the *Mourning Garment* to the Earl of Cumberland will not help us. In spite of his prolonged absences from England, the Earl was at home all 1587, except during his brief expedition to Flanders in August. (Compare the accounts of his voyages in Purchas, *Pilgrims*, Lib. vi., c. 1.) And he was at home also during the whole of 1590. So he might have accepted the dedication in either year. It is more to the point to remark, that if the *Farewell* had been four years in the printer's hands, Greene would probably have told us. He does so with regard to *Orpharion*.[1] 'The printer had it long since; marry, whether his press were out of tune, paper dear, or some other secret delay drave it off, it hath lien this twelve-month in the suds; now at last it is crept forth.' Again, so rapid a writer as Greene is not likely to have rewritten his productions, merely because their publication was delayed. If, therefore, we find in the body of such a work a reference to another, it will be probable that this other was already in existence. But in the internal structure of the *Farewell* there are such references and allusions to the *Mourning Garment*. For instance, whereas the latter (sig. D, verso) has an elaborate story to illustrate the word misprinted *Antipechargein*, in the *Farewell* there is only this brief allusion (sig. B2, verso) : 'Themistocles wore in his shield a stork, his motto *antipelargein*, for that he would not be stained with ingratitude.' Hence the *Mourning Garment* would appear to have been already written when the *Farewell* was registered in 1587. Once more, there are three of Greene's works which have all one drift, the abjuration of love. These are *Never too late* (two parts), 1590; the *Mourning Garment*, first known edition 1590; the *Farewell to Folly*, first known edition 1591. This must have been their order, if the two latter were not published till 1590 and 1591, for in the *Farewell* Greene seems to speak of the *Mourning Garment* as his last work. In this case

[1] Registered 1589, first known edition 1599.

Never too late would be the first of the series, the earliest announcement of the author's repentance. But it is quite evident, both from the prefatory matter and from the internal structure of the novel, that the *Mourning Garment* is the earliest of the series, the book in which the writer broke new ground, and for the first time came out in a new character. It is evident also that the dedication contains an indication of the date in its unquestionable reference to the drama on the subject of Jonah and the Ninevites, which Greene wrote in conjunction with Lodge. This drama must have been written before 1589, when Lodge declares that Glaucus bound him by oath,

' To write no more of that whence shame doth grow,
Or tie my pen to Pennie-knaves delight,
But live with fame, and so for fame to write.'

That is, to write no more for the stage. (*Scillaes Metamorphosis*, last stanza before l'envoy, 1589.) The following passages seem to have been written while *The Looking-glass for England and London* was fresh in memory. They are from Greene's dedication of his *Mourning Garment* to the Earl of Cumberland, and show that the book they introduce was his first essay in doing public penance. ' While wantonness overweaned the Ninevites, their surcoats of bisse were all polished with gold: but when the threatening of Jonas made a jar in their ears, their finest sendall was turned to sackcloth. . . . Having myself over-weaned with them of Nineveh in publishing sundry wanton pamphlets, and setting forth anxioms of amorous philosophy, *tandem aliquando* taught with a feeling of my palpable follies, and hearing with the ears of my heart Jonas crying *except thou repent*, as I have changed the inward affects of my mind, so I have turned my wanton words to effectual labours, and pulling off their vain-glorious titles have called this my *Mourning Garment.'* The 'Epistle to the Gentlemen scholars' can leave little doubt of this being the earliest of the repentant series. 'Sudden changes of mens affects crave great wonder but little belief, and such as alter in a moment win not credit in a month. These premisses (gentlemen) drives me into a great quandary, fearing I shall hardly insinuate into your favours with changing the title of my pamphlets, or make you believe the inward metamorphosis of my mind by the exterior show of my works, seeing I have ever professed myself Love's philosopher.' Then, after a reference to Ovid's *Tristia*, he continues, 'Then Gentlemen let me find like favour, if I that wholly gave myself to the discoursing of amours be now applied to better labours. Think, though it be *Sero* yet it is *serio*, and although my showers come in autumn, yet think they shall continue the whole year. Hoping you will grace me with your favourable suspense till my deeds prove my doctrine, I present you with my *Mourning Garment*. Wherein, Gentlemen, look to see the vanity of youth so perfectly anatomized, that you may see every vein, muscle, and artery of her unbridled follies. Look for the discovery of wanton love, wherewith ripe wits are soonest inveigled, and scholars of all men deepest entangled. Had Ovid been a dunce he had never delivered such amorous precepts... Scholars have piercing insights, and therefore they overween in their sights, feeding their eyes with fancy that should be peering on the principles of Plato: they read of Venus, and therefore count every fair face a goddess, and grow so religious that they almost forget their God. They count no philosophy like love, no author so good as Ovid, no object so good as beauty, nor no exercise in schools so necessary as courting of a fair woman in a chamber. But please you gentlemen to put on my mourning garment, and see the effects that grow from such wanton affects, you will leave Ovid's art and fall to his remedy... You will think women *mala*, although they be to some kind of men *necessaria;* you will hold no heresy like love, no infection like fancy, no object so prejudicial as beauty... I wish to you as I would to myself, new loves, not to Venus but to Virtue... If you enter into the depth of my conceit, and see how I have only with humanity moralized a divine history,[1] and some odd scoffing companion that hath a commonwealth of self-love in his head say every painted cloth is the subject of this pamphlet[2]; I answer him with a common principle of philosophy, *Bonum quo communius eo melius;* and if that will not serve, let him either amend it or else sit down and blow his fingers till he find his *Memento* will serve to shape my garment after a new cut. I know, gentlemen, fools will have bolts, and they will shoot as well at a bush as at a bird; and some will have frumps, if it be but to call their father whoreson: but howsoever, I know *facilius est μωμησεται* quam *μιμησεται;* and a dog will have a barking tooth though he be warned: to such I write not....'

It will be seen by this Introduction that the *Mourning Garment* was Greene's first penitential production. The same conclusion may be drawn from a comparison of it with the two similar novels which he afterwards published, *Never too late*, containing the story of Francesco's fortunes, in 1590, and the *Groatsworth of wit*, con-

---

[1] The novel is the story of the *Prodigal Son*, embroidered with additions. In fact, we learn by *Histriomastix*, that Shakspere did write a drama of the *Prodigal Son*. If it is the same as that of which a translation into German was published among the *English comedies* in 1620, and outlined above, the memory of the dramatist had somewhat availed itself of Greene's shaping of the story. [See *ante*, pp. 12, 91.—G.]

[2] *i. e.* that the story might be read on any piece of old tapestry.

taining Roberto's adventures, in 1592. Philador, the prodigal in the *Mourning Garment*, Francesco in *Never too Late*, and Roberto in the *Groatsworth of wit*, are all more or less autobiographical sketches. But of these sketches Philador is the most rudimentary, and Roberto the most finished. Philador is evidently the first, which by its success encouraged its author to carry out the idea in two other novels of the same form. If this was all, we might conclude that the *Mourning Garment* was first published in 1587, before June, when the *Farewell to Folly* was also registered and published.

But the evidence on the other side is stronger. Not only was the *Mourning Garment*, published just before the *Farewell to Folly*, registered in 1590, but also the dedication and the Epistle prefixed to the *Farewell* contain two notes of time which force us to date it in 1590 or 1591. In the Epistle, Greene says that the whole impression of the *Mourning Garment* had been sold, and that the pedlar, finding it too dear, had been forced to buy 'The life of Tomlivolin, to wrap up his sweet powders in those unsavoury papers.' Tomlivolin is an obvious misprint for Tamburlain. Marlowe's plays on the subject, though written in 1587, were not published till 1590; nor is there any entry of ballads on the subject in the Stationers' register, though, truly, ballads may have been published without registration. Greene was at one time an adversary of the 'atheist Tamburlain,' as may be seen from his preface to *Perimedes* in 1588. The other note of time is decisive. He says: 'I cannot Martinize—swear by my fay in a pulpit, and rap out gogs-wounds in a tavern.' That is, he cannot do like Martin Mar-Prelate; assume sanctity in church, and bring out blasphemous and scurrillous libels through the press. Martin's first appearance was early in 1589, and Greene could not have used the word to *Martinize* in this sense in 1587. We might fancy a Catholic forming such a verb from the name of Martin Luther, but Greene was not a Catholic; and I know of no example of the word so used before 1589.

We must therefore conclude, that though the *Farewell to Folly* was designed, probably written, and registered in 1587, there is no evidence that it was then published. And if it was so published, it must have been without the dedication, and probably, also, without the Epistle to the Readers which we find in the edition of 1591. And yet I imagine that the *Farewell to Folly*, as designed to be published in 1587, had in the Introduction some such reference to *Faire Em* as is now found in the Introduction to the edition of 1591. My reason is, that in the *Penelope's Web*, a work which Greene seems to have given to Aggas, the Stationer, instead of his *Farewell to Folly*—possibly because he was not yet fully prepared to publish his penitential series—he betrays in what he calls his 'mystical speech' the same jealousy of a playwright, whose 'rudeness' he affects to despise, as we find in the *Farewell:* 'They which smiled at the *Theatre* in Rome, might as soon scoff at the rudeness of the scene, as give a plaudite at the perfection of the action.' He pretends to doubt whether the applause at the Theatre at Shoreditch in London—Rome was the canting name for London—was in mockery at the rude ignorance of the dramatist, or in admiration of the perfect acting of the players. We see already the rude and self-taught wit beginning to supplant in popularity the technical and pedantic university scholar, who thought his degree gave him the monopoly of play-books, and the exclusive privilege of pleasing.

Greene's other work, in 1587, was *Euphues his Censure to Philautus,* a philosophical combat between Hector and Achilles on the virtues of a gentleman and the perfection of a soldier. Both this book and the *Penelope's Web* are of a different texture from Greene's usual amatory pastorals, one being designed to exhibit the virtues of woman, 'Obedience, Chastity and Silence,' and the other the virtues of the gentleman and soldier. They are such books as a man might have written after bidding his farewell to folly. In *Euphues Censure*, Greene abandoned his old posy, *omne tulit punctum*, and adopted another, *Ea habentur optima quæ et jucunda honesta et utilia*.

In 1588, Greene's earliest publication was *Perimedes the Blacksmith*. By its Introduction we learn that the change in his posy had been made a joke of, and that some one of his plays had been ridiculed on the stage. 'I keep my old course still,' he says, 'to palter up something in prose, using mine old posy still, *omne tulit punctum*: although lately two gentlemen poets made two madmen of Rome beat it out of their paper bucklers, and had it in derision, for that I could not make my verses jet upon the stage in tragical buskins, every word filling the mouth like the fa-burden of Bow-bell, daring God out of heaven with that atheist Tamburlain, or blaspheming with the mad priest of the sun. But let me rather openly pocket up the ass at Diogenes' hand than wantonly set out such impious instances of intolerable poetry. Such mad and scoffing poets that have poetical spirits as bred of Merlin's race, if there be any in England that set the end of scholarism in an English blank-verse, I think either it is the humour of a novice that tickles them with self love, or too much frequenting the hot-house (to use the German proverb) hath sweat out all the greatest part of their wits.' The meaning of this 'dark speech,' as he calls it, is not far to seek. Greene had hitherto, whether in his tales or plays, confined himself to amatory subjects. This had been made a subject of criticism; he therefore, first on the stage, afterwards as a romance-writer, professed to change his subject, and to abjure love's lazy languishment. The play in which he did this is still extant. His *Comical history of Alphonsus King of Arragon* begins with Venus's offer to Calliope to be her scholar, and to write of deeds of war—

> 'And this my hand, which used for to pen
> The praise of Love, and Cupid's peerless power,
> Will now begin to treat of bloody Mars,
> Of doughty deeds and valiant victories.'

The result was a play manifestly written in imitation and emulation of *Tamburlain*. The hero's history is built on the same model; he is a beggar's son, who by prowess, impudence, and adroitness, wins crowns and kingdoms. Greene's challenge to Marlowe was not successful; and he attributes his failure to the absence of blasphemy in his lines. The criticism of the 'gentlemen poets,' however, was evidently that there was 'no point' in his poetry. They made two of their characters, 'two madmen of Rome,' beat his motto, *omne tulit punctum*, out of their paper bucklers. We can fancy the kind of jest here referred to; one like that with which Shakspere in *Love's Labour Lost* (v. 2, 276) makes Maria spoil the point of Dumain's words:

> 'Dumain was at my service, and his sword.
> "No point," quoth I; my servant straight was mute.'

But Greene could not stand a joke; he returned to his prose again, and wrote his gibe at the 'novices', 'that set the end of scholarism in an English blank verse.'

The two 'madmen of Rome' I suppose to be a kind of cant

term for two players. Greene, as we have seen in *Perimedes*, when he wished to criticize the London Theatre, talks of the Theatre in Rome. So in his *Never too late*, when he talks of the London actors, he pretends only to speak of Roscius and the actors of Rome. In the pedlar's French of the day, Rome-vyle was London, and Rome-mort the Queen.

It is to be noticed that the tale of Gradasso in *Perimedes* is in many parts almost word for word the same as 'Venus Tragedy,' or the tale of Valdrako in *Planetomachia*. The last-mentioned was the first immature sketch of the Saturnist; the picture in *Perimedes* is revised and augmented, superior both in volume and finish to the first sketch.

Greene's other publication of 1588 was *Pandosto, The Triumph of Time*. It has a double posy—*Temporis filia veritas*, and *omne tulit punctum*. It is dedicated to the Earl of Cumberland. Greene tells the Earl 'they which fear the biting of vipers do carry in their hands the plumes of a Phœnix,' and he shrouds his pamphlet under the Earl's patronage, 'doubting the dint of such envenomed vipers as seek with their slanderous reproaches to carp at all, being oftentimes most unlearned of all;' he assures himself, also, that the Earl's name will protect him 'from the poisoned tongues of such scorning sycophants.' In the Epistle to the readers, also, he hopes that 'though fond, curious, or rather currish, barkers breathe out slanderous speeches,' yet courteous readers will requite his travail, at least with silence.

The contest we see was becoming bitter; and it did not sweeten with time. Greene had fondly imagined that the cry went on him for the best playwright, but his pre-eminence was challenged; and when he found his rivals becoming more popular than he was, he wrote his *Menaphon* (1589), to show that if his plays were not the best in their kind, he was at least still unrivalled in what he was pleased to think a higher kind of writing, the prose romance. *Menaphon* was accordingly introduced to the world with an extraordinary flourish of trumpets. It had two commendatory copies of verses, one by Henry Upchear, gentleman, who says, that as far as he can see, Delos is no better than Arcadia—

'[Where] feeds our Menaphon's celestial muse—
There makes his pipe his pastoral report,
Which strained now a note above his use
Foretells, he'll ne'er more chant of Choas sport.'

This looks as if Greene, like his partner playwright Lodge, now declared that he would never more write for the stage. The other copy of verses, by Thomas Brabine, Gent, is plainer—

'Come forth you wits that vaunt the pomp of speech,
And strive to thunder from a stageman's throat;
View *Menaphon*, a note beyond your reach,
Whose sight will make your drumming descant doat.
Players, avaunt! you know not to delight;
Welcome, sweet shepherd, worth a scholars sight.'

The story itself was intended by Greene to bear a part in the controversy between himself and the players. If, says he, in the Epistle to the Readers, 'you find dark enigmas or strange conceits, as if Sphinx on the one side and Roscius on the other were playing the wags,' I 'desire you to take a little pains to pry into my imagination.' It would not have been easy for us to discover his imagination, if he had not employed Thomas Nash to write an epistle, addressed to 'the gentlemen students of both universities,' as a preface to his pastoral. Nash had been rusticated from Cambridge in

1586, for his share in some satire, which, though resented by the authorities, had served to discover his powers to his friends. Afterwards he went to Ireland and Italy, and from Italy he seems to have been summoned to take part with Lily, Greene, and the rest employed by Archbishop Whitgift, through Bancroft, to oppose Martin Mar-Prelate with his own weapons of scurrility and lampoon. It appears from Nash's first production in this kind, his *Countercuffe given to Martin Junior by . . . Pasquil of England*, which he dates 'from Gravesend Barge, the 8th of August, the first and last year of Martinism,' that after spending two years abroad, he had come 'lately over sea into Kent,' and from thence had 'cut over into Essex from Gravesend.' After so long an absence it is not likely that he could have been an original authority for literary affairs which had occurred while he was away. He was in demand for his style, and his business was to reduce to pointed form the matter furnished him by others. Hence his publications of 1589 must be supposed to represent, not the fruits of his own experience, but the ideas decanted into him. Greene may be assumed to have crammed him with what had to be said as introduction to *Menaphon*; and the identity of idea, as well as of phrase, between Nash's epistle and things which Greene subsequently wrote will prove this assumption to be correct. We shall see that the actor-author here attacked by Nash is assailed in the same phrases as the one attacked by Greene three years later, in his *Groatsworth of Wit*. But in the latter case it is Shakespeare who is thus assailed. Therefore it is probably, also, Shakespeare in the former case.

Nash begins by recommending to the university men the 'scholar-like shepherd' who wrote *Menaphon*, as one of themselves;

implying that his opponent was neither scholar-like nor a university man. He immediately goes on to complain that university scholarship is being eclipsed by the example and teaching of the stage. The 'gowned age' has grown eloquent, and every 'mechanical mate abhors the English he was born to, and plucks, with solemn periphrasis, his *ut vales* from the ink-horn.' This comes not, he says, from art and study, but from 'the servile imitation of our vain-glorious tragedians,' who study not grace of action, but mouthing of words, and who delight 'to embowel the clouds in a speech of comparison; thinking themselves more than initiated in poets' immortality if they once get Boreas by the beard, and the heavenly Bull by the dewlap.' This phrase serves to identify the 'vain-glorious tragedian' of Nash with the 'Roscius' who, as Greene tells us, plays the wag in *Menaphon*. In that pastoral this personage appears under the name of the shepherd Doron, and the following 'speech of comparison' is put into his mouth to describe Samela, the heroine. 'We had an ewe amongst our rams whose fleece was white as *the hairs that grow on father Boreas' chin*,[1] or as the *dangling dewlap of the silver bull*; her front curled like the Erimanthian boar, and spangled like to the worsted stockings of Saturn; her face like Mars treading upon the milk-white clouds ... her eyes like the fiery torches tilting against the moon.' This affectation of actors and audience, Nash continues, 'is all traceable to their idiot art-masters,' that is, the self-dubbed masters of the art, who have no university degree, 'that intrude themselves ... as the alchemists of eloquence, who (mounted on the stage of arro-

---

[1] This seems copied from *Taming of a Shrew*, p. 22, where Ferando compares Kate to the white hairs on Boreas' chin; Hyperion's curls (*Hamlet*), not Erymanthian boar's; 'worsted-stocking knave' (*Lear*).

gance) think to outbrave better pens with the swelling bombast of bragging blank verse.' It will be remembered that Greene afterwards says of the stage-man, Shake-scene, that he 'supposes he is as well able to bombast out a blank verse as the best of you.' Nash proceeds—' Indeed it may be the ingrafted overflow of some kill-cow conceit, that overcloyeth their imagination with more than drunken resolution, being not extemporal in the invention of any other means to vent their manhood, commits the digestion of their choleric encumbrances to the spacious volubility of a drumming decasyllabon.' Killing the cow, or the calf, was a kind of extemporal performance of vagrant actors, and the tradition about Shakespeare was that 'he would kill a calf in high style.' Nash says that the person of whom he writes, instead of venting his kill-cow conceit in the usual extemporal way, would commit it to the drumming blank-verse. 'Amongst this kind of men,' he proceeds, 'that repose eternity in the mouth of a player' (seek the poets' immortality in the passing popularity of the unprinted play), 'I can but engross some deep-read schoolmen or grammarians' (whose reading is so deep that it stopped at the grammar-school), 'who having no more learning in their skull than will serve to take up a commodity' (to keep a tradesman's books), 'nor art in their brains than was nourished in a serving-man's idleness, will take upon them to be the ironical censurers of all, when God and poetry doth know they are the simplest of all,'—which is evidently a mere paraphrase of a sentence of Greene's previously quoted from *Pandosto*, about men who 'carp at all, being oftentimes most unlearned of all.'

Nash then passes from these lacklatins, whom he leaves 'to the mercy of their mother-tongue, that feed on nought but the crumbs that fall from the translator's trencher,' to Greene's *Menaphon*,

which he praises, first, for the rapidity of its composition, and
secondly, for being original, and not stolen from a foreign source;
and then he digresses into an abuse of Martin Mar-Prelate, and its
supposed author Penry. But he soon returns to lighter literature,
and to the subject of 'our trivial translators,' and those who feed
from their trencher, among whom he cannot resist once more en-
grossing the actor-poet whom he has already attacked. 'It is a
common practice,' he says, 'now-a-days, amongst a sort of shifting
companions, that run through every art and thrive by none, to
leave the trade of *noverint* whereto they were born, and busy themselves with the endeavours of art, that could scarcely latinize their
neck-verse, if they should have need. Yet English Seneca read by
candle-light yields many good sentences, as "blood is a beggar,"
and so forth; and if you intreat him fair in a frosty morning, he
will afford you whole Hamlets, I should say handfuls, of tragical
speeches.' 'But... what's that which will last always?... Seneca,
let blood line by line, and page by page, at length must die to our
stage, which makes his famished followers ..... leap into a new
occupation, and translate two-penny pamphlets from the Italian,[1]
without any knowledge even of its articles.' 'And no matter .....
for what can be hoped of those that thrust Elisium into Hell, and
have not learned, so long as they have lived in the spheres, the just
measure of the horizon without an hexameter? Sufficeth it them
to botch up a blank-verse with *ifs* and *ands*.' From this abuse of
the translators and adapters from the Italian, Nash proceeds, following Ascham's *Schoolmaster*, which had also been Lily's text-book
for his *Euphues*, to talk about the lights of St John's College, Cambridge, and about Trinity College, which was only a *Colonia deducta*

[1] *i.e.* take the plots of their plays from Italian sources.

from it, and about the evil of epitomes and compendiums. Then he returns to the puritanical 'divinity-dunces,' and then gives a list of the English poets whom he approves. After some paragraphs upon them, he comes to 'George Peele, the chief supporter of pleasaunce now living, the atlas of poetry, and *primus verborum artifex;* whose first increase, *the Arraignment of Paris*, might plead . . . his pregnant dexterity of wit and manifold variety of invention, wherein (*me judice*) he goeth a step beyond all that write.'

Nash was unable to mention a play and its writer without making a third attack on the players, and their own poet, who, by his works, maliciously enumerated here, is identified with the player-poet attacked by Greene in his *Groatsworth of Wit*. 'Sundry other sweet gentlemen I do know, that we [sic] have vaunted their pens in private devices, and tricked up a company of taffaty fools with their feathers,[1] whose beauty, if our poets had not pecked' [*sic;* apparently it should be 'decked'] 'with the supply of their perriwigs, they might have anticked it until this time up and down the country with *The King of Fairies*, and dined every day at the pease-porridge ordinary with *Delfrigus*.' The *King of Fairies* and *Delfrigus* are the plays for which the player-poet in the *Groatsworth of Wit* is famous, as will be seen below. Nash proceeds: 'But Tolasso hath forgotten that it was sometime sacked, and beggars[2] that ever they carried their fardels on footback; and in truth no

---

[1] Notice this; it proves that when Greene, three years later, called Shakespeare 'an upstart crow, beautified with our feathers,' he need not have meant anything more than that he was an actor, who had gained his reputation by speaking the verses that the poets had written for him.

[2] See Jonson's *Poetaster*, III. i., where Tucca says to Histrio, 'If he pen for thee once, thou shalt not need to travel with pumps full of gravel any more, after a blind jade and a hamper, and stalk upon boards and barrell-heads to an old crackt trumpet.'

marvel, whereas the deserved reputation of one Roscius is of force to enrich a rabble of counterfeits. Yet let subjects, for all their insolence, dedicate a "de profundis" every morning to the preservation of their Cæsar, lest their increasing indignities return them ere long their juggling to mediocrity, and they bewail in weeping blanks the wane of their monarchy.' This sentence implies that the players had been very successful, in spite of, perhaps because of, their neglect of Greene, Peele, and the University crew; but Nash warns them, that as their first successes were in the plays which these authors wrote for them, so the ultimate consequence of their ceasing to write will be the ruin of the players. Nash then speedily comes to an end; he calls the preface he has just written 'the firstlings of his folly,' his first published work, and announces another work, the *Anatomy of Absurdity*, in which he will go on persecuting the idiots who have made art bankrupt.

The *Anatomy of Absurdity* was published under the same circumstances as the preface just analyzed. Nash was recently arrived, and too busy to have been capable of forming an independent critical judgment of the state of literature. The new work was just as much dictated to him by Greene as the old one. The prime idea of it was to inveigh against women, condemning almost all by the example of one whose severity had caused him to fly his country two years before. It was dedicated to Sir Charles Blunt, to whom at the end of the preceding year Greene had dedicated his *Alcida*, a book of similar argument, discovering 'the anatomy of women's affections, setting out as in a mirror how dangerous his hazard is, that sets his rest upon love.' In the parts of his new book that relate to literature, Nash repeats the ideas, almost the phrases, that he had published in Greene's *Menaphon*. He talks of those 'that obtrude themselves as the authors of eloquence and fountains of our finer phrases' . . . . . . who, he says, resemble 'drums, which, being empty within, sound big without.' There is the same gird at those who depend on translations, 'whose threadbare knowledge, being bought at second hand, is spotted, blemished, and defaced through translators' rigorous rude dealing,' and the ignorant sonnetteers and ballad-makers (under which term we are also to understand play-makers) are thus attacked: 'What politic counsellor or valiant soldier will joy or glory of this, in that some stitcher, weaver, spendthrift or fiddler, hath shuffled or slubbered up a few ragged rhymes in the memorial of the ones prudence or the others prowess? It makes the learned sort to be silent, whereas they see unlearned sots so insolent. These buzzards think knowledge a burden, tapping it before they have half tunned it, venting it before they have filled it. . . . They come to speak before they come to know. They contemn arts as unprofitable, contenting themselves with a little country grammar knowledge.' Again: 'Far more ardent is the desire of knowing unknown things than of repeating known things. This we see happen in stage players, in orators . . . . . Many there be that are out of love with the obscurity wherein they live, that to win credit to their name . . . encounter with them on whose shoulders all arts do lean' (such as Peele, the 'Atlas of Poetry'). 'These upstart reformers of arts . . . will seem wise before their time, that now they both begin to counterfeit that which they are not, and to be ashamed of that which they are' (*i. e.* to counterfeit being poets, and to be ashamed of being players) . . . . . 'He that estimates arts by the insolence of idiots, who profess that wherein they are infants, may deem the university nought but the nurse of folly, and the knowledge of arts nought but the imitation of the stage.' Here we see plainly Greene's inspiration, and the hatred which he infused into Nash of the upstart crow, the unlearned country wit, who was not contented with his place, but took upon him to usurp the functions of the licenciates of the Universities, and to instruct the people in novel principles of art.

Doron, in Greene's *Menaphon*, whom we have already identified with the poet-actor whom he wishes to criticize, is not a very important person in the plot, nor are his several entrances very consistent with each other. His poetical description of Samela satisfies the courtly Melicertus, who says it is worthy of Paris on Helen. The 'jig' of 'plain Doron, as plain as a packstaffe', is ordinary pastoral. The joint eclogue of Doron and Carmela is simple clownery, and justifies his being called the 'homely blunt shepherd.' Nothing more can be extracted from this, than that Greene wished to represent his 'vain-glorious tragedian' as a boor and a clown. So, three years later, he classes 'Shakescene' among the 'peasants.'

In the same year, 1589, Greene published his *Ciceronis Tamor* or *Tullies Love*, and dedicated it to Ferdinando, Lord Strange.[1] He professes that it was meant, however unsuccessfully, to be an imitation of Cicero. And he thus apologizes for its inferiority, if it is inferior, to *Menaphon:* 'If my method be worse than it was wont to be, think that skill in music marred all; for the cleive was so dissonant from my note, that we could not clap a concord together by five marks. Chiron the Sagittory was but a feigned conceit, and men that bear great shapes and large shadows, and

---

[1] This dedication is one of the points of evidence. Lord Strange's players were the actors of *Fair Em*.

have no good nor honest minds, are like the portraitures of Hercules drawn upon the sands. If I speak mystically, think 'tis musically.' It is useless to attempt to give any certain explanation of these dark sayings, but the romance is important, for the drama of *Faire Em*, in which the loves of William the Conqueror and the Marquess Lubeck for Mariana and Blanche, are the counterparts of the loves of Lentulus and Tully for Terentia and Flavia in the story. Lentulus is the conqueror whose fancy is inflamed for Terentia by the soldier's description of her. He employs his friend Tully to woo for him. Tully, himself enamoured of her, loyally urges his friend's suit, making sacrifice of his own love. But the lady will not be thus bandied about. At length Lentulus, seeing that he cannot win Terentia, is won by Flavia's constant but hitherto slighted affection, and so leaves Terentia to Tully. There is certainly a general resemblance between the play and the romance, but this resemblance does not decide which was the earlier. My own impression is that the situation, and its appropriate passion, are more characteristic of Shakespeare than of Greene, as will appear farther on.

The Spanish Masquerado (1589), a pamphlet occasioned by the defeat of the Armada in the previous year, requires a passing notice. Greene was a little late in the field, but it appears from some Latin verses prefixed to *Alcida*, that in 1588 he was in the country, sick of a tedious fever. From the Epistle introducing the *Masquerado*, it is clear that Greene had not hitherto printed any of his penitential books. 'Hitherto, gentlemen, I have written of love, and I have found you favourable ... now, lest I might be thought to tie myself wholly to amorous conceits, I have adventured to discover my conscience in Religion.' At this time he was employed with Nash by Bancroft to lampoon Martin Mar-Prelate. An unwonted opening to high society was thus given to the two satirists; Nash brags of it in his *Pierce-Pennilesse;* the following lines of Lodge addressed to Greene and prefixed to the *Masquerado* speak of him as the scourge of the seditious puritans, and as having thereby become a companion for the gods—

> 'Ton nom (mon Greene) animé par mes vers
> Abaisse l'œil des gens seditieux.
> Tu, de mortel, es compagnon de Dieux.'

We come now to the series of penitential pieces, the *Mourning Garment, Never too Late,* and *Farewell to Folly;* the two first dated in 1590, the last written in 1587, but not published till 1591. I have already spoken of the *Mourning Garment,* the first of the series; the second, *Never too Late,* is divided into two parts, both, however, published the same year, 1590. Both are dedicated to Thomas Burnaby, and both introduced by commendatory verses by Ralph Sidley and Richard Hake. The first part has Greene's old posy ' *Omne tulit punctum;* ' the second a new one, taken from the Introduction to the *Mourning Garment,* ' *Sero sed serio.*' Sidley's lines prefixed to the first part seem to refer to the same book—

> 'There you may see repentance all in black,
> Scourging the forward passions of fond youth.'

Both parts contain an account of 'Francesco's fortunes,' related by a youthful and beautiful Palmer, who has reached Bergamo in his pilgrimage from England to Venice, by way of France, Germany, and the Rhine (B3 verso). The Palmer is evidently the same as Francesco; and Francesco, as Mr Dyce has shown in his life of the poet, is Greene. He was 'wandering in a strange land to satisfy the follies committed in England, travelling through many countries to make other men learn to beware of his harms.' He resolved how he would behave, and what he would say if he came amongst youth, amongst courtiers, or amongst lovers. In accordance with this triple division, his *Mourning Garment* is sent 'to all young gentlemen that wish to wean themselves from wanton desires,' that is, to lovers; his *Never too Late* 'to all youthful gentlemen;' and his *Farewell to Folly* to courtiers and scholars. I have hazarded an opinion that Greene's tour must be placed in 1586. It must have been made before August, 1589, since he says that he saw in Paris 'a king fit for so royal a regiment, if he had been as perfect in true religion as politic in martial discipline.' In fact, it must have been before May, 1588; when Henry III fled from Paris, which he was never to enter again. And it must have been considerably before that date, as Greene describes a court altogether undisturbed by proximate dangers. He had travelled in Spain and Italy before 1583; but afterwards he saw France, Germany, Poland, and Denmark; and this was, I suppose, in 1586. Greene's sketch of his own life tells us how after his marriage he had occasion to go to London,[1] where he was entangled in the snares of Infida, a

[1] 'At Cambridge, I light amongst wags as lewd as myself, with whom I consumed the flower of my youth, who drew me to travel into Italy and Spain, in which places I saw and practised such villany as is abominable to declare... At my return into England, I ruffled out in my silks, in the habit of malcontent... but after I had by degrees proceeded Master of Arts (1583) I left the University and away to London, where (... after a short time ...) I became an author of plays, and a penner of love-pamphlets... Once I felt a fear and horror in my conscience... This inward motion I received in Saint Andrew's Church in the city of Norwich, at a lecture or sermon ... being new-come from Italy... But this good motion lasted not long in me... Nevertheless, soon after I married a gentleman's daughter of good account, with whom I lived for a while; but ... after I had a child by her I cast her off... then left I her at six or seven, who went into Lincolnshire, and I to London.' It is clear, however, that his travels were more than to Spain and

woman who flattered him till he had spent all his money, and then cast him off. He goes on to tell us how Francesco (as he calls himself), in his poverty, cast about for means of getting bread, and in this humour 'fell in amongst a company of players, who persuaded him to try his wit in writing of comedies, tragedies, or pastorals, and if he could perform anything worthy of the stage, then they would largely reward him for his pains.' Thereupon Francesco 'writ a comedy, which so generally pleased all the audience, that happy were those actors in short time that could get any of his works, he grew so exquisite in that faculty.' As his wealth returned, Infida tried to lure him back; but he had learned wisdom, and therefore returned instead to his wife Isabel, who would not allow him to utter his self-reproaches. 'I see thou art penitent,' she said, 'and therefore I like not to hear what follies are past. It sufficeth for Isabel that henceforth thou wilt love Isabel; and upon that condition, without any more words, welcome to Isabel.'

The mention of the players was an occasion for venting his discontent with them, which Greene could not afford to let slip. He therefore makes one of the interlocutors ask about them, and then gives this elaborate answer, which, under the mask of a fictitious history, conveys his own personal feelings towards the contemporary stage. 'Although that some, for being too lavish against that faculty, have for their satirical invective been well canvassed; yet seeing here is none but ourselves, and that I hope what you hear shall be trodden under foot, I will flatly say what I can, both even

Italy. He says in his *Notable discovery of Cosenage*, 'I have smiled with the Italian ... eaten Spanish mirabolanes ... France, Germany, Poland, Denmark, I know them all.'

by reading and experience. The invention of comedies were first found amongst the Greeks and practised at Athens, some think by Menander, whom Terence so highly commends in his *Heauton-Timorumenos*. The reason was, that under the covert of such pleasant and comical events they aimed at the overthrow of many vanities that then reigned in the city; for therein they painted out in the persons the course of the world, how either it was graced with honour or discredited with vices. There might you see levelled out the vain life that boasting Thrasos use, smoothed up with the self-conceit of their own excellence; the miserable state of covetous parents, that rather let their sons taste of any misfortunes, than to relieve them with the superfluity of their wealth;[1] the portraiture of parasitical friends which sooth young gentlemen subtilly in their follies as long as they may *ex eorum sullo* [sic] *vivere*, was set out in lively colours. In these comedies the abuse of bauds that made sale of honest virgins, and lived by the spoil of women's honours, was deeply discovered; to be short, letchery, covetousness, pride, self-love, disobedience of [sic] parents, and such vices predominant both in age and youth, were shot at, not only with examples and instances to feed the eye, but with golden sentences of moral works to please the ear. Thus did Menander win honour in Greece with his works, and reclaim both old and young from their vanities by the pleasant effect of his comedies. After him this faculty grew to be famous in Rome, practised by Plautus, Terence, and other that excelled in this quality, all aiming, as Menander did, in all their works to suppress vice and advance virtue. Now so highly were comedies esteemed in those days, that men of great honour and account were the actors, the senate and the consuls

[1] But look in *Cassiodorus*, IV, Vinfi.

continually present as auditors at all such sports, rewarding the author with rich rewards, according to the excellency of the comedy. Thus continued this faculty famous, till covetousness crept into the quality, and that mean men, greedy of gains, did fall to practise the acting of such plays, and in the theatre presented their comedies but to such only as rewarded them well for their pains. When thus comedians grew to be mercenaries, then men of account left to practise such pastimes, and disdained to have their honours blemished with the stain of such base and vile gains; insomuch that both Comedies and Tragedies grew to less account in Rome, in that the free sight of such sports was taken away by covetous desires. Yet the people (who are delighted with such novelties and pastimes) made great resort, paid largely, and highly applauded their doings; insomuch that the actors, by continual use, grew not only excellent, but rich and insolent. Amongst whom, in the days of Tully, one Roscius grew to be of such exquisite perfection in his faculty, that he offered to contend with the orators of that time in gesture, as they did in eloquence, boasting that he would express a passion in as many sundry actions as Tully could discourse it in variety of phrases. Yea, so proud he grew by the daily applause of people, that he looked for honour and reverence to be done him in the streets, which self-conceit, when Tully entered into with a piercing insight, he quipped at in this manner.

'It chanced that Roscius and he met at a dinner, both guests unto Archias the poet, where the proud comedian dared to make comparison with Tully; which insolency made the learned orator to grow into these terms. "Why, Roscius, art thou proud with Æsop's crow, being pranked with the glory of others' feathers? Of thyself thou canst say nothing; and if the cobler hath taught thee to say *Ave Cæsar!* disdain not thy tutor because thou pratest in a king's chamber. What sentence thou utterest on the stage flows from the censure of our wits; and what sentence or conceit of the invention the people applaud for excellent, that comes from the secrets of our knowledge. I grant your action, though it be a kind of mechanical labour, yet well done, 'tis worthy of praise; but you worthless, if for so small a toy you wax proud."

'At this Roscius waxed red, and bewrayed his imperfection with silence. But this check of Tully could not keep others from the blemish of that fault, for it grew to a general vice among the actors, to excel in pride as they did exceed in excellence, and to brave it in the streets as they brag it on the stage. So that they revelled it in Rome in such costly robes that they seemed rather men of great patrimony than such as lived by the favour of the people, which Publius Servilius very well noted; for he, being the son of a senator, and a man very valiant, met on a day with a player in the streets richly apparelled, who so far forgat himself, that he took the wall of the young nobleman, which Servilius, taking in disdain, counter-checked with this frump. "My friend" (quoth he), "be not so brag of thy silken robes, for I saw them but yesterday make a great show in a broker's shop." At this the one was ashamed, and the other smiled; and they which heard the quip, laughed at the folly of the one and the wit of the other. Thus, sir, have you heard my opinion briefly of plays; that Menander devised them for the suppressing of vanities, necessary in a commonwealth as long as they are used in their right kind; the playmakers worthy of honour for their art; and players men deserving both praise and profit as long as they wax neither covetous nor insolent.' (Ed. 1590, sig. B4, recto and verso, and C recto.)

It seems that this attack on the players in the first part of *Never too Late* renewed the old quarrels, and subjected Greene to reprisals; to these Richard Hake alludes at the end of his lines prefixed to the second part—

'But envy lives too much in these our days—*Virtutis comes invidia.*'

And Ralph Sidley still more clearly—

'The more it works, the quicker is the wit;
The more it writes, the better to be 'steem'd.
By labour ought men's wills and wits be deem'd,
Though dreaming dunces do inveigh against it.
But write thou on, though Momus sit and frown;
A Carter's jig is fittest for a clown.
Bonum quo communius eo melius.'

The 'carter's jig' was probably some country drama in which Greene was glanced at. And as in *Menaphon* he had shown up, as Doron, the Roscius who had offended him, so in the second part of *Never too Late* he introduces an episode at the end, 'The Host's tale,' in which the same jig-maker and player is more virulently attacked under the name of Mullidor. The story is,—A beautiful shepherdess, Mirimida, is woo'd by three lovers; Eurymachus the shepherd, Radagon the courtier, and Mullidor the clown. The last will be seen to be identical with Doron in *Menaphon* by any one who will take the trouble to compare the two novels. He is said to be 'a fellow that was of honest parents, but very poor; and his personage was as if he had been cast in Æsop's mould; his back like a lute, and his face like Thersites', his eyes broad and tawny, his hair harsh and curled like a horse-mane, his lips were of the largest size in folio... The only good part that he had to grace his visage was his nose, and that was conqueror-like, as beaked as an eagle... Into his great head [Nature] put little wit, that he knew rather his sheep by the number, for he was never no good arithmetician, and yet he was a proper scholar, and well seen in ditties' (sig. G3). The speeches put into his mouth, and the letter he is supposed to write, are the things which serve to identify him with Doron. Thus his address to Mirimida (sig. H), 'Here is weather that makes grass plenty and sheep fat; by my troth, there never came a more plenteous year; and yet I have one sheep in my fold that's quite out of liking... The other day as he was grazing he spied a spotted ewe feeding before him; with that he fell to gaze on her, and that so long, that he wagged his tail for very joy, and with a sheepish courtesy courted her; the ewe was coy and butted him,' &c... 'You are the ewe that hath so caught Mullidor captive.' ... Again (sig. H3), 'Oh love, thou art like a flea which bitest sore, and yet leapest away and art not to be found; or to a pot of strong ale that maketh a man call his father whoreson.' Again (sig. K), 'Mullidor the malcontent, with his pen clapt full of love, to his Mistress Mirimida, greeting. After my hearty commendations remembered, hoping you be in as good health as I was at the making hereof. This is to certify you that love may be compared to a bottle of hay ... or to a cup full of strong ale... After the furious flames of your two eyes had set my poor heart on the coals of love, I was so scorched on the gridiron of affection that I had no rest till I was almost turned to a coal; and after I had tasted of the liquor of your sweet phisnomy, I never left supping of your amiable countenance till with love I am almost ready to burst.' That which is common to Doron and Mullidor is the simple country clownery which eschews, because it knows not, the refinements of pedantry and scholarship. It is not very consistent that Mullidor's madrigal should have a French refrain.

Whether this episode was an answer to *Faire Em*, or whether the story of *Faire Em* and her three lovers was a reply to this episode, I cannot tell. But it is certain that about this time the play of *Faire Em* was in existence, for in his next publication Greene attacked it with great virulence. The probability is that it was already an old play, written perhaps in 1587, before the *Farewell to Folly* was entered on the Stationers' registers. It was meant for a country play, written for Lord Strange's men to act in Lancashire and Cheshire. The references to the 'good Sir Edmond Trafford' would be hardly intelligible elsewhere, and Greene's attack upon it would scarcely be made till it had been played on the London boards, and become known to the Londoners, for whom he wrote his pamphlets.

The play is built on two plots interwoven together. The secondary plot tells of the loves of William the Conqueror, and discusses in the manner of Greene's *Arbasto* and his *Tully's Love* the question, 'What happens when a man loves a lady who dislikes him, and dislikes another who loves him?' The chief plot tells the story of *Faire Em*, the miller's daughter of Manchester, and her three lovers, Mandeville, the Manchester gentleman, and Mounteney and Valingford, the nobles of William's court. The desertion of Em by Mandeville, after gaining her heart, is a feature also contained in the episode of Alexis and Rosamund in the *Mourning Garment*. Rosamund, like Em, was beloved by all who saw her, whether king, courtier, or clown. Brought into court to choose her mate, she fixed on the shepherd Alexis; he carried her home in triumph, but soon secretly transferred his affections to Phillida.

This 'at last came to the ears of Rosamund, but she, incredulous, would not believe, nor Alexis confess it, till at last Sydaris [Rosamund's father] espied it, and told it to his daughter, wishing her to cast off so inconstant a lover. But love that was settled in the centre of her heart made her passionate, but with such patience that she smothered the heat of her sorrows with inward conceit, pining away as a woman forlorn, till on a day Alexis, over-doating in his fancies, stept to the church and married himself to Phillida.' Rosamund then sings her swan-song and dies; and Alexis goes down to the water-side and hangs himself in a willow-tree.

In the play, Em is soon consoled for the loss of Mandeville, but in other respects the foregoing extract is a good summary of some of its scenes. In the last act, where Mandeville, repentant, seeks to return to Em, and is rejected both by her and by his new love, comes what Greene perhaps considered the greatest insult. Mandeville rejects love entirely, just as Greene does in the *Mourning Garment*. Women, he says, are evils; he will none of them. As Philador says to the lover whom he saves from suicide in the *Mourning Garment*, 'did'st thou know what a world of woes thou dost enter into by taking a wife, thou would'st say, "Fie on love, and farewell to women!" Be she never so fair, thou shalt find faults enow in her face shortly to mislike . . . . they are sullen; and be *Morosæ* . . . . or scolds . . . . or froward . . . . deceitful, flattering, sick with the puff of every wind, and lowering at the show of every storm.'

The play, however, has a symbolical meaning. Both branches of the plot refer to events in the history of the stage. William the Conqueror is William Kempe, who in 1586 went as head of a company to Denmark to espouse the princess Blanch, that is, to make himself the master of the Danish stage. But on his arrival there he was more struck with the chances of another career, and very soon eloped to Saxony, to turn his histrionic talents to more account there. Mounteney and Valingford are two of his company whom he would have taken with him, but who preferred to stay behind, and contend for the prize of the Manchester stage, which Lord Strange's players were then bringing into repute.[1]

And the second part of the plot carries on the history of this Manchester contention. The windmill, with its clapper and its grist, is the type of the theatre; the wind is either the encouraging breath of the audience, or the voice of the actors,[2] the clapper the applause, and the grist the gains. The miller's daughter is the prize; he who wins her bears the bell as play-wright. Her three wooers are, 1. Mandeville, Greene, the double-man with two mistresses, who knows not whether to devote himself to the play or the pastoral tale, and at last falls between two stools, is rejected by both, and in return rejects both. 2. There is the stilted Mounteney

---

[1] Look into the histories of Manchester and Lancashire for any notices of the stage, or of town festivals and shows there.

[2] Without favour art is like a windmill without wind. Danish proverb, Bohn's Handbook, p. 270.

Also B. R.'s dedication of '*Greene's News both from Heaven and Hell*' to Gregory Coole, to recall him 'from that melancholy conceit that hath so long pestered your brains for the loss of a mill dismembered and shaken down by the rage of a felling puff of wind; but such a paltry tempest should not dismay a man of your spirit.'

The *Windmill* is the tavern where the wedding supper is given in Jonson's *Every man in his humour*.

Buckle notices that 'a windmill' is mentioned in the Council Register of Aberdeen in 1602. (Posthumous Works, iii. p. 593, No. 684.)

The player to Roberto in Greene's *Groatsworth of Wit*, 'So I am [i.e. a substantial man] where I dwell, reputed able at my proper cost to build a *windmill*.'

with his highflying rodomontade, always losing his head in the clouds. This is Marlowe. 3. There is also the plain-spoken and homely Valingford, who is Shakespeare. Mandeville is the first love of Em, the first to gain a transient reputation as the most eminent dramatist; Em will look on no other, but feigns herself deaf and blind, to prevent the advances of Mounteney and Valingford. Mandeville and Mounteney come to think her really deaf and blind, so they forsake her. Valingford sees through the pretence, and by his constancy and perseverance wins her. Mounteney and Valingford conclude with making a scorn of Mandeville.

This satire moved Greene's indignation, and he replied in the introduction to his next work, the *Farewell to Folly*. In the bitter conclusion he tells the writer of *Faire Em*, that so far from being the first dramatist, he is a dunce who draws his plots from ballads, and cannot write English without the help of parish clerks. The introduction is as follows:

'Gentlemen and students (my old friends and companions), I presented you alate with my *Mourning Garment*. How you censure of the cloth or cut I know not; but the printer hath passed them all out of his shop, and the pedlar found them too dear for his pack, that he was fain to bargain for the life of Tomlivolin [Tamburlain] to wrap up his sweet powders in those unsavoury papers. If my garment did any gentleman good I am glad; if it offended none, I am proud; if goodman Find-fault, that hath his wit in his eyes, and can check what he cannot amend, mislike it, I am careless; for Diogenes hath taught me that to kick an ass when he strikes were to smell of the ass for meddling with the ass. Having, therefore, gentlemen (in my opinion), mourned long enough for the misdeeds of my youth, lest I should seem too pharisaical in my fasts, or, like our dear English brethren, that measure their prayers by the hour-glass, fall asleep in preaching of repentance, I have now left off the intent and am come to the effect, and after my mourning, present you with my farewell to follies, an ultimum vale to all youthful vanities, wishing all gentlemen, as well courtiers as scholars, to take view of those blemishes that dishonour youth with the quaint show of pleasant delights. What a glorious show would the spring present if the beauty of her flowers were not nipped with frosts! How would autumn boast of her fruits if she were not disfigured with the fall of the leaf! And how would the virtues of youth shine (polished with the ripe conceit of wit) if they were not eclipsed with the cloud of vanity! Then, sweet companions and love-mates of learning, look into my *Farewell*, and you shall find the poisons which infect young years, and, turning the leaf, read the antidotes to prevent the force of such deadly confections. Lay open my life in your thoughts, and beware by my loss; scorn not in your age what you have learned in your accidence; though stale, yet as sure a check—*felix quem faciunt aliena pericula cautum*. Such wags as have been wanton with me, and have marched in the Mercers book to please their mistress eye with their bravery, that, as the frolic phrase is, have made the tavern to sweat with riotous expenses, that have spent their wits in courting of their sweet-hearts, and emptied their purses with being too prodigal, let them at last look back to the follies of their youth, and with me say farewell unto all such vanities. But those young novices that have not yet lost the maidenhead of their innocency, nor have not heard the melody of such alluring syrens, let them read, that they may loathe, and that, seeing into the depth of their folly, they may the more detest that whose poisoned sweetness they never tasted. Thus, generally, I would wish all to beware by me, to say with me, farewell to folly. Then should I glory that my seed, sown with so much good-will, should yield a harvest of so great advantage.

'But, by your leave, gentlemen, some, overcurious, will carp and say, that if I were not beyond I would not be so bold to teach my betters their duty, and to show them the sun that have brighter eyes than myself. Well, Diogenes told Alexander of his folly, and yet he was not a king. Others will flout and over-read every line with a frump, and say 'tis scurvy, when they themselves are such scabbed lads that they are like to die of the *fazion*[1]; but if they come to write, or publish anything in print, it is either distilled out of ballets,[2] or borrowed of Theological poets,[3] which, for their calling and gravity being loth to have any prophane pamphlets pass under their hand, get some other Batillus to set his name to their verses. Thus is the ass made proud by this underhand brokery. And he that cannot write true English without the help of clerks of parish churches will needs make himself the father of interludes. O 'tis a jolly matter when a man hath a familiar style, and can endite a

---

[1] Fazion, *i.e.* the fashions, a disease of horses, like glanders. See *Taming of the Shrew*, iii. 2. It is usually derived from Ital. *farcina*, Fr. *farcin*. *Fasch*, in German, is the thrush, ulcers in children's throats. This, perhaps, is more akin to the disease which Greene evidently alludes to.

[2] Part of the plot of *Faire Em* was probably distilled from the ballad licensed to Henry Carre, March 2, 1580-1, under the title of *The Miller's Daughter of Manchester*.

[3] There are pieces of piety in *Faire Em* worthy of the Elizabethan pulpit, and quite justifying Greene's reference to the Theological poets. That Shakespeare had been compared to an unletter'd clerk by his rival, appears from Sonnet 85, where he says he can only—

'Like unletter'd clerk still say Amen
To every hymn that able spirit affords.'

whole year, and never be beholding to art. But to bring Scripture to prove anything he says, and kill it dead with the text in a trifling subject of love, I tell you is no small piece of cunning. As, for example, two lovers on the stage arguing one another of unkindness, his mistress runs over him with this canonical sentence, "A man's conscience is a thousand witnesses"; and her knight again excuseth himself with that saying of the Apostle, "Love covereth the multitude of sins." I think this was simple abusing of Scripture. In charity be it spoken, I am persuaded the Sexton of St Giles without Cripplegate would have been ashamed of such blasphemous rhetoric. But not to dwell on the imperfection of these dunces, or trouble you with a long commentary of such witless cockscombs, Gentlemen, I humbly intreat pardon for myself, that you will favour my Farewell, and take the presentation of my book to your judicial insights in good part; which courtesy if I find at your hands, as I little doubt of it, I shall rest yours, as I have ever done, Robert Greene.'

Greene was never careful to be accurate. The lines he quotes are from the closing scene of *Faire Em*, but are not bandied between two lovers as he describes. Blanche has run away with the man she wants to marry, and begs her father's pardon. He answers, that though she deserves punishment—

' Yet love, that covers multitude of sins,
  Makes love in parents wink at children's faults.' sc. xvii, l. 1271-2.

And then, a little way on, when Manville is being examined, whether it was to Em or to Elinor that he first made love, and he says it was to Em, Elinor replies,

'Yea, Manville, but there was no witness by.'

And Em retorts,

'Thy conscience is a thousand witnesses.' sc. xvii, l. 1308.

Greene, we see, here pretends that Shakespeare could not have written the play himself: it was written by some Theological poet, and fathered by him. For himself, he could not write true English without the help of a parish clerk, and the sexton of St Giles' Cripplegate would have been ashamed to have had a hand in such blasphemy as this. These insinuations are nothing extraordinary in the polemics of the period. When Decker began to ridicule Ben Jonson for his 'lime and hair,' *i. e.* his trade of a bricklayer, under the mask of Emulo in *Patient Grissel*, he ventured to say of the scholar that a challenge sent by him was not his own, but that 'he gave a sexton of a church a groat to write it, and he set his mark to it, for the gull can neither write nor read.' In the satirists of this period we must not always look for truth, however distorted. It was rather their cue to abuse with the most grotesque and improbable lies.

In this *Farewell to Folly* Greene changed his usual 'posy' *omne tulit punctum*, into *sero sed serio*, a sentence adopted from the Introduction to his *Morning Garment*. He dedicated it to Robert Cary, son of Lord Hunsdon, who had been a fellow-collegian at Oxford with his friend Lodge, through whom, perhaps, he obtained the introduction to him. In the dedication he says that he is 'indebted to all gentlemen, that with favours have overslipt my follies. Follies I term them, because their subjects have been superficial and their intents amorous, yet mixed with such moral principles that the precepts of virtue seemed to crave pardon for all those vain opinions love set down in his periods.' But age, he says, compels him *petere graviora ;* and he writes his *Farewell to Folly* to satisfy the hope of his friends, and to make the world privy to his private resolution. In this work he 'renounces love for a fool, and vanity as a vein too unfit for a gentleman.' But, he adds, 'some are so peremptory in their opinion, that if Diogenes stir his stumps they will say it is to mock dancers, not to be wanton; that if the fox preach, it is to spy which is the fattest goose, not to be a ghostly father; that if Greene write his *Farewell to Folly,* 'tis to blind the world with folly, the more to shadow his own folly. My reply to these thought-searchers is this—I cannot Martinize, swear by my fay in a pulpit, and rap out gogs-wounds in a tavern, feign love when I have no charity, or protest an open resolution of good when I intend to be privately ill; but in all public protestations my words and my deeds jump in one sympathy, and my tongue and my thoughts are relatives.'

This dedication to Robert Cary is evidently posterior to the dedication to him of *Orpharion* (licensed in 1589), when Greene had no other knowledge of his patron but what he had heard, probably from their common friend Lodge. . . . 'Hearing your worship to be indued with such honourable virtues and plausible qualities as draws men to admire and love such united perfection, I embolden myself to trust upon your worships courteous acceptance, which if it be such as others have found and I hoped for,' &c.

Greene declared that his *Farewell to Folly* was 'the last of such superficial labours,' and he told his readers to look for graver matter at his hands. This graver matter was his attack on coney-catchers, contained in several pamphlets, one of them a mere piracy from Harman's *Caveat to cursitors*[1]. In his *Repentance* (1592, sig.

---

[1] See the edition by Mr Viles and Mr Furnivall, Early English Text Society.

C3) he thanked God for having put this course into his head; because these discourses were his only publications which he could hope would do good. He did not, however, long confine himself to his new trade. Early in 1592 he published his *Philomela*, and in the address he wrote: 'I promised, Gentlemen, both in my *Mourning Garment* and *Farewell to Folly*, never to busy myself about any wanton pamphlets again . . . but yet am I come, contrary to vow and promise, once again to the press with a labour of love, which I hatched long ago, though now brought forth to light.' The *Quip for an upstart Courtier* published the same year is not 'a labour of love,' and so argues no breach of promise, though it is a flat piracy from the anonymous dialogue between velvet breeches and cloth breeches.[1] Not so, however, his posthumous publication, written shortly before his death in September, 1592 (he was buried on the 4th of that month), *A Groatsworth of wit bought with a million of repentance*.[2] This novel is to most intents a reproduction of Francesco's fortunes in *Never too Late*; its great interest centres in the letter to his brother play-wrights which the author appended to it, addressed 'To those gentlemen his quondam acquaintance, that spend their wits in making plays, R. G. wisheth a better exercise, and wisdom to prevent his extremities.' First he addresses Marlowe, the 'famous gracer of tragedians,' whom he implores to abandon his 'pestilent Machiavelian policy.' 'The broacher of this diabolical atheism is dead,' he says, . . . 'ended in despair,' and 'inherited the portion of Judas.' It was a favourite myth that Machiavelli had died by suicide. Malone made a bad guess when

---

[1] Not Francis Thynne's. The written F. T. on the title is a forgery. See my edition of Thynne's *Animadversions*.—F. J. F.
[2] Reprinted in New Shakspere Soc.'s *Allusion-Books*, 1874.

he supposed that Kett, who was burnt for heresy at Norwich in 1589, was the person here referred to. After Marlowe, Greene addresses 'young Juvenal, that biting Satirist, that lastly with me writ a comedy,' and calls him 'Sweet boy.' This is generally supposed to be Thomas Lodge, who was even at this time a satirist, for his book, *A Fig for Momus*, 1595, was only a selection from voluminous manuscripts that he had by him; he also had written a comedy, *A looking glass for London and England*, in conjunction with Greene. Dr Farmer thought the man referred to was Nash; but Malone thought this impossible, as Chettle, the publisher of the *Groatsworth of Wit*, laboured to vindicate Nash from being the writer of it, which he would not have needed to do, if any part of it had been professedly addressed to Nash. Yet I think it was Nash: for, first, Lodge was absent from England; he had sailed with Cavendish on the 26th of August, 1591; on the 13th of September, 1592, the ships got sight of the South Sea, and after cruel storms hardly escaped. One of the vessels reached Ireland June 11, 1593. Lodge can scarcely have been in England much before; and at the time when Greene is supposed to have been addressing him he was being buffetted in the Straits of Magellan. Secondly, Greene would scarcely have dwelt so strongly on Lodge's youth, or called him 'sweet boy,' when Lodge was his elder by about two years. Nash, on the other hand, was younger than Greene by seven years. Once more, the 'young Juvenal' does not seem to have been a professed play-writer, and is only addressed as such by Greene because he had 'lastly with him together writ a comedy.' Lodge and Greene's joint play was probably some five years old in 1592. But Greene and Nash had been since associated together in writing biting satires on Mar-Prelate and the puritans. Some of these satires were 'May games' exhibited on the stage. I would even go so far as to risk the conjecture that the *Knack to know a Knave*,[1] as we have it now, is the very comedy which was patched up by Nash and Greene out of an older play, as an attack on Martinism. On the other hand, Chettle's ignorance of Lodge and Nash is no marvel. He was unacquainted also with Shakespeare. Moreover, those who thought Nash the author of the *Groatsworth of Wit* may well have thought that he addressed himself as a device to blind readers to his authorship.

The third of the persons addressed by Greene is George Peele; and then comes the joint address to all three of them : ' base minded men all three of you, if by my misery ye be not warned; for unto none of you, like me, sought those burs to cleave; those puppets I mean that speak from our mouths, those antics garnished in our colours. Is it not strange[2] that I to whom they all have been beholding—is it not like that you to whom they all have beholding, shall, were ye in that case that I am now, be both of them at once forsaken? Yes, trust them not; For there is an upstart crow beautified with our feathers, that with his *tigres heart wrapt in a players hide*, supposes he is as well able to bombast out a blank-verse as the best of you ; and being an absolute Johannes-fac-totum, is in his own conceit the only Shakescene in a country. Oh that I might intreat your rare wits to be employed in more profitable courses, and let these apes imitate your past excellence, and never more acquaint them with your admired inventions! . . . seek

[1] The *Knack to know a Knave* was acted, as a new play, by Lord Strange's men, in June, 1592. The *Looking glass* was acted by them, as an old play, on the 8th of March, three months previously. The date of the *Knack* thoroughly well agrees with Greene's expression *lastly*.
[2] *i. e.*, If it is not.

you better masters; for it is pity men of such rare wits should be subject to the pleasures of such rude grooms.

'In this I might insert two more that both have writ against these buckram gentlemen; but let their own work serve to witness against their own wickedness if they persevere to maintain any more such peasants. For other new comers, I leave them to the mercy of these painted monsters... Trust not then... such weak stays, for they are as changeable in mind as in many attires. Well, my hand is tired, and I am forced to leave where I would begin; for a whole book cannot contain their wrongs, which I am forced to knit up in some few lines of words.'

The quarrel, which thus at last found articulate utterance, had been long brewing. There can be very little doubt that the Shake-scene who 'supposes he is as well able to bombast out a blank-verse as the best of you,' is the same man whom Nash, under Greene's instructions, had attacked three years before as one of the 'idiot art-masters' of the players, 'that intrude themselves... as the alchemists of eloquence, who (mounted on the stage of arrogance) think to outbrave better pens with the swelling bombast of bragging blank-verse.' The idea 'beautified with our feathers' had been constantly used both by Greene and Nash. In Nash's Preface to *Menaphon*, 1589, the actors were 'taffata fools tricked up with our feathers;' in *Never too Late*, 1590, Greene makes Cicero say to Roscius, 'Why art thou proud with Æsop's crow being pranked with the glory of others feathers?' The phrase, therefore, does not necessarily mean that Shakespeare had altered and appropriated 'certain plays which had been written either separately or conjointly, by Greene, Marlowe, Lodge, [Nash] or Peele,' as Mr Dyce says. It simply means that he was an actor, who had acted in plays written by those men, and was thus dressed out in their feathers. And although the obscure author of *Greene's Funerals*, who thought Greene Jove for judgment, Apollo for learning, Mercury for eloquence, and Guy for courtesy, chooses to interpret the passage, 'the men that so eclipsed his fame purloined his plumes,' yet Chettle who had published the accusation had to retract it, and to confess that 'divers of worship have reported his [Shakespeare's] uprightness of dealing which argues his honesty, and his facetious grace in writing that approves his art.' Shakespeare, he says, had too much honesty to steal, and too much facility in writing to need to steal.

So much for the epistle annexed to the *Groatsworth of Wit*. In the novel itself, Greene gives us a new and improved version of his first introduction to the players, and his subsequent life. In *Never too Late* he called himself Francesco; here he calls himself Roberto, and opens the story with his marriage, his desertion of his wife, and his attachment to a courtezan, on whom he wasted all his substance. When he is reduced to poverty his leman discards him; he sits like an outcast under a hedge, and bemoans his wretched plight. 'On the other side of the hedge sat one that heard his sorrow, who, getting over, came . . . and saluted Roberto. . . "If you vouchsafe such simple comfort as my ability will yield, assure yourself that I will endeavour to do the best that . . . may procure your profit . . . the rather, for that I suppose you are a scholar; and pity it is men of learning should live in lack." Roberto . . . uttered his present grief, beseeching his advice how he might be employed. "Why easily," quoth he, "and greatly to your benefit; for men of my profession get by scholars their whole living." "What is your profession?" said Roberto. "Truly, sir," said he, "I am a player." "A player!" quoth Roberto; "I took you rather for a gentleman of great living; for if by outward habit men should be censured, I tell you you would be taken for a substantial man." "So am I, where I dwell," quoth the player, "reputed able at my proper cost to build a windmill. What though the world once went hard with me, when I was fain to carry my playing fardel a foot-back? *Tempora mutantur*—I know you know the meaning of it better than I, but I thus construe it—*It is otherwise now;* for my very share in playing apparel will not be sold for two hundred pounds." "Truly," said Roberto, "it is strange that you should so prosper in that vain practice, for that it seems to me your voice is nothing gracious." "Nay, then," said the player, "I mislike your judgment; why, I am as famous for *Delphrygus* and *The King of Fairies* as ever was any of my time; *The twelve labours of Hercules* have I terribly thundered on the stage, and played three scenes of the Devil in *The Highway to Heaven*." "Have ye so?" said Roberto; "then I pray you pardon me." "Nay, more," quoth the player, "I can serve to make a pretty speech, for I was a country author, passing at a Moral; for it was I that penned *The Moral of Man's wit*, *The Dialogue of Dives*, and for seven years space was absolute interpreter of the puppets. But now my almanac is out of date:

    'The people make no estimation
    Of morals, teaching education—'

Was not this pretty for a plain rhyme extempore? If ye will ye shall have more." "Nay, it is enough," said Roberto; "but how mean ye to use me?" "Why, sir, in making plays," said the other, "for which you shall be well paid, if you will take the pains." Roberto, perceiving no remedy, thought it best to respect his present necessity, [and,] to try his wit, went with him willingly; who lodged him at the town's end in a house of retail . . . there by conversing with bad company, he grew *a malo in pejus*, falling from one vice to another. . . But Roberto, now famoused for an arch- playmaking poet, his purse, like the sea, sometime swelled, anon, like the same sea, fell to a low ebb; yet seldom he wanted, his labours were so well esteemed. Marry, this rule he kept, whatever he fingered beforehand, was the certain means to unbind a bargain; and being asked why he so slightly dealt with them that did him good, "It becomes me," saith he, "to be contrary to the world. For commonly when vulgar men receive earnest, they do perform. When I am paid anything aforehand, I break my promise."'

This last sentence, taken in conjunction with the following paragraph from Cuthbert Cony-catchers *Defence of Cony-catching*, 1592, easily justifies the actors in their conduct to Greene. 'What if I should prove you a cony-catcher, Master R[obert] G[reene], would it not make you blush at the matter? . . . Ask the Queen's players if you sold them not *Orlando Furioso* for twenty nobles, and when they were in the country sold the same play to the Lord Admiral's men for as many more? . . . But I hear, when this was objected, that you made this excuse; that there was no more faith to be held with players than with them that valued faith at the price of a feather; for as they were comedians to art, so the actions of their lives were Camelion-like; that they were uncertain, variable, time-pleasers, men that measured honesty by profit, and that regarded their authors not by desert, but by necessity of time.'

It is singular that Greene should here select Delphrygus and the King of Fairies as the note of the actor whom he denounces, just as Nash had done three years before in his preface to *Menaphon*.

Whether Delphrygus is the 'laureate bachelor Del Phrygio' mentioned by Guilpin in his *Skialetheia*, or a mistake for *Belphegor*, maliciously foisted on the actor, I know not. Belphegor, Oberon, the Devil in the *Highway to Heaven*, Merlin and his spirit father (referred to in *Perimedes*), are all characters which we may well suppose the youthful Shakespeare meditated upon. What he has done with Oberon we all know. There are scenes in the *Birth of Merlin*, one of the plays attributed to him, that are almost worthy of his pen. Even the scenes respecting Belphegor in *Grim the Collier* may retain something of the corrections and alterations of the managing *Johannes-fac-totum*. But to leave such mere conjectures, and to come to more safe ground. Whoever studies this series of quotations from Greene's publications will see that this attack on Shakespeare in 1592 is no sudden thought, no isolated ebullition, without antecedents and preparation, but that it is the crowning blossom of a long jealousy, which began with Greene's first introduction to the actors, and his discovery that there were those among them who dared to pen interludes and morals, and to write speeches to be introduced into the plays. His enormous idea of his own genius, his jealousy, his dictatorial nature, and his intolerance of critic or rival, are discoverable in his earliest writings, and he seems to have entered into engagements with the players on the assumption that he and his fellow-scholars were to have the monopoly of writing, as the players had the monopoly of acting what he wrote. This was his idea of the just division of labour, and the player who transgressed these limits was to be treated as an intruder and trespasser, and attacked with any scurrility that could be found at the bottom of his inkhorn. Greene was as thoroughly unscrupulous in his literary relations as in his domestic and social life. As he made no scruple of selling the same play to two sets of actors, so he made no scruple of stealing the printed dialogue between 'velvet and cloth breeches' and Harman's 'revelations of rogues,' and publishing them as his own. We have seen by his remarks on *Faire Em* how totally untrustworthy he is as a critic. He was a man whose direct assertions upon oath were not worthy of credit, and whose insinuations are no foundation for any conclusion in favour of the truth of the particular circumstances he wishes to insinuate. Yet it is upon these insinuations that most of the current surmises about the early authorship of Shakespeare are founded. That he appropriated and refurbished other men's plays; that he was a lacklatin who had no acquaintance with any foreign language, except perhaps French, and lived from the translator's trencher, and such like. Throughout we see Greene's determination not to recognize Shakespeare as a man capable of doing anything by himself. At first, Greene simply fathers some composition of his upon 'two gentleman poets,' because he, in Greene's opinion, was incapable of writing anything. Then as to *Faire Em*, it is either distilled out of ballads, or it is written by some theological poet who is ashamed to set his own name to it; it could not have been written by one who cannot write English without the help of a parish clerk. Then at last, Greene owns that his rival might have written a speech or two, might have interpreted for the puppets, have indited a Moral, or might be even capable of penning the *Windmill*—the *Miller's Daughter*[1]—without help; but Greene will not own that the man is capable of having really done that which passes for his; all that can be said is, that in his self-

---

[1] So I interpret the words before quoted, 'reputed able at my proper cost to build a windmill.'

conceit he supposes he is able to bombast a blank verse, or that he is the first of Shakescenes. Here is a long and vain struggle of five years against the growing popularity of a rival whom Greene was determined never to recognize, but sooner to withdraw from writing plays at all, and to persuade all his friends to do the same.

Such, then, is the external evidence for attributing *Faire Em* to Shakespeare. It remains to inquire how far the play itself is consistent with his authorship.

1. The play was written for the company of actors that belonged to Lord Strange, to whom Greene dedicated his *Tullies Love*, a book which seems to have been glanced at by the dramatist in one portion of his double plot. That Shakespeare was known to Lord Strange is clear from Spencer's words about him[1] in his *Teares of the Muses*, 1591, dedicated to the wife of Lord Strange, then Earl of Derby, ' *Our* pleasant *Willy*, ah! is dead of late.' According to tradition, Shakespeare was employed by the family to write the fine epitaph on Sir Thomas Stanley in Tonge Church. Shakespeare's mother, if she belonged to the Cheshire Ardens, as the arms sketched by Dethicke indicate, would have been a connection of the Stanleys. Perhaps, also, the play may have been written during the time when, according to Spenser, Shakespeare was dead to the London stage, that is, in 1589 and 1590, while the Martinist controversy filled the theatres with theological scurrility. The play was written for Lancashire. Not only are the chief scenes at Manchester, with references to Chester and Liverpool, but it has allusions which would be unintelligible in London, or, if understood, flat and uninteresting. In the second scene the Miller of Manchester reveals to

---

[1] The general opinion of the best critics now is, that these words do *not* refer to Shakspere, but probably to Lilly.—F.

the audience that he is not a miller, but a knight, obliged so to disguise himself on account of the Norman invasion—and then he says—

> 'Why should not I content me with this state,
> As good Sir Edmond Trafford did the flail?'

The tradition in the Trafford family is, that during a struggle with the Norman invaders the Trafford of the day had to disguise himself as a thresher, and was found with the flail by the soldiers. Hearne (*Curious Discourses*, i. 262, 8°. 1771) says, 'The ancientest [armorial device] I know or have read is that of Trafords or Trafard in Lancashire, whose arms [crest] are a labouring man with a flail in his hand threshing, and this written mott, *Now Thus*, which they say came by this occasion: that he and other gentlemen opposing themselves against some Normans who came to invade them, this Traford did them much hurt, and kept the passages against them; but that at length the Normans having passed the river came suddenly upon him, and then he, disguising himself, went into his barn, and was threshing when they entered; yet being known by some of them, and demanded why he so abased himself, answered "Now Thus".' In Flower's *Visitation of Lancashire*, 1567, this crest is said to have been granted to the family by Lawrence Dalton, Norroy. This makes its date about the middle of the 16th century. At that time several of the great Chester and Lancashire families made similar additions of crests to the plain prescriptive coat-armour which they had previously borne. Sir Edmond Trafford was the head of the family at the period of the play, a well-known man, more than once sheriff of the county, and keeper of the prison for recusants at Manchester. Sir Thomas

Goddard, on the contrary, is, so far as Lancashire is concerned, a mythical personage, and Trafford's name is only connected with his in order to give an air of local probability to the story.

2. When we come to estimate the internal evidence of authorship we are at once confronted with this difficulty. . The play has come to us badly edited from a bad manuscript, which was probably no transcript from the original, but only from some stenographic report made by a zealous spectator. It was not printed till forty years after its first production, and is probably no better a representation of its author's mind than some of the early and defective quartos of Shakespeare's known works are of the works as he really wrote them. In examining *Faire Em* it must not be compared to *Hamlet* or the *Merry Wives of Windsor* as we have them, but to those plays in the quartos of 1603 and 1602. But even as the play stands there is much, both in its general structure and its details, that is Shakespearian.

The plot, like the plots of many of Shakespeare's known plays, is a not unskilful combination of two stories. These are conducted independently of each other in alternate scenes, like the serious and comic parts in 1 *Hen. IV.*, till in the last scene they unite. The two plots are similar, and at the same time contrasted. One gives the story of one man contracted to two women, and losing them both; the other tells of one woman contracted to two men, and successfully palming off a substitute on the less favoured lover. This lover is made, in the last scene, the judge of the inconstant man of the former plot, by which means the several issues of their loves stand out in stronger contrast; and it is at last by the decision that celibacy is the fit punishment for the jealousy and fickleness of the inconstant man, that the judge is reconciled to a woman fraudulently imposed upon him. This weaving together of distinct plots into a unity is eminently Shakespearian in its broad principles.

3. And the same thing must be said of some of the special points in the conduct of the plot. Thus the identity of effect produced first upon Mounteney, and then upon Valingford, by the feigned blindness and deafness of Em, in Scene VII., which raises in each, independently of the other, the same suspicions, and the same determination, has its exact counterpart in *Much Ado about Nothing*, II. sc. 3, and III. sc. 1, where Benedick and Beatrice are imposed on by the same device. Stevens remarks that this is an imperfection similar to that which Dr Johnson has pointed out in the *Merry Wives of Windsor*:—'the second contrivance is less ingenious than the first:—or, to speak more plainly, the same incident is become stale by repetition.' It is interesting to observe how the repetition of similar situations was one of Shakespeare's principles of art, to be used, not always, but in proper place and time. The same remark applies to the two enamoured men overhearing each other's soliloquies, in Scene iv., and thereby finding each other out—an incident similar to that in *Love's Labour Lost*, iv. sc. 3.[1] (The same thing occurs in *Richard III*.)

4. In the method of exposition of the plot, *Faire Em* is quite Shakespearian. There is hardly a drama older than 1591 which does not set forth its story either epically, by narrative, or pantomime-like, by a dumb show, with or without the interpretation of a chorus. One of the great characteristics of Shakespeare's art is, that he did away with this artless method, and

---

[1] Also the two similar episodes of the son who has killed his father, and the father who has killed his only son, in 3 *Hen. VI*, 2. 5.

showed how to make the exposition grow naturally and by degrees out of the dialogue, without formal narrative or dumb show. This was one of the steps in his great design of simplifying the materials of his dramas, and of doing away with all that was incongruous. The audience finds itself gradually becoming acquainted with all necessary preliminaries, not directly, by any formal process, but indirectly, through the chance references of the speakers. In *Faire Em* the exposition of the plot is of this simple character.

5. This reform in the exposition of the plot stands in close connection with a similar reform in the exposition of the characters of the persons of the drama. With our earlier dramatists the principles of the dumb show, or rather puppet show, affect the whole form of their dramas. As poets, they speak rather like interpreters to the puppets than like dramatists. An example will best show what is meant. A puppet, let us say, is brought on the stage for Friar Bacon. The interpreter, who has to speak for him, beholding his own assumed personality objectively before him, naturally speaks in the third person—

> 'Bacon can by looks
> Make storming Boreas thunder from his cave—
> The great Arch-ruler, potentate of hell,
> Trembles when Bacon bids him.'

And so forth. But a human being acting the part, and entering into the character subjectively, would desire to say all this in the first person. The professional and scholastic poets, who probably held aloof from acting, were much scandalized when an actor usurped their function, and undertook to write dramas. But the actor knew what was wanted better than they. They were not used to transfuse their souls into their characters, and speak behind the mask. They contemplated the outside of the characters which they manufactured rather than created. They set about making speeches for them by the written rules of rhetoric, not by any secret formative psychological process. In their dramas it often seems as if the speaker of the words and the actor of the part were two different beings, whom the dramatists did not see the necessity of uniting into one. Each character is divisible into actor and speaker, and the speaking soul addresses the acting soul as a distinct entity. Bacon enters, addresses himself, 'Now, Bacon, rouse thy slumbering courage, address thee to thy task,' and so forth, and then turns to the audience, and tells them who Bacon is, and what Bacon does or will do. Is he in difficulties? He exhorts himself, and uses the same rhetoric to himself that he would use to another. Does he threaten? He tells what he will do, as if it was to be done not by him, but by another. This pedantic and scholastic method is characteristic of Lily, and the Euphuists. Traces of it occur now and then in Shakespeare; but he uses it not as a permanent form, but as a transient figure of speech. Each of his dramatic persons has his own self-consciousness, and says, like a reasonable being, 'I am hungry,' not like an idiot, 'Poor Tom's a-cold.' Perhaps in *Faire Em* the figure in question is used somewhat oftener than in Shakespeare's acknowledged dramas, yet it occurs but seldom, and then only as a transient figure, and with a good psychological reason for its use. As when in Scene VIII Lubeck persuades his affianced lover, Mariana, to take William instead, she asks, 'Wherein hath Mariana given you occasion?' and complains, 'Lubeck regards not Mariana.' Feminine modesty prompts such a change of person when a woman is holding a man to his bargain of marriage.

6. Another of the characteristics of Shakspere is his unerring common sense; his feeling of congruity, whether in manners or morals, in taste or in feeling. With all his inexhaustible wealth of imagination, and his daring use of it, he has always the fear of the ridiculous before his eyes, and never gets upon stilts. His imagery may be colossal, it is never disproportioned. The moon-raking grandiloquence of Marlowe, Greene, and Peele, Shakespeare only laughed at, or treated with 'ironical censure.' Peele's invention of Mahamet robbing a lioness of a lump of flesh to feed his fainting Callipolis was a perpetual amusement to him, and he patches together Pistol's speeches with the tatters of this tawdry eloquence. That *Faire Em* is not generally at fault on this score is proved by the sense of incongruity with which we stumble on this figure in Scene IV.—

> 'Her beauty and her virtues may suffice
> To hide the blemish of her birth in hell,
> Where neither envious eyes nor thought can pierce,
> But endless darkness ever cover it.'

It is true that this speech is given to Mounteney, who, in accordance with his name, is often tall in talk, like a mountain in labour. But the violent contrast and far-fetched image which makes a girl's beauty hide her low birth in hell is almost too much even for Greene. Once more, a characteristic of our earlier dramatists is their absurd manner of making each character his own trumpeter, by applying to himself the most glorious epithets. Of this practice there is one apparent example in *Faire Em*, where William says, in reference to his fancy suddenly fired by the sight of a picture—

> 'No sooner had my sparkling eyes beheld
> The flames of beauty blazing on this piece,
> Than suddenly,' &c.

But here 'sparkling' is clearly contrasted with 'blazing' and 'flames' in the next line, and is consequently used rather in a modest than a vainglorious sense, disparaging the embryo fires of his own eyes in comparison to the blaze of Blanch's beauty.

7. Closely connected with Shakespeare's artistic moderation and common sense is his moral uprightness, rectitude of judgment, and soundness of feeling. Moral surprises are as frequent as artistic plunges in Marlowe, Greene, and Peele. One is never sure of a character. Actions are heaped up together, not as growing out of a man's nature, but as if he was a mere puppet obliged to do what circumstances suggested, without any choice of his own. When once such a theory was admitted, the more violent the surprises, the more effective they would be; and doubtless it would be considered quite grand to make a man in peril begin his prayer—

'O Gods and stars—damned be the gods and stars!'

or to make him kill himself at the end of a scholastic exposition of the guilt of self-murder. In *Faire Em*, though there are platitudes enough, as when the 'Denmark King' says of Duke William,

'I so admire the man
As that I count it heinous guilt in him
That honours not Duke William with his heart.'

Yet these blemishes are in the corrupt and defective dialogue. In the plot itself, the moral developments are all thoroughly natural, and the reader is never shocked, or affected with incredulous surprise, at the forced sequence of moral cause and effect. Perhaps the most unusual moral situation is where Lubeck woos his own affianced bride for Duke William (scene viii.). But this is taken from Greene's romance of *Tullie's Love*, and is, moreover, in itself Shakespearian. It is like Valentine resigning all his part in Silvia to Proteus, in *The two Gentlemen of Verona*, and is justified by the philosophy of Shakespeare's Sonnets, one of the chief lessons of which is, that friendship between two men is greater than love between man and woman, and that friendship gives and forgives things which love itself would jealously guard and revenge.

8. When from the generalities of the plot and the characterization we come down to the more special forms of speech, we still, in spite of the copyist and printer, find much that may remind us of Shakespeare. Shakespeare was a great creator in language; yet the constant criticism which his contemporaries, from Greene to Ben Jonson, passed on him was that he was ignorant of language, and no scholar. This may be true, for there is more than one kind of ignorance. There is a crass ignorance, both of form and matter, which can create nothing; and there is an ignorance of detail, joined with a knowledge of form, which may be the parent of a matchless strength. If it were not for a kind of judicious forgetfulness, there could be neither philosophy nor poetry. Generalization would be impossible if every accidental detail were as vividly represented to the mind as the more general forms. There must be a voluntary or involuntary oblivion of individualities, in him who forms to himself the idea of the species. And as it is in philosophy, so it is also in poetry. The figures and images of the poet,—who paints with words, and tells you what he means not so much by sounds as by signs, by pictures conjured up before the eye rather than by the wonted significance of the words that enter the ear,—would be almost impossible if an abstract mode of thought always presented him on the instant with the proper generalized word to express his meaning. The forgetfulness, the want of instantaneous power in

one direction, obliges him to put out his strength in another direction. Thus the philosopher's abstract thought is the compensation for a 'difficulty in instantaneously recalling the concrete details, and the poet's pictorial and concrete exposition is the compensation for his habitual oblivion of the philosophical abstract. The poet and the philosopher each has his weak side; and this weakness is, as it were, the matrix of his strength. Sir William Hamilton's philosophy assigns to the limitation and impotence of the faculty a great part in the genesis of its universal ideas. As in morals, humility is at the root of grandeur of character, so in philosophy and poetry there is a weakness which generates strength.

It is not difficult to imagine how ignorance of linguistic details, in a mind rich in ideas, and travailing with the domineering necessity of expressing them, should produce new forms and methods of expression, some perhaps doomed to immediate and deserved oblivion, others at once seized on by the popular mind, and assimilated to the common speech. In a language like ours, which borrows so largely of other tongues, the scholar feels constrained not to wander too far from the native meaning and use of the borrowed word; but the orator, or poet, who is not a scholar, will venture on combinations which scholars would never dare produce, and the result will be happy according to his genius. In such a man we should be likely to see a laborious endeavour, a struggle to make words mean something which commonly they do not mean, and to twist them and coil them together so as to condense a long thought into a short phrase. We find this in Shakespeare; and to some extent also in *Faire Em.* Thus (Scene i. l. 11):

'I amorously do bear to your intent,'

where 'bear' is for 'bear myself,' and the line means, 'I accept your intentions with all love.' In the same scene William describes the effect produced on him by Blanch's picture, borne by Lubeck:

> 'A sense of miracle
> Imagined on thy lovely mistress face,
> Made me abandon bodily regard,
> And cast all pleasure on my wounded soul.'
> [p. 408, l. 37, *et seq.*]

Meaning 'the picture made me imagine a miraculous beauty in the original; and this imagination caused me to abandon all regard for the bodily feats of the tournament, and to find my pleasure only in the fresh wound love had given my soul.' In the same scene,

> 'Advance your drooping spirits,'

reminds one more directly of Shakespeare. In the next scene—

> 'Our harmless lives, which, led in greater port,
> Would be an envious object to our foes.'

Port of course means carriage, or career; it is a word common enough. But the phrase 'envious object,' for 'object of envy,' is quite characteristic. So is this line—

> 'Thralled to drudging, stayless of the world.' [p. 412, l. 114.]

'To whom the world affords no stay.' So in scene iv. l. 285—

> 'He ruminates on my beloved choice.'

'On her whom I have chosen to love.' In scene v. we have 'testies' for testimonies, and 'suspicious' for suspected. In scene vi., 'It might be alleged to me of mere simplicity,' for 'I might well be called a simpleton for it.' In scene vii.—

> 'I should ghostly give my life to sacred prayers.' [l. 600.]

'I should become a nun, and dedicate my spiritual life to prayer.'
In scene viii. l. 747—

> 'Lest that suspicion, conscious of our weal,
> Set in a foot to hinder us.'

There seems something beyond the common in thus making a vague guess equivalent to the consciousness or full knowledge of personified suspicion. In scene x.—

> 'And get we once to sea, I force not then
> We quickly shall attain the English shore.' [ll. 810-11.]

'To force' in passages like this usually means 'to regard,' 'to heed,' as 'I force not argument a straw.' But Shakespeare uses the word just in those border spaces where the meaning of 'heed' passes over into that of 'doubt.' 'You force not to forswear' (*Love's Labour's Lost*, V. ii., 440), 'you doubt not,' 'you boggle not,' rather than 'you heed not,' or 'regard not.' So in the lines of *Faire Em*, 'I doubt not we shall soon reach England.' Observe, too, the absolute infinitive in the passage in scene xii. l. 916—

> 'she likewise loved the man,
> Which he, to blame, did not at all regard.'

In scene xiii. we have 'revengement' for revenge; and in scene xiv., 'I betake you to your journey,' for 'I commend you,' or 'I bid you betake yourself.' In scene xvi., 'Because I shall complete my full resolved mind,' for 'In order that I may fully carry out my resolutions.' Here we find also 'reproachment' for 'reproach.' In scene xvii. we have 'competitors' in the sense of fellow-seekers, associates, not rivals (cf. Shakespeare, *Richard III*, iv. 4). And here also occurs the characteristic line when Mandeville turns from

Em, who rejects him, to Elinor, who, as he supposes, will accept him.

'Then fare-well, frost! well-fare a wench that will!' [l. 1358.]

Cases of the substantive used as an adjective, such as 'the Britain Court,' 'the Denmark King,' and of the adjective for the substantive, as 'Duke of Saxon,' are scarcely characteristic enough to need quotation.

9. To pass from words and figures of speech to forms of thought and imagery, we need only make cursory reference to the studied antithesis, which, as being no more special to Shakespeare than to Lily and the Euphuists, are of no value in determining a question of authorship. Such an antithesis as—

'I turn my conquering eyes
To cowards looks and beaten fantasies' [p. 408, l. 14]—

is rather characteristic of the time than of any particular author. If, however, it were required to produce from *Faire Em* passages which have the true Shakespearian ring in them, it would be difficult to do so. It is true that the chain of precepts given by the miller to his daughter, in Scene ii., is similar to that given by Polonius to Laertes in *Hamlet*, and by the Countess to Bertram in *All's Well that Ends Well*, and the concluding lines of the advice might pass for Shakespeare's—

'Chaste thoughts and modest conversations,
Of proof to keep out all enchanting vows,
Vain sighs, forced tears, and pitiful aspects,
Are they which make deformèd ladies fair,
Poor, rich: and all enticing men
That seek of such but only present grace,
Shall, in persév'rance of a virgins vow,

Prefer the most refusers, to the choice
'Of such a soul as yielded what they sought.'
[p. 413, ll. 141, &c.]

So might William's reflections when he first sees Mariana—

'Not very fair, but richly decked with favour;—
A sweet face;—an exceeding dainty hand;—
A body—were it fram'd of wax
By all the cunning artists of the world,
It could not better be proportioned.' [p. 417, ll. 228—32.]

This reference to artists is quite a characteristic touch. Another hint of Shakespeare's æsthetics is given later on when he speaks of sweet Em as one in whom

'Nature, in her pride of art,
Hath wrought perfections.' [p. 427, ll. 474-5.]

The following lines also from scene iv. [ll. 265—9] may be quoted in this relation—

'Ah, Em! the subject of my restless thoughts—
The anvil whereupon my heart doth beat,
Framing thy state to thy desert—
Full ill this life becomes thy heavenly look,
Wherein sweet love and virtue sits enthroned.'

And, if we are seeking for the Shakespearian ring, it must, we think, be owned that the whole of scene viii., where Lubeck courts Mariana for William, and the concluding scene of all, are neither of them quite unworthy of our great poet.

If, however, it be asked whether *Faire Em* is on the whole a play which, from internal evidence, would seem to be Shakespeare's, the candid answer must be, No. On the other hand, its defects, so far as they are not fairly attributable to defective editing and printing, are not greater than those of the older parts of *Pericles* and

Timon of Athens, or the whole of *The troublesome raigne of King John*, and not much greater than those of the *Hamlet* of the quarto of 1603. That is to say, the internal evidence, though not sufficient by itself to establish Shakespeare's claim to the play, is not inconsistent with its being his, if there is competent witness that it is so. The fact that the first scene in the play is a rather inferior imitation of the first scene of Greene's *Friar Bacon* rather confirms than invalidates the conclusion drawn above, that it is a play written by Shakespeare upon Greene.

A question may arise, whether, if we give any value to the evidence of the 'bookbinder' who included *Faire Em* in vol. i. of Shakespeare's works, the same evidence will not oblige us to confess that *Mucedorus* and the *Merry Devil of Edmonton* are also his. As for *Mucedorus*, although the old play, as we have it in the editions of 1598 and 1606, is too bad to be Shakespeare's, unless it was written in his very earliest days, yet the additions in the edition of 1610, which contain a manager's apology for an offence given by his company, have in them a ring quite consistent with Shakespeare's authorship, who, though too good an artist to patch cloth of frieze with cloth of gold, yet could hardly help showing a fibre of his golden vein in anything that he scribbled. These additions are, Scene i. after the Induction; the scene beginning on Sign. D3; the part relating to the entrance of 'the Valentia Lord,' on Sig. F2, verso; and the whole concluding scene between Comedy and Envy except the fifteen opening lines.[1] As for the *Merry Devil of Edmonton*, though it was entered on the Stationers' books in 1608 by Hunt and Archer as 'written by T. B.,' yet

---

[1] See Mr Simpson's Paper on *Mucedorus* and *Faire Em* in the *New Shakspere Society's Trans.*, 1875-6, pp. 157—180.

in 1653 H. Moseley entered it as the production of Shakespeare. Perhaps a proper investigation might find evidences of his hand in parts of this play also. At any rate Moseley's entry proves that the tradition did not arise simply from the carelessness of a book-binder.

It might be worth while to gather up the traditional fragments concerning the connection between William I. and Sven Esthrithson, K. of Denmark. The Berkeley tradition says that Robert Fitz-Harding was son of Harding, Mayor of Bristol, Governor of Bristol, son of the King of Denmark, and a follower of William the Conqueror. See the *Berkeley Legend* in the *Antiquary*.

A PLEASANT COMEDIE OF FAIRE EM,

The Miller's Daughter of Manchester.

DRAMATIS PERSONÆ.

WILLIAM THE CONQUEROR, *afterwards disguised as Robert de Windsor.*
MARQUESS LUBECK, *a Danish nobleman.*
MOUNTENEY, } *Gentlemen of William's Court.—*
VALINGFORD, } *Suitors to Faire Em.*
MANDEVILLE, *a gentleman of Manchester.*
DUKE DIROT, } *Norman nobles,*
DE MARCH, } *left governors of England during William's absence.*
SIR THOMAS GODDARD, *disguised*

as the Miller of Manchester.
FAIR EM, *his daughter.*
TROTTER, *his man.*
King of Denmark (Sweyn).
BLANCH, *his daughter.*
MARIANA, *a Swedish captive of Sweyn, beloved by Lubeck.*
Messenger.
ROSILIO, *courtier of King of Denmark.*
Ambassador from Sweyn to William.
Soldiers—Attendants.
Citizen of Chester.
ELINOR, *his daughter.*

A PLEASANT COMEDIE OF FAIRE EM,

The Miller's Daughter of Manchester;

WITH THE LOVE OF WILLIAM THE CONQUEROR.[1]

ACTUS PRIMUS. SCÆNA PRIMA.

Enter WILLIAM THE CONQUEROR; MARQUES LUBECK, *with a picture;* MOUNTNEY; MANVILE; VALINGFORD; *and* DUKE DIROT.

Marques. What means faire Britaines mighty Conqueror
So suddenly to cast away his staff,
And all in passion to forsake the tilt?
D. Dirot. My Lord, this triumph we solemnize here[2]   4
Is of mere love to your increasing joys,
Only expecting cheerful looks for all[3];
What sudden pangs then moves your majesty
To dim the brightness of the day with frowns?   8
W. Conqueror. Ah, good my Lords, misconster not the cause;
At least, suspect not my displeased brows:
I amorously do bear to your intent[4],
For thanks; and all that you can wish, I yeeld.   12

---

[1] See Note 1, p. 467. [2] we have here set forth (Chetwood).
[3] For similar absolute use of at all, see p. 421, l. 334.
[4] See *Introd.*, p. 399.

But that which makes me blush and shame to tell
Is cause why thus I turn my conquering eyes
To cowards looks and beaten fantasies.

 Mountney. Since we are guiltless, we the less dismay 16
To see this sudden change possess your cheer,
For if it issue from your own conceits
Bred by suggestion of some envious thoughts,
Your highness wisdom may suppress it straight. 20
Yet tell us (good my Lord) what thought it is
That thus bereaves you of your late content,
That in advice we may assist your Grace,
Or bend our forces to revive your spirits. 24

 W. Con. Ah, MARQUES LUBECK, in thy power it lies
To rid my bosom of these thraled[1] dumps[2]:
And therefore, good my Lords, forbear awhile
That we may parley of these private cares, 28
Whose strength subdues me more than all the world.

 Valingford. We go, and wish thee[3] private conference
Public affects[4], in this accustomed peace.

      [*Exit all but* WILLIAM *and the* MARQUES.

 William. Now, MARQUES, must a conqueror at arms 32
Disclose himself thrald[5] to unarmed thoughts,
And, threatened of a shadow, yield to lust[6].
No sooner had my sparkling eyes beheld
The flames of beauty blazing on this piece, 36
But suddenly a sense of miracle,
Imagined on thy lovely mistress[7] face,

   [1] Thralled [2] woes (Ch.) [3] the
  [4] effects [5] thralled [6] love (Ch.). [7] maistres

Made me abandon bodily regard,
And cast all pleasures on my wounded soul [1]: 40
Then, gentle MARQUES, tell me what she is,
That thus thou honourest on thy warlike shield;
And if thy love and interest be such
As justly may give place to mine— 44
That if it be, my soul with honour's wings
May fly into the bosom of my dear—
If not, close them, and stoop into my grave!

   Marques. If this be all, renowned Conqueror, 48
Advance your drooping spirits and revive
The wonted courage of your conquering mind;
For this fair picture painted on my shield
Is the true counterfeit of lovely BLANCH, 52
Princess and daughter to the King of DANES,
Whose beauty and excess of ornaments
Deserves another manner of defence,
Pomp, and high person to attend her state 56
Than MARQUES LUBECK any way presents.
Therefore her virtues I resign to thee,
Already shrin'd in thy religious breast,
To be advanced and honoured to the full. 60
Nor bear I this [2] an argument of love,
But to renown fair BLANCH, my Sovereign's child,
In every place where I by arms may do it.

   William. Ah, MARQUES [3], thy words bring heaven vnto my
    [4] soul! 64

---

   [1] See *Introd.*, p. 400.   [2] this as.—G.
 [3] friend (Ch.)   [4] Word out: soul is in Ch.

And had I heaven to give for thy reward,
Thou shouldst be throned in no unworthy place—
But let my uttermost[1] wealth suffice thy worth,
Which here I vow : And to aspire the bliss   68
That hangs on quick achievement of my love,
Thyself and I will travel in disguise,
To bring this lady to our Brittain court.

 Marques. Let WILLIAM but bethink what may avail,   72
And let me die if I deny my aid.

 William. Then thus—The DUKE DIROT, and th' Earl DIMARCH[2].
Will I leave substitutes to rule my Realme,
While mightie love forbids my being here ;   76
And in the name of SIR ROBERT of *Windsor*[3]
Will go with thee unto the Danish Court.
Keep WILLIAM's secrets, MARQUES, if thou love him.
Bright BLANCH, I come! Sweet fortune, [4]favour me[4],   80
And [5]I will laud thy name eternally[5]!   [*Exeunt.*

[SCENE II.]

Enter the Miller, and EM *his daughter.*

 Miller. Come, daughter, we must learn to shake off pomp,
To leave the state that erst beseemed a knight
And gentleman of no[6] mean discent,   84
To undertake this homely millers trade :

---

[1] utmost (Ch.)   [2] Dimach (Bodleian, no date).
[3] dele *Sir.* Ch. has,—feigned name of Robert Windsor.
[4]—[4] smile on me. Ch.
[5]—[5] altars shall be raised to worship thee. Ch.
[6] dele *no* (Ch.) not a·?:

Thus must we mask to save our wretched lives,
Threatened by Conquest of this hapless Isle,
Whose sad invasions by the Conqueror, 88
Have made a number such as we subject
Their gentle necks unto their[1] stubborn yoke
Of drudging labour and base peasantry.
SIR THOMAS GODDARD now old GODDARD is, 92
GODDARD the miller of fair Manchester.
Why should not I content me with this state,
As good Sir Edmond TROFFERD did the flail?
And thou, sweet EM, must stoop to[2] high estate 96
To join with mine, that thus we may protect
Our harmeless lives, which, led in greater port,
Would be an envious object to our foes,
That seek to root all Britain's Gentry [up] 100
From bearing countenance against their tyranny[3].

Em. Good father, let my full resolved thoughts
With settled patience to support this chance
Be some poor comfort to your aged soul; 104
For therein rests the height of my estate—
That you are pleased with this dejection[4],—
And that all toils my hands may undertake
May serve to work your worthiness content. 108

Miller. Thanks, my dear daughter. These thy pleasant words
Transfer my soul into a second heaven:
And in thy settled mind my joys consist,
My state revived[5], and I in former plight. 112

---

[1] the [2] *to high* probably a misprint for *to like*.
[3] These two lines out of Ch. [4] Line out of Ch. [5] Revives

Although our outward pomp be thus abased,
And thrall'd to drudging, stayless of the world¹,
Let us retain those honourable minds
That lately governed our superior state, 116
Wherein true gentry is the only mean
That makes us differ from ²base millers born².
Though we expect no knightly delicates,
Nor thirst in soul for former sovereignty, 120
Yet may our minds as highly scorn to stoop,
To base desires of vulgars worldliness,
As if we were in our precedent way. .
And, lovely daughter, since thy youthful years 124
Must needs admit as³ young affections,
And that sweet love unparti-al perceives⁴
Her dainie⁵ subjects thorough every part⁶,
In chief receive these lessons from my lips, 128
The true discoverers of a Virgin's due,
Now requisite, now that I know thy mind
Something inclined to favour MANVILS suit,
A gentleman, thy lover in protest; 132
And that thou mayst not be by love deceived,
But try his meaning fit for thy desert,
In pursuit of all amorous desires,⁷
Regard thine honour. Let not vehement sighs, 136

---

¹ *Stayless of the world* out of Ch. See *Introd.*, p. 400.
²—² plebeian birth (Ch.) ³ of (Ch.)
⁴ 'perceives' is clearly wrong: perhaps *deceives*, or *peruses*, or *pursues*, or *perverts;* a dissyllable is wanted if we read *un-par-ti-al*, a trisyllable if *un-par-tial*.
⁵ Of course *dainty*.
⁶ These two lines out of Ch. ⁷ This line out of Ch.

ACT I.]   OF FAIRE EM.   413

Nor earnest vows importing fervent love,
Render thee subject to the wrath of lust¹.
For that, transformed to former² sweet delight,
Will bring thy body and thy soul to shame.   140
Chaste thoughts and modest conversations,—
Of proof to keep out all enchanting vows,
Vain sighs, forced tears, and pitiful aspects—
Are they that make deformed ladies fair,   144
³Poor wretch³, and all⁴ enticing men,
That seek of such but only present grace,
Shall in perseverance of a Virgins due⁵
Prefer the most refusers, to the choice   148
Of such a soul as yielded what they ⁶thought⁷—
But ho! where's TROTTER⁸?

Here enters TROTTER, *the Miller's man, to them: and they within call to him for their grist.*

Trotter. Where's TROTTER? why, TROTTER is here. I' faith, you and your daughter go up and down weeping and wamenting, and keeping of a wamentation, as who should say, the Mill would go with your wamenting.

---

¹ love (Ch.)
·² form of. The use of former is a proof that the copy was taken by short-hand, from hearing, not from a MS.
³—³ And poor ones rich;
⁴ *all* here should be *such*, and such in next line should be *all*.
⁵ ? vow   ⁶ ? sought.
⁷ Compare this entire speech with Polonius' advice to Laertes (*Hamlet*, 1603, C2), and to Ophelia (Ib., same leaf, *verso*). In that play the precepts are more concentrated than here. It is clearly a later performance. See also *Introd.* p. 402.   ⁸ These six lines are out of Ch.

Miller. How now, TROTTER, why complain'st thou so?   155

Trotter. Why, yonder is a company of young men and maids, keep such a stir for their grist, that they would have it before my stones be ready to grind it. But, i' faith, I would I could break wind enough backward: you should not tarry for your grist, I warrant you.   160

Miller. Content thee, TROTTER, I'll[1] go pacify them.   <small>Here he taketh *Em* about the neck.</small>

Trotter. I wis you will when I cannot. Why look, you have a mill—why, what's your mill without me? Or rather, Mistress, what were I without you?   164

Em. Nay, TROTTER, if you fall a chiding, I will give you over.

Trotter. I chide you, dame, to amend you. You are too fine to be a Miller's daughter; for if you should but stoop to take up the toll-dish, you will have the cramp in your finger at least ten weeks after.   169

Miller. Ah, well said, TROTTER. Teach her to play the good huswife, and thou shalt have her to thy wife, if thou canst get her good will.   172

Trotter. Ah, words! wherein I see Matrimony come loaden with kisses to salute me: Now let me alone to pick the mill, to fill the hopper, to take the toll, to mend the sails, yea, and to make the mill to go with the very force of my love.   176

[*Here they must call for their grist within.*]

I come, I come! I' faith, now you shall have your grist, or else *Trotter* will trot and amble himself to death.

[*They call him again. Exit.*

---

[1] I will (B. n. d.)

[SCENE III.]

Enter KING OF DENMARK, *with some attendants;* BLANCH, *his daughter;* MARIANA; MARQUES LUBECK; WILLIAM, *disguised.*

King of Denmark. Lord MARQUES LUBECK, welcome home.
Welcome, brave Knight, unto the *Denmark* King,   180
For WILLIAM'S sake, the noble *Norman* Duke,
So famous for his fortunes and success,
That graceth him with name of Conqueror;
Right double welcome must thou be to us.   184
    Rob. Windsor. And to my Lord the King shall I recount
Your graces courteous entertainment,
That for his sake vouchsafe to honour me,
A simple knight, attendant on his grace.   188
    King Den. But say, Sir Knight, what may I call your name?
    Rob. Win. ROBERT WINDSOR, and like your majesty.
    King. Den. I tell thee, ROBERT, I so admire the man
As that I count it heinous guilt in him   192
That honours not DUKE WILLIAM with his heart.
BLANCH, bid this stranger welcome, good my girl.
    Blanch. Sir,
Should I neglect your highness charge herein   196
It might be thought of base discourtesy.
Welcome [1], Sir Knight, to [2]*Denmark*, heartily [2].
    Robert Wind. Thanks, gentle lady. LORD MARQUES, what is
        she?   200

---

[1] Blanch's speech commences with *Welcome* in Ch.
[2—2] Denmark's royal court (Ch.).

Lubeck. That same is BLANCH, [the] daughter to the King,
The substance of the shadow that you saw.

Rob. Wind. May this be she for whom I cross'd the seas?
I am ashamed to think I was so fond—   204
In whom there's nothing that contents my mind—
[1] Ill head, worse featured [2], uncomely, nothing courtly;
Swart and ill-favoured, a collier's sanguine skin.
I never saw a harder favour'd slut [3];   208
Love her? for what? I can no whit abide her!

King of Den. MARIANA, I have this day received letters
From SWETHIA, that lets me understand
Your ransom is collecting there with speed,   212
And shortly shall be hither sent to us.

Mariana. Not that I find occasion of [4] mislike
My entertainment in your graces court,
But that I long to see my native home.   216

King Den. And reason have you, Madam, for the same [5].
LORD MARQUES, I commit unto your charge
The entertainment of SIR ROBERT here;
Let him remain with you within the Court,   220
In solace and disport to spend the time.

Rob. Wind. I thank your highness, [6] whose bounden I remain [6].

[*Exit* KING OF DENMARK.

Blanch (*speaketh this secretly at one end of the stage*).
Unhappy BLANCH, what strange effects are these
That works within my thoughts confusedly?   224

---

[1] See note to next p., with quotation from *Comedy of Errors.*
[2] face [3] maid (Ch.)
[4] to [5] This line not in Ch. [6]—[6] Not in Ch.

That still, methinks, affection draws me on,
To take, to like, nay more, to love this knight.

Rob. Wind. A modest countenance; no heavy sullen look [1];
Not very fair, but richly deck'd with favour;
A sweet face; an exceeding dainty hand;
A body, were it framed [2] of wax
By all the cunning Artists of the world,
It could not better be proportioned [3].

Lubeck. How now, SIR ROBERT? In a study, man?
Here is no time for contemplation.

Rob. Wind. My Lord, there is a certain odd conceit
Which on the sudden greatly troubles me.

Lubeck. How like you BLANCH? I partly do perceive
The little boy hath played the wag with you.

Sir Robert. The more I look the more I love to look.
Who says that MARIANA is not fair?
I'll gage my gauntlet 'gainst the envious man
That dares avow there liveth her compare.

Lubeck. SIR ROBERT, you mistake your counterfeit—
This is the lady which you came to see.

Sir Rob. Yea, my Lord: she is counterfeit indeed,
For there's the substance that best contents me [4].

Lubeck. That is my love. SIR ROBERT, you do wrong me.

---

[1] *looking at Mariana.* [2] all of
[3] It is characteristic that the writer looks to art, not to nature, for the highest beauty. See my MS. on the Sonnets, p. 27. Cf., or contrast, *Comedy of Errors*, iv. 2. 20—
'Ill fac'd, worse bodied, shapeless everywhere;
Vicious, ungentle, foolish, blunt, unkind;
Stigmatical in making, worse in mind.' See also *Introd.* p. 403.
[4] doth best, &c. *Or*, substance best contenteth me.

Robert. The better for you, sir, she is your love— 248
As for the wrong, I see not how it grows.

Lubeck. In seeking that which is anothers right.

Robert. As who should say your love were privileged,
That none might look upon her but yourself. 252

Lubeck. These jars becomes not our familiarity,
Nor will I stand on terms to move your patience.

Rob. Why, my Lord,
Am not I of flesh and blood as well as you? 256
Then give me leave to love as well as you.

Lub. To love, SIR ROBERT; but whom? not she I love.
Nor stands it with the honour of my state
To brook corrivals with me in my love. 260

Rob. So, Sir, we are thorough[1] for that L[ady][2].
Ladies, farewell. LORD MARQUES, will you go?
I'll find a time to speak with her I trow[3].

Lubeck. With all my heart. Come, ladies, will you walk? 264
[*Exit.*

[SCENE IV.]

Enter MANVILE *alone, disguised.*

Manv. Ah, EM! the subject of my restless thoughts—
The anvil whereupon my heart doth beat,
Framing thy state[4] to thy desert—
Full ill this life becomes thy heavenly look, 268
Wherein sweet love and virtue sits enthroned[5]—

---

[1] *Thorough,* a mistake—perhaps thwart. 'So, sir, we're thwart for.'
[2] dele Ch.   [3] dele Ch.
[4] lowly state (Ch.)   [5] See *Introd.,* p. 403.

Bad world! where riches is esteemed above them both [1];
In whose base eyes nought else is bountiful!
A millers daughter, says the multitude, 272
Should not be loved of a gentleman—
But let them breathe their souls into the air [2],
Yet will I still affect thee as myself,
So thou be constant in thy plighted vow. 276
But here comes one—I'll listen to his talk.

[MANVILE *stays, hiding himself.*

Enter VALINGFORD *at another door, disguised* [3].

Valing. Go, WILLIAM CONQUEROR, and seek thy love—
Seek thou a minion in a foreign land,
Whilst I draw back and court my love at home— 280
The Millers daughter of fair Manchester
Hath bound my feet to this delightsome soil,
And from her eyes do dart such golden beams
That holds my heart in her subjection. 284
Manv. He ruminates on my beloved choice:
God grant he come not to prevent my hope.
But here's another, him I'll listen to.

Enter MOUNTNEY, *disguised, at another door.*

L. Mount. Nature unjust, in utterance of thy art, 288

[1] 'bove both are esteemed most (Ch.)
[2] 2 H6, III. ii. 391 : 'Here could I breathe my soul into the air.' (It is in the l. *Cont.*, p. 46.)
[3] Something like the scene in *Love's Labour's Lost*. See *Introd.*, p. 393.

To grace a peasant with a prince's fame[1]!
Peasant am I, so to misterm my love:
Although a Millers daughter by her birth,
Yet may her beauty and her virtues well suffice 292
To hide the blemish of her birth in hell,
Where neither envious eyes nor thought can pierce,
But endless darkness ever smother it[2].
Go, WILLIAM CONQUEROR, and seek thy love, 296
Whilst I draw back and court mine own the while,
Decking her body with such costly robes
As may become her beauty's worthiness;
That so thy labours may be laughed to scorn, 300
And she thou seekest [out] in foreign regions
Be darkened and eclipsed when she arrives
By one that I have chosen nearer home.

 Manv. What comes he to[3], to intercept my love? 304
Then hie thee, MANVILE, to forestall such foes. [*Exit* MAN.

 Mount. What now, LORD VALINGFORD, are you behind?
The King hath chosen you to go with him.

 Val. So chose he you, therefore I marvel much 308
That both of us should linger in this sort.
What may the King imagine of our stay?

 Mount. The King may justly think we are to blame:
But I imagin'd I might well be spared, 312
And that no other man had borne my mind.

 Val. The like did I: in friendship then resolve
What is the cause of your unlookt for stay?

---

[1] frame.—Ch.   [2] See *Introd.*, p. 396.
[3] too (Ch.)

ACT II.] *OF FAIRE EM.* 421

Mount. LORD VALINGFORD, I tell thee as a friend: 316
Love is the cause why I have stayed behind.
   Val. Love, my Lord? of whom?
   Mount. EM, the millers daughter of Manchester.
   Val. But may this be? 320
   Mount. Why not, my Lord? I hope full well you know
That love respects no difference of state,
So beauty serve to stir affection.
   Val. But this it is that makes me wonder most, 324
That you and I should be of one conceit,
In such a strange unlikely passion.
   Mount. But is that true? My Lord[1], I hope you do but jest.
   Val. I would I did; then were my grief the less. 328
   Mount. Nay, never grieve; for if the cause be such,
To join our thoughts in such a sympathy,
All envy set aside. Let us agree
To yield to either's fortune in this choice. 332
   Val. Content, say I: and whatsoe'er befall,
Shake hands, my Lord, and fortune thrive at all[2].   [*Exeunt.*

SCENE V. [ACT II. CH.]

Enter EM *and* TROTTER, *the Millers man, with a kerchief on his head, and an urinal in his hand.*

   Em. TROTTER, where have you been?
   Trot. Where have I been? Why, what signifies this? 336
   Em. A kerchief, doth it not?

---

[1] dele Lord.   [2] ? o'er all. See also supra, Act I. l. 6.

Trot. What call you this, I pray?

Em. I say it is an Urinal.

Trot. Then this is mystically to give you to understand, 340
I have been at the Phismicaries house.

Em. How long hast thou been sick?

Trot. Ifaith, e'en as long as I have not been half[1] well, and that hath been a long time. 344

Em. A loitering time, I rather imagine.

Trot. It may be so: but the Phismicary tells me that you can help me.

Em. Why, anything I can do for recovery of thy health be right well assured of. 349

Trot. Then give me your hand.

Em. To what end?

Trot. That the ending of an old indenture is the beginning of a new bargain.

Em. What bargain?

Trot. That you promised to do anything to recover my health.

Em. On that condition I give thee my hand. 356

Trot. Ah, sweet EM! [*Here he offers to kiss her.*

Em. How now, TROT[2]! your master's daughter?

Trot. I'faith, I aim at the fairest. Ah, EM, sweet EM!
    Fresh as the flower, 360

---

[1] *half*, dele Ch.

[2] Trotter (B. n. d.)
    'Of me, poor thief,
      In prison bound—
    So all your rhyme
      Lies on the ground.'

The third line must have rhymed with the first, according to all rules of capping verses.—See the last scene of Rowley's II.8.

ACT II.]   *OF FAIRE EM.*   423

  That hath [the] power
  To wound my heart,
  And ease my smart,
  Of me, poor thief, in prison bound—   364
Em. So all your rime lies on the ground.
But what means this?
Trot. Ah, mark the device—
For thee, my love, full sick I was, in hazard of my life,   368
Thy promise was to make me whole, and for to be my wife.
  Let me enjoy my love, my dear,
  And thou possess thy TROTTER here.
Em. But I meant no such matter.   372
Trot. Yes, woos, but you did. I'll go to our Parson, Sir John, and he shall mumble up the marriage out of hand.
Em. But here comes one that will forbid the bans.

   Here enters MANVILE *to them.*

Trot. Ah, sir, you come too late.   376
Manv. What remedy, TROTTER?
Em. Go, TROTTER, my father calls.
Trot. Would you have me go in, and leave you two here?
Em. Why, darest thou not trust me?   380
Trot. Yes, faith, e'en as long as I see you.
Em. Go thy ways, I pray thee heartily.
Trot. That same word (heartily) is of great force. I will go. But I pray, sir, beware you; come not too near the wench. [*Exit.*
Man. I am greatly beholding to you.   385
Ah, [1]Mistress, sometime I might have said, my love,

  [1] Four lines commencing with this are in two in original.

But time and fortune hath bereaved me of that,
And I am[1] abject in those gracious eyes,
That with remorse erst saw into my grief,—
May sit and sigh the sorrows of my heart.

Em. Indeed my MANVILE hath some cause to doubt,
When such a swain is rival in his love.

Man. Ah, EM, were he the man that causeth this mistrust,
I should esteem of thee as at the first.

Em. But is my love in earnest all this while?

Man. Believe me, EM, it is not time to jest,
When others 'joys what lately I possest.

Em. If touching love my MANVILE charge me thus,
Unkindly must I take it at his hands,
For that my conscience clears me of offence.

Man. Ah, impudent and shameless in thy ill,
That with thy cunning and defraudful tongue
Seeks[2] to delude the honest-meaning mind!
Was never heard in Manchester before,
Of truer love than hath been betwixt[3] us twain:
And for my part how I have hazarded
Displeasure of my father and my friends,
Thyself can witness; yet[4] notwithstanding this,
Two gentlemen attending on DUKE WILLIAM,
MOUNTNEY, and VALINGFORD, as I heard them named,
Ofttimes resort to see and to be seen
Walking the street fast by thy father's door,
Whose glancing eyes up to [thy[5]] windows cast

---

[1] an.   [2] Seekese. B. n. d.   [3] 'twixt. Ch.
[4] dele yet.   [5] the (B. n. d.)

Give testies of their Masters amorous heart.
This, EM, is noted, and [is] too much talked on—
Some see it without mistrust of ill— 416
Others there are that, scorning, grin thereat,
And saith, 'There goes the Millers daughters wooers.'
Ah me! whom chiefly and most of all it doth concern—
To spend my time in grief, and vex my soul, 420
To think my love should be rewarded thus,
And for thy sake abhor all women[1]-kind!

Em. May not a maid [then] look upon a man
Without suspicious judgment of the world? 424.

Man. If sight do move offence, [2]it is the[2] better not to see.
But thou didst more, unconstant as thou art,
For with them thou hadst talk and conference.

Em. May not a maid talk with a man without mistrust? 428

Man. Not with such men suspected amorous.

Em. I grieve to see my MANVILE's jealousy.

Man. Ah, EM[3], faithful love is full of jealousy.
So did I love thee true and faithfully, 432
For which I am rewarded[4] most unthankfully.

[*Exit, in a rage: Manet* EM.

Em. And so away? What, in displeasure gone,
And left me such a bitter sweet to gnaw upon[5]?
Ah, MANVILE[6], little wottest thou 436
How near this parting goeth to my heart.
Uncourteous love, whose followers reaps reward

---

[1] maiden kind (Ch.).   [2—2] 'tis   [3] Dele *Em.*
[4] So I'm rewarded.   [5] on
[6] *Manville* duplicated. Ch.

Of hate, disdain, reproach and infamy,
The fruit of frantic, bedlam jealousy! 440

Here enters MOUNTNEY *to* EM.

But here comes one of these suspicious[1] men :
Witness, my God, without desert of me,
For only MANVILE honour I in heart,
Nor shall unkindness cause me from him to[2] start! 444

   Mount. For this good fortune, Venus, be thou blest,
To meet my love, the mistress of my heart,
Where time and place gives opportunity,
At full to let her understand my love. 448

   [*He turns to* EM, *and offers to take her by the hand, and she goes from him.*

Fair mistress, since my fortune sorts so well,
Hear you a word. What meaneth this?
Nay, stay, fair EM.

   Em. I am going homewards, sir. 452

   Mount. Yet stay, sweet love, to whom I must disclose
The hidden secrets of a lovers thoughts,
Not doubting but to find such kind remorse
As naturally you are enclined to. 456

   Em. The gentleman, your friend, sir,
I have not seen him this four days, at the least.

   Mount. Whats that to me?
I speak not, sweet, in person of my friend, 460
But for myself, whom, if that love deserve
To have regard, being honourable love,

---

[1] *i. e.* suspected   [2] Dele to

Not base affects of loose lascivious love,
Whom youthful wantons play and dally with,
But that unites in honourable bands of holy rites,
And knits the sacred knot that Gods— [*Here* EM *cuts him off.*

  Em. What mean you, sir, to keep me here so long?
I cannot understand you by your signs;
You keep a prattling with your lips,
But never a word you speak that I can hear.
  Mount. What? is she deaf? a great impediment!
Yet remedies there are for such defects.
Sweet EM, it is no little grief to me,
To see, where Nature, in her pride of art,
Hath wrought perfections rich and admirable.
  Em. Speak you to me, Sir?
  Mount. To thee, my only joy.
  Em. I cannot hear you.
  Mount. O plague of fortune! Oh[1], hell without compare!
What boots it us to gaze and not enjoy[2]?
  Em. Fare you well, sir. [*Exit* EM. *Manet* MOUNTNEY.
  Mount. Farewell, my love, nay, farewell life and all!
Could I procure redress for this infirmity,
It might be means she would regard my suit.
I am acquainted with the Kings physicians,
Amongst the which there's one, mine honest friend,
Signor Alberto', a very learned man—
His judgment will I have[3] to help this ill.
Ah, EM, fair EM, if art can make thee whole,

---

[1] Dele oh. [2] Probably *and not to hear?* so to rhyme with *compare.*
[3] ? crave

I'll buy that sense for thee, ¹although it¹ cost me dear.
But, MOUNTNEY, stay : this may be but deceit,
A matter feigned only to delude thee,   492
And, not unlike, perhaps by VALINGFORD.
He loves fair² EM as well as I—
As well as I? ah, no, not half so well—
³Put case : yet may he be thine enemy³,   496
And give her counsel to dissemble thus.
I'll try the event, and if it fall out so,
Friendship, farewell : Love makes me now a foe. ·[*Exit* MOUNTNEY.

[SCENE VI.]

Enter MARQUES LUBECK *and* MARIANA.

Mar. Trust me, my Lord, I'm sorry for your hurt.   500
Lub. Gramercy, Madam ; but it is not great :
Only a thrust, prick't with a rapier's point.
Mar. How grew the quarrel, my Lord?   503
Lub. Sweet lady⁴, for thy sake. There was, this last night, two masks in one⁵ company; myself the foremost : the other strangers were; amongst the which, when the music began to sound the measures, each masker made choice of his lady ; and one, more forward than the rest, stept towards thee, which I perceiving, thrust him aside and took thee myself. But this was taken in so ill part that at my coming out of the court gate, with justling together, it was my chance to be thrust into the arm. The doer

---

¹—¹ though 't   ² the lovely. Ch.
³—³ Yet he may prove thy favoured friend. Ch. Delius (ed. 1874) prints this substituted Chetwood line before l. 496 above.
⁴ Dele lady. Ch.   ⁵ our

thereof, because he was the original cause of the disorder at that inconvenient time, was presently committed, and is this morning sent for to answer the matter. And I think here he comes. What, SIR ROBERT OF WINDSOR, how now? 515

[*Here enters* SIR ROBERT OF WINDSOR, *with a jailor. B. n. d.*]

   Sir Rob. I'faith, my Lord [1], a prisoner: but what ails your arm?
   Lub. Hurt the last night, by mischance.
   Sir Rob. What, not in the mask at the Court gate? 518
   Lub. Yes, trust me, there.
   Sir Rob. Why, then, my Lord, I thank you for my nights lodging.
   Lub. And I you for my hurt, if it were so. Keeper, away; I [2] discharge you of your prisoner. [*Exit the Keeper.*
   Sir Rob. LORD MARQUES, you offered me disgrace to shoulder me. 525
   Lub. Sir, I knew you not, and therefore [3]you must pardon me[3]: and the rather, it might be alleged to me of mere simplicity to see another dance with my Mistress, disguised, and I myself in presence. But seeing it was our haps to damnify each other unwillingly, let us be content with our harms, and lay the fault where it was, and so become friends. 531
   Sir Rob. I'faith, I am content with my nights lodging, if you be content with your hurt.
   Lub. Not content that I have it, but content to forget how I came by it. 535
   Sir Rob. My Lord, here comes LADY BLANCH; lets away.

[1] Dele my Lord   [2] Dele I   [3]—[3] crave excuse. Ch.

Enter BLANCH.

Lub. With good will. Lady, will you stay?

[*Exit* LUBECK *and* SIR ROB.

Mar. Madam— 538

Blanch. MARIANA, as I am grieved with thy presence so am I not offended for thy absence; and, were it not a breach to modesty, thou shouldest know before I left thee.

Mar. How near is this humour to madness? If you hold on as you begin, you are in a pretty way to scolding.

Blanch. To scolding, huswife [1]? 544

Mar. Madam, here comes one. [*Here enters one with a letter.*

Blanch. There doth indeed. Fellow, would's thou have anything with anybody here?

Messenger. I have a letter to deliver to the LADY MARIANA.

Blanch. Give it me.

Mess. There must none but she have it. 550

[BLANCH *snatcheth the letter from him, Et exit Messenger.*

Blanch. Go to, foolish fellow. And therefore, to ease the anger I sustain, I'll be so bold to open it. Whats here? SIR ROBERT greets you [2] well! You Mistress, his love, his life! Oh, amorous man, how he entertains his new Mistress, and bestows on LUBECK, his odd [3] friend, A horn nightcap to keep in his wit. 555

Mar. Madam, though you have discourteously read my letter, yet, I pray you, give it me.

Blanch. Then take it, there, and there, and there. 558

[*She tears it; Et exit* BLANCH.

[1] madam? Ch. ' [2] Ed. your [3] old. Ch. 'od (B. n. d.)

Mar. How far doth this differ from modesty! Yet will I gather up the pieces which, haply, may show to me the intent thereof, though not the meaning. 561

[*She gathers up the pieces and joins them.*
'Your servant and love[1], SIR ROBERT OF WINDSOR, ALIUS WILLIAM THE CONQUEROR, wisheth long health[2] and happinesse.' Is this WILLIAM the CONQUEROR, shrouded under the name of SIR ROBERT OF WINDSOR?—Were he the monarch of the world he should not dispossess LUBECK of his love. Therefore I will to the Court, and there, if I can, close to be friends with LADY BLANCH; and thereby keep LUBECK, my love, for myself, and further the LADY BLANCH in her suit, as much as I may. [*Exit.*

[SCENE VII.]

Enter EM, SOLUS.

[Ah], Jealousy, that sharps the lovers sight, 570
And makes him conceive and conster his intent,
Hath so bewitched my lovely MANVILES senses
That he misdoubts his EM, that loves his soul,
He doth suspect corrivals in his love— 574
Which, how untrue it is, be judge, my God[3]!
But now no more—Here cometh VALINGFORD;
Shift him off now, as thou hast done the other.

Enter VALINGFORD.

Val. See how fortune presents me with the hope I lookt for!
Fair EM! 579

[1] *lover:* Delius.—G. [Needless. See *Merch. of Ven.* IV. i. 277.—F.]
[2] *life:* Delius.—G.   [3] high heaven! Ch.

Em. Who's that?

Val. I am VALINGFORD[1], thy love and friend.

Em. I cry you mercy, sir; I thought so by your speech.   582

Val. What aileth thine eyes?

Em. Oh blind, sir, blind, stricken blind, by mishap, on a sudden!

Val. But is it possible you should be taken [2]on such a sudden[2]? Infortunate VALINGFORD, to be thus crost in thy love! Fair EM, I am not a little sorry to see this thy hard hap, yet nevertheless I am acquainted with a learned physician, that will do anything for thee, at my request; to him will I resort, and enquire his judgment, as concerning the recovery of so excellent a sense.   590

Em. O Lord, Sir! and of all things, I cannot abide physic: the very name thereof to me is odious.

Val. No? not the thing will do thee so much good? Sweet EM, hither I came to parley of[3] love,[4] hoping to have found thee in thy wonted prosperity; and have the Gods so unmercifully thwarted my expectation, by dealing so sinisterly with thee, sweet EM[4]?   596

Em. Good sir, no more.   It fits not me
To have respect to such vain phantasies
As idle love presents my ears withal,
More reason I should [5]ghostly give my life[5]   600
To sacred prayers, for this my former sin,
For which this plague is justly fall'n upon me,
Than to[6] hearken to the vanities of love.

Val. Yet, sweet EM[7], accept this jewel at my hand, which I bestow on thee[8] in token of my love.   605

[1] Dele Valingford   [2—2] thus. Ch.
[3] Dele of. Ch.   [4—4] dele. Ch.
[5—5] myself. Ch. and B. n. d.   [6] Dele to   [7] Dele *Em*
[8] Dele on thee. Ch.

ACT III.] *OF FAIRE EM.* 433

Em. A jewel, sir! what pleasure can I have
In jewels, treasure, or any worldly thing
That want mine sight that should discern thereof? 608
Ah, sir, I must leave you,
The pain of mine eyes is so extreme,
¹ I cannot long stay in a place. I take my leave. [*Exit* EM.

Val. Zounds, what a cross is this to my conceit! But, VALING-
FORD, search the depth of this device. Why may not this be some²
feign'd subtlety, by MOUNTENYS invention, to th' intent that I
seeing such occasion should leave off my suit, and not any more
persist to sollicit her of love? ³I'll try th'event.³ If I can by any
means perceive the effect of this deceit to be procured by his means,
friend MOUNTENY, the one of us is like to repent our bargain.

[*Exit.*

SCENE VIII. [ACT III. CH.]

Enter MARIANA *and* MARQUES LUBECK.

Lub. Lady,
Since that occasion, forward in our good, - 620
Presenteth place and opportunity,
Let me intreat your wonted kind consent
And friendly furtherance in a suit I have.

Mar. My Lord, you know you need not to intreat, 624
But may command MARIANA to her power,
Be't no impeachment to my honest fame.

· The reduplication of the same situation, when Mountney finds Em deа
in scene v., and Valingford finds her blind in scene vi., is something like the
reduplication in *Much Ado* criticized by Johnson.
² Dele some. Ch., and B. n. d. ³.—³ Dele. Ch.

VOL. II. 28

Lub. Free are my thoughts from such base villany
As may in question, Lady, call your name;
Yet is the matter of such consequence,
Standing upon my honourable credit,
To be effected with such zeal and secresy
As, should I speak and fail my expectation,
It would[1] redound greatly to my prejudice.

Mar. My Lord, wherein hath MARIANA
Given you[2] occasion that you should mistrust,
Or else be jealous of my secresy?

Lub. MARIANA, do not misconster me:
I not mistrust thee, nor thy secresy;
Nor let my love misconster my intent,
Nor think thereof but well and honourable[3]—
Thus stands the case:
Thou knowest from England hither came with me
ROBERT OF WINDSOR, a noble man at arms,
Lusty and valiant, in spring time of his years,
No marvel then though he prove amorous.

Mar. True, my Lord, he came to see fair BLANCH.

Lub. No, MARIANA, that is not it—his love to BLANCH
Was then extinct, when first he saw thy face.
'Tis thee he loves: yea, thou art only she
That's mistress and commander of his thoughts.

Mar. Well, well, my Lord, I like you: for such drifts
Put silly Ladies often to their shifts[4].
Oft have I heard you say you loved me well,

---

[1] 'twould   [2] Dele you
[3] honourably [4] Two lines ending here omit. Ch.

Yea, sworn the same, and I believed you too.
Can this be found an action of good faith
Thus to dissemble where you found true love? 656
   Lub. MARIANA, I not dissemble on mine honour,
Nor fails my faith to thee. But for my friend,
For princely WILLIAM, by whom[1] thou shalt possess
The title of estate and majesty, 660
Fitting the[2] love and virtues of thy mind—
For him I speak, for him do I intreat,
And, with thy favour, fully do resign
To him the claim and interest of my love— 664
Sweet MARIANA, then, deny me not:
Love WILLIAM, love my friend, and honour me,
Who else is clean dishonoured by thy means.
   Mar. Born to mishap, myself am only she 668
On whom the sun of fortune never shined:
But planets ruled by retrograde aspect
Foretold mine ill in my nativity!
   Lub. Sweet Lady, cease, let my intreaty serve 672
To pacify the passion of thy grief,
Which well I know proceeds of ardent love.
   Mar. But LUBECK now regards not MARIANA.
   Lub. Even as my life, so love I MARIANA. 676
   Mar. Why do you post me to another then?
   Lub. He is my friend, and I do love the man.
   Mar. Then will DUKE WILLIAM rob me of my love?
   Lub. No, as his life MARIANA he doth love. 680
   Mar. Speak for yourself, my Lord, let him alone.

      [1] b'whom   [2] thy. Ch.

Lub. So do I, Madam, for he and I am one.

Mar. Then loving you I do content you both.

Lub. In loving him you shall content us both— 684
Me, for I crave that favour at your hands,
Him, [1] for he hopes that comfort at your hands [2]—

Mar. Leave off, my Lord, here comes the LADY BLANCH.

Enter BLANCH *to them* [3].

Lub. Hard hap, to break us off our talk so soon!
Sweet MARIANA, do remember me. [*Exit* LUBECK.

Mar. Thy MARIANA cannot choose but [4] remember thee.

Blanch. MARIANA, well met. You are very forward in your love. 692

Mar. Madam, be it in secret spoken to your self, if you will but [5] follow the complot [6] I have invented you will not think me so forward as yourself shall prove fortunate.

Blanch. As how? 696

Mar. Madam, as thus: It is not unknown to you that SIR ROBERT OF WINDSOR, a man that you do not a little esteem, hath long importuned me of love. But rather than I will be found false or unjust to the MARQUES LUBECK, I will, as did the constant lady PENELOPE, undertake to effect some great task.

---

[1] He for hopes. B. n. d.

[2] The two lines ending here are omitted in Ch.

[3] This scene, between Blanch and Mariana, is printed in verse-lines in the original.—L. T. S.

[4] This idea, that love is to be sacrificed to friendship, because friendship among men is greater than the love of man to woman, is found in *The Two Gentlemen of Verona*, where Valentine gives up Silvia to Proteus, and lies at the foundation of Shakspere's sonnet philosophy. See my book, p. 18, and p. 58. Also Vernon, in the first act of *Stukley :* ante, vol. i. p. 161, l. 93.   [5] Dele but. Ch.   [6] plot. Ch.

Blanch. What of all this? 702

Mar. The next time that SIR ROBERT shall come in his wonted sort, to solicit me with love, I will seem to agree, and like of anything that the knight shall demand, so far forth as it be no impeachment to my chastity[1]. And, to conclude, point some place for to meet the man, for my conveyance from the DENMARK court: which determined upon, he will appoint some certain time for our departure: whereof, you having intelligence, you may soon set down a plot to wear the English crown, and then—

Bl. What then? 711

Mar. If SIR ROBERT prove a King and you his Queen, how then?

Bl. Were I assured of the one as I am persuaded of the other there were some possibility in it. But here comes the man.

Mar. Madam, begone, and you shall see I'll work to your desire and my content. [*Exit* BLANCH.

William Conq. Lady, this is well and happily met; for [2] Fortune hitherto hath been my foe, and though I have oft sought to speak with you, yet still I have been crost with sinister[3] haps. 720
I cannot, Madam, tell a loving tale[4],
Or court my Mistress with fabulous discourses[5],
That am a soldier sworn to follow arms—
But this I bluntly let you understand— 724
I honour you with such religious zeal
As may become an honourable mind.
Nor may I make my love the siege of Troy,

---

[1] honour. Ch.   [2] for, not in orig.   [3] pron. 'sinster.'
[4] Compare Henry Vth's courtship: *Hen. V.* v. 2, ll. 98 *et seq.*
[5] Otherwise.—or with discourses fabulous court my mistress. Ch. has 'false vows of love.'

[1] That am a stranger in this country [1]. 728
First, what I am I know you are resolved,
For that my friend hath let you t' [2] understand,
The MARQUES LUBECK, to whom I am so bound
That whilst I live I count me only his. 732
    Mar. Surely you are [3] beholding to the MARQUES [3],
For he hath been an earnest spokesman in your cause.
    Wm. And yields my lady then, at his request,
To grace DUKE WILLIAM with her gracious love? 736
    Mar. My lord, I am a prisoner, and hard it were
To get me from the court.
    Wm. An easy matter, to get you from the Court,
If case that you will thereto give consent. 740
    Mar. Put case [4] I should, how would you use me then?
    Wm. Not otherwise but well and honourably.
I have at sea a ship that doth attend,
Which shall forthwith conduct us into England; 744
Where, when we are, I straight will marry thee.
We may not stay deliberating long,
Lest that suspicion, conscious [5] of our weal,
Set in a foot to hinder our pretence. 748
    Mar. But this I think were most convenient,
To mask my face, the better to scape unknown.
    Wm. A good device. Till then farewell, fair love.
    Mar. But this I must intreat your grace— 752

    [1]–[1] Line omitted in Ch.   [2] that to, in orig.
    [3]–[3] beholden to that lord. Ch.
    [4] Bodc. n. d. also has Put case I; but Ch. has What if I.
    [5] envious. Ch. and B. n. d.

You would not seek by lust unlawfully
To wrong my chaste determinations.

   Wm. I hold that man most shameless in his sin
That seeks to wrong an honest ladys name,   756
Whom he thinks worthy of his marriage bed.

   Mar. In hope your oath is true,
I leave your grace till the appointed time.   *[Exit* MARIANA.

   Wm. O happy WILLIAM, blessed in thy love [1],   760
Most fortunate in Mariana's love!—
Well, LUBECK, well, this courtesy of thine
I will requite, if God permit me life.   *[Exit.*

[SCENE IX.]

Enter VALINGFORD *and* MOUNTNEY *at two sundry doors, looking angerly each on other with rapiers drawn.*

   Mount. VALINGFORD, so hardly I digest an injury thou'st
    proffered me,   765
As, wer't not I detest
To do what stands not with the honour of my name,
Thy death should pay the ransom of thy fault.   768

   Val. And, MOUNTNEY, had not my revenging wrath,
Incensed with more than ordinary love,
Been such for to deprive thee of thy life,
Thou hadst not lived to brave me as thou dost.   772
Wretch as thou art [2],
Wherein hath VALINGFORD offended thee?

---

     [1] ? fortune   [2] Line omitted by Ch.

That honourable bond which late we did
Confirm in presence of the gods, 776
When with the Conqueror we arrived here,
For my part hath been kept inviolably.
Till, now, too much abused by thy villany,
I am enforced to cancel all those bands, 780
By hating him which I so well did love.

    Mount. Subtle thou art, and cunning in thy fraud,
That, giving me occasion of offence,
Thou pick'st a quarrel to excuse thy shame. 784
Why, VALINGFORD, was't [1] not enough for thee,
To be a rival 'twixt me and my love,
But counsel her, to my no small disgrace,
That, when I came to talk with her of love, 788
She should seem deaf, as feigning not to hear?

    Val. But hath she, MOUNTNEY, used thee as thou sayest?

    Mount. Thou knowest too well she hath—wherein
Thou couldst not do me greater injury. 792

    Val. Then I perceive we are deluded both,
For when I offered many gifts of gold,
And jewels, to entreat for love,
She hath refused them with [2] coy disdain [3], 796
Alleging that she could not see the sun.
The same conjectured I to be thy drift,
That feigning so she might be rid of me.

---

    [1] it in orig.   [2] a coy in orig.
   [3] The three lines ending here, like many others in this text, are differently divided in the original.—L. T. S.

ACT III.]   OF FAIRE EM.   441

    Mount. The like did I by thee. But are not these   800
Natural impediments?
    Val. In my conjecture merely counterfeit:
Therefore let's join hands, in friendship once again,
Since that the jar grew only by conjecture.   804
    Mount. With all my heart: yet let us[1] try the truth thereof.
    Val. With right good will. We will straight unto her father,
And there to learn whether it be so or no.   [*Exeunt.*

[SCENE X.]

Enter WILLIAM, *and* BLANCH *disguised with a mask over her face.*

    Wm. Come on, my love, the comfort of my life.   808
Disguised thus, we may remain unknown,
And get we once to seas, I force[2] not then
We quickly shall attain the English shore.
    Blanch. But this I urge you with your former oath—   812
You shall not seek to violate mine honour
Until our marriage rights be all performed.
    Wm. MARIANA, here I swear to thee by heaven,
And by the honour that I bear to arms,   816
Never to seek or crave at hands of thee
The spoil of honourable chastity,
Until we do attain the English coast,
Where thou shalt be my right espoused Queen.   820
    Blanch. In hope your oath proceedeth from your heart,
Let's leave the Court, and betake us to his power

---

    [1] let 's in orig.   [2] doubt. Ch.

That governs all things to [1] his mighty will,
And will reward the just with endless joy, 824
And plague the bad with most extreme annoy.

Wm. Lady, as little tarriance as we may,
Lest some misfortune happen by the way. [*Exeunt.*

[SCENE XI.]

Enter the Miller, his man TROTTER, *and* MANVILE.

Mil. I tell you, sir, it is no little grief to me you should so hardly conceit of my daughter, whose honest report, though I say it, was never blotted with any title of defamation.

Man. Father *Miller*, the repair of those gentlemen to your house hath given me great occasion to mislike. 832

Mil. As for those gentlemen, I never saw in them any evil intreaty; but should they have proffered it her chaste mind hath proof enough to prevent it.

Trot. Those gentlemen are as honest as ever I saw. For i'faith one of them gave me sixpence to fetch a quart of seck [2].—See, master, here they come. 838

Enter MOUNTNEY *and* VALINGFORD.

Mil. TROTTER, call EM. Now they are here together I'll have this matter thoroughly debated. [*Exit* TROTTER.

Mount. Father, well met. We are come to confer with you.

Man. Nay, with his daughter rather.

Val. Thus it is, father, we come to crave your friendship in a matter. 844

---

[1] by. Ch.   [2] Falstaff was charged 8½d. a quart for sack.

Mill. Gentlemen, as you are strangers to me, yet by the way of courtesy you shall demand [1] any reasonable thing at my hands.

Man. What, is the matter so forward they come to crave his goodwill? 848

Val. It is given us to understand that your daughter is suddenly become both blind and deaf.

Mil. Marry, God forbid! I have sent for her. Indeed she hath kept her chamber this three days, it were no little grief to me if it should be so.

Man. This is God's judgment for her treachery! 854

Enter TROTTER *leading* EM.

Mil. Gentlemen, I fear your words are two true: see where TROTTER comes leading of her. What ails my EM? not blind, I hope? 857

Em. MOUNTNEY and VALINGFORD both together! and MAN-VILE, to whom I have faithfully vowed my love! Now, EM, suddenly help thyself. 860

Mount. This is no dissembling, VALINGFORD.

Val. If it be it is cunningly contrived of all sides.

Em. TROTTER, lend me thy hand; and as thou lovest me, keep my counsel, and justify whatsoever I say, and I'll largely requite thee. 865

Trot. Ah, that's as much as to say you would tell a monstrous, terrible, horrible, outrageous lie, and I shall sooth it—No, [2]by our[2] lady! 868

Em. My present extremity wills me, if thou love me, TROTTER.

Trot. That same word love makes me to do anything [3].

[1] ? command.   [2—2] b'er orig.
[3] Grim, the Collier of Croydon, is a Clown with many of the same cha-

Em. TROTTER, where's my father? 871

Trot. Why what a blind dunce are you, can you not see? He standeth right before you. [*He thrusts* EM *upon her father.*

Em. Is this my father? Good father, give me leave to sit where I may not be disturbed, sith God hath visited me both of my sight and hearing. 876

Mil. Tell me, sweet EM, how came this blindness? Thy eyes are lovely to [1] look on, and yet have they [2] lost the benefit of their [3] sight? What a grief is this to thy poor father!

Em. Good father, let me not stand as an open gazing stock to every one, but in a place alone, as fits a creature so miserable.

Mil. TROTTER, lead her in: the utter overthrow of poor GODDARD's joy and only solace! 883

[*Exit the Miller,* TROTTER, *and* EM.

Man. Both blind and deaf! Then is she no wife for me; and glad am I so good an [4] occasion is happened. Now will I away to *Manchester* [5], and leave these gentlemen to their blind fortune.

[*Exit* MANVILE.

Mount. Since fortune hath thus spitefully [6] crost our hope, let us leave this guest [7], and hearken after our king, who is at this day landed at *Lirpoole.* [*Exit* MOUNTNEY.

Val. Go, my Lord, I'll follow you. Well, now MOUNTNEY is

---

racteristics as Trotter. Note especially the way in which he receives any kind word of Joan's. Thus, Act II. sc. i.:

'Oh, Mr Parson, write down this sweet saying of hers in Grim's commendation. She hath made my heart leap like a hobby-horse.' And again, a little farther on: 'If I love thee, Joan! Those very words are a purgation to me.'

[1] yet to. Ch.   [2] they not in Ch.   [3] their not in Cb.
     [4] an not in B. n. d.   [5] Chester.
     [6] spiteful. Ch.   [7] ? gear, or quest.

gone, I'll stay behind to solicit my¹ love; for I imagine that I shall find this but a feigned invention, thereby to have us leave off our suits². 893

[SCENE XII.]

Enter MARQUES LUBECK *and the* K. OF DENMARK, *angerly, with some attendants.*

Zweno. K. Well, LUBECK, well, it is not possible
But you must be consenting to this act.
Is this the man so highly you extolled? 896
And play a part so hateful with his friend?
Since first he came with thee in to the Court,
What entertainment and what countenance
He hath received none better knows than thou— 900
In recompense whereof he quits me well
To steal away fair ³ MARIANA my prisoner ³,
Whose ransom, being lately ⁴ 'greed upon ⁴,
I am deluded of by this escape. 904
Besides, I know not how to answer it,
When she shall be demanded home to Swethia.

Lub. My gracious Lord, conjecture not, I pray,
Worser⁵ of LUBECK than he doth deserve: 908
Your highness knows MARIANA was my love,
Sole paragon and mistress of my thoughts.
Is't likely I should know of her departure,
Wherein there's no man injured more than I? 912

Zweno. That carries reason, MARQUES, I confess.

¹ fair love. Ch.   ² All this scene is printed as verse in original.—G.
³—³ Marian, my captive. Ch.   ⁴—⁴ fixed on. Ch.   ⁵ More ill. Ch.

Call forth my daughter. Yet I am persuaded
That she, poor soul, suspected not her going;
For as I hear, she likewise loved the man,
Which he, to blame, did not at all regard [1].

Rocilia. My Lord, here is the Princess MARIANA;
It is your daughter is conveyed away.

Zweno. What, my daughter gone!
Now, MARQUES, [now] [2] your villany breaks forth;
This match is of your making, gentle sir,
And you shall dearly know the price thereof.

Lub. Knew I thereof, or that there was intent
In ROBERT thus to steal your highness daughter,
Let heavens in justice presently confound me!

Zweno. Not all the protestations thou canst use
Shall save thy life. Away with him to prison;
And, minion, otherwise it cannot be
But you are an agent in this treachery,
I will revenge it throughly on you both.
Away with her to prison!—
Here's stuff indeed! My daughter stolen away!
It booteth not thus to disturb myself,
But presently to send to English WILLIAM,
To send me that proud knight of Windsor hither,
Here in my Court to suffer for his shame,
Or at my pleasure to be punished there,

---

[1] *Merry Wives*, 1602, p. 35, l. 8:
'You know my answer, sir; she's not for you;
Knowing my vow, to blame to use me thus.'
[2] now not in orig.

Act III.]   *OF FAIRE EM.*   447

Withal that BLANCH be sent me home again,
Or I shall fetch her unto *Windsor's* cost,   940
Yea, and WILLIAM's too, if he deny her me.   [*Exit* ZWENO.

[SCENE XIII.]

Enter WILLIAM, *taken with soldiers.*

Wm. Could any cross, could any plague be worse?
Could heaven or hell, did both conspire in one
To afflict my soul, invent a greater scourge   944
Than presently I am tormented with?
Ah, MARIANA, cause of my lament!
Joy of my heart, and comfort of my life,
For thee[1] I breathe my sorrows in the air   948
And tire myself, for[2] silently I sigh,
My sorrows[3] afflicts my[4] soul with equal passion.

Soldier. Go to, sirrah, put up, it is to small purpose.

Wm. Hence, villains, hence! Dare you [to] lay your hands
Upon your sovereign!   953

Sol. Well, sir, we will deal for that.
But here comes one will remedy all this.   [*Enter* DEMARCH.
My lord, watching this night in the camp   956
We took this man, and know not what he is;
And in his company was a gallant dame,
A woman fair in outward show she seemed,
But that her face was masked we could not see   960

[1] ? Whether.   [2] ? or.
[3] griefs. Ch.   [4] me. n. d.

The grace and favour of her countenance.

De March. Tell me, good fellow, of whence and what art thou?

Sol. Why do you not answer my lord?

He takes scorn to answer! 964

Demarch. And tak'st thou scorn to answer my demand?
Thy proud behaviour very well deserves
This misdemeanour at the worst be construed.
Why dost thou neither know, nor hast thou heard, 968
That in the absence of the Saxon Duke [1]
DEMARCH is his especial substitute,
To punish those that shall offend the laws?

Wm. In knowing this, I know thou art a traitor; 972
A rebel and [a] mutinous conspirator.
Why, DEMARCH, knowest thou who I am?

Dem. Pardon, my dread Lord, the error of my sense,
And misdemeanor to your princely excellency! 976

Wm. Why, DEMARCH, what is the cause my subjects are in arms?

Dem. Free are my thoughts, my dread and gracious Lord,
From treason to your state and common weal; 980
Only revengement of a private grudge,
By LORD DIROT lately proffered me,
That stands not with the honour of my name,
Is cause I have assembled for my guard 984
Some men in arms, that may withstand his force
Whose settled malice aimeth at my life.

---

[1] He was Norman. William is variously termed King and Duke William, Duke of Saxony, Normandy, and Duke of Britain. Do not these differences show different hands in the play?

ACT III.]   *OF FAIRE EM.*   449

Wm. Where is LORD DIROT?
Dem. In arms, my gracious Lord,   988
Not past two miles from hence,
As credibly I am ascertained.
Wm. Well, come, let's go.
I fear I shall find traitors of you both.   [*Exit.*

[SCENE XIV[1].]

Enter the Citizen of Manchester[2], *and his daughter* ELNER, *and* MANVILE.

Cit. Indeed, sir, it would do very well if you could intreat your father to come hither; but, if you think it be too far, I care not much to take horse and ride to Manchester. I am sure my daughter is content with either. How sayest thou, ELNER, art thou not?

Eln. As you shall think best I must be contented.   997

Man. Well, ELNER, farewell. Only thus much, I pray: make all things in a readiness, either to serve here, or to carry thither with us.   1000

Cit. As for that, sir, take you no care: and so I betake you to your journey—   [*Enter* VALINGFORD.
But soft, what gentleman is this?

Val. God speed, sir. Might a man crave a word or two with you?

Cit. God forbid else, sir; I pray you speak your pleasure.

Val. The gentleman that parted from you, was he not of Manchester, his father living there of good account?

[1] Act IV. Ch.
[2] Are they not at Chester, and should not this be Citizen of Chester?

Cit. Yes, marry is he, sir. Why do you ask? Belike you have had some acquaintance with him? 1009

Val. I have been acquainted, in times past, but, through his double dealing, I am growen weary of his company; for, be it spoken to you, he hath been acquainted with a poor miller's daughter, and divers times hath promised her marriage, but what with his delays and flouts he hath brought her into such a taking that I fear me it will cost her her life. 1015

Cit. To be plain with you, sir, his father and I have been of old acquaintance, and a motion was made between my daughter and his son, which now is throughly agreed upon, save only the place appointed for the marriage, whether it shall be kept here or at Manchester; and for no other occasion he is now ridden.

Elner. What hath he done to you, that you should speak so ill of the man? 1022

Val. Oh, gentlewoman, I cry you mercy: he is your husband that shall be.

Elner. If I knew this to be true, he should not be my husband were he never so good. And therefore, good father, I would desire you to take the pains to bear this gentleman company to Manchester, to know whether this be true or no. 1028

Cit. Now trust me, gentleman, he deals with me very hardly, knowing how well I meant to him. But I care not much to ride to Manchester, to know whether his father's will be he should deal with me so badly. Will it please you, sir, to go in? We will presently take horse and away. 1033

Val. If it please you to go in, I'll follow you presently. [*Exit* ELNER *and her father.*] Now shall I be revenged on MANVILE, and by this means get Ēm to be my wife[1]; and therefore I will straight to her fathers, and inform them both of all that has [2] happened[3]. [*Exit.*

[SCENE XV.]

Enter WILLIAM, *the Ambassador of Denmark*, DEMARCH, *and other attendants.*

Wm. What news with the Denmark embassador? 1038
Emb. Marry, thus: the King of Denmark, and my Sovereign,
Doth send to know of thee what is the cause, 1040
That, injuriously, against the law of arms,
Thou hast stolen away his only daughter, BLANCH,
The only stay and comfort of his life?
Therefore, by me 1044
[4] he willeth thee to send his daughter BLANCH [4],
Or else forthwith he will levy such an host,
As soon shall fetch her in despite of thee.

Wm. Embassador, this answer I return thy King. 1048
He willeth me to send his daughter BLANCH,
Saying, I conveyed her from the Danish Court,
That never yet once did as think thereof.
As for his menacing and daunting threats, 1052
I will regard him nor his Danish power;
For if he come to fetch her forth my realm
I will provide him such a banquet here,
That he shall have small cause to give me thanks. 1056

---

[1] be not in orig.   [2] is. Bode. n. d.
[3] All this scene is printed as verse in the original.—G.
[4]—[4] he wills thee send her back. Ch.

Emb. Is this your answer, then?

Wm. It is; and so begone.

Emb. I go; but to your cost. [*Exit Ambassador.*

Wm. DEMARCH, 1060
Our subjects, erst levied in civil broils,
Muster[1], forthwith, for to defend the Realm.
In hope whereof, that we shall find you true,
We freely pardon this thy late offence. 1064

Dem. Most humble thanks I render to your grace. [*Exeunt.*

[SCENE XVI.]

Enter the Miller and VALINGFORD.

Mil. Alas, gentleman, why should you trouble yourself so much, considering the imperfections of my daughter, which is able to withdraw the love of any man from her, as already it hath done in her first choice. MASTER MANVILE hath forsaken her, and at Chester shall be married to a mans daughter of no little wealth. But if my daughter knew so much, it would go very near her heart, I fear me. 1072

Val. Father miller, such is the[2] entire affection to your daughter, as no misfortune whatsoever can alter. My fellow MOUNTNEY, thou seest, gave quickly over; but I, by reason of my good meaning, am not so soon to be changed, although I am borne off with scorns and denial[3]. [*Enter* EM *to them.*

Mil. Trust me, sir, I know not what to say. My daughter is not to be compelled by me; but here she comes herself: speak to

---

[1] Mustered. n. d.   [2] ? my
[3] The four lines ending here are omitted by Ch.

her and spare not, for I never was troubled with love matters so much before. 1081

Em. Good Lord! shall I never be rid of this importunate man? Now must I dissemble blindness again. Once more for thy sake, MANVILE, thus am I enforced, because I shall complete my full resolved mind to thee. Father, where are you? 1085

Mil. Here, sweet EM. Answer this gentleman, that would so fain enjoy thy love.

Em. Where are you, sir? will you never leave this idle and vain pursuit of love? Is not England stored enough to content you but you must still trouble the poor contemptible maid of Manchester? 1091

Val. None can content me but the fair maid of Manchester.

Em. I perceive love is vainly described, that, being blind himself, would have you likewise troubled with a blind wife, having the benefit of your eyes. But neither follow him so much in folly, but love one in whom you may better delight. 1096

Val. Father Miller, thy daughter shall have honour by granting me her love. I am a gentleman of KING WILLIAM's court, and no mean man in KING WILLIAM's favour.

Em. If you be a Lord, sir, as you say, you offer both yourself and me great wrong; yours, as apparent, in limiting your love so unorderly, for which you rashly endure reproachment; mine, as open and evident, when, being shut out from the vanities of this world, you would have me as an open gazing stock to all the world; for lust, not love, leads you into this error. But from the one I will keep me as well as I can; and yield the other to none but to[1], my father, as I am bound by duty. 1107

[1] to, is from the n. d. copy.

Val. Why, fair EM, MANVILE hath forsaken thee, and must at Chester be married: which if I speak otherwise than true, let thy father speak what credibly he hath heard. 1110

Em. But can it be MANVILE will deal so unkindly to reward my justice with such monstrous ungentleness? Have I dissembled for thy sake, and dost thou now thus requite it? Indeed these many days I have not seen him, which hath made me marvel at his long absence. But, father, are you assured of the words he spake were concerning MANVILE? 1116

Mil. In sooth, daughter, now it is forth I must needs confirm it: MASTER MANVILE hath forsaken thee, and at Chester must be married to a mans daughter of no little wealth. His own father procures it, and therefore I dare credit it; and do thou believe it, for trust me, daughter, it is so. 1121

Em. Then, good father, pardon the injury that I have done to you, only causing your grief, by overfond affecting a man so trothless. And you likewise, sir, I pray hold me excused, as I hope this cause will allow sufficiently for me: my love to MANVILE, thinking he would requite it, hath made me double with my father and you, and many more besides, which I will no longer hide from you: that inticing speeches should not beguile me, I have made myself deaf to any but to him; and lest any man's person should please me more than his, I have dissembled the want of my sight: both which shadows of my irrevocable affections I have not spared to confirm before him, my father, and all other amorous solicitors—wherewith not made acquainted, I perceive my true intent hath wrought mine own sorrow, and seeking by love to be regarded am cut off with contempt and despised. 1136

Mil. Tell me, sweet EM, hast thou but feigned all this while[1] for his love, that hath so discourteously forsaken thee? 1138

Em. Credit me, father, I have told you the truth; wherewith I desire you and LORD VALINGFORD not to be displeased. For aught else I shall say, let my present grief hold me excused. But, may I live to see that ungrateful man justly rewarded for his treachery, poor EM would think herself not a little happy. Favour my departing at this instant; for my troubled thought desires to meditate alone in silence. [*Exit* EM.

Val. Will not EM show one cheerful look on VALINGFORD?

Mil. Alas, sir, blame her not; you see she hath good cause, being so handled by this gentleman[2]: and so I'll leave you, and go comfort my poor wench [3] as well as I may [3]. [*Exit the Miller.*

Val. Farewell, good father[4]. [*Exit* VALINGFORD.

[SCENE XVII[5].]

Enter ZWENO, *King of Denmark, with* ROSILIO *and other attendants.*

Zw. ROSILIO, is this the place whereas 1151
The DUKE WILLIAM should meet me?

Ros. It is, and like your grace.

Zw. Go, captain! Away, regard the charge I gave: 1154
See all our men be marshalled for the fight;
Dispose the wards, as lately was devised;

---

[1] only. Ch. [2] This line not in Ch.
[3]—[3] Omitted by Ch.
[4] All the prose in this scene is printed as verse in the original.—G.
[5] Act V. Ch.

And let the prisoners, under several guards,
Be kept apart, until you hear from us. 1158
Let this suffice, you know my resolution.
If WILLIAM, Duke of Saxon,[1] be the man,
That by his answer sent us he would send [2]—
Not words, but wounds; not parleis, but alarms, 1162
Must be decider of this controversy.
ROSILIO, stay with me. The rest begone. [*Exeunt.*

Enter WILLIAM, *and* DEMARCH, *with other attendants.*

Wm. All but DEMARCH go shroud you out of sight;
For I'll go parley with the prince myself. 1166
Dem. Should ZWENO, by this parley, call you forth,
Upon intent injuriously to deal,
This offereth too much opportunity.
Wm. No, no, DEMARCH, 1170
That were a breach against the law of arms.
Therefore begone, and leave us here alone. [*Exeunt.*
I see that ZWENO is master of his word.
ZWENO, WILLIAM OF SAXONY [3] greeteth thee, 1174
Either well or ill according to thy intent.
If well thou wish to him and Saxony [4],
He bids thee friendly welcome as he can;
If ill thou wish to [5] him and Saxony [5], 1178
He must withstand thy malice as he may.
Zweno. WILLIAM, for other name and title give I none

---

[1] Normandy. Ch. [2] Seem.
[3] England. Ch. [4] Englands crown. Ch.
[5]—[5] this my realm. Ch.

To him, who, were he worthy of those honours
That fortune and his predecessors left,   1182
I ought, by right and human courtesy,
To style his grace the duke of Saxony [1];
But, for I find a base, degenerate mind,
I frame my speech according to the man,   1186
And not the state that he unworthy holds.
 Wm. Herein, ZWENO, dost thou abase thy state,
To break the peace which by our ancestors
Hath heretofore been honourably kept.   1190
 Zw. And should that peace for ever have been kept
Had not thy self been author of the breach:
Nor stands it with the honour of my state,
Or nature of a father to his child,   1194
That I should so be robbed of my daughter,
And not, unto the utmost of my power,
Revenge so intolerable an injury.
 Wm. Is this the colour of your quarrel, ZWENO?   1198
I well perceive the wisest men may err—
And think you I conveyed away your daughter, BLANCH?
 Zw. Art thou so impudent to deny thou didst,
When that the proof thereof is manifest?   1202
 Wm. What proof is there?
 Zw. Thine own confession is sufficient proof.
 Wm. Did I confess I stole your daughter, BLANCH?
 Zw. Thou didst confess thou hadst a lady hence.   1206
 Wm. I have, and do.

---

[1] In Mr Simpson's MS the line stands as here printed, but the original reads—To grace his style with, &c.—G.

Zw. Why, that was BLANCH, my daughter.

Wm. Nay, that was MARIANA;
Who wrongfully thou detainest prisoner.   1210

Zw. Shameless persisting in thy ill!
Thou dost maintain a manifest untroth,
As she shall justify unto thy teeth.
ROSILIO, fetch her and the MARQUES hither.   1214

[*Exit* ROSILIO *for* MARIANA.

Wm. It cannot be I should be so deceived.

Dem. I hear this night among the soldiers
That in their watch they took a pensive lady,
Who, at the appointment of the Lord Dirot,   1218
Is yet in keeping. What she is I know not:
Only thus much I overheard by chance.

Wm. And what of this?

Dem. It may be BLANCH, the King of Denmark's daughter.

Wm. It may be so; but on my life it is not: 1223
Yet, DEMARCH, go and fetch her straight.

Enter ROSILIO *with the* MARQUES.

Ros. Pleaseth your highness, here is the MARQUES and MARIANA.

Zw. See here, DUKE WILLIAM, your competitors,   1226
That were consenting to my daughter's scape:
Let them resolve you of the truth herein.
And here I vow and solemnly protest,
That in thy presence they shall lose their heads,   1230
Unless I hear whereas my daughter is!

Wm. O, MARQUES LUBECK, how it grieveth me,

That for my sake thou shouldst endure these bonds!
Be judge, my soul, that feels the martyrdom! 1234
 Marques. DUKE WILLIAM, you know it's for your cause
It pleaseth thus the King to misconceive of me,
And for his pleasure doth me injury.

    Enter DEMARCH *with the* LADY BLANCH.

 Dem. May it please your highness, 1238
Here is the Lady you sent me for.
 Wm. Away, DEMARCH! what tellest thou me of Ladies [1]?
I so detest the dealing of their sex,
As that I count a lovers state to be 1242
The base and vildest slavery i' th' world!
 Dem. What humours are these? Here's a strange alteration!
 Zw. See, DUKE WILLIAM, is this BLANCH or no?
You know her if you see her, I am sure. 1246
 Wm. ZWENO, I was deceived, yea, utterly deceived.
Yet this is she—this same is LADY BLANCH.
And for mine error, here I am content
To do whatever ZWENO shall set down. 1250
Ah, cruel MARIANA, thus to use
The man which loved and honoured thee [2] with 's heart [2]!
 Mar. When first I came into your highness court,
And WILLIAM oft' importing me of love, 1254
I did devise, to ease the grief your daughter did sustain,
She should meet SIR WILLIAM masked, as I it were.

 [1] Cf. *Twelfth Night*, IV. ii. 29.—'Out hyperbolical fiend! how vexest thou this man! Talkest thou nothing but of ladies?'
 [2]—[2] so much. Ch.

This put in proof did take so good effect,
As yet it seems his grace is not resolved,   1258
But it was I which he conveyed away.

Wm. May this be true? It cannot [1] be but [1] true.
Was 't LADY BLANCH which I conveyed away?
Unconstant MARIANA, thus to deal   1262
With him which meant to thee nought but faith!

Blan. Pardon, dear father, my follies that are past,
Wherein I have neglected my [2] duty,
Which I in reverence ought to show your grace;   1266
For led by love I thus have gone astray,
And now repent the errors I was in.

Zw. Stand up, dear daughter. Though thy fault deserves
For to be punished in the extremest sort,   1270
Yet love, that covers multitude of sins [3],
Makes [4] love in [4] parents wink at childrens faults.
Sufficeth [5], BLANCH, thy father loves thee so,
Thy follies past he knows, but will not know.   1274
And here, DUKE WILLIAM, take my daughter to thy wife,
For well I am assured she loves thee well.

Wm. A proper conjunction!
As who should say, lately come out of the fire,   1278
I would go thrust myself into the flame.
Let Mistress nice go saint it where she list,
And coyly quaint it with dissembling face;
I hold in scorn the fooleries that they use: 1282

[1]—[1] but be   [2] this my. Ch.: me. n. d.
[3] This is one of the lines censured by Greene. See *Introd.*, p. 379.
[4]—[4] loving. Ch.   [5] Suffice it

I being free, will ne'er subject myself
To any such as she is underneath the sun [1].

Zw. Refusest thou to take my daughter to thy wife?
I tell thee, DUKE, this rash denial may bring   1286
More mischief on thee than thou canst avoid.

Wm. Conceit hath wrought such general dislike,
Through the false dealing of MARIANA,
That utterly I do abhor their sex.   1290
They're all disloyal, unconstant, all unjust:
Who tries as I have tried, and finds as I have found,
Will say there's no such creatures on the ground.

Blanch. Unconstant Knight, though some deserve no trust,
There's others faithful, loving, loyal, and just!   1295

Enter to them VALINGFORD, *with* EM *and the Miller, and*
MOUNTNEY, *and* MANVILE, *and* ELNER.

Wm. How now, L. VALINGFORD, what makes these women here?

Val. Here be two women, may it please your grace,   1298
That are contracted to one man, and are
In strife whether shall have him to her [2] husband.

Wm. Stand forth, women, and say
To whether of you did he first give his faith.   1302

Em. To me, forsooth [3].

Elner. To me, my gracious Lord.

Wm. Speak, MANVILE: to whether didst thou give thy faith?

---

[1] Otherwise—To any she is underneath the sun.
[2] their in orig.   [3] my liege. Ch.

Man. To say the troth, this maid had first my love. 1306
Elner. Yea, MANVILE, but there was no witness by.
Em. Thy conscience, MANVILE, [1] is a thousand[1] witnesses[2].
Elner. She hath stolen a conscience to serve her own turn—
But you are deceived, i' faith, he will none of you. 1310
    Man. Indeed, dread Lord, so dear I held her love
As in the same I put my whole delight;
But some impediments, which at that instant
Happened, made me forsake her quite; 1314
For which I had her father's frank consent.
    Wm. What were th' impediments?
    Man. Why, she could neither hear nor see.
    Wm. Now she doth both. Maiden, how were you cured? 1318
    Em. Pardon, my Lord, I'll tell your Grace the troth—
Be it not imputed to me as discredit.
I loved this MANVILE so much, that still methought,
When he was absent, did present to me 1322
The form and feature of that countenance
Which I did shrine an idol in my heart,
And never could I see a man, methought,
That equalled MANVILE in my partial eye. 1326
Nor was there any love between us lost,
But that I held the same in high regard,
Until repair of some unto our house,
Of whom my MANVILE grew thus jealous 1330
As if he took exception, I vouchsafed
To hear them speak, or saw them when they came:

[1]—[1] a hundred. n. d.
[2] This is the other line censured by Greene. See *Introd.*, p. 378.

On which I straight took order with myself,
To void the scruple of his conscience   1334
By counterfeiting that I neither saw nor heard
Any ways to rid my hands of them.
All this I did to keep my MANVILE's love,
Which he unkindly seeks for to reward.   1338
 Man. And did my EM, to keep her faith with me,
Dissemble that she neither heard nor saw?
Pardon me, sweet EM, for I am only thine!
 Em. Lay off thy hands, disloyal as thou art!   1342
Nor shalt thou have possession of my love,
That canst so finely shift thy matters off!
Put case I had been blind, and could not see—
As often times such visitations falls   1346
That pleaseth God, which all things doth dispose—
Shouldst thou forsake me in regard of that?
I tell thee, MANVILE, hadst thou been blind,
Or deaf, or dumb,   1350
Or what impediments else might befal man [1],
EM would have loved, and kept, and honoured thee;
Yea, begged, if wealth had failed, for thy relief.
 Man. Forgive me, sweet EM!   1354
 Em. I do forgive thee, with my heart,
And will forget thee too, if case I can:
But never speak to me, nor seem to know me!
 Man. Then fare-well, frost! well-fare a wench that will!   1358
Now, ELNER, I'm thine own, my girl.
 Elner. Mine, MANVILE? thou never shalt be mine;

[1] Ed. or else what impediments might befal to man.

I so detest thy villany,
That whilst I live I will abhor thy company! 1362
   Man. Is 't come to this? Of late I had choice of twain,
On either side, to have me to her husband,
And now am utterly rejected of them both.
   Val. My Lord, this Gentleman, when time was, 1366
Stood something in our light,
And now I think it not amiss
To laugh at him that sometime scorned at us.
   Mount. Content, my Lord, invent the form. 1370
   Val. Then thus [1]—
   Wm. I see that women are not general evils—
BLANCH is fair: Methinks I see in her
A modest countenance, a heavenly blush. 1374
ZWENO, receive a reconciled foe,
Not as thy friend, but as thy son-in-law,
If so that thou be thus content.
   Zw. I joy to see your grace so tractable— 1378
Here, take my daughter, BLANCH;
And after my decease the Denmark Crown.
   Wm. Now, sir, how stands the case with you?
   Man. I partly am persuaded as your grace is [2]— 1382

---

[1] 'Then thus.' Cf. 2 H6. II. 2. 9. where the same words are a line by themselves as here. 'Then thus'—was probably followed by some 'scorn,' the nature of which may be surmised from the scorn put upon Horace in Dekker's *Satiromastix*, or on Crispinus in Jonson's *Poetaster*. [This 'scorn' may be the *badinage* following a little later, and commencing with Valingford's ' Sir, may a man be so bold.'—G.]

[2] It is evident that this should come before William accepts Blanch, while he is still resolved to be a bachelor. [Or perhaps Manville has not heard William's half-aside conversion, owing to his being engaged with the other lords' 'scorn,' which probably is printed a little out of place.—G.]

My Lord, he's best at ease that meddleth least.

Val. Sir, may a man
Be so bold as to crave a word with you?

Man. Yea, two or three. What are they?

Val. I say, *this* maid will have thee to her husband.

Mount. And I say *this :* and thereof will I lay
An hundred pound.

Val. And I say *this :* whereon I'll lay as much.

Man. And I say neither: what say you to that?

Mount. If that be true, then are we both deceived.

Manvile. Why, it is true, and you are both deceived.

Marques. In mine eyes,
This is the properest wench. Might I advise thee,
Take her to [1] thy wife?

Zwe. It seems to me she hath refused him.

Marques. Why, there's the spite.

Zw. If one refuse him, yet may he have the other.

Marques. He'll ask but her good will, and all her friends.

Zw. Might I advise thee? Let them both alone.

Man. Yea, that's the course: and thereon will I stand;
Such idle love henceforth I will detest.

Val. The foxe will eat no grapes, and why?

Mount. I know, full well, because they hang too high.

Wm. And may't be a Millers daughter by her birth?
I cannot think but she is better born.

Val. SIR THOMAS GODDARD hight this reverend [2] man
Famed for his virtues, and his good success,
Whose fame hath been renowmed through the world.

---

[1] Ed. unto. [2] Ed. *reverent.*

Wm. Sir Thomas Goddard, welcome to thy Prince;
And, fair Em, frolic [thou¹] with thy good father;
As glad am I to find Sir Thomas Goddard,
As good Sir Edmond Treford, on the plains,   1414
He like a shepherd, and thou our country Miller.

Mill. And longer let not Goddard live a day
Than he in honour loves his sovereign.

Wm. But say, Sir Thomas, shall I give thy daughter?   1418

Mill. [Sir Thomas] Goddard, and all that he hath,
Doth rest at the pleasure of your Majesty.

Wm. And what says Em to lovely Valingford?
It seemed he loved you well that for your sake   1422
Durst leave his King.

Em. Em rests at the pleasure of your highness:
And would I were a wife for his desert.

Wm. Then here, Lord Valingford, receive faire Em.   1426
Here take her, make her thy espoused wife.
Then go we in, that preparation may be made,
To see these nuptials solemnly performed.

                [*Exeunt all. Sound drums and trumpets*².

Finis.

---

¹ thou not in original.

² In the *London Prodigal*, also attributed to Shakspere, is a line which also occurs in this play: [p. 460, l. 1264.]
'Pardon, dear father, the follies that are past.' Act v., p. 247, of Hazlit's ed.
Similarly supra, p. 26, l. 11:
      'Pardon, my dread lord, the error of my sense.'
See above, p. 448, l. 975. Another line is also very similar:
      'Never come near my sight or look on me.' Act iii. sc. 3, p. 232.
See above, p. 463, l. 1357:
      'But never speak to me, nor seem to know me.'

NOTES.

1. THE 1631 edition of *Faire Em*, which, in the main, is here reproduced, is not divided into scenes or acts. The division into scenes here given is by Mr Simpson. Prof. Delius, in his reprint (*Pseudo-Shakspere'sche Dramen, II. band:* Elberfeld, 1874), follows the division into acts of Chetwood's edition (as indicated in the present reprint). Prof. Delius's scenes correspond with Mr Simpson's, except that he has a fresh scene—his scene ii. Act V.—commencing at line 1165. In the 1631 edition most of the prose is printed in verse-lines. In the present reprint Prof. Delius's division into prose and verse has been adopted.—G.

2. *Manchester Stage:* (vide footnote, Introduction, p. 374.)—A cursory glance into some of the authorities which might be supposed capable of affording information under this head yields very little, owing to the fact, that most of the writers have evidently viewed the local stage events of the period in question as being unworthy of notice. The histories of Cheshire, however (and Lord Strange's company played in Chester about the time they played in Manchester), yield a little more than those of Lancashire. Ormerod's *Cheshire* (3 v. folio, 1819) and Hemingway's *City of Chester* (2 v. 8vo, 1831) give accounts of the 'Playes of Chester called Whitsun Playes,' the 'Midsummer Show,' and the plays and pageants of the local trades—tne immediate precursors of the stage-performances of noblemen's companies of professional actors such as the company of Lord Strange. These histories also give, amongst their extracts from the *Vale Royal*, a few notices of Lord Strange, and his predecessors and successors as local men. One of

these refers to the Lord Strange whose company played *Faire Em*, and to whom Greene dedicated his *Tullies Love*, in 1589 (*ante*, p. 362), as follows :—' 1587—Ferdinando Lord Strange was made an alderman, who received the same very honorably, and made a rich banquet in the Pentice.' It is likely enough that at this, or some similar aldermanic festival, by, or in honour of, Lord Strange, his lordship's company of players figured with *Faire Em* and their other plays. Previously, under the one date of 1577, occurs the record of the following two events—connecting, as will be seen, in that one year Lord Strange and some local play-acting: —' 1577.—The Earl of Derby, with lord Strange, and many others, came to the city (Chester) and were honorably received by the mayor and citizens.'—'The Shepherds' play was played at the High Cross, and other triumphs at Rood-eye. —G.

INDEX AND GLOSSARY.

Accomodate, associate, ii. 164/174
Actors. *See* Players.
Actors, Apology for, Heywood's, ii. 213
Adreamt, I was, I dreamed, i. 172/359
Afore, because, or, and for, i. 235/1943
Alarum for London, i. 139, 154; ii. 211. (*See also Shoemaker's Holiday.*)
Alcazar, Battle of, i. 134, 144, 268
Alcida, Greene's, ii. 360
Ale, Nut-brown. Ale browned on the top with nutmeg (and having ginger in it), ii. 21/114
All, any, any at all, ii. 304/901
All, at all, and for all = o'er all, or, with all, ii. 407/6, 421/334
All's Well that Ends Well; Countess to Bertram, cf. with Miller to Em, in *Fair Em*, ii. 402, 413/141
Alphonsus King of Arragon, Greene's, ii. 352
ALVA, Duke of, i. 139, 215
Amatist, amethyst, ii. 48/143
Anaides, name for Dekker in Jonson's *Cynthia's Revels*, ii. 129
Anatomy of Absurdity, Nash's, ii. 359
ANTONIO, DON, of Portugal, lost play on, i. 140
Apple-squire, a bawd, ii. 314/1158
Arbasto, Greene's, ii. 341, 372
ARCHIGALD (or Archigallo). *See* British Kings.
Arden of Faversham, 1592, attributed to Shakspere, ii. 211
Armes, Law of (*see* Law of armes).
AYLMER, Bp of London, i. 271

Bald man, a, is an honest man because 'there's not a haire betwixt him and heaven,' ii. 167/21
Bale of dice, a pair of dice, i. 337/1512
Ballad. *See* Ballating, and Ballet.
Ballating, ballad making, ii. 165/350
Ballet, a, a dittie or little song, ii. 161/249
——— singer, sings a ballet, ii. 31
Banbery cheese, a, 'nothing but paring,' ii. 173/178
BANCROFT, Bp, and Mar-Prelate (which see).
Bankes's horse, ii. 145/292
Bar sizeaces, false dice, which see.
Barmie, yeasty, ii. 128, 136/35, 199/108
Barrater, a wrangler, a quarreller, i. 167/229
Baven, brushwood, ii. 136/42
Bear, I do bear = I bear myself, ii. 399, 407/11
Become = gone to, ii. 142/210
Beef, Indian, ii. 147/326
Berwick, Thos Stucley's captaincy in, i. 29
Bespawle, to = to deride, ii. 128, 146/302
Betake, I betake you = I leave you to, or I dismiss you to, ii. 449/1001
Bewrayed, covered, ii. 369
Bezelers, guzzlers, tipplers, ii. 135/26
Birchin-lane, i. 294/440
Bird in a box, saying, i. 339/1571
Birth of Merlin, in part attributed to Shakspere, ii. 388
'Blacke Bowle, the,' song. (*See* 'Gentle Butler, balley moy.')

INDEX AND GLOSSARY.

Black patches, why worn, ii. 203/220
Blind Beggar, Chapman's, i. 357
BOLEYN, ANNE, and Hen. VIII.,
 Dr Sanders's charges against in
 his book against the Reformation
 in England, i. 124
Bones a Dod! an oath. (?) God's
 bones! or good God! i. 158/6,
 160/45
Bonny clabbo, sour butter milk (Irish),
 i. 192/844
Boulogne, siege of (1544), i. 7
Bourbon locks, locks of hair, ii. 147/
 340
Bowzing, drinking, ii. 135/22, 142/
 214
BRADINE, T. ii. 354
Bradfard's Meditations, ii. 334/1681
Brag, a, proud, ii. 369
Brag it, to, to show-off, or swell about,
 ii. 369
Brawle, a French, a dance, ii. 199/128
*Breeches, Velvet and Cloth Breeches,
 Dispute Between*, the second title
 of Greene's *Quip for an Upstart
 Courtier* (which see).
Brisle dice, false dice, i. 337/1522
British Kings, Monmouth's *Chronicle
 of*, the history of Archigald, Elidure, Peridure, and Vigent treated
 in *Nobody and Somebody*, i. 269
BROWNE, Capt., murderer of Mr Sanders (*Warning for Faire Women*), ii.
 209, *et seq*. (*See also* Sanders, Geo.)
Buccaneering by Queen Elizabeth,
 —Stucley, Hawkins, and Cobham
 buccaneers in her interest, i. 34
——————— Expedition to Florida
 by Thomas Stucley, i. 32
Buffone, Carlo, ii. 61/132
Bumbast, stuffing in dress, i. 354/
 1945
BUONCOMPAGNO, Giacomo, the Pope's
 scheme for making him King of
 Ireland, i. 119
Buske, the bones of a woman's stays,
 ii. 182/22
Butchers, Maunday Thursday and the,
 ii. 275/166
' Buttoned his cap, Ale has,' *i. e.* made
 him drunk, ii. 31/71

Cabbaleers, Cavaliers, roystering,
 swaggering ruffians, ii. 291/589

Calais, Stucley's disclosure of the
 French King's designs upon, in Ed.
 VIth's reign, i. 12, 13, 16
Cales, Cadiz, i. 230/1807
'Calf, killing the' (or the cow), 'a
 kind of extemporal performance of
 vagrant actors,' ii. 357
Canning Street, ? Cannon Street, i.
 292/378
Cannon (?) or Canning Street, i. 292/
 378
Cape-merchant (?) i. 232/1862
Cards, cheating at, i. 337/1525, 354/
 1946
CAREW, Sir Peter, cousin of Thos
 Stucley, he recovers the Barony of
 Odrone, i. 53
Carkanet, a jewel, ii. 49/148
Carlo Buffone, i. 60/132
Carpet-coward, same as carpet-soldier,
 &c., i. 201/1050
Cashel, Fitzgibbon, the Catholic
 Archbp of. *See* Fitzgibbon.
Catholic plots against Queen Elizabeth's life. *See* Stucley's life generally.
Caveat to Cursitors, Harman's, ii. 380
CECIL (Burleigh), his account of,
 friendship for, and subsequent enmity to Thomas Stucley, i. 40, 109,
 136. —Thomas Stucley's scandalous reports against him (as retailed by Rigsby, S's discarded
 servant), i. 75. —his party that of
 the civilians, as opposed to the
 soldiers' party led by Essex, i. 143,
 144, 155
CHAPMAN is (possibly) *Musus*, alluded to in *Jack Drum*, ii. 131,
 183/40
——— his *Blind Beggar*, i. 357
Chester, plays at : ' Witsun Plays,'
 'Midsummer Show,' the ' Shepherd's Play,' plays and pageants
 of the local trades, &c., ii. 467.
 —Lord Strange at, and possibly his
 players at, *ibid*.
CHETTLE, and his vindication of
 Shakspere, ii. 383—5
Cheverell, stretching, like kid-leather,
 ii. 64/29
Children (Player) of Paul's, and
 Queen's Revels. (*See* Player Children.)

INDEX AND GLOSSARY. 471

'Chorus' characters in plays. *See* Drama.
'Chorus' in *Stucley* (play of) like Chorus in *Hen. V.*, i. 359
Ciceronis Tamor, or *Tullie's Love*, Greene's, ii. 362, 372, 397
Citizens *v.* Soldiers, rival parties of Cecil and Essex, i. 143, 154, 155
Claque men, or applauders of the Players called Ingles, ii. 33, 67/89, 93, etc.
Clawback, name for a sycophant, i. 293/416
Clergyman, 'Sir John' a, ii. 423/373
Cluttered bloud, clouted, or clotted, blood, ii. 159/216
Coarsie: 'To haue a great hurt or damage which we call a *corsey* to the herte,' *Eliotes Dictionarie*, 1559, in *Nares*, ii. 231, 332/1651
Cobham, Lord, Sycophant in *Nobody and Somebody* possibly meant for him, i. 274
COBHAM'S piracies, i. 34, 39
Coin, base, evil of, in 1598, i. 349/1814
Collier of Croydon: see *Grim the Collier*, etc.
Comedy of Errors, iv. 2, 20,—cf. with *Faire Em*, ii. 403, 416/206
Comedy, no point, none at all (Fr.), ii. 54, 266, 149/389, 352
—— contest of with Tragedy in Shakspere's time, ii. 241/1
Comet of Nov. 9, 1577, its application as a warning of the pending disastrous Battle of Alcazar, i. 123, 134, 147, 249
Competitors, confederates, ii. 458/1226
Complements, a combat of, between Brabant signior and Puffe in *Jack Drum*, ii. 169/76
Coney-catcher, Cuthbert, his *Defence of Coney-catching*, a defence of the actors against Greene, ii. 380, 387
Consort, musician, accompanyist, ii. 66/74
Coresie. *See* Coarsie.
Cork, all its inhabitants kin, i. 1
—— not captured by Thos Stucley, i. 60
Corn 2/6*d.* a quarter in time of plenty, ii. 31

Cotton, to, to take to, i. 169/290
Cought, coughed, or spit, i. 227/1732
Counter, the prison, and other London prisons, i. 301/613
Countercuffe to Martin Junior, Nash's, ii. 355
Court, Porters at, their great gains, i. 320/1105
Coyle, tumult, ii. 162/272
Crack-breech, a nickname, i. 165/190
Cripplegate, St Giles's, 'the Sexton of' (R. Crowley), ii. 377-8
Crispinus, Rufus, name for Marston in Jonson's *Poetaster*, ii. 128
Critic, or Censurer, judgment on, in the person of Brabant signior (*Jack Drum*) meant for Jonson, ii. 129, 207/325
Cromwell, Thos Lord, the play, possibly in part by Shakspere, i. 139
Crowley, R., ii. 378
Cunnicatching, cheating, i. 338/1545
CURTIS, Alderman (and Lord Mayor) Sir Thos, i. 25, 144, 158, 239/2044
Cut, New, a card game, i. 338/1534
Cynthia's Revels, Jonson's, ii. 129
Cyvilt, Seville, i. 244/2154

Dagge, pistol, ii. 198/82
Dagger, dudgen, a box-handled dagger, i. 188/744
Dagger pies, ii. 66/70
Daniel is (possibly) *Musus* alluded to in *Jack Drum*, ii. 131, 183/40
DAVILA, Sancho, i. 139, 215
Decius, name of Drayton in *Jack Drum*, ii. 131, 183/42
Dejected, deposed, rejected, i. 297/509
Dekker and Ben Jonson, ii. 5
—— not the original of Thersites in *Troilus and C.*, ii. 7
—— and Marston, their quarrel with Jonson. (*See* Marston.)
—— is Anaides in Jonson's *Cynthia's Revels*, ii. 129
—— his attacks upon Jonson, ii. 379
—— and Wilson's *Shoemaker's Holiday*, ii. 154
—— his *Fortunatus*, i. 357
Delius, Prof., his ed. of *Faire Em*, ii. 467

Deloney's *Gentle Craft*, i. 154
Demi-bars, false dice, i. 337/1517
Devonshire, Duke of, Hen. VIII's attempt to dispark his Okehampton Park, i. 9
Dice, false, i. 336/1502 *et seq*, 353/1914, *et seq*.
Dismal day, 'in the almanack' (March), ii. 290/556
Distinguishing, extinguishing, i. 217/1474
Doron, in *Menaphon*, is Shakspere, ii. 340, 356
Drama, decline of, in Greece, in Rome, in England, R. Greene's account of, ii. 367—369
—— Greene's letter to his brother playwrights (in his posthumous *Groatsworth of Wit*) addressed to Marlowe, Lodge (or Nash), Peele, and Shakspere, ii. 381-2
—— the Martinist controversy upon the stage, 1589-90; ii. 390
—— Shakspere's reforms of the, (1) By substituting dramatic action for the didactic exposition of the 'Euphuists,' and (2) By discarding 'dumb-show' and 'chorus' evolvements of plot, ii. 393—5. *See also* Stage, Players, &c.
Dramatists, Elizabethan, generally wrote in the Essex interest, i. 274
—— Taine on their style, i. 358
Drayton is *Decius* alluded to in *Jack Drum*, ii. 131, 183/42
Dreams of 'green meadows' a sign of death, &c., ii. 277/204
Dress, fashionable, men's, ii. 48/124, etc.
—— women's, ii. 49/137, etc., 53, 248
Drinking 'their skinnes full,' ii. 36/182
—— Dutch, ii. 165/364
—— 'Lion drunk'? = 'pot valiant,' ii. 166/3
Drury, Mrs Anne, one of the murderers of Mr Sanders (*Warning for Faire Women*), ii. 209, *et seq*. (*See also* Sanders, Geo.)
Dudley, Arthur, who professed to be a son of Q. Elizabeth and the Earl of Leicester, i. 6.
Dumb shows and Pantomime, in *Warning for Faire Women*, ii. 269, 284, *et seq*. *See also* Drama.
Dundalk, Capt. Stucley's defence of (in the play), i. 49, 190.
'Dutch drinking,' ii. 165/364
'—— Ancient,' epithet for an impostor, ii. 172/174
Dye, a dairy-woman, ii. 141/162
Dyer's, Sir Edward, *Praise of Nothing* (1585), i. 270

Easter sermons at the Spittle, ii. 275/159
Edward III, cf. with play of *Stucley*, i. 359
Elidure. *See* British Kings.
Elizabeth, Queen, and Leicester, Arthur Dudley claimed to be their son, i. 6
—— her final rejection of the Earl's suit, i. 31—38
—— piracy and privateering in her reign, some of it being in her interest, i. 22, 32, 34, 38, 39, 69, 81, and life of Stucley generally (which see).
—— Catholic and Spanish plots against her. *See* Stucley's life.
—— her ejection of Thomas Stucley from his office and lands in Ireland, i. 41, 82; Stucley's scandalous reports against her, i. 75; she complains to Philip of Spain, of his harbouring Stucley and other rebels, i. 85, 91, 93
—— time of, abuses of, reflected upon in *Nobody and Somebody*, i. 269, *et seq*.; decay of hospitality, racking of rents, extortions of usurers, and offences against protectionist code, i. 348, *et seq*.
—— dramatists of her time generally in the interest of Earl of Essex, i. 274
—— London prisons in her time, i. 301/613
—— is Astræa in *Histrio-Mastix*, ii. 3, 86/259
—— hospitality in her time, ii. 35/172
—— her 'bounty,' or good cheer, 'to all comers,' ii. 292/604
Elizabethan Poets, Nash on, ii. 359

INDEX AND GLOSSARY. 473

England in Elizabeth's time. *See* Elizabeth, Q., time of.
——— hospitality in; expenses of a Lord's establishment in time of plenty(temp. Eliz.), ii. 35/172
Englefield, Lord Francis, his part in the Spanish Papal plot against Q. Elizabeth, i. 111
English, the, are 'hardy but rash, witty but overweaning,'—views of a Spaniard, i. 238/2023
Essex, Earl of, his party that of the soldiers, as opposed to the civilian party which was led by Cecil, i. 143, 154, 155
——————— in Ireland, i. 209/1257
——————— his enemy, Lord Cobham, probably satirised in character of Sycophant in *Nobody and Somebody*, i. 274
——————— dramatists of Elizabethan era generally in his interest, i. 274
Esternulio, Sir Thomas Stucley (which see).
Esther and Haman, and *Hester and Ahasuerus*, i. 356-7, ii. 12
'Euenuch'd Vicaridge, or,' fitter for a younger brother than marriage, ii. 129, 172/157
Euphues, his Censure to Philautus, Greene's, ii. 344, 351
'Euphuist' school of dramatists, their method driven out by Shakspere's method, ii. 393—5. *See also* Drama.
Every Man in His Humour, Jonson's, its prologue, ii. 216
Execution of the murderers of Mr Sanders, at Smithfield, May, 1573, ii. 226
——————— an, on the Stage, in *Warning for Faire Women*, ii. 326/1470, 336

Faire Em, A Pleasant Comedie of, the *Miller's Daughter of Manchester ; with the Love of William the Conqueror :* 1631, the text, ii. 337.
—various editions of, ii. 339, 467.
—Introduction to, ii. 339. —Summary of the play, ii. 338 and 392.
—attributed to Shakspere, ii. 13, 339, 390—405. —attributed to Greene, ii. 339. —resemblance to it of Greene's *Arbasto*, ii. 342, 372, *Tullie's Love*, ii. 362, 372, and *Mourning Garment*, ii. 372. —its story, ii. 372. —its plot, and symbolical meaning, ii. 373-4.—characters in ; *Mandeville* is meant for Greene ; Mountenay for Marlowe ; Valingford for Shakspere ; William the Conqueror for Will Kempe, &c., ii. 373-4. —is a satire on Greene, and is attacked as such in Greene's *Farewell to Folly*, ii. 372, 375-7-8, 404. —is in part from ballad of *Miller's Daughter of Manchester*, ii. 377.
—Greene attacks it and its author (Shakspere), ii. 372, 377-8. —the play internally examined and compared with Shakspere's work, ii. 13, 390—405. —different hands in the play, ii 448/969
Falstaff's babbling 'of green fields' an omen of his death, ii. 277/204
Famoused, made famous, ii. 387
Fardel, pack, or burden, ii. 359, 386
Farewell to Folly, Greene's, ii. 340, 344, 345, 346, 362, 375
Fazion, or fasions, a disease of horses like glanders, ii. 377
Fetch, a, a pretence, ii. 327/1495
Fig for Momus, Lodge's, ii. 88
Finsbury, the Bailif of, his dealings with frays in the 'Theatre-fields,' i. 182/610
Fitzgibbon, Catholic Archbishop of Cashel, account of, i. 61, 70
——————— he quarrels with Thos Stucley, i. 74
——————— he gives account of and a warning against Thos Stucley to Philip of Spain, and then betrays cause of the Irish Catholics who wished for a Spanish Prince, i. 88—90
——————— plots with Alva for invasion of Ireland, i. 90
Flail, the, in the arms of the Trafford family, ii. 390
Fletcher, Bp, father of the dramatist, i. 271
Florida, Stucley's buccaneering expedition to, taken in interest of Q. Elizabeth, i. 32, 81

Flush, abounding in money, i. 179/538
Fond, credulous, i. 239/2040
Foot-back-a, on foot, ii. 386
Force, I force not, I care not; no force, no matter, i. 209/1255; ii. 441/810
Fore-prizzing, surprising, i. 236/1961
Forslowed, delayed, ii. 224
Fortunatus, i. 357
—————— Dekker's, *ibid.*
'Founder! God bless the,' ii. 36/183
Four Sons of Aymon, Shawe's and a possible older one, ii. 214, 216
Foutre! = 'a fig for!' i. 243/2130; ii. 168/44
Fox, a—A sword with a fox engraved on the blade, i. 169/275, 181/174
Freeze, Upsey, Dutch, or hard, drinking, ii. 165/364. (*See* Upsey freeze.)
Frenchman, John fo de King, a caricature of a, and teacher of French, in *Jack Drum*, ii. 147/328, *etc.*
Friar Bacon, Greene's, ii. 339
Friar Francis, ii. 214—16
Friendship, Shakspere's view of its superiority to love, as shown in his *Sonnets*, &c., ii. 397-8, 436/690
Froude, Mr, his 'characteristic idea,' 'that whatever is new (and discovered by himself) must also be true,' i. 64
Frump, a, a critical censure, ii. 377
Fulloms, low and high, loaded dice, i. 337/1512, 354/1952

Galliard, a, a dance danced by a Page, ii. 200/130
Garden-allies, the suburb streets of London, full of brothels about Elizabeth's time, i. 352/1891
Genius, difference of, in the Poet and the Philosopher—the one has the genius to dispense with details, the other to use them : Shakspere illustrates poetic genius, for his very ignorance of technicalities helped him to his larger insight and knowledge, ii. 398
'Gentle Butler, balley moy,' John, Elliss's 'high Dutch' song in *Jack Drum*: a repetition song, introducing the names of tavern liquor vessels from the 'black bowle' to the 'tunne,' ii. 204/237
Gentle Craft, Deloney's, i. 154
Gentleman, Post-haste's (Shakspere's (?)) definition of a—'A gentleman is a gentleman that hath a clean shirt on, with some learning,' ii. 37/214
Gentry, decline of their hospitality, i. 343/1648
Geraldine, James, his part in O'Desmond's scheme of invasion of Ireland, i. 124
German Collection of English Plays (1620), i. 356, ii. 12
Germany, Shakspere's company in, i. 356, ii. 15
'Gip, Mistresse! or 'Gup, Mistress!' —'Gee up!' or 'Hullo' mistress! ii. 58/65, 55/291, 241/13
Glib, easily, or smoothly, got, ii. 53/267
Glibbery, slippery, smooth, ii. 128, 139/127
Glooming, gloomy, ii. 155/93
Godwarde, in Newgate, cell in which condemned criminals were left for confession and death, ii. 227
Gorge, stomach, i. 354/1945
Gosson's *School of Abuse* (an attack upon the Stage), an answer to it, *Strange News out of Afric*, i. 144
Gourds, loaded dice, i. 354/1952
Gradasso, Greene's, ii. 353
Grant, consent, i. 293/413
Greene, R., his life and works, and his attacks upon Shakspere and the players, ii. 11, 12, 339—90. — *Faire Em* attributed to him, ii. 339. —his *Friar Bacon*, ii. 339. —*Faire Em* a satire upon him by Shakspere, and attacked by Greene in consequence, ii. 340, 344, 362, 375, *et seq.* —his *Mamillia*, ii. 340. —his *Youth seeing all his ways, etc.*, ii. 340. —his *Gwidonius*, ii. 341. —his *Arbasto*, ii. 341, 372; its resemblance to *Faire Em*, ii. 342. —his *Morando*, ii. 342. —his *Planetomachia*, with its denunciation of the 'Saturnists,' and por-

trait of Valdraco (possibly Shakspere), ii. 342, 353. —his travels, ii. 343, 365. —his *Penelope's Web*, ii. 344, 351. —his *Euphues, his Censure to Philautus*, ii. 344, 351. —his *Perimedes*, ii. 344, 351, 353. —his *Orpharion*, ii. 345, 380. —his repentance, and works in consequence, viz. *Never too Late*, ii. 346, 348, 364, 365, 370; *Farewell to Folly*, ii. 344, 345, 346, 362, 365, 375, 379; *Mourning Garment*, ii. 344, 345, 346, 348, 364, 365, 372, 379; and *Groatsworth of Wit*, ii. 348, 381. —his works abjuring Love, ii. 345. —his and Lodge's drama on *Jonah*, ii. 346, 383. — his Francesco in *Never too Late*, Philador in *Mourning Garment*, and Roberto in *Groatsworth of Wit* are autobiographical sketches, ii. 349. —he is employed (in conjunction with Nash and Lily) by Archbp Whitgift to write down Martin Mar-Prelate (which see), ii. 349, 355, 364. —his *Alphonsus King of Arragon*, an unsuccessful imitation of *Tamburlaine*, ii. 352. —his tale of *Gradasso* in *Perimedes* nearly the same as his 'Venus Tragedy,' or Valdrako in *Planetomachia*, ii. 353. —his *Pandosto*, ii. 353. —his *Menaphon*, and Nash's preface to it, ii. 354. —Nash joins him in his attacks upon Shakspere and the Players, ii. 354. —his *Alcida*, ii. 360. —*Ciceronis Tamor; or, Tullie's Love*, and its likeness to *Faire Em*, ii. 362, 372, 397. —his *Spanish Masquerado*, ii. 363. —Sidley and Hake's verse in his honour, ii. 364, 370. —his sketch of his own life; how he deserted his wife, &c., ii. 365; fell in with the players, and so got to write for them, &c., ii. 366, 384. —his account of the decadence of playing, and attack upon players, ii. 367—70, 384. —points of likeness of four of his works to *Faire Em*, ii. 373. —his view of women as evils, ii. 373. —*Mandeville* in *Faire Em* meant for him, ii. 374. —his mendacity, ii. 378. —his *Coney-catching* pamphlets; one a piracy of Harman's *Caveat*, ii. 380. —his *Quip for an Upstart Courtier*, a piracy upon *Dialogue between Velvet Breeches and Cloth Breeches*, ii. 35/179, 381. —his *Philomela*, ii. 381. —his death, and *Groatsworth of Wit*, with the letter to his brother playwrights contained in the latter, ii. 381—5. —his and Lodge's conjoint work, ii. 346, 383. —*Knack to Know a Knave*, perhaps by him and Lodge, ii. 383. —*Greene's Funerals*, an anonymous panegyric upon Greene, ii. 385. —his quarrel with the actors, and Cuthbert Coney-catcher's defence of them against him, ii. 386-7. —Cuthbert Coney-catcher accuses him of cheating the players by selling his *Orlando Furioso* to two companies, &c., ii. 387. —his lifelong attacks upon Shakspere, ii. 339—405. —his character summarized and condemned, ii. 388. —his and Peele's and Marlowe's grandiloquent style superseded by Shakspere's common-sense style, ii. 396. —Shakspere's ridicule of this grandiloquence in Pistol's speeches, *ibid*.

Greene's Funerals an anonymous panegyric of Greene, ii. 385

Grim the Collier of Croydon, in part attributed to Shakspere, ii. 388. —cf. with *Faire Em*, ii. 443/870

Gripple, griping, i. 223/1623

Groatsworth of Wit, Greene's, ii. 348, 349, 381

Grope, to, to catch by tickling, ii. 147/323

'Gup, Mistress!'—*See* 'Gip, Mistresse!'

Gwidonius, Greene's, ii. 341

Hair, to press one's = to put on one's hat, ii. 170

Hair, bourbon locks of, ii. 147/340

Hake, R., his verse commendatory of R. Greene, ii. 364, 370

Halter-sack, slip-string, i. 167, 231

Hamlet, ii. 216

——— i. 357

——— 'Hyperion's curls,' ii. 356

Hamlet, iii. 2, 111—' to kill so capital a calf,' ii. 357
——— Nash's allusion to it, ii. 358
——— Polonius's counsel, cf. with *Faire Em*, ii. 402, 413/141
——— the ed. of 1589, ii. 212.
Harman's *Caveat to Cursitors*, Greene's piracy of it, ii. 380
'Hart!' interjection = 'Heart o' me!' or 'Dear heart!' ii. 145/377, et seq.
Harward's *Solace for the Soldier and Sailor*, ii. 88
Hawkins, Cobham, and Stucley, buccaneers in the interest of Q. Eliz., i. 34.
——— his plot with Philip of Spain for invasion of England, i. 96.
Hedon, name for Marston in Jonson's *Cynthia's Revels*, ii. 129.
Hen. II. of France, his friendship for Thos Stucley, and letter to Edward VI. in his praise, i. 11
——— his alleged designs on Calais and England, as disclosed by Thos Stucley, i. 11, 16
Hen. IV., Pt 2. Pistol's speeches are satires upon the grandiloquence of Marlowe, Peele, Greene, &c., ii. 396
Hen. V., ii. 216
——— II. iii. 17, Falstaff's death in. (*See* Falstaff.)
——— *See* Pistol's speeches.
——— *Chorus* in, compared with same in play of *Stucley*, i. 359
Hen. VI., Part 1, I. iii. 141, cf. with *Nobody and Somebody*, i. 359
——— II. 2, 9, cf. with *Faire Em*, ii. 464/1371
——— III. ii. 391, cf. with *Faire Em*, 419/274
Henry VIII., tradition that Sir T. Stucley was his illegitimate son, i. 5
——— his mistresses, i. 5
——— at siege of Boulogne, i. 7
——— and Anne Boleyn, Dr Sanders's charges against, in his book against the Reformation in England, i. 124
Henslowe's Diary, i. 357, ii. 6, 7
Hensman, henchman, a page, ii. 147/337

'Herb John in broth, unexpected kindness is like,' because 'it may as well be laid aside as used,' ii. 254/331
Hester and Ahasuerus, and *Esther and Haman*, i. 356-7, ii. 12
Heywood, Thos, i. 272
——— his *Apology for Actors* (1612), ii. 213
Histrio-Mastix, or the Player Whipt, the text, ii. 17. —summary of its story, ii. 2. —notes to, ii. 89. —importance of, in history of the stage, ii. 3. —Marston's work in, ii. 3, 50/191. —allusion to, by Jonson, ii. 5. —its main intention to show the unworthiness of actors, ii. 9. —original play by Peele, ii. 10. —idea forming plan of the play (viz. that Peace and Plenty bring War and Poverty, and that War and Poverty bring Peace and Plenty) traced to Minfant's *Fatal Destiny* (quoted by C. Marot), Lodge's *Fig for Momus*, Jhean de Mehune, and Harward's *Solace for the Soldier and Sailor*, ii. 88, 348
Hoddy-doddy—'all breech and no body,' i. 292/376
Hodge, a name for Roger, ii. 257/411
Holder, to, to be unable to bear or support, ii. 171/149
Hole, debtor's prison, i. 346/1730
Holinshed's Chronicles, Vowel, alias Hooker, of, i. 53
Holloway and Highgate, scene of *Jack Drum* laid there, ii. 134/3
Horse and foot, mine—*i.e.* mine completely, i. 170/311
Hospitality, and feeding the poor in olden time, i. 289/308
——— of Q. Elizabeth, ii. 292/604
'Hospitals and Spittles,' one not the other, i. 289/304
Huffing parts, ranting parts, ii. 63/186
Humour, his = his disposition, ii. 148/353

Imbrothery, embroidery, ii. 49/163
Immanity, monstrosity, ii. 303/873

Influent, flowing—from your influence, ii. 198/93
Ingles, players, *claque* men, or applauders, ii. 33, 67/89/93, etc.
Intend, to—to plan, i. 226/1714
Interponents, intermediaries, go-betweens, i. 279/49
Ireland, Thos Stucley in, his efforts to purchase offices of Marshall, &c., of, frustrated by Cecil, i. 41—55.
—charges against Thos Stucley in, and his departure from, i. 58.
—Catholics offer crown of, to Don Alfonso, brother of Philip of Spain, i. 60, 68, 72. —the Pope's view of this plot, i. 71. —Stucley's description of, to Philip of Spain, when urging that monarch to invade it, i. 68. —the lands Thos Stucley claimed in, i. 77. —Thos Stucley, when in Spain, called Duke of Ireland, i. 77-8. —Fitzgibbon, Catholic Archbp of Cashel, plots with Alva for invasion of, i. 90. —the Duke of Guise's plot for invasion of, i. 90. —Sir Thos Stucley and the Pope's plot of invasion of, i. 93-5. —O'Desmond's projected invasion of, the assistance accorded it by Sir Thos Stucley, Dr Sanders, the Pope, Philip of Spain, and others, and its ultimate failure through the defection of Stucley, i. 119, 120, 124—126, 132, 138. *See also* O'Desmond.
—project for making Giacomo Buoncompagno, Pope Gregory XIIIth's illegitimate son, King of, a part of O'Desmond's project of rebellion, i. 119, 124. —Dr Sanders' reasons for supporting O'Desmond's scheme of invading it, i. 120, 124. —Irish titles given to Sir Thos Stucley by the Pope, i. 128. —Sir Thos Stucley's reported saying that nothing was to be got there but hunger and lice, i. 130. —wastes soldiers, ii. 141/161.
—soldiering to, ii. 166/13. —Earl of Essex in, i. 209/1257. —state of, topic of the time (1599), ii. 244/94

Jack Drum's Entertainment; or the *Comedie of Pasquil and Katherine:* 1601 and 1616, ii. 127.
—1616, the text, ii. 133. —Introduction to, ii. 127. —Summary of its plot, ii. 126. —Notes to, ii. 208. —Marston wrote it, ii. 123.
—its first title (*J. D.'s E.*) a proverbial expression for ill-treatment, ii. 133/2, 140/156, 208.
—supports ministers of the day, ii. 136/49 —Planet in, perhaps meant for Shakspere, ii. 131. —Brabant Signior in, meant for Ben Jonson, ii. 129, 207/325. —alludes to poets of the time, ii. 131, 183/40. —Mamon in, like Shylock, ii. 140/156, 180/381, 208.
Jacke, probably a 'Black Jack,' a large black leathern drinking vessel. The use of this vessel gave rise to the Frenchman's report, that 'the English drink out of their boots,' ii. 292/607
James I., his lavish distribution of Knighthoods, viz., to 2323 persons, i. 273, 290/325
Jerkt, beaten, ii. 297/724
'Jests, single,' small, poor jests, ii. 52/225
Jet, to, to strut, ii. 47/112, 57/36, 58/67
Jewels—Amethyst; Carkanet; Ruby rocks, &c., ii. 48/137, 49
Joan a Noke. *See* John a Noke.
John a Nokes, and John a Style, fictitious names used in the Law; empty names, i. 169/290; ii. 57/51, 58/79
'John, herb.' *See* Herb John.
Jolly—'a jolly matter,' a pleasant state of things, ii. 377
Jonah, Greene and Lodge's play on, ii. 346
Jone a Noke. *See* John a Noke.
Jonson, Ben, is Crysoganus in *Histrio-Mastix*, ii. 4, 30
———— his *Poetaster, Satiro-Mastix*, &c., and the characters therein meant for Marston and Dekker, ii. 4, 5, 127
———— his *Richard Crookback* (1600) the first play sold at so high a price as £20, ii. 7.
———— the introducer of the method

of placing the author in a chorus, or moralizing, character of a play, ii. 7

Johnson, Ben, and 'Bottle Ale,' ii. 51/203

——— his quarrel with Marston and Dekker, ii. 379. (*See also* Marston.)

——— his *Return from Parnassus*, ii. 129

——— his *Cynthia's Revels*, ii. 129

——— he is Brabant signior in *Jack Drum*, ii. 129

——— his *Every Man in His Humour*, the prologue, ii. 216

——— *Julio and Hypolita*, form of *Two Gentlemen of Verona*, ii. 12.

Kemb'd, kempt, combed, ii. 178/325, 180/378

Kempe, Will, William the Conqueror in *Faire Em* meant for him, ii. 373

Kempe's Morice, ii. 127, 136/45, 137/53

Kick-showes, toys, ii. 151/325

King Lear, cf. with *Menaphon*, ii. 356

Knack to Know a Knave, i. 272; ii. 383

Knack to Know an Honest Man, i. 272

Knighthood, lavish distribution of the honour by James I., for sake of the fees paid, i. 273, 290/325

Lackey, to, to flatter, ii. 43/13

Lancashire, Trafford family of, ii. 390, 411/95

Lantado, Customs officer of Spain, i. 232/1858

Law, indictment for murder in Westminster Courts, 1573; ii. 315/1193, 319/1276

Laws of armes, the, 'as much law as arms are able to lay on,' *i.e.* a beating, i. 291/369

Leesings, lyings, lies, i. 353/1913

Leicester, Earl of, an early friend of Thos Stucley, i. 10

——— his suit for Q. Elizabeth's hand favoured by Thos Stucley, i. 30

——— Arthur Dudley claimed to be his son and Q. Elizabeth's son, i. 6

Leicester, his suit for Q. Elizabeth's hand rejected, i. 31—38

Lepanto, Battle of, i. 94

Libel: A slander with the writer's name to it no libel, i. 353/1923

Lily and the 'Euphuist' school of dramatists, their method driven out by Shakspere's method. *See* Drama.

——— his, and Nash, and Greene's writings against Mar-Prelate (which see).

Lion drunk = 'pot valiant,' ii. 166/3

Lirpoole, Liverpool, ii. 444/889

Lisle's *Nothing for a New Year's Gift* (1603), i. 270

Lodge and Greene's play on *Jonah*, ii. 346, 383

——— his *Fig for Momus*, ii. 88

——— his *Looking-glass for England and London*, ii. 346, 383

——— his abjuration of the stage, ii. 346

——— his Introduction to Greene's *Spanish Masquerado*, ii. 364

——— (or Nash) is addressed by Greene in *Groatsworth of Wit*, ii. 381-2

——— *Knack to Know a Knave*, perhaps by him and Greene, ii. 383

London, prisons in Elizabeth's time, i. 307/781

——— Cannon Street, i. 292/378

——— Smithfield, executions in, (1573) ii. 226

——— Newgate, ii. 227

——— the Temple, i. 164; ii. 171/123

——— Alderman and Lord Mayor Sir T. Curtis, which see.

——— the Thames, i. 321/1120

——— plagues in, 1593 and 1603; i. 307/4

——— attempt to establish an Academy in, for the better culture of noblemen, made by Raleigh, Heriot, and others, ii. 10, 19/53, 24/179

——— Woolwich to, in 1573, dangers of travelling, ii. 275/163

——— Shooter's Hill, ii. 209, 217

——— Morefields. *See* Mooreditch.

——— Birchin Lane, i. 294/440

London Prodigal, ii. 12, 466

——————— cf. with *Faire Em*,

ii. 466. *See also* Shakspere's doubtful plays, ii. 12, &c.
Looking Glass for England and London, Lodge's, ii. 346, 383
Love, lover, ii. 431/562
—— Greene's works abjuring, ii 345
—— Shakspere's view of its inferiority to friendship, as shown in his *Sonnets*, &c., ii. 397-8, 436/690
Love's Labour's Lost, cf. with *Faire Em*, ii. 393, 419/278, 433/611
Lucky man, Beware a, saying, i. 338/1542

Macbeth, ii. 216
—— cf. with *Warning for Faire Women*, ii. 272/98, 336
Malice used as a verb, i. 240/2068
Mamillia, Greene's, ii. 340
Mamon, character in *Jack Drum*, somewhat like *Shylock*, ii. 140/156, 180/381, 208
Manchester Stage, and Lord Strange's players there, ii. 374, 467
Marafastot, an oath (Irish), i. 192/844
March, 'Dismal day' in, ii. 290/556
Markets, Clerk of the, ii. 31
Marlowe, his *Tamburlaine*, ii. 349, 352, 375
—— *Mountenay* in *Faire Em* is meant for him, ii. 374
—— addressed by Greene in his warning to playwrights (*Groatsworth of Wit*), ii. 381-2
—— his grandiloquent style superseded by Shakspere's commonsense style, ii. 396
Marmady—Maravedi—a small Spanish coin, i. 242/2115
Mar-Prelate, Martin (supposed to have been Penry), and his tracts, ii. 349, 355, 358, 364. *See also* Martinist.
Marston, his *Troilus* in *Histrio-Mastix* a parody on Shakspere's, ii. 3, 4, 39
—— is Crysoganus in *Histrio-Mastix*, sometimes, and sometimes the character is meant for Jonson, ii. 4, 30/64
—— his work and quarrels with Jonson, ii. 5, 127
—— is part author of *Histrio-Mastix* with Peele, ii. 10, 50/191
Marston, one of the imitators of Shakspere, ii. 3, *et seq.*, 14
—— is author of *Jack Drum*, ii. 123
—— is satirized by Jonson in *Poetaster* (as *Crispinus*), in *Cynthia's Revels* (as *Hedon*), and in *Return from Parnassus*, ii. 127—9
—— draws himself in character of Brabant, junr. (*Jack Drum*), ii. 127-8
—— is the poet *Mellidus* alluded to in *Jack Drum*, ii. 131, 183/37
Martinist Controversy upon the stage, 1589-90, and its effects upon Shakspere and contemporary playwrights, ii. 390
Martinize, to, verb expressing mode of writing of Martin Mar-Prelate, ii. 349. *See also* Mar-Prelate.
Mary, Queen, shows favour to Thos Stucley, i. 18
—— the Duke of Savoy at her Court, i. 22
MARY STUART, the Pope and Sir Thos Stucley's plot for making her Queen of England, i. 93—5
Masque, a, given before a nobleman (in *Histrio-Mastix*), ii. 54/278
Maunday Thursday and the butchers, ii. 275/166
Maw, card game, i. 337/1525
May, the Merry Month of, song, ii. 171/140
Mazors, large and fine drinking bowls. Mazarines are 'little dishes to be set in the middle of a large dish.'—*Bailey*, ii. 268/21
Medicine, woman professor of, Mrs Drury, the murderer of Geo. Sanders (which see), ii. 264/625
Mell, a suspended clergyman, his love for, and efforts to procure pardon for, Mrs Sanders, charged with the murder of her husband (*see* Sanders, Geo.), and his punishment on the pillory, ii. 227, 326/1474
Mellidus, name of Marston in *Jack Drum*, ii. 131, 183/37
Menaphon, Greene's, ii. 340, 354
—— cf. with *Taming of Shrew*, *Hamlet*, and *Lear*, ii. 356
Merchant of Venice, likeness of

Mamon, the usurer in *Jack Drum*, to Shylock, ii. 140/156, 180/381, 208

Merlin, Birth of, possibly in part by Shakspere, ii. 388

Merry Devil of Edmonton, ii. 339, 404

—— perhaps partly by Shakspere, ii. 404

Merry Wives of Windsor. See Pistol's speeches.

—— cf. with *Faire Em*, ii. 446/917

Miching, lurking, or prowling, i. 191/834

Middleton's *A mad World my Maisters*, i. 307/777

Midsummer Night's Dream, its incidental play of *Pyramus and Thisbe*, ii. 89

'Midsummer Show,' Chester, which see.

Miller's Daughter of Manchester, the second title of *Faire Em*, ii. 337

—— ballad, *Faire Em* in part founded on it, ii. 377

Minikin, fiddle, ii. 135/14, 170/113

Montmorency, Constable of France, i. 14

Moore-ditch (Morefields)—allusion, i. 306/754

Moors, Sebastian of Portugal's expedition against. *See* Portugal.

Morando, Greene's, ii. 342

More, Sir Thos, play, possibly in part by Shakspere, i. 139

Morglay, Sir Bevis's sword, i. 309/826

Morice Dance, Kempes, at Whitsuntide, ii. 127, 136/45, 137/53

—— Dancers, ii. 35, 127, 136

MORLEY, Lord, his quarrel with Sir Thos Stucley, i. 104

Mourning Garment, Greene's, ii. 344, 345, 346, 348, 349, 364, 372

Mucedorus, ii. 339, 404

—— the additions to ed. 1610 are Shakspere's, ii. 404

Mullidor, the player attacked by Greene in *Never too Late, Part 2*, is Shakspere, ii. 370

Munday and Chettle's account of Sebastian of Portugal's African expedition, i. 268

Murder, indictments for, in Courts of Westminster, in 1573; ii. 315/1192, 319/1276

Murdered man's wounds break out at approach of murderer, ii. 309/1036

Murders confessed through seeing plays, ii. 213-14

Murders dramatized (including *Yorkshire Tragedy* and *Arden of Faversham*) attributed to Shakspere, ii. 211

Musus, name of Chapman, or Daniel, in *Jack Drum*, ii. 131, 183/37

Nash, his and Peele and Greene's attacks upon Shakspere and the other player-poets, ii. 11, 12, 355, *et seq.*, 384. —his rise and career, ii. 354, *et seq.* —his work with Greene against the players, and against Mar-Prelate, ii. 349, 355, *et seq.*, 384. —on the poets of his time, ii. 359. —his *Countercuffe*, ii. 355. —he is 'Pasquil,' ii. 355. —his *Anatomy of Absurdity*, ii. 360. —his *Pierce Penniless*, ii. 364. —he (or Lodge) is 'Young Juvenal,' addressed by Greene in the warning to playwrights in *Groatsworth of Wit*, ii. 381-2

Never too Late, Greene's, ii. 346, 348, 349, 365

New-cut, card game, i. 338/1534

Newgate, Godwarde cell in, ii. 227

Nicholas Nemo, A Letter of (1561), i. 270

Nitty brogetie, (?) splendid embroidery (L. nitidus), ii. 54, 274

Nobody, The Return of Old Well-Spoken (1568), i. 270

Nobody, the picture of, i. 272

—— 'Hoddy-doddy,' i. 292/376

Nobody and Somebody, i. 275. —Summary of its story, 269. —its plot in part from British History (reigns of Archigald, Elidure, &c.), and in part a satirical narration of the doings of *Nobody* and *Somebody* in the community, i. 270. —Sycophant in, possibly meant for Lord Cobham, i. 274. —its date probably 1592; but perhaps revised and rewritten in reign of James I., i. 272. —allusion to in *Tempest*, i. 272.

INDEX AND GLOSSARY. 481

—translation of it in German collection of English plays, 1620, i. 273. —cf. with *Hen. VI*, pt. I, i. 359. —missing stage directions for, i. 359. —Tieck on, i. 356
Nokes, John a. *See* John a Nokes.
'No point:' *see* 'Point, no.'
Nothing for a New Year's Gift, Lisle's, i. 270
Nothing, Praise of, Dyer's, i. 270
Numme, numbed, ii. 18/33, 67/112
Nut-browne Ale—the Players' song, ii. 21/112

Obedience preferable to majesty, *i.e.* sovereign rule, i. 295/455, 296/486
O'Desmond, James Fitzgerald Fitzmorris, and his abortive Catholic invasion of Ireland, i. 119, 120, 124—126, 132, 134. —Cecil's account of him, i. 137
Okehampton Park, Hen. VIII's attempt to dispark it, i. 9
Oldcastle, Sir John, the Life of, ii. 6
Omens. Yellow spots on the fingers, ii. 264/609. Stumbling at setting forth, ii. 275/168, &c., &c.,|290/556. (*See also* Dreams.)
O'Neill, Shane, his visit to Q. Elizabeth's Court, i. 30
——— his friendship for Thos Stucley, i. 38
——— Stucley's mission from Q. Eliz. to, i. 41
——— his attack upon Dundalk, and Stucley's successful defence of the town (in the play), i. 49, 190
Orlando Furioso, Greene's, ii. 387
Orpharion, Greene's, ii. 345, 380
Ought, owned, i. 233/1875
'*Owle i'th Ivybush*,' — Sir Oliver Owlet's and his company's ' sign,' ii. 31/87
Owlet, Sir Oliver. (*See* Owlet's Men.)
'*Owlet's Men, Sir Oliver*,' company of Players in *Histrio-Mastix*, ii. 22/148, 83/230

'Packstaffe, plain as a,' ii. 362
Page, or hensman, or henchman, office of, ii. 147/337, 200/130
'Paid on the petticoate,' (?) stricken dead, ii. 81/2
VOL. II.

Palmistry, woman professor of, Mrs. Drury (which see), ii. 264/624
'Pancras (or Pancridge) Knights,' show knights, ii. 34/157
Pandosto, the Triumph of Time, Greene's, ii. 353
Pantomime and Dumb Show action, in *Warning for Faire Women*, ii. 268, 284, *et seq. See also* Drama.
Parks, Hen. VIII's scheme for disparking them, i. 9.
Pasht, smashed, ii. 139/123
Pasquil and Katherine, the sub-title of *Jack Drum*, ii. 125-6
Pasquil of England, a pseudonym of Nash, ii. 355
Paul's, St, collection for the steeple, after burning down in 1561, allusion to it in *Nobody and Somebody*, i. 270, 306/754
——— Player children of. *See* Player Children.
'Peace and Plenty bring War and Poverty, and War and Poverty bring Peace and Plenty,' this aphorism the ground-work of *Histrio-Mastix* (after other works), ii. 86
Peaceth, holds his peace, ii. 62/164
Peate, a small person, ii. 248/188
Pedlar's Prophecy, The, i. 270
Peele, G., his *Battle of Alcazar*, i. 4, 141, 151, 268. —is the author of first form of *Histrio-Mastix*, ii. 10. —his *Honour of the Garter* (1593), ii. 10. —his and Greene and Nash's attacks upon Shakspere and the other player-poets, ii. 11, 12. —is George Pyeboard, ii. 14. —is satirized in *Puritan*, ii. 12. —addressed by Greene in his warning to playwrights (*Groatsworth of Wit*), ii. 381—3. —his and Greene's and Marlowe's grandiloquent style superseded by Shakspere's common sense style, ii. 396
Penelope's Web, Greene's, ii. 344/351
Penry, supposed author of Mar-Prelate pamphlets (which see).
Pericles, Shakspere's part in, i. 139
PERIDURE. *See* British Kings.
Perimedes, Greene's, ii. 344, 351, 353
Philip is treading, song, ii. 171/140
PHILIP of Spain (*see also* Spain), his procrastination, i. 100. —his be-

31

trayal of Sebastian of Portugal, in the expedition against the Moors, i. 122, 134, 215. (Play of *Stucley*.) —his reception of Thos Stucley, i. 234/1903. (Play of *Stucley*.) —Stucley's rebuke to his 'niggardice,' i. 242/2120

Philomela, Greene's, ii. 381

Philosopher, the, contrasted with the Poet. *See* Genius.

Phismicary, apothecary, ii. 422/341, 346

Pierce Penniless, Nash's, ii. 14, 364

Pight, pitched, set on foot, i. 149/12

'Pip, fine pip,' Irishman's (street ?) cry, ii. 147/339

Piracy and Privateering in Elizabeth's reign: for subject generally see entire life of Stucley; for ditto particularly see i. 22, 32, 34, 38, 39, 69, 81

Pistol's speeches are satires upon the grandiloquence of Marlowe, Peele, Greene, &c., ii. 396

Plagues in London, 1593 and 1603, i. 307/4

Planet, the *Jaques*-like philosopher in *Jack Drum*, is possibly meant for Shakspere, ii. 131

Planetomachia, Greene's, ii. 342, 343, 353

Platte, and platforme, a plot, scheme, plan, or platform, ii. 227-8

Player Children of Paul's, ii. 130, 199/102. —*Jack Drum* a play by them, ii. 127, 133. —children of the Queen's Revels, ii. 130

Player-poets v. Scholar-poets, Peele, Greene, and Nash's war against former in interest of latter, ii. 11, 12, 63/195, 393—5

Players, Chamberlain's men and Admiral's (Earl of Nottingham's) men in opposition, i. 358. (*See also* Plays, Stage, &c.) —*Henslowe's Diary*, i. 357; ii. 6, 7. —main intention of *Histrio-Mastix* to show unworthiness of Actors, ii. 9. —Men versus Boys: the men actors and boy actors continually buffeting each other, ii. 9. —Song, the, ii. 21/114. —in *Histrio-Mastix*, a company of mechanics out of work with the 'Poet' Post-hast for their writer, ii. 21/122, etc. —Politics the arena of, ii. 22/128—146. —'Sir Oliver Owlet's men,' *i. e.* company so called, ii. 22/148. —their Ingles, or claquers, ii. 33, 67/89, 93, etc. —Friday a good night with, ii. 34/141. —playing to a Lord preferred to playing to a town Mayor, ii. 34/145. —dissolutions of companies frequent, ii. 38, 82/208. —are common rogues and vagabonds by Act of 1597, cap. iv., an allusion to the Act, ii. 52/244. —3s. 4d. the fee to a company of players acting before a Lord about 1592, ii. 41/320. Fee for same increased between 2nd & 3rd acts of *Histrio-Mastix* (a year or two only, but in the reign of Plenty) to £10, ii. 53/266. —Rehearsal amongst, in *Histrio-Mastix*, ii. 62/164. —sharers v. hired men; comparative cost of their dinners, ii. 82/196. —their dissolute life, ii. 82/208. —their 'Tyerman,' or dresser, ii. 133. —the Lord Chamberlain's company, didactic and educational character of their plays, illustrated in *Warning for Faire Women*, ii. 211. —and Earl of Sussex's players, ii. 211—213. —Shakspere at the head of the Lord Chamberlain's men, ii. 216. —English, in Holland, ii. 214. —Greene's attacks upon Shakspere and the, ii. 339—405. —Nash's attacks upon Shakspere and the, ii. 354, *et seq.*, 384. —vagrant, Jonson (in *Poetaster*) on, ii. 360. —Greene's account of his falling in with, and writing for them, ii. 365, 384 ; the same writer's account of origin and decline of acting in Greece, Rome, and England ; of how players came to be 'mercenaries,' &c., ii. 367—369, 384. —their quarrel with Greene, ii. 386. —defence of them by Cuthbert Couey-catcher against Greene's aspersions, ii. 387. —Lord Strange's company at Manchester and Chester, ii. 374, 467. —'killing the calf' amongst: see *Calf, killing the*.

Playhouse Yard, a pickpocket in, hoisted upon the stage there and 'shamed about it,' i. 352/1894

Plays. (*See also* Players, Stage, &c.) German collection of English plays (1620); probably these were played in Germany by a travelling detachment of Shakspere's company, i. 273; ii. 12—15. —ten pounds a high price for supplying a company of players with one, ii. 5, 50/180, 52/231. — those with 'chorus,' or moralizing, characters first done by Ben Jonson, ii. 7. — and theatre audiences (Elizabethan), ii. 199/102. — 'guilty creatures sitting at,' stories of such, who have confessed murders, including those in *Hamlet* of 1589, and in Heywood's *Apology for Actors* (1612), ii. 213-14. —at Chester, viz., 'Whitsun Plays,' 'Midsummer Show,' 'Shepherd's Play,' trade plays, &c., ii. 467.
—'Chorus' characters. *See* Drama.
—'Dumb-show' action in. *See* Drama.

Pleasures, pleasantries, ii. 134/29

Ployden's Coffin, an Inn of Court, or part of one (may-be that part of the Temple now called Plowden's Buildings), ii. 171/123

Pocket up, to, and set, and poke, as laundresses and starchers do, i. 318/1050

Poet, the, contrasted with the Philosopher. *See* Genius.

Poetaster, Jonson's, ii. 4, 30, 127-9

Poets criticised in *Jack Drum*, viz. *Mellidus* (Marston); *Musus* (Chapman, or Daniel); and *Decius* (Drayton), ii. 131, 183/37.—Player-poets *v.* Scholar-poets. *See* Player-poets.

'Poets, Your, and your pots!' Posthaste's (Shakspere's) 'song extempore' in praise of poets and potting, ii. 40.

'Point, no,' and 'no point comedy,' none at all (Fr.), ii. 54/266, 149/389, 352

Poke, to—to poke and set and pocket up, as laundresses do, i. 318/1050

Politics talked in ale-houses, ii. 135/22

POLLARD, Judge, i. 1
—— Sir R., and his scheme for disparking the country, tried by Hen. VIII, i. 9

Poor, feeding the, in olden time, i. 289/308

Pope (Pius V.), his plot with Sir Thos Stucley for invasion of Ireland and England, and the placing of Mary Stuart on Q. Elizabeth's throne, i. 93—5. —his wars against the Turks; and Battle of Lepanto, i. 94, 97, 100

—— (Gregory XIII.), 'indulgences' granted by him to Sir Thos Stucley and others helping towards the 'delivery of Mary Queen of Scotland, the reduction of England, Scotland, and Ireland to Catholicism, and the extirpation of heretics,' i. 106.
—his assistance to O'Desmond's project of invasion of and rebellion in Ireland, i. 119. —his project for making his illegitimate son, Buoncompagno, King of Ireland, i. 119. —his support of Sebastian of Portugal in expedition against the Moors, i. 121. *See also* Rome.

Portugal; Sebastian, King of, and his expedition against the Moors, i. 114. —Pope Gregory XIII favours him, and assists it, i. 121. —Philip of Spain promises aid for the expedition, but actually opposes it, i. 122, 134—215 (play of *Stucley*). —Stucley joins the expedition, i. 127, 236 (play of *Stucley*), which is 'warned' by a comet, i. 123, 134, 147 (ballad), 219 (play), but proceeding, ends in the disastrous Battle of Alcazar, and death of Sebastian, Stucley, &c., i. 134. —Antonio Sebastian's successor, and the lost play on his life, i. 140, 263 (play of *Stucley*). —story that Sebastian was not killed, appearance of a claimant to his personality. —*Strange News of the return of Don Sebastian*, a book on this story, i. 154.

Post and paire, card-game, i. 338/1533

Post-haste, in *Histrio-Mastix*, is

Shakspere, ii. 11, 12, 32/93.
—characteristics of, ii. 33/130, 87.
—the 'gentleman and scholar' who writes for the players, ii. 37/209. —his affectations of the gentleman, ii. 37/212, and of the poet, 22/141, 23/157. —his self-sufficiency and boasting, ii. 33/121, 126, 40/292. —his definition of a gentleman, one 'that hath a clean shirt on with some learning,' ii. 37/215. —his 'song extempore,' in praise of 'Your poets and your pots,' ii. 40/292. —'dangerous to read his name at a play door,' ii. 62/166. —his ballad-making, ii. 67/91, 83/235
Pot, to go to the = to go to destruction, ii. 143/218
Premero, card-game, i. 338/1530
Prison pestilences in 16th century, i. 228/1759
Prisons, London, in Elizabeth's time, i. 307/781
Privateering by Thos Stucley against Protestants, Spain supplying ships, &c., i. 69. (*See also* Piracy.)
Prodigal Child. See *Prodigal Son.*
Prodigal Son, sub-play in *Histrio-Mastix*, ii. 3, 11, *et seq.*, 32/93, 89, 90. —original possibly by Shakspere, ii. 12, 15. —like Greene's *Mourning Garment*, ii. 15, 348.
Promoter, an Informer (in Law), ii. 135/8.
Propitioner, a, a good-giver, ii. 330/1597
Puffe, a character in *Jack Drum* who is 'a perpetuitie of complement,' ii. 147/335, *et seq.*
Puffes, Polyphemian, some fashion of dress, ii. 128, 139/124
Pug, a, a dog, i. 315/1215
Puritan, The, in its hero Peele is satirized. *See* Shakspere's doubtful plays, ii. 12, &c.
Purposes, making, making plans, ii. 171/133
Pyeboard, Geo. (Peele), ii. 14
Pyramus and Thisbe, the incidental play in *Mid. Night's Dream*, ii. 89.

RALEIGH, SIR W., his attempt (in conjunction with Heriot and Northumberland) to set up an Academy in London, ii. 10, 19/53, 24/179
Rascand, to shake, i. 169/278
Ratcliffe, Egremond, his quarrel with Sir Thos Stucley, i. 108.
Rebato-pinner, a pinner up of headdresses, a lady's maid, ii. 192/273
Record (verb), declare, i. 313/934
Reformation in England, Dr Sanders's book against, and Sir R. Shelly's reply to it, i. 124
Resolved, informed, ii. 438/729
Respective, adj. respected, ii. 271/78
Return from Parnassus, Jonson's, ii. 129
'Retail, house of,' (?) shop, brothel, or public-house, ii. 387
Richard III, ii. 216
——— *Crookback*, Jonson's, ii. 7
Robert de Windsor, alias used by William the Conqueror in *Faire Em*, ii. 410/77
Roger, Trusty (Roger Clement) one of the murderers of Mr Sanders (*Warning for Faire Women*), ii. 209, *et seq.* (*See also* Sanders, Geo.)
Rome, Sir Thos Stucley in, where he (along with Sir R. Shelly) acts as 'inquisitor' into the lives of the English living there, i. 105—7, 125. *See also* Pope.
'Rome, Theatre in' = Theatre in London, ii. 350
Rome-vyle, London; Rome-mort, the Queen (Pedlar's French), ii. 353
Romeo and Juliet, cf. with *Warning for Faire Women*, ii. 302/863, 336
——— cf. with *Nobody and Somebody*, i. 328/1314
——— cf. with play of *Stucley*, i. 358
Roscius, the actor, Cicero's rebuke to, ii. 368
Rose (white) in murderess's (Mrs Sanders's) bosom at trial turns red on her being convicted, ii. 322/1369
Ruby rocks, a kind of jewellery, ii. 49/149
Ruling powers, majesty of the, ii. 135/23
——— Shakspere's view of, i. 295/455, 296/486, ii. 208
Russetings, poor peasants, ii. 69/147

Sack sixpence a quart, Falstaff was charged 8½d., ii. 442/837
Sanders, Dr, and his participation in Papal plots against Elizabeth, i. 98—100. —his reasons for O'Desmond's invasion project, i. 120, 124. —his book against the Reformation in England and Hen. VIII, and Anne Boleyne, and Sir Richard Shelly's reply to it, i. 124. —Cecil's account of him, i. 137
Sanders, Geo., Merchant, murdered by Capt. Browne (*Warning for Faire Women*), ii. 209, *et seq.*
——— account of his murder, and trial and execution of his murderers, from Stowe, ii. 217
——— from 'a Briefe Discourse of,' &c., 1573, ii. 220
——— other accounts, ii. 219, 239
Sanders, Mrs Anne, implicated in murder of Geo. Sanders (*Warning for Faire Women*), ii. 209, *et seq.* (*See also* Sanders, Geo.)
Savoy, Duke of, at the Court of Queen Mary, i. 22
Satiro-Mastix, Jonson's, ii. 2, 4, 5, 127
'Saturnists,' Greene's anatomy of the, ii. 342, 353
Saunt, card-game, i. 338/1533
Scand-pouch, (?) scant-pouch, nickname for a parsimonious person, i. 165/198
Scorn, a, a censuring, or ridiculing, ii. 464
Scots, Mary Queen of, Papal 'indulgences' granted to her partisans, i. 106
Seamen, in Q. Eliz.'s time, Thos Stucley's men, i. 67
Sebastian, King of Portugal, and his disastrous expedition against the Moors. *See* Portugal, Sebastian, King of.
Servants, growth of luxury amongst, ii. 46/84
Set, to, 'to set and poke and pocket up,' as laundresses and starchers do, i. 318/1050
Sewer, officer who placed meat on the table of a king or lord, ii. 36/186, 193.

Shakspere, the biographical plays of *Stucley, Sir Thomas More, and Thomas Lord Cromwell*, played by Lord Chamberlain's men, possibly by him, i. 139, 142. —reference to in *Histrio-Mastix* ('shakes his furious speare'), ii. 3, 39/273. —Marston one of his imitators, ii. 3, *et seq.*, 14. —his *Troilus* parodied by Marston in *Histrio-Mastix*, ii. 3, 4, *et seq.*, 39. —his Thersites in *Troilus and Cressida*, meant for author of *Histrio-Mastix*, ii. 7. —he is Post-haste in *Histrio-Mastix*, ii. 11, 12, 32/93. (*See also* Post-haste.) —as *Johannes Factotum*, Shakscene, &c., Greene, Peele, and Nash's attacks upon him, and S.'s return blows, ii. 11, 12, 14, 354, 381—5. —began his career as a ballad-maker, ii. 12. —his doubtful plays, *Prodigal Son, Faire Em, London Prodigal, Puritan,* and *Yorkshire Tragedy*, all reflect upon his enemies, Greene, Peele, and Nash, and may have been levelled at them by S., ii. 12. —detachment of his company probably played in Germany, ii. 15. —*Prodigal Son*, original of, possibly by S., ii. 15. —(Post-haste) his name unpopular, ii. 62/166. —' the upstart crowe,' ii. 75/8, 359 —his worship of ruling powers, ii. 208 (which see). —*Planet*, the *Jaques*-like philosopher in *Jack Drum*, perhaps meant for him, ii. 131. —*Yorkshire Tragedy* and *Arden of Faversham* attributed to him, ii. 211. —his *Rich. III, Hen. V, Macbeth*, and *Hamlet*, apparent fling at them on his own stage, in Induction to *Warning for Faire Women*, ii. 216, 241. —his large-heartedness, and fearlessness of criticism, ii. 216. —Jonson's attack on, in prologue to *Every Man in His Humour*, ii. 216. —R. Greene's attacks upon him and the players, ii. 339. *Faire Em, Merry Devil of Edmonton*, and *Mucedorus*, attributed to him, ii. 339, 405. —*Faire Em* was written by him as a satire upon Greene, and as such was attacked by the latter in his *Farewell to Folly*, ii. 340, 344, 362, 365, *et seq*. —*Faire Em* compared with his. work generally, ii. 390—405. —he is Doron, in Greene's *Menaphon*, ii. 340, 356, 370. —early authorship of, ii. 342. —Valdraco in Greene's *Planetomachia* possibly meant as a satire upon him, ii. 342, 353. —*Prodigal Son*, attributed to him, is perhaps formed upon Greene's *Mourning Garment*, ii. 348. —Nash's attacks upon, ii. 11, 354, *et seq*., and 384. —as an actor, ii. 357—60, 387-8. —'upstart crowe' epithet explained, also Dyce's explanation, ii. 359. —he is *Mullidor*, the player attacked by Greene in *Never too Late*, Part II. —he is *Valingford* in *Faire Em*, ii. 374. —his want of learning, Greene's reflections upon, &c., ii. 377. — classed with the 'theological poets,' and accused of working for 'the Sexton (Rector) of St Giles without Cripplegate' (R. Crowley), ii. 377-8. —attacked by Greene and accused of blasphemy as author of *Faire Em*, ii. 377-8. —(as 'Shakescene') is addressed by Greene in *Groatsworth of Wit*, ii. 381—5. — Chettle's vindication of him against Greene's aspersions, ii. 383—5. —his identity with the actor in Greene's *Groatsworth of Wit* surmised, ii. 385—7. —*Birth of Merlin* and *Grim the Collier of Croydon*, possibly in part by him, ii. 388. —and Lord Strange's company of players, ii. 390. —his mother perhaps one of the Cheshire Ardens, and so a connection of Lord Strange's family (the Stanleys), ii. 390. —and the Martinist Controversy upon the stage, ii. 390. —his reform of play-writing by (1) substituting his own *dramatic* method for the scholastic or *didactic* method of Lily and the 'Euphuists;' and (2) discarding 'dumb-show' and 'chorus' evolvements of play-plots, ii. 393-5. —his common sense style contrasted with the grandiloquence of his predecessors, Marlowe, Greene, and Peele, which grandiloquence he ridicules in Pistol's speeches, ii. 396. —the philosophy of his *Sonnets*, viz., that love between men is greater than love between man and woman; and that friendship gives and forgives things which love would retain and revenge, ii. 397-8, 436/690. —his lack of scholarship more than balanced by the knowledge his genius helped him to, ii. 398. (*See also* Genius.) —on art versus nature, ii. 403, 416/206, 417/233, 418/269. (See also under heads of his several plays, &c.)

Shamrocks are meat, i. 192/844

Shawe's, R., *Four Sons of Aymon*, ii. 214, 216

SHELLY, Sir Richard, his reply to Dr Sanders's book upon the Reformation in England, and the favour it procured him at Rome, i. 124. —he is employed with Sir Thos Stucley as inquisitor of English residents in Rome, i. 125

'Shepherds' Play,' the, at Chester (which see).

Shewing-horne, (?) show-trumpet, ii. 135/26

Shoemaker's Holiday, the (Dekker and Wilson's), and Deloney's *Gentle Craft*, plays in honour of shoemakers, and glorifying citizen soldiers as preferable to professional soldiers; *Stucley* and *Alarm for London* being plays taking opposite views, i. 154

Shogs, trots, goes, ii. 154/77

Shooters Hill (1573), murder of Mr Sanders there, ii. 209. (*See* G. Sanders.)

Shoreditch, ii. 165/359

——— Theatre at, ii. 350, 352

Sidley, Ralph, his verse commendatory of R. Greene, ii. 364, 370

Single jests, small, poor jests, ii. 52/225

Sizcaces, false dice, i. 337/1520

Skreene, woman's veil, ii. 40/277

Slicke, sleek, i. 355/1977

Slopt, clothed, ii. 139/125

Smithfield, execution for murder at, (1573), ii. 226

Soldiers v. Civilians : the Essex party

were for the first, and their opponents, the Cecil party, were for the last, i. 143, 154-5
Somebody, the picture of, i. 272, 337/1511
——— old joke that a man with little legs is ' a gentleman,' because he is—Somebody, i. 273
SOMERSET, Protector, i. 9
——— his plot of rebellion, 1551, i. 11
Somner, Sompnour, summoning officer of an Ecclesiastical Court, ii. 135/8
Spain invited to invade Ireland by Archbp of Cashel, Stucley, and other Catholics, i. 60, 68—72. —rejects the plan, i. 91. —Thos Stucley's entertainment at Court of K. Philip, and his getting knighted there, i. 74—78. —Sir T. Stucley teaches the Spaniards to fashion their ships like the English, i. 97
——— Philip of, his plot with Sir J. Hawkins for invasion of England, i. 96. —Philip's great fleet for the Invasion of England, 1574, i. 102. —reasons for his lukewarmness in the cause of the Irish Catholics, i. 122. (*See also* Philip.)
Spanish Masquerado, Greene's, ii. 363
Sparrows a penny a dozen, ii. 31/77
Speaks small, *i. e.* shrilly, ii. 147/338
Spend-good, a, a spendthrift, i. 162/109
Spinsters, married women so termed, ii. 319/1278
'Spittles and Hospitals,' one not the other, i. 289/304
Spittle Sermons in Easter week, ii. 275/159
Square, to, to fight, ii. 172/151
Squirril's skin, a shoeing-horn, i. 170/321
Stage. (*See also* Players, Plays, &c.) —'*Strange News out of Afric*,' a defence of the Stage in answer to Gosson's ' School of Abuse,' i. 144. —importance of *Histrio-Mastix* in history of, ii. 3. —Devil and Vice on the, ii. 40. —in Shakspere's time, contests of Tragedy, Comedy, and History (or Spectacle) ; ' luggage and foppery,' and ' fiddling tricks ' of two last denounced, ii. 241/1. ' —is hung with black for Tragedy, ii. 244/74. —Pantomime and Dumb Show action in *Warning for Faire Women*, ii. 249, 284, *et seq.* —an execution on, in *Warning for Faire Women*, ii. 326/1470, 336. —'Theatre in Rome' often used by Elizabethan writers to express Theatre in London, ii. 350. —of Manchester and Chester, Lord Strange's players there, ii. 374, 467. (*See also* Tragedy, Comedy, &c.) —Coney-catcher's *Defence of Coney-catching*, a defence of the Stage, ii. 380, 387. —frays in Theatre fields, Finsbury, i. 182/610
Stale, a, a trap, or decoy, i. 332/1391
Stammell peticoate, a red woollen peticoate, ii. 151/8
Stanley family, possibly connected with Shakspere, through his mother, ii. 390
State, the, praised in *Jack Drum*, ii. 136/48
Stationers' Registers, dates 1571—75 are lost, ii. 219
' Statute rogues,' common players, &c., so termed by Act of 1597, ii. 52/244
Stemme, race, or generation, ii. 85/281
Steretchley, Sir Thos Stucley (which see)
Sternville, Sir Thos Stucley (which see)
Sternvillio, Sir Thos Stucley (which see)
Stewtley, a play on life of Stucley, i. 153
Still, always, ii. 310/1061
Strange, Lord, his players play *Faire Em*, ii. 337, 362, 390, and *Knack to Know a Knave*, &c., ii. 383 —they play *Andronicus*, &c., i. 357. —they play at Manchester and Chester, ii. 374, 467. —this company and Shakspere, ii. 390. —Strange's family (the Stanleys) perhaps allied to Shakspere through the poet's mother, ii. 390
Strange News out of Afric, a defence

of the Stage, in answer to Gosson, i. 144
Stucley, History of Stout (play), i. 156
STUCLEY, Sir Thomas, Biography of, i. 1. —his family, i. 1, 2, 160. —various spellings of the name, viz., Steretchley, Strevokley, Stratcheley, &c., i. 1, 2. —his ancestor, Judge Pollard, i. 1. —Ballads on, i. 4, 123, 144, 147, 156. —as hero of Peele's play, the *Battle of Alcazar*, i. 4. —tradition that he was born in London, i. 4. —tradition that he was an illegitimate son of Hen. VIII, i. 5. —not in Wyat's rebellion, i. 7, 19, 199/113. —is present, as retainer of Duke of Suffolk, with Hen. VIII at Siege of Boulogne (1544), i. 7. —his uncle, Sir Richard Pollard, i. 7. —he enters service of Lord Hertford, afterwards Protector Somerset, i. 9. —at Court (1550), i. 10. —probably a friend of Earl of Leicester (when Mr Dudley) at Court of France, i. 10. —compromised by Duke of Somerset's abortive plot of rebellion, 1551, and flies to France, i. 11. —in King of France's (Hen. II) service in the war against Emp. Charles V (1552); and enjoys Hen. II's friendship, i. 11. —returns to England, and goes to Edward VI's Court, i. 11. —discloses to Edward French King's designs upon Calais and England, i. 12, 13. —friendship with Constable Montmorency, i. 14. —his disclosures of French King's designs discredited, and he imprisoned in Tower for deceit; his information probably genuine, i. 16. —his military genius and patriotism, i. 17/788 (play). —released and in favour with Mary at her accession, i. 18. —goes to Emperor's Court, 1553, i. 18. —writes to Q. Mary, offering his and his band's service, i. 18. —serves Duke of Savoy against France, i. 19. —returns to England and attends Duke of Savoy at Mary's Court, 1555, i. 22. —stories about his buccaneering enterprises, i. 22.

—marriage with daughter of Alderman Sir T. Curtis, i. 25, 144 (ballads), 158 (play), 239/2044. —libels on, i. 25. —musters men for Q. Eliz. in Berkshire, i. 26. —a Catholic, i. 28, 82. —appointed to Captaincy in Berwick, i. 29. —great reputation as model officer and soldiers' friend, i. 30, 185/671. —entertains Shane O'Neill during that chief's visit to Court of Elizabeth, 1561-2, i. 30. —his efforts for Leicester as suitor for Queen Elizabeth's hand, i. 30. —his buccaneering expedition to Florida, a project in the interest of Q. Elizabeth; the attendant piracies, i. 32, 81, 148, 151. —Fuller's (*Worthies*) and Westcote's accounts of him, i. 32, 134. —charged with piracies, and acquitted, i. 38. —Shane O'Neill's friendship for him, i. 38. —Cecil's friendship for, and subsequent enmity to him, i. 40. —Cecil's account of him, i. 109, 136. —in Ireland: mission to Shane O'Neill, i. 41, 185 (play). —his offer to purchase office and lands of Sir Nicholas Bagnall, Marshall of Ireland, for £3000 refused the Queen's assent, i. 41, 82. —dramatists' account of his defence of Dundalk against O'Neill, i. 49, and play of *Stucley*, i. 190. —again in Ireland: Buys office and lands of Seneschall of Wexford, but is refused the assent of the Court to the transfer, i. 49—55. —Nicholas White, a creature of Cecil's, appointed in his stead, i. 55. —enmity of White against him, i. 58. —charges of abusing the Queen, helping the rebels, and 'lifting' the widow Kavanagh's cattle brought against him; upon which he is imprisoned, i. 58. —the story of his having taken Cork false, i. 60. —joins Fitzgibbon, Archbishop of Cashel, and other Catholics in offer of crown of Ireland to Don Alfonso, brother to King of Spain, i. 60, 70—2. —Mr Froude's unfavourable account of him, i. 64, 68. —offers a plot against England to

France, which is not accepted, i. 66. —sets sail for Spain with a crew of English seamen, i. 67, 209 (the play). —lays plan for invasion of Ireland before Philip of Spain, i. 68. —his description of Ireland to Philip, i. 68. —his project for invading Ireland not accepted by Philip, who, however, gives him three ships for privateering against Protestants, English, Dutch, and French, i. 69, 91. —Walsingham's opinion of him, i. 72, 84, 86. —his magnificent entertainment at King of Spain's Court, i. 74, 78, where he is knighted (of the religious order of Calatrava) by the King, i. 78, 87, 104. —he quarrels with Fitzgibbon, Archbp of Cashel, i. 74, 103. —Rigsby, his man, leaves him, and returning to England informs upon him, i. 75. —his scandalous accounts of Q. Eliz., Cecil, and others, as given at English Court by Rigsby, i. 75, —his own account (according to Rigsby) of the lands he claimed in Ireland, i. .77. —called Duke of Ireland in Spain, i. 77—8. —Don Francesco Merles assigned his companion at Court of Philip, i. 78. —Oliver King's information against him sent to Cecil, i. 78. —projects going to Rome, i. 80. —Fitzgibbon exposes him to Philip of Spain, i. 80—85. —Philip's harbouring of him and other 'rebels' complained of by Q. Eliz., i. 85, 91, 93, 105. —his project for invading Ireland finally declined by the Spanish King; his consequent departure to the Papal Court, i. 91, 237/1980 (the play). —King Philip's account and commendations of him, i. 91. —Murdin's account of him, i. 92. —his plot with the Pope for the invasion of Ireland and England, and for making Mary Stuart queen, i. 93—5. — Laderchi's account of him, i. 93. —serves the Pope in the league against the Turks, at Battle of Lepanto, i. 94. —returns to Court of Spain, i. 94—6. —he teaches the Spaniards to fashion their ships like the English, i. 97. —Philip of Spain's preparations for invading England, i. 102. —Lord Morley quarrels with him, i. 104. —again in Rome, where he is granted privileges and indulgences, i. 105—7, and where he and Sir Richd Shelly act as 'inquisitors' into the lives of the English there, i. 125. —his correspondence with Mistress Julyan, i. 106. —Munday's allusions to him, i. 107-8. —his quarrel with Egremond Ratcliffe, i. 108. —his old servant Renold Digby exposes him to Cecil, i. 108. —Sebastian of Portugal's expedition against the Moors, i. 114, et seq., 215 (the play). —goes with Don John into Flanders, i. 115. — his part in O'Desmond's projected pro-Catholic invasion of Ireland, and the Pope's assistance therein, i. 119, et seq. — his ship-load of troops from Rome to assist this plot is taken instead to Lisbon, and he is there induced to join Sebastian's expedition against the Moors, i. 127. —Irish titles he received from the Pope, i. 128, 248 (play). —is called Sternville, Sternvillio, and Esternulio by Spanish and Portuguese historians, i. 129 (note). —Pillens's account of his professions of loyalty to Elizabeth, and of his having said that there was nothing to be got in Ireland but hunger and lice, i. 130. — Turquet's opinion of him, i. 130 (note). —his expedition with Sebastian against the Moors, historians' accounts of, i. 134, 236 (the play). —his death, at Battle of Alcazar, i. 134, 144. —his family pensioners of Spanish Court for two generations after his death, i. 136. —was a popular hero with the partizans of the soldiers', or Essex, party, as opposed to the partizans of the civilians, or Cecil, party, i. 143, 154, 155. —his life and character as shown in *Stewtley*, another play on his life, i. 153. —where information about him may be found, i. 156. —*History of Stout Stucley*, i.

156. —his rebuke of King Philip for his 'niggardice,' i. 242/2120 (the play)
Stukeley, the Play of:—*Life and Death of Captain Thomas Stukeley*, &c., the text, i. 157. —summary of it, i. xiii. —accounts of it, i. 105, 114, 123, 134, 139. —'Chorus' in, like 'chorus' in *Hen. V,* i. 359. —cf. with *Edward III, Romeo and Juliet,* and *Titus Andronicus,* i. 358-9. —cf. with *Two Gent. Verona* and *Faire Em,* ii. 436/690. —possibility of its being partly by Shakspere, i. 139; ii. 398, 436/690. —belongs to same political school as *Alarm for London,* i. 139, 154. —fragments of lost play on *Don Antonio* interwoven in it; also other fragments, i. 140. —four hands in it, one a writer of great diffuseness and some power, i. 142. —compared with Peele's *Battle of Alcazar,* i. 141, 268. —is a glorification of professional soldiers as against citizen soldiers, and so opposed to the Cecil party, i. 154. —*Historia De bello Africano,* the supposed original of the play's account of battle of Alcazar, i. 268
Stumbling. (*See* Omens.)
Style, John-a. *See* John-a-Nokes.
Surreinde, over-reined, over-driven, ii. 183/44
Suspicious, suspected, ii. 426/441
Sweb, to, to swoon, or faint, ii. 391/567
Swiftness, curtness of manner, ii. 141/169
Switzars, guards in attendance upon royalty, ii. 139/125
Sycophant, Lord, in *Nobody and Somebody,* possibly meant for the Earl of Essex's enemy, Lord Cobham, i. 274

Tabling-house, (?) gambling-house, i. 165/189
Taine on the style of the Elizabethan dramatists, i. 358
Take day, to, to take time, i. 174/412
Tall-men and low-men, false dice, i. 354/1952

Tamburlaine, Marlowe's, an early allusion to, ii. 73/142; ii. 349, 352, 375
Taming of the Shrew, cf. with Greene's *Menaphon,* ii. 356
Tapestry, old, ii. 348
Tavern liquor vessels, named in the song, 'Sing, Gentle Butler,' ii. 204/237
Tempest, allusion to *Nobody and Somebody* in, i. 272
Temple, the, i. 164/149, ii. 171/123
Thames, river, i. 321/1120
Theatre. *See* Stage, Players, &c.; *also* Play-house Yard.
——— at Shoreditch, ii. 350, 352
Theatre-fields at Finsbury, frays in, i. 182/610
Three Ladies of London, The, i. 270
Three Lords and Three Ladies of London, The, i. 270
Thynne, F., not the author of *Dialogue between Velvet Breeches and Cloth Breeches,* ii. 381
Timon of Athens, allusion to, ii. 146/314
Titus Andronicus, i. 357, ii. 12
——— cf. with play of *Stucley,* i. 359
——— played in Germany, ii. 15
Titus and Vespasian, i. 357
Toades, oil of, a poison poured over Katherine by Mamon (*Jack Drum*), ii. 178/343
Tobacco smoking, allusions to, ii. 143/236, 145/276, 168/57, 243/52
Touch, to keep-touch, to keep faith, i. 239/2030
Traduce ace, cheating cards, i. 354/1952
Trafford family of Lancashire, and the flail in their arms, ii. 390, 411/95
Tragedy, Comedy, and History (or Spectacle), their contests for prevalence on the stage in Shakspere's time, ii. 241/1
——— acts as *Chorus* in *Warning for Faire Women,* and introduces Dumb Shows and Pantomime action, ii. 241, 268, 284
——— personified on the stage with a bowl of blood in her hand, ii. 268/1
Translated pockets, *i. e.* turned-out pockets, i. 353/1933

INDEX AND GLOSSARY. 491

Trashe, counterfeits, i. 354/1950
Troilus and Cressida, Thersites in, meant for author of *Histrio-Mastix,* ii. 7
——— the sub-play in *Histrio-Mastix,* a hit at Shakspere's *Troilus,* ii. 3, 4, 39, 89
Troynovant, London, i. 320/1104
Turks, the Pope's wars against them, and Battle of Lepanto, i. 94, 97, 100
Twelfth Night, IV. ii. 29, cf. with *Faire Em,* ii. 459/1240
Two Gentlemen of Verona, version called *Julio and Hypolita* played in Germany, ii. 15
——— Valentine's resignation of Silvia and similar resignation by Lubeck in *Faire Em* compared, both illustrative of Shakspere's opinion, as shown in his *Sonnets,* that love between two men is greater than love between man and woman, ii. 398, 436/690. Similar idea shown in *Stucley, ibid.*
Tycrman, the, or players' dresser, ii. 133

Ulster in 1566, under Shane O'Neill; and Thos Stucley's mission relative to it, i. 42—44
Umberst, umber coloured, ii. 276/198
Unwreaked, unavenged, i. 208/1219
Upchear, H., in 354
Upsee Dutch, or Upsee Freeze (Frice =Dutch), 'A cant phrase of tipplers for being intoxicated. * * * Op-zyn-fries means in the Dutch fashion.'—*Nares,* ii. 165/364
Ure, use, ii. 270/66
Usury punished, in character of Mamon (*Jack Drum*), who lent at 'thirtie in the hundred,' ii. 181/408

Valdraco, in Greene's *Planetomachia,* a possible satire upon Shakspere, ii. 342, 353
Valingford, in *Faire Em,* is meant for Shakspere, ii. 374
Velvet Breeches and Cloth Breeches, not by F. Thynne, ii. 381
Venus's Tragedy, Greene's, ii. 353
'Vicarage, An euenuch'd,' fitter for a younger brother than marriage, ii. 129, 172/157
VIGENIUS (or Vigent). *See* British Kings.
VOWEL, JOHN, alias Hooker, the compiler of the later portion of the Irish annals of *Holinshed's Chronicles,* his visit to Ireland in interest of Sir Peter Carew, i. 53

War and Poverty, and Peace and Plenty — the moral of *Histrio-Mastix,* ii. 86
'Ward, be my' = be my fool, or subservient follower, ii. 149/380
Warning for Faire Women; containing the Murther of Mr Sanders, consented unto by his owne wife, acted by M. Browne, Mistris Drewry and Trusty Roger, &c., 1599, the text, ii. 209. —summary of the play, ii. 210. —Introduction, ii. 211. —illustrates didactic and educational intention of the Lord Chamberlain's (Shakspere's) players, ii. 212. — cf. with *Macbeth,* ii. 272/99, 336. — apology for it as a play, ii. 335/1708, and note 4, p. 336. —cf. with *Romeo and J.,* ii. 302/863, and note 1, p. 326. —follows original accounts of murder of Mr Sanders very closely, ii. 332/1644, and note 3, p. 326. —and its chief character (Browne) criticised, ii. note 4, p. 326
'What lack you?' traders' cry, ii. 56/8
Whenas, when, ii. 261/519
Whereas, whereat, ii. 244/95
WHITE, NICHOLAS, the supplanter and enemy of Thos Stucley in Ireland, i. 55, 58
Whitgift (Archbp) and Bancroft's employment of Greene, Nash, and Lily to write down Martin Marprelate, ii. 349, 355, 358, 364
'Whitsun Plays,' Chester, which see.
Whitsuntide, Morice at, ii. 136/52
Whooded, puffed out, ii. 54/294
William the Conqueror, Love of, part title of *Faire Em,* which see.
——— and the King of Denmark. *See Faire Em.*
——— the Berkeley legend, ii. 405

Windmill, the, in *Faire Em, the Miller's Daughter of Manchester*, its symbolical meaning, ii. 374

Wit combat, a, between Brabant Signior and M. Puffe in *Jack Drum*, ii. 169/69

Woe worth him! Woe be to him!— Bad luck to him! ii. 291/583

Woman professing medicine, Mrs Drury (which see), ii. 264/625

Women, R. Greene's view that they are evils, ii. 373

'Wood, way to the'—used for way out of the wood, i. 170/302

Woolwich to London in 1573, dangers of travelling, ii. 275/163

'Worth, take it in' = take it in current money, or sterling, ii. 302/850

Wrack—to hold wrack, to hold parley (? reck, care), i. 255/2426

Wrecks, law of, i. 232/1859

Wyat's rebellion, i. 7, 19

Yarking, hallooing, i. 254/2409

Yawle, howl, ii. 50/189

Yellow spots. (*See* Omens.)

Yeoman, a serving-man so termed, ii. 319/1278

Yesty, yeasty, ii. 135/22

Yorkshire Tragedy, 1608, attributed to Shakspere, ii. 211. (*See also* Shakspere : Doubtful Plays.)

Young Juvenal, in Greene's *Groatsworth of Wit*, is either Lodge or Nash, most likely Nash, ii. 382

CLAY AND TAYLOR, PRINTERS, BUNGAY.

www.ingramcontent.com/pod-product-compliance
Lightning Source LLC
Chambersburg PA
CBHW021416300426
44114CB00010B/511